Library of Old English and Medieval Literature

CHAUCER
Essays and Studies

CHAUCER
ESSAYS AND STUDIES

A Selection From the Writings
of
OLIVER FARRAR EMERSON
1860—1927

———

 BOOKS FOR LIBRARIES PRESS
FREEPORT, NEW YORK

First Published 1929
Reprinted 1970

STANDARD BOOK NUMBER:

8369-5311-8

LIBRARY OF CONGRESS CATALOG CARD NUMBER:

78-114907

PRINTED IN THE UNITED STATES OF AMERICA

CONTENTS

	PAGE
Foreword	vii
Introduction	9
Some of Chaucer's Lines on the Monk	39
The Suitors in Chaucer's Parlement of Foules	58
The Suitors in the Parlement of Foules Again	90
What is the Parlement of Foules?	98
A New Note on the Date of Chaucer's Knight's Tale	123
A New Chaucer Item	174
Chaucer's First Military Service—A Study of Edward Third's Invasion of France in 1359–60	182
Chaucer's Testimony as to his Age	247
"Seith Trophee"	263
English or French in the Time of Edward III	271
The old French Diphthong EI (EY) and Middle English Metrics	298
Chaucer's "Opie of Thebes Fyn"	312
Chaucer and Medieval Hunting	320
Some Notes on Chaucer and some Conjectures	378
Saint Ambrose and Chaucer's Life of Saint Cecilia	405
Appendix	421
Bibliography of the Writings of Oliver Farrar Emerson	431
Bibliography. List of the More Important Authors, Books, and Articles Referred to in the Text and Footnotes	446

FOREWORD

The Emerson Memorial Volume is published by
the colleagues, students, and other friends of the late
Professor Oliver Farrar Emerson, for the purpose
of preserving in substantial and convenient form
some of his more than one hundred fifty fugitive
articles, which have hitherto been accessible to readers only in the files of scholarly periodicals. To
finance the publishing of this book, an Emerson
Memorial Fund has been created, to which former
students, professional associates, and interested
friends have contributed generously. The Emerson
family—Mrs. Annie Logan Emerson, Olive Emerson
(Mrs. Halbert Payne), College for Women, 1918,
and Harold Emerson, Adelbert College, 1914—have
given Professor Emerson's library of Old and Middle English works, to be the nucleus of a collection
for the use of future graduate students at Western
Reserve University.

Although the articles here selected for republica-
tion represent only a small part of the rich and
varied scholarly activity of the author, over a period
of thirty-five years, yet it has seemed wise to the
editors to limit the contents of this volume to Chaucer studies. Professor Emerson was keenly interested
in all phases of human life which found any sort of
expression in literature. He wrote on as diverse
topics as "ghost words," Scott's translation of Bürger's 'Lenore,' and the text of Johnson's 'Rasselas,'
with the same unflagging interest and the same devotion to truth. Yet, after his 'History of the Eng-

8   FOREWORD

lish Language' and his 'Middle English Reader,' both
standard works for more than a quarter of a century, the papers on Chaucer, taken as a group, probably constitute his most substantial and interesting
contribution to English scholarship.

WALTER GRAHAM.

INTRODUCTION

I

This book originated from the pertinent suggestions of Professor Walter Graham (now of the University of Illinois) during the summer and fall of the year 1927. He first conceived the idea of a memorial volume to Professor Emerson and he, after consultation with the present writer and others, came to the conclusion that a collection of Professor Emerson's Chaucer papers would most fittingly represent the best work of his busy life to his friends and to the outside world of interested scholars and students. Professor Graham, moreover, worked out all the details of the plan for publishing the volume in the course of the academic year, 1927–28; and he also personally drew up the letter which when sent, at his suggestion, to several hundreds of Mr. Emerson's former friends and students, resulted in a subscription fund of sufficient size to defray virtually all the expenses of publication.

Professor Emerson's books have all been catalogued and each of them is supplied with a neat and attractive bookplate which was designed from the Emerson family coat-of-arms, and which will always distinguish the "O. F. Emerson" books from all others of the Western Reserve University libraries. The books, moreover, have been placed together on shelves in the English Seminary room of the Graduate School Library, where, it is hoped, they will be most convenient and serviceable to every student and member of the Faculty.

It was the intrinsic value of the Chaucer articles of Professor Emerson perhaps more than anything else that was mainly responsible for the desire to have them made accessible in easily obtainable book form. For they were originally printed in some half dozen different periodicals, all of which could be easily found only in the complete files of the larger university library collections. Their comparative inaccessibility has probably kept them hitherto unknown to many of the leading Chaucer students in America and Europe, in spite of their undeniably great importance in the up-to-date investigations of questions about Chaucer's life and work. At any rate, entire familiarity with the contents of Emerson's contributions leaves one in amazement at the apparent neglect of them, or a complete failure to utilize them, by the authors of some of the more important recent books about Chaucer, in anything like the measure they deserve. It is hoped that this book will make the neglect of his fine array of Chaucer articles inexcusable in the future, since its convenient form and price should make it accessible to every college and university library in the country. The collection should, moreover, find a place in the private libraries of numerous English teachers and scholars in all parts of the world: it is our sincere hope that it will.

It was at Professor Graham's request that the writer agreed, more than a year ago, to undertake the in no respect simple task of doing whatever editorial work should be found advisable in preparing the book for publication. Professor Emerson had himself already materially helped to make the edi-

torial task less onerous by collecting, some time
before his death, specimen copies of everything he
had published in the form of "papers" or essays during the period 1892–1925, and, after arranging them
in chronological order, by having them bound together in two volumes for convenience of reference.
So far as content, style, and diction are concerned,
the contributions have been reprinted without
change, except in a comparatively few instances of
evident mistakes in printing which have caught the
eye of one or the other of the proof readers and been
corrected. Since, moreover, the essays and papers
included in this volume appeared originally in several
different scholarly publications whose press-room
practices show a considerable number of variations,
it has seemed advisable to normalize the most noticeable of the typographical differences in this reprint.
The original footnotes of each article have been reproduced as exactly as possible. Very few explanatory or other footnotes have been added. It is believed that the individual essays and studies are in
the main sufficiently explicit in themselves to require
no further editorial explanation. The guiding purpose has been throughout to let his own work—the
characteristic presentation of his own thoughts and
ideas—speak for Professor Emerson. If, however,
any interested reader of the book should wish to
delve more deeply into some of the rather abstruse
Chaucer problems here considered, or presented in
fresh guise, he will find ample additional references
and pertinent suggestions in the excellent 'Bibliography of the Writings of Oliver Farrar Emerson,'
compiled by Professor Clark S. Northup of Cornell

University, originally to accompany his fine necrological account of Professor Emerson *(PMLA* XLII, December, 1927), which he has carefully revised and consented to have printed in the Memorial Volume.

The editorial work has, it may be truly said, been generously shared by several of Professor Emerson's former colleagues, who were only too glad to have such an opportunity to show their real appreciation of the man and his work. While the writer agreed to be mainly responsible for arranging and preparing the several articles for publication, and while he is entirely responsible for all the errors and shortcomings of the book which an editor would be expected to correct or remove, he has nevertheless been greatly assisted by several colleagues. Professor Graham deserves to be mentioned first and might justly be designated 'Editor-in-Chief'; next in order are Professor Barrow and Professor Bourland who carefully read the proof and gave most valuable advice on numerous occasions; Professor Bourland and Mr. Strong (the librarian of Adelbert College Library) have given freely of their expert advice about the selection of format, paper, print, and binding of the book.

All business matters connected with the actual printing were ably arranged by Mr. Zettelmeyer and the Treasurer of the University, Mr. Sidney S. Wilson.

WILLIAM H. HULME.

April 22, 1929.

II

Professor Emerson might at any time in the last
few years of his life have impressed the stranger,
meeting him for the first time, as lacking somewhat
in physical vigor, if not as being in delicate health.
But to his friends, constantly associated with him,
this was rarely if ever noticed. To some of us he
had always appeared thin and spare physically, and
not to grow thicker or thinner with increasing years.
But he was withal wiry and apparently capable of
much physical endurance. He was a constant walker
and remained fond of the out-of-doors to the last.
He particularly enjoyed puttering around the house
and in the garden of his lake-shore country home in
summer vacations. His untimely death was, therefore, all the more surprising because it seemed almost
contrary to the justifiable expectations of his family
and friends.

Oliver Farrar Emerson was descended from an-
cestors of early New England and still earlier English stock. His father, Rev. Oliver Emerson, migrated
westward in the first half of last century, for the
purpose of completing his theological studies at Lane
Theological Seminary, Cincinnati; and he was destined eventually to enter the service of the Home
Missionary Society of the Congregational Church
in the state of Iowa.

The first member of this branch of the Emerson
family to come to the United States seems to have
been Thomas Emerson, who crossed over from Bishop's Stortford, Hertfordshire, England, in the second
quarter of the seventeenth century (about the year
1636) and settled at Ipswich, Massachusetts. Then,

from the son Joseph and his wife Elizabeth (Bulk-
ley) Emerson the direct line of descent may be traced
through Ebenezer and Mary (Bontwell) Emerson,
Ebenezer II and Rebecca (Putnam) Emerson, Daniel and Lucy (Pratt) Emerson, Oliver and Elizabeth
(Brown) Emerson, Oliver II and Maria (Farrar)
Emerson. Professor Emerson's mother, whose maid-
en name was Maria Farrar, was a native of Iowa
and his father's second wife.

The immediate forbears of Oliver Farrar Emerson were thus all genuine New Englanders, his
mother Maria Farrar excepted. She was a woman
of remarkable personality and character, who seems
to have been the ideal wife for her notable pioneer
missionary husband, and the ideal mother for such
a truly noble and notable son.

Rev. Oliver Emerson enjoyed the best educational
opportunities of the New England of the first half
of the nineteenth century. He was prepared for college at Philips (Andover) Academy; and then graduated from Waterville (now Colby) College, Maine,
as well as from Lane Theological Seminary, Cincinnati. Soon after the completion of his training for
the ministry (in 1840) he migrated to and settled in
Iowa (Danville), where he spent the remainder—
more than forty years—of his life in home missionary work of the most strenuous and varied kind,
necessary in those pioneer days for the devoted, zeal-
ous servant of the Christian church.

At the time of Oliver Farrar's birth (May 24th,
1860) his parents were living in Wolf Creek (now
Traer), Iowa. There in the public schools of Sabula
and the academy at Denmark, Lee County, he was

prepared for college, and there at Iowa College (now Grinnell College) he received the A.B. degree in 1882, after completing the usual four year course of study. There also he served his apprenticeship in teaching for six years, first in the public schools of Grinnell and Muscatine for three years, and subsequently for another three years as principal and teacher of Latin in the academy of Iowa College.

With this valuable experience as teacher in and director of secondary schools to his credit, young Emerson began to feel stronger and stronger the urge toward higher education. This resulted in his applying for a fellowship in Cornell University in the year 1888 and his election as Goldwin Smith Fellow in English for the academic year 1888–89. Meanwhile his Alma Mater had conferred on him the degree of A.M. *honoris causa* (1885), and he had fully decided to devote the time necessary to obtain the Ph.D. from Cornell in the immediate future. He was, moreover, greatly encouraged and materially assisted in carrying out his ambitious plans by reappointment to the Goldwin Smith Fellowship for the year 1889–90, and also by appointment to an instructorship in the department of English in Cornell University for the same year, while he was still a graduate student.

In writing to a friend (in 1923) about these years of preparation he says: "My years at good old Denmark were followed by college at Grinnell — Iowa College as we then called it—from which my brother Bartlett had graduated, of which my father was a trustee for many years, and to which my sister and myself naturally went, with no regret let me add...

After graduation I remained two years at the head
of the Grinnell schools, a position I owed in no small
degree to Professor Edson, then a professor of ped-
agogy at the College.   At the end of those years I
received a call to the larger schools of Muscatine,
Iowa, where, however, I remained but one year, a
call then coming to return to Grinnell as principal
of the College academy."

At Cornell, then, "I remained as fellow, instructor,
and assistant professor for eight years (1888–96),
studying, taking my Doctor's degree (1891), and
teaching the English language and literature."

During his third year at Cornell (1891), after
being promoted to an assistant professorship in the
department of English, he was happily married to
Miss Annie L. Logan of St. Louis, Mo.   So, with a
congenial, sympathetic companion for life, the long-
coveted badge of higher graduate training, and pro-
fessorial rank as teacher of his chosen subject in one
of the best universities of the country, fortune was
undoubtedly smiling most graciously upon him.
Prospects for the future seemed to beckon him on,
courage he never lacked, and

> Hope like the gentle taper's light,
> Adorned and cheered his way.

III

In trying to form a just estimate of the first half—
thirty-five years—of Emerson's life, of the incen-
tives and impulses and ambition which led him to
hope for, dream about, and yearn for a career of
high attainment and splendid achievement as teacher
and scholar, much that is prophetically suggestive

and intensely interesting may be gleaned from a
unique diary or journal which he kept in French
throughout the year 1887. This journal, neatly written on some seventy of the large foolscap pages of an
ordinary blank book, was discovered not long ago by
the writer in one of the many files of Emerson's numerous notebooks, letters, and papers of all sorts. It
was, it would seem, previously unknown to any of his
family or intimate friends. It covers just one year,
but a crucial year, of his early career. It is, strangest
of all, written entirely in French,—seldom in good,
correct French, perhaps, but always in such form
and words that their meaning or purport can be
easily divined by anyone who reads French. He jot-
ted down in those pages, day by day, accounts and
descriptions of the subjects, events, and people, that
were at the time most interesting to him, apparently
most strongly affecting his life, and were probably
unconsciously developing what came to be the domi-
nant moral and intellectual tastes and tendencies of
his mature years. The diary seems to have been undertaken at the suggestion of his French teacher at
the time, a woman at Grinnell. It begins with "5 Jan-
vier 1887" and concludes with the "31 Décembre."
And while it is not a daily record of his life—for not
infrequently the diarist apologises to "mon journal"
for having neglected it for periods of several days
at a time—it nevertheless seems to include virtually
everything, however insignificant, that touched his
life during the course of the year. Many of the
entries are quite long and are recorded with numerous details; many of them are most interesting,

2

entertaining, and amusing. Virtually every entry
throws some revealing light on the many phases
of Emerson's personality and character. He was
then in his twenty-seventh year,—the time of
life when talent and genius have already begun to
show unmistakable signs of existence in the intellect and soul of a human being, if they do really exist
and have not hitherto been deprived of all opportunities to make themselves known.

So, in the pages of the journal we find out about
the interesting books young Emerson was reading
and the impressions made on his mind by each of
them. We know that he liked French lyric poetry,
Molière, Victor Hugo's 'Les Misérables,' and George
Sand's 'La Mare au Diable', but that he could not become enthusiastic about the French drama in general. He enjoyed the reading of Gogol's 'Taras Bulba,'
but he thought it nevertheless a "horrible story of
blood and thunder." He was greatly impressed by
Tolstoi's 'Anna Karenina.' It was to him "a remarkable book, filled with thought and well written." The
story possessed for him "a charming simplicity, and
the freshness of green woods and delightful fields."
The entire story, style, nature descriptions, and
character portrayal made him believe that Russian
literature was destined to take high rank among the
literatures of the world.

We learn from the diary that Emerson was an
active member of the Grinnell Browning Club and
much occupied with reading 'The Ring and the Book,'
of which poem he made his first significant critical
study that was honored by publication.[1] It was

---

[1] See 'Bibliography' for specific references.

apparently in the same year, that he first "committed the sin of rhyme," as Burns once said of himself. At any rate, we have no reference to any thing of the kind in print earlier than his Latin verse translation of the popular church hymn, 'Onward Christian Soldier,' which appeared in *Education*, Vol. IX, p. 187 (1889). And he thought it, he tells us in the journal, a pretty good bit of work, which gave him great pleasure and was indeed a "labor of love." He suggests, however, in a delightfully humorous manner, that he can hardly expect this effort of his to rival Gladstone's Latin version of 'The Rock of Ages.' Here indeed in this journal we learn for the first time of Emerson's genuine interest in poetical composition, or better said perhaps, verse-making. In those early years he enjoyed "dabbling" in poetry occasionally and found a certain fascination in arranging thoughts and words in attractive poetical form. It was not much later than the diary year (1887) that the muse of poetry apparently began to haunt his spirit quite persistently. For during the four or five years immediately following, several of his sonnets on a variety of subjects were published in the columns of *The Chautauquan, The Cornell Magazine,* and *The Cornell Era.*[2]

Emerson had already shown at that time by his studies in the academy and at college, and especially by his success in teaching and in his management of secondary schools during the years immediately following upon his graduation from college, that he

---

[2] All these sonnets have just been collected and reprinted in *The Western Reserve University Bulletin* (July, 1929, Vol. XXXII, No. 13, pp. 5–11).

possessed a very alert and active mind, as well as
unusual talent bordering on genius. He was an
indefatigable and intelligent reader of good literature from the early years of his youth. And at the
time he was keeping his French journal, judging
from the continuous references to the many and the
great variety of books he was reading, he must have
been almost as persistent a reader as his great master Chaucer describes himself as being in one of his
important poems:

> But of thy verray neyghebores,
> That dwellen almost at thy dores,
> Thou herest neither that ne this;
> For whan thy labour doon al is,
> And hast y-maad thy rekeninges,
> In stede of reste and newe thinges,
> Thou gost hoom to thy hous anoon;
> And, also domb as any stoon,
> Thou sittest at another boke,
> Til fully daswed is thy loke,
> And livest thus as an hermyte.[3]

But Emerson was always too fond of men, of
human associations, the out-of-doors, and certain
kinds of sport ever to become a reader of the book-
worm type. He enjoyed tennis especially, and he
was one of the champion tennis players of south central Iowa during his years as student and teacher at
Grinnell. He was also interested in base ball, and he
continued to participate actively in these popular
ball games long after he came to Cleveland. Riding
the bicycle, sometimes on long trips, through the

[3] *The Hous of Fame*, ll. 141–151, Skeat's *Student's Chaucer*,
1896.

country round Grinnell, was perhaps his most delightful pastime in those early years, because possibly, bicycling afforded him the best opportunities for combining physical exercise with a sort of spiritual exhilaration in the enjoyment of the beauty of country scenery.   June 27th, the day on which he bought himself a cyclometer, receives especial notice in the journal: "Monday I purchased my cyclometer which registers the number of miles I ride.   It gives me great satisfaction to know how many miles I go each day, and I imagine I ride farther sometimes just to increase the number.   Professor G— told me that he rode more than a thousand the first year, and I hope to surpass that number!"

The journal records many incidents connected with Emerson's daily activities as master of and teacher in the academy.   He refers frequently to his readings in Caesar, Cicero, Sallust, and Vergil; not infrequently he speaks of the progress of some one of his pupils.   Being the son of a devout preacher and missionary of the Christian church, he naturally took much interest in the services of the church he attended and in the work of the Y.M.C.A. at Grinnell.   He occasionally assisted in a service, and at one period that year he delivered a series of lectures before the members of the Y.M.C.A.   We learn from the same source that he greatly enjoyed music and art—that is painting—through the many references to the paintings of a friend in Grinnell, and to concerts in which he occasionally took part.

This journal for 1887 is a splendid tribute to his capacity for making friends, so many of whom are discussed by name again and again and in various

relationships in the interesting life-record of that
annus mirabilis. It is the only year of his life of
which we possess a complete account recorded by
himself, and was verily the crucial year of his ambitious, vigorous young manhood. Indeed, the French
diary does seem to contain some record of everything
physical, intellectual, and spiritual in which the man
Emerson took any—even a passing—interest. As
has already been suggested, we may read in its
pages about his games and sports, his occupation as
teacher and master in the Grinnell Academy, his
public lectures before the Y.M.C.A. and at summer
teachers' institutes in Iowa and Nebraska, about the
many and various books he was reading, his studies
in the field of philosophy, and the gradual development of his own philosophy of life. Rarely, indeed,
has any man of Emerson's station and profession
and importance as teacher and scholar left behind
such a significant account of the keystone year of his
well-rounded arch of life.

His first published article seems to have appeared
in March, 1887, in an educational journal in Iowa.
The article was entitled 'The Study of Latin,' and
was apparently a reprint of a paper read some
time earlier in the year (or perhaps in the previous
year, 1886) before the annual meeting of an Iowa
Masters' (or Teachers') Association. The reference
in the journal to the publication is rather vague.

It is from the journal that we first learn something definite about his dreams and plans for continuing his graduate studies at some eastern university in the near future. In the record for March 10
he writes, "I am at present thinking about my stu-

dies for next year. If possible I intend to go to
Johns Hopkins or Cornell. I am planning to study
the English language, and I hope to obtain the
degree of Doctor of Philosophy before I return. It
goes without saying that it will be impossible for me
to come back here to teach. When I think of that it
makes me unhappy; but my plan appears to me to
be the best one, nevertheless. I have just received
a letter from W——, and he advises me to go to Johns
Hopkins, but he tells me that the work there is very
difficult and at times very discouraging. Sometimes
I think it is all a mistake; that I have overestimated
my ability; that I am nothing above mediocrity intel-
lectually; that it will be a waste of time, nothing
more; that it would be better for me to build a home
and settle down there for the rest of my life. If I
could only *know!*"

He was also thinking much in the spring of 1887
about traveling in Europe at some time in the next few
years, for he says "The idea of a trip to Europe before many years pass, occupies my thoughts more
than ever. I think it would be possible for me to do
it; and I am thinking of going in the year 1889 or
1890, if it is possible. At that time I should be able
to go and retain my position in the college here at
the same time." Near the end of the year, as we
also learn from the journal, after he had been
offered and had refused three or four good school
positions and an invitation to become president or
principal of a small college in Dakota, he applied for
and received, as has already been stated, the Goldwin Smith Fellowship in English at Cornell University for the academic year 1888–89.

This fortunate event almost entirely changed "the current of his being" by helping him to realize in hitherto unexpected ways his ardent hopes and vivid dreams of the preceding years. His success at Cornell was immediate and beyond a doubt. Before he had been in the university three years he had fully established himself as a teacher of great power and a scholar second to none of his years and experience for exactness and thoroughness, though shown in the somewhat limited field of his doctoral dissertation. And before three more years had passed he had placed himself in the front rank of English scholars and investigators in America by the publication (1894) of his almost epoch-making 'History of the English Language.' It was this book along with 'The Ithaca Dialect, A Study of Present English' (1891), that was mainly responsible for the invitation he received (and accepted) from Adelbert College of Western Reserve University in 1896 to become Professor of Rhetoric and English Philology; and this position with only a slight change in the title, he held with marked distinction for the remainder of his life, more than thirty years.

IV

Previous to his appointment in Adelbert College Emerson's active mind, tireless energy, and thirst for exact knowledge had led him far afield by many different paths in the extensive realm of English scholarship. He had tried out his intellectual equipment on verse translation, sonnet-writing, book-reviewing, essays on grammar, literary criticism, brief studies of different kinds of English verse, pedagogical philosophizing, historical criticism of Shakespearean drama, an occasional excursus on phonetics, and a thoroughgoing study of language and dialects, represented especially by the two books previously mentioned. But down to that time he had barely touched Chaucer—in the illuminating review of Lounsbury's 'Studies in Chaucer.'[4] If, however, he later had *one* favorite subject in the broad field of English literature which he pursued with love and assiduity and ever increasing interest for almost twenty-five years, that subject was Geoffrey Chaucer's life and work. All his previous studies of the English language and dialects, whether in Old, Middle, or Modern English, served as admirable preparation for what is without doubt his own best work, and some of the finest American scholarship has produced, in the field of accurate and reliable, as well as distinctly informing and illuminating, investigation.

But during the first ten or twelve years of his career as college teacher, his most promising pieces of literary investigation, in addition to his great work on the history of the English language, were concerned with a wide range and remarkable variety of subjects. The work of this period is well illustrated by such titles as Browning's 'The Ring and the Book'; Shakespeare's 'Antony and Cleopatra,' which won him "The Barnes Shakespeare Prize" at Cornell University in 1889 and was published in *Poet-Lore* for February–April, 1890; 'English in Secondary Schools,' which, published in the *Academy* (Syracuse) for June, 1889, received a prize offered by that

---

[4] *The Dial* for February, 1892 (XII. 351-2).

journal for the best paper on the subject; extensive articles on English in 'Johnson's Universal Cyclopaedia,' Vols. V–VI (1894–5) ; 'Relations of Literature and Philology' in the *Educational Review* for 1893; 'A Parallel between the ME Poem Patience and an early Latin Poem Attributed to Tertullian,' in *PMLA*, Vol. X (1895) ; college editions of two well-known eighteenth century prose books: 'The History of Rasselas, Prince of Abyssinia' (1895) and 'The Life and Writings of Edward Gibbon' (1898) ; and finally 'Transverse Alliteration in Teutonic Poetry' (1900).

These important contributions, besides a second edition of 'The History of the English Language' (1895), 'A Brief History of the English Language' (1896, 267 pp.), and about seventy other publications of less significance, generally speaking, fill the thirteen years from 1889 to 1903 rather full for an otherwise busy, effective, and conscientious college teacher. This long list of published works shows, beyond doubt, Emerson's enthusiastic love of learning, a capacity for taking infinite pains in the search for truth, untiring patience and indefatigable intellectual energy, eternal vigilance in detecting and pointing out the errors of other scholars in his field, but at the same time the exercise of strict justice and courteous consideration in refuting opposing views and theories. All these qualities, eminently characteristic of the mature scholar and true gentleman Emerson, were already easily detectable in his more youthful productions.

Emerson's more than thirty years in Adelbert College and Western Reserve University were filled with valuable accomplishments as teacher, scholar,

counsellor, and citizen, which reflected great honor
upon his college and university and upon American
scholarship, as well as upon himself and his family.
His intense zeal in the search for truth was no
more notable a characteristic of the man than his
sympathetic interest in his numerous students, many
of whom live to bless his name by their work and
fame, and to cherish lasting memories of the sage
and courteous and kindly advice they frequently received from his lips.   Everywhere, whether as teacher
in college or as citizen in the non-collegiate circle
of his home, he was always ready to give freely
from his rich store of suggestions and experience,
if he felt that he could be helpful in any way.   Busy
as he always was with constantly increasing college
duties and the time-consuming investigations of
numerous literary problems, he was ever ready to
serve the community in which he lived in any helpful
capacity.   He remained through life true and loyal
to the religious principles and precepts he had received from his remarkable missionary father.   He
never refused to lend a hand wherever he could be
of assistance in the work of the church of which he
was a faithful attendant.

He founded and was for many years the unobtru-
sive guiding spirit of the "Novel Club of Cleveland,"
for which he helped to edit a modest volume of
'Papers' in the year 1899.   His contribution to the
attractive little volume of some one hundred twenty-
five pages, entitled 'Novel Club Papers,' consists of
the introductory essay of about ten pages on 'The
Place of the Novel in Literature.'   As the book was
privately "Published by the Club," it has not per-

haps received the attention from the reading public which its merits and interest deserve.

A few years before his death he organized the "English Club" among the members of the English faculties of Western Reserve University and of other colleges of Greater Cleveland, and later invited members of the English faculties of the colleges of Northern Ohio that were conveniently located, to become members or to attend and take part in the monthly meetings as frequently as possible. In the foundation of these organizations there was always the modest but enthusiastic and almost instinctive wish to arouse fresh interests in English studies and keep alive old ones among the members of the English teaching staffs of the several colleges, who he felt might in that way easily be brought together for at most two hours in informal evening meetings once every few weeks during the academic year. These meetings served the further useful purpose of giving convenient opportunities for the ever increasing and constantly changing personnel of the faculties concerned to become better acquainted and to exchange opinions, enthusiasms, and suggestions about their respective work in the field of English investigation or their similar pedagogical problems and experiences. Once the club was established, he modestly but effectively kept it going from year to year by regular attendance at the meetings and by serving in any useful capacity. Moreover, he was always ready with a never-failing supply of pertinent and encouraging suggestions which were shrewdly and modestly calculated, no doubt, to keep up interest in and call forth opinions and arouse ideas on the various subjects and papers presented at the meetings, from many individuals who would otherwise have remained silent.

The forcefulness of Emerson's charming personality, coupled with his keen intellect, inspiring enthusiasm, and profound learning made him a valued adviser and leader in the councils of the many national societies and associations (of which he was a member) for the promotion of English scholarship in America.   The effectiveness of his work in this broad national, even international, field, and the high esteem in which he and his services were held by fellow-members, are shown by his election to positions of honor in several of the societies during the long period of his active career.   He was secretary of the American Dialect Society from 1898 to 1905, during which period he edited *Dialect Notes,* the official publication of the society, and he was president from 1906 to 1909.   He was also a life member of the Modern Language Association of America, of the Central Division of which he was elected chairman for the year 1907–1908; and he later, in 1922, was made President of the Association for the ensuing year.   Moreover, he served several terms as member of the Executive Council of the Association.

Being deeply interested in the purpose and the problems for the solution of which the Simplified Spelling Board, the Linguistic Society of America, and the Humanities Research Association were mainly established, he became an active member of each society almost from the date of its organization.   He was seldom absent from annual meetings of those societies, on which occasions he rarely failed

to do his part by address, paper, discussion, or committee service in promoting the success and increasing the general interest of the meetings.

In addition to his interest in the purpose and work
of each of the previously named organizations for
the promotion of the more comprehensive study of
English in American schools and colleges, Emerson
was a member of the American Association of University Professors from its organization. He was,
in fact, among the comparatively few American college professors and scholars whose counsel was
sought as to the advisability of establishing such an
association.

V

As has already been pointed out, Emerson's real
and abiding interest in Chaucer did not show itself
definitely in his published work until the first decade
of the present century. But from about 1905 on for
the next ten years, Chaucer in some form was
rarely absent for any length of time from his
serious studies, and the list of his publications for
this period shows that a year seldom passed for him
without one or more "notes" or articles or books on
the subject appearing in print. The critical discussion of 'Some of Chaucer's Lines on the Monk'
(1903) was followed by 'A Middle English Reader'
(1905), his most extensive and scholarly piece of
editorial work. Then followed in quick succession
'A New Note on the Date of Chaucer's Knight's
Tale' (1910), 'The Suitors in Chaucer's Parlement of
Foules' (1910), 'A New Chaucer Item' (1911),
'Poems of Chaucer; Selections from His Earlier and

Later Works' (1911), the climax in printed form of his Chaucer enthusiasm; 'The Suitors in the Parlement of Foules Again' (1911); 'Chaucer's First Military Service' (1912); and 'Chaucer's Testimony as to his Age' (1913). After this, Chaucer articles appeared with longer intervals between, down to the close of his life.

It must not be imagined, however, that his Chaucer studies occupied even the major portion of the time that he always somehow managed to find for scholarly investigation, in spite of the heavy burden of college and class-room responsibilities and duties, during the last twenty years and more of his active life. A cursory glance at the list of publications for the years 1905–1925 reveals the fact that the multiplicity of his scholarly interests, so clearly shown in the published work of the earlier fifteen years, continued to exercise a determinative influence to the very end. As a scholar, he certainly did not have a "one-track mind." He was never satisfied to settle down for years, or even months, at a time to the solution of some one big problem, or a set of closely related problems in the same field, to the exclusion of interest in and specific study of problems in other fields very widely separated, in time at least. He could, and did, frequently concentrate his mind and energy upon a single question or problem of study that interested him intensely for weeks or months in succession. But he seems always to have kept a multitude of slightly different pieces of research lying on his desk, close at hand, to any one of which he could turn from his principal work or task at any time a particular mood or frame of

mind demanded, for relaxation and mental recrea-
tion. Emerson was hardly the man and scholar to
devote all the years of a long life to the study of say
the particle *ne* to the exclusion of every other attractive subject of study.

So, it probably came about that he, with his all-
embracing desire for fresh knowledge, his active,
never satiated mind, continued through life to make
and publish the results of researches in a half dozen
or more, frequently rather distantly related, fields
in the broad realm of English literature and philology. We find, for example, the following extraordinary list of scholarly, serious articles—not mere
"notes" of a few lines in extent—credited to his
name in the years from 1914 to 1925: 'What is the
Parlement of Foules?' (16pp.); 'The Earliest English Translations of Bürger's Lenore' (120 pp.);
'English or French in the Time of Edward III'
(16 pp.); 'More Notes on Patience' (10 pp.); 'The
Shepherd's Star in English Poetry' (20 pp.); 'The
OF Diphthongs ei (ey) and ME Metrics' (8 pp.);
'Spenser, Lady Carey, and the Complaints Volume'
(16 pp.); 'Spenser's Virgil's Gnat' (24 pp.); 'ME
Clannesse' (28 pp.); 'Grendel's Motive in Attacking
Heorot' (6 pp.); 'Chaucer and Medieval Hunting'
(35 pp.); 'Notes on Sir Gawain and the Green
Knight' (47 pp.); 'Some Notes on the Pearl' (41
pp.); 'Monk Lewis and His Tales of Terror' (5 pp.);
'Shakespeare's Sonneteering' (25 pp.); 'Some Notes
on Chaucer and Some Conjectures' (15 pp.); 'Notes
on OE' (6 pp.); 'The Early Life of Sir Walter
Scott' (90 pp.); 'Notes on Gilbert Imlay, Early
American Writer' (33 pp.); 'John Dryden and a

British Academy' (13 pp.); 'Shakespearean and Other Feasts' (22 pp.).

This list would not be easy to parallel in the annals of modern American scholarly investigations in English or any other subject. And the list could easily be more than doubled for the same period by including his contributions of from one to three or four pages in length. It is moreover probably true that no critic of Emerson's work, however severe he may have been, ever accused him with justice of being careless or superficial.

What has just been said about the great variety of his scholarly investigations, as shown by the list of his most significant publications during the ten years from 1914 to 1925, may be applied with equal aptness to any ten years of his active career as investigator from 1892 to 1927. It may easily be seen by examination of the 'Bibliography' published in this volume, that several volumes of equal extent, if not altogether of equal importance, could be compiled with little difficulty from the upwards of one hundred and fifty contributions of all kinds which he made to the study of English during more than thirty years.

It is, therefore, a fact worthy of note that the essays and studies reprinted in the present volume give only a very incomplete estimate of Emerson's scholarly interests and activities in other fields of English literature than that of Chaucer. He touched no subject, moreover, no matter to which century it belonged, without adding some light by means of new discovery or fresh suggestion from his rich store of exact information and his tireless

3

researches among original and hitherto untapped sources. Nevertheless, a glance at the list of his contributions published after about 1903 will serve to show how much more of his time and attention was devoted to the study of Chaucer than of any other single author or subject. The Chaucer studies, perhaps, more than any of the many subjects of investigation that aroused his intellectual interest during the years of his entire devotion to teaching and research, afforded him the best opportunities for the exercise of his excellent training and rich experience. Classical mythology, ecclesiastical polities and policies, as well as medieval history, legend, and learning of all sorts, found in his Chaucer studies the finest field for their adequate exploitation. It would probably not be extravagant to assert that no scholar in this country and very few students of Chaucer in any part of the world have been more admirably equipped for the study and appreciation of Chaucer from every point of interest than Emerson was. Thorough grounding in Latin and Greek, intimate knowledge of the entire periods of Old and Middle English, philologically and historically considered, entire familiarity with general medieval history, an easy reading knowledge of French, German, and Italian, —these constituted the most noteworthy features of his unique endowment as a Chaucerian scholar.

Emerson was always conservative about changing theories of long standing or advancing new ones in the interpretation of Chaucer problems. He had little patience with the hit or miss guesses of several otherwise brilliant contemporary students of Chaucer. Nothing aroused his innate fighting spirit more quickly than the publication from time to time of the threadbare sophistries of over-venturesome scholars. And in conversation more than in his published work he showed his intense pleasure at every opportunity he had of detecting error and laying bare evident sophistry, where truth should have been the only goal. But his love of truth never caused him to forget his inborn courtesy and fine sense of justice. Nothing disturbed his gentle spirit as man and scholar more than the injection of "personalities" into the discussion of literary and philological questions.

No Chaucer scholar of recent times has probably shown himself to be such a clarifying and effective annotator of obscure words, lines, and passages. His love of annotation was, indeed, almost a passion. And how well this characteristic is illustrated in the present 'Studies' and the "Notes" to his 'Poems of Chaucer,' not to mention his 'Middle English Reader' and the numerous articles devoted to the clarification of Old and Middle English masterpieces. The minutely painstaking manner in which he, already in the beginning of his career as a teacher of Old English, covered the fly-leaves of his interleaved copy of Harrison's 'Beowulf' with almost numberless but always pertinent annotations, is an excellent case in point.

Annotation meant for him, however, something very different from the popular text-book exploitation of encyclopaedias by inexperienced and incompetent editors. Emerson's notes are almost always and essentially interpretative, whether they are in the main linguistic or historical or literary. More-

over, they always go to the bottom of things where
the sources of information are accessible to him. It
was very rare for him to be caught napping in annotations, or to be found guilty of error or careless
oversight. It might, indeed, be asserted without injustice that his effectiveness and ability as interpretative critic virtually always emanated from his an-
notative interest in the subject. All his best editorial
work, whether in connection with Bürger, Johnson,
Gibbon, Scott, or with Chaucer and Middle English
poetry, might well be considered as centering in his
peculiarly comprehensive and incisive power of, and
intense zeal for, illustrative annotation. Emerson's
mind was also eminently historical and logical, qualities which are readily noticeable in his Chaucer
studies.

His English is always clear, concise, and to the
point. He never wrote merely or mainly for literary effect. He was little given to the cultivation of
the graces of style; no one would speak of the
magic of Emerson's style. The generally serious
character of his writings rarely permitted him to
sprinkle them with the spice of wit and humor.
He avoided unnecessary repetition, reserving this
stylistic peculiarity for the occasions in which he
wished to drive his points home with most emphasis.
Long experience in teaching, and in writing about
composition and rhetoric, as well as natural in-
clination, made his style best and strongest in
exposition. He seems to have had little facility in
narration. He was, however, a pleasing and interesting conversationalist, with a rich vein of native
wit and humor which found their natural outlet

most readily in genial conversation with his close friends. With them and with his college classes from year to year who learned to love and appreciate him as teacher, scholar, and man his wit sparkled and his humor flashed in their own peculiar manner.

VI

In conclusion, it would be difficult to characterize the man Emerson and his work better and more tersely than has been done by Professor Northup in the following paragraphs from *In Memoriam,* appended to 'More Notes on Pearl,' *PMLA* XLII, No. 4, December, 1927, and published several months after Professor Emerson's death, March 12, 1927:

"As a teacher Professor Emerson is remembered and honored by a large number of pupils because of his enthusiasm for his chosen field, his wise and sane views of life, his quickness in puncturing the bubbles of sham and pretense, his fine sense of humor, his clear exposition of the science of language, and his acute and just criticism of literature.

"As a scholar Emerson was painstaking, accurate, and thorough to the last degree. Besides these qualities he had the vision and the daring of the explorer. He knew how to formulate a hypothesis and test it; and if he found his hypothesis untenable he was great enough to abandon it, although it was not often that he had occasion to do this. If he was not actually the first to mark out the field of the historical study of the English tongue, he was one of the pioneers; and his acumen has enriched our scholarship with many facts and discoveries in the field of linguistics and the history of letters. Though a doughty champion of his own views, he was withal a courteous and fair opponent. He had few enemies and many friends.

"Language he regarded as a growth, to be regulated or guided, not by the dogmatism of the jurist but by the sane thought of reasonable and large-minded leaders in the march of culture. He saw the importance of the scientific study of language as an index not only of individual but also of communal and racial traits. For him the modern languages were on the same plane as the ancient classical languages. He urged the literary study of the classics; but he insisted that side by side with this should be studied the evolution of the modern spirit. Either study without the other tended to become futile, and exclusive generalizations from either were not to be trusted . . . . The study of language was his favorite field; but he recognized the fact that too exclusive attention to linguistic study is conducive to narrowness. Accordingly he made many excursions into the field of literary study. Students of Johnson, Gibbon, Milton, Chaucer, Shakespeare, Spenser, and Scott, as well as of other authors, are indebted to him for important contributions to their knowledge.

"The tributes paid to him by his pupils and colleagues testify how highly they thought of him as a man. They perceived his sense of proportion, the sanity of his philosophy of life, his fearlessness of death, his gentleness, his generosity, his optimism. To us, to whom he has passed on the torch, his life will be an unfailing inspiration."

W. H. H.

SOME OF CHAUCER'S LINES ON THE MONK*

I

He yaf nat of that text a pulled hen,
That seith that hunters been nat holy men.
—*CT*, 177 f.

Upon this passage Professor Skeat says, in substance, that "text" means any remark in writing;
that the allusion is to Nimrod (*Gen.* x, 9), who was
described as a very bad man; and that the Canons
of Edgar (No. 64) say, "We enjoin that a priest be
not a hunter, nor a hawker, nor a dicer." The impression left by the note is that there is nothing
more to be said. Nor must I omit to mention
Professor Flügel's article,[1] which discusses the Nimrod legend at some length, though that article was
preceded in publication by Professor Skeat's note. In
passing I may remark that Professor Flügel has
apparently missed some of the important relations
of the Nimrod legend, for he need have gone no
farther than Josephus to find that the Hebrews regarded Nimrod as a tyrant. One tradition says that
Abraham left Ur of the Chaldees (*Gen.* xi, 31) because of the oppression of Nimrod.[2]

---

* *Mod. Philol.* Vol. I, pp. 105–115 (1903).

[1] *Journal of English and Germanic Philology*, Vol. I, p. 126.
Cf. also his notes in *Anglia*, Vol. XXIV, p. 448.

[2] Baring-Gould, *Legends of the Patriarchs and Prophets.*

It has not been noticed, however, that there is something more than an excellent commentary on the Chaucer lines above—to explain an older by a more recent writer—in the first chapter of Walton's *Angler*. Here Piscator, in praising his art, says:

> And let me tell you that, in the Scripture, angling is always taken in the best sense, and that, though hunting may be sometimes so taken, yet is but seldom to be so understood. And let me add this more: he that views the ancient ecclesiastical canons shall find hunting to be forbidden to churchmen, as being a turbulent, toilsome, perplexing recreation; and shall find angling allowed to clergymen as being a harmless recreation, a recreation that invites them to contemplation and quietness.—Bethune's edition, p. 45.

Upon this passage, the American editor Bethune first added this note:

> I have alluded to this in the Bib. Pref. In a collection of canons by St. Ives (Yves, Yvon, Yon), at the close of the eleventh century, he gives the decree of Gratian forbidding hunting, founded upon the passage ascribed to St. Jerome on xc (in King James's version xci) Psalm (which I have given in my Bib. Pref., commencing Esau, the usual way of quoting canon law). The reasons for angling being preferred

are either conjectured by Walton or supplied by
St. Ives the compiler.   I quote from the *Corpus
Juris   Canonici*   of   Gregory   XIII,   ed.   1682
(where the decree is found *Dist*. lxxxvi, c. 11),
which has been kindly lent me by a well-read
friend.   This reference has not been made by
any previous commentator on Walton.

In his bibliographical preface (p. xxix) Bethune
says:

> According to the observation of St. Ives, the
> compiler of Ecclesiastical Canons, angling is a
> thing simple and innocent, no ways repugnant
> to the clerical character: non inveniri, in Scrip-
> turis sanctis, sanctum aliquem venatorem; pis-
> catores inveniri sanctos (Esau, c, 86).

This note is by no means very effective when we
consider the possibilities of expounding the Angler
passage, and besides makes no allusion to Chaucer's
Monk; but at least it leads us to the 'Decretals' themselves.   Turning to the *Decretum* of Gratian, more
comprehensive than the earlier work of St. Ives, we
find in *Decreta Pars Prima, Distinctio* lxxxvi, at
least four canons against hunters (c. viii–xi).   Of
these, the one referred to by Bethune reads as follows:

> C. XI.   Hieronymus in Psalm xc, ad vers:
> Sperabo in Domino. Esau venator erat, quoniam
> peccator erat.   Et penitus non invenimus, in

Scripturis sanctis, sanctum aliquem venatorem;
piscatores invenimus sanctos.[3]

Now this, I think we may safely infer, is the
"text" itself which Chaucer had in mind, or the most
reasonable source of it. The 'Decretals' were of
course well known in his time, and especially such
departures from them as were frequently laid at the
door of the religious orders. The very next remark of
Chaucer, that comparing a monk who is "recchelees"
to a "fish that is waterlees" has its more immediate
source in these same ecclesiastical canons.[4] While
Chaucer may have had in mind, as Professor Flügel
thinks, John of Salisbury's *Polycraticus*,[5] the remark
"Interroga patres tuos, et annuntiabunt tibi, majores
tuos, et dicent se nusquam sanctum legisse venatorem" is surely based on Jerome's words above, or
possibly on another form of his comment, as I shall
show. In any case, it is not as direct or forcible as
that I have pointed out, which assumes a more immediate basis in Scripture itself and had behind it
the authority of the whole medieval church. This

---

[3] In St. Ives (Migne, *Patrologia*, CLXI, 810) the statement
of the canon does not differ essentially. It reads: "Pars XIII,
cap. xxxiii. Quod sancti inveniantur piscatores, nulli venatores."

Hieronymus super *Ps.* xc (ad vers. 2). *Dist.* lxxxvi, c. Esau.
Esau, etc., as already quoted.

[4] For the remoter sources see Professor Skeat's note on the
passage.

[5] Lib. I, c. iv, *De Venatica;* Migne, pp. 199, 395.

comment of Jerome was also in the mind of the genial
Walton when he saw how easily it could be used to
support the claims of his own gentle art, while at
the same time bearing most heavily upon his chance
acquaintance Venator.[6]

The decretal based on Jerome is found in the *Breviarium in Psalmos* which, with the *Commentarium*
on Job, was formerly attributed to St. Jerome and
was doubtless regarded as genuine in medieval
times.[7]   The passage reads:

---

[6] A word should be added regarding Professor Skeat's quotation of the English canon against hunting, though its word-
ing shows no special relation to Chaucer's "text."   There are
at least three such canons which may be cited.   The first is
in *Liber Poenitentialis Theodori Archiepiscopi Cantuariensis
Ecclesiae*, xxxii, 4:

"Si clericus venationes exercuit, i annum poeniteat; diaco-
nus ii; presbiter iii annos poentiteat."   *Ancient Laws and Institutes of England*, Vol. II, p. 43.

This belongs to the last half of the seventh century, as
Theodore died in 690.   A second comes to us from the eighth
century, in the Canons of Ecgbert, Archbishop of York (d.
766), Book xiv, 32:

"Gif hwylc gehadod man on huntaþ fare, gif hit beo cleric,
forga xii monaþ flæsc; diacon, ii geara; mæssepreost, iii;
and bisceo, vii." *Ibid.*, Vol. II, p. 214.

Finally, in the tenth century, there is the canon of King
Edgar (lxiv) which Professor Skeat quotes in part:

"And we læraþ þæt preost ne beo hunta, ne hafecere, ne
tæflere, ac plege on his bocum swa his hade gebiraþ." *Ibid.*,
Vol. II, p. 259.   It will be clearly seen that none of these can
be regarded as the original of Chaucer's "text," and it is
probable that no one of them was in his mind when he wrote.

[7] Appendix to Jerome's Commentaries on various books of
the Bible, Migne, *Jerome*, Vol. VII; *Patrologia*, XXVI, 1097.
A footnote on the decretal says that the comment is not found
in Jerome's works, and gives no direct reference to the place
in which it occurs.   The note, of course, means that the passage does not occur in genuine works of Jerome.   But in such

"Quoniam ipse liberabit me de laqueo venantium." Multi sunt venatores in isto mundo, qui animam nostram venari conantur. Denique et Nimrod ille gigas; magnus in conspectu Dei venator fuit (Gen. x, 9), et Esau venator erat (Gen. xxvii, 3) quoniam peccator erat; et penitus non invenimus in Scripturis sanctis, sanctum aliquem venatorem. Piscatores invenimus sanctos.

It will be noticed that both Nimrod and Esau are mentioned, though the decretal takes account of the latter only. This was natural, since Nimrod was associated with tyranny and other vices, while Esau was a hunter in the more restricted sense, and his name was more properly associated with a canon against hunting. This also is some reason for believing that Chaucer knew the ecclesiastical canon only, rather than some passage like that in John of Salisbury, who includes an account of hunting among the classical peoples, besides referring to Nimrod and Esau.

If Jerome did not write the *Breviarium in Psalmos* mentioned above, he expresses the same idea in his *Commentarium in Machaeam*, cap. v, vers. 6 (Migne XXV, 1201): "Quantum ergo possum mea

---

cases we must consider, not what is now known as to the genuineness of works belonging to the early Christian period, but what was believed in medieval times.

recolere memoria, nunquam venatorem in bonam partem legi."

This, it will be seen, is very close to the language of John of Salisbury, and is probably the passage which the latter had in mind when writing the sentence already quoted.

Further back than Jerome, or the *Breviarium* attributed to him, the same thought is similarly expressed by Ambrose, *Expositio in Psalmum* cxviii [cxix], vs. 61. Funes peccatorum:

> Haec sunt sceleratorum vincula quae dure peccatores ligant, hoc est, diabolus et ministri ejus, vel certe Nemrod, hoc est, amaritudo, vel certe Esau, hoc est, terrenus et callidus. Isti enim venatores erant, qui feras laqueis captare consueverunt, et muta animantia vinculis illigare. Inutiles venatores, qui capiant bestias, quae pompam spectaculo populari praebeant, ministerium crudelitati. Denique nullum invenimus in divinarum serie Scripturarum de venatoribus justum.[8]

The reference in this passage to the hunters of wild beasts for the circus has its parallel several times in the writings of St. Augustine, who expresses the abhorrence of early Christians for those gladiatorial shows in which so many of their own number had

---

[8] Migne, *Ambrose*, Vol. I, p. 1380; *Patrologia*, Vol. XV. Cf. preceding page, footnote 7.

suffered martyrdom. It is sufficient here to mention
the Canon based on a passage of Augustine in comment on *Ps.* cii, 6. This has the heading "Nil esse
dandum venatoribus et histrionibus" in the *Decretals of Ives* (Pars XIII, cap. xxxi),[9] and is taken
from the *Enarratio in Psalmos,* cii [ciii], vs. 6
(Migne, XXXVII, 132).

I return to the *Breviarium* attributed to Jerome
in order to mention another part of the commentary
on *Ps.* xci,3, because it has almost equal significance for other passages in medieval literature. Immediately following the part already quoted occurs
this passage:

"Quoniam ipse liberabit me de laqueo venantium. Anima nostra sicut passer erepta est
de laqueo venantium. Laqueus contritus est, et
nos liberati sumus" *(Ps.* cxxiii, 7). Qui est
iste laqueus qui contritus est? Dominus, inquit,
conterat Satanam sub pedibus nostris velociter
(Rom. xvi, 20) ; et Apostolus dicit: Ut libe-
ramini a laqueo diaboli *(II Tim.* ii, 26). Vides
ergo quoniam iste venator est, qui animas nos-
tras venari cupit ad perditionem? Multos habet
diabolus laqueos, et diversos habet laqueos.
Avaritia diaboli laqueus est: ira, detractio, etc.
The hunter is here made a type of the devil and this

---

[9] Migne, *Patrologia*, CLXI, 810. Compare Gratian, Pars Prima, *Distinctio* LXXXVI, c. ix.

is a common conception of medieval writers. Compare Chaucer himself in the *Second Nun's Tale:*

> Wel oghten we to don al oure entente,
> Lest that the feend thurgh ydelnesse us hente.

> For he, that with his thousand cordes slye
> Continuelly us waiteth to biclappe,
> Whan he may man in ydelnesse espye,
> He kan so lightly cacche hym in his trappe,
> Til that a man be hent right by the lappe,
> He nys nat war the feend hath hym in honde;
> Wel oghte us werche and ydelnesse withstonde.[10]

This explains, also, a line in the Middle English Bestiary (Nature Leonis, Significacio prime nature), which reads:

> Migte nevre divel witen   ðog he be derne hunte.

Here "divel" refers to the Latin "venatorem" in the Physiologus of Theobaldus.

The common interpretation of the above-mentioned passage from the Psalms, and similar allusions in

---

[10] *Cant. Tales, G,* 6 f.   For a similar interpretation of the hunter as the devil see the passage from Ambrose already quoted on p. 45.   In his *Enarratio in Psalmos*, Augustine comments as follows on *Ps.* xc [xci],3: Tendit diabolus et angeli ejus, tanquam venantes tendunt muscipulas; et longe ab ipsis muscipulis ambulant homines qui in Christo ambulant. Migne, XXXVII, 1151.   Without attempting to go further, also, I note this passage from Rabanus Maurus, *De Universo,* Lib. VIII, c. i. De Bestiis: Venator diabolus, in cujus figura Nemrod ille gigas venator coram Domino, ut in Genesi *(Gen.* x) ; venatores pravi homines, ut in propheta: Venantes ceperunt me, quasi avem, inimici mei gratis (Thren. III).

other parts of the Bible, directly affected early translations of the Psalter. The interlinears are not
influenced, it is true, but the freer translations introduce instead of "hunter" a more or less clear reference to the devil. This seems to be intended in the
poetical version of the Psalms printed by Thorpe in
1835 and later by Grein,[11] in which Ps. xc [xci], 3
reads:

> For ðon he me alysde   of laðum grine,
> huntum unholdum,   hearmum worde.

As there is nothing in the original requiring "unhol-
dum," and as the noun "unholda" means the devil, it
seems reasonable to believe that the Old English
paraphrast had in mind some such commentary as I
have quoted. Be this as it may, there can be no
doubt of the translation in Middle English, known
as the West Midland Prose Psalter. In this *Ps.* xc
[xci], 3 reads:

> For he delivered me from þe trappes of
> fendes and fram asper word of men.

Similarly *Ps.* cxxiii[cxxiv], 6, 7 is translated:

> Oure soule is defended as þe sparowe from
> þe gnare of þe fouler. Þe trappes of þe fend is
> tobroke wyþ þe deþ of Crist, and we ben deliv-
> ered fro dampnacioun.

It thus becomes evident that the passage in the

---

[11] Wülker's Grein, *Angelsächsische Poesie*, III, 391.

Breviarium in Psalmos attributed to Jerome explains not only the "text" in Chaucer's description of the Monk *CT*, A, 177–180), but more fully than has been done the allusion to the ecclesiastical canons in Walton's *Angler*, and finally the free translations of parts of the Psalms in at least one, probably two, of the early English Psalters.

II

I return to Chaucer's Monk in order to comment on another difficulty connected with the lines immediately following those already explained. Those lines are:

> Ne that a monk, whan he is recchelees,
> Is lykned til a fissh that is waterlees;
> This is to seyn, a monk out of his cloystre;
> But thilke text heeld he nat worth an oystre.

It will be remembered that the word "recchelees," in the first line of this passage, has been regarded as inadequate or incorrect. Professor Skeat adopts the reading "cloisterles," found only in the Harleian MS, and explains the apparent tautology of the third line by assuming that "cloisterles" was "a coined word" and hence needed explanation. The editors of the "Globe" Chaucer retain "recchelees," note the "cloysterles" of the Harleian MS, and add, "neither reading is satisfactory." Liddell has the following note:

4

Recchelees seems to have a peculiar meaning here, "careless of regulations," so that Chaucer has to explain what he means in vv. 181, 182. Various emendations have been suggested, "rewlelees," "cloysterles" of H₄, "recetless," i. e. refugeless, but no emendation is necessary in view of vv. 181, 182.[12]

Just why the reading "recchelees" has been regarded as so unsatisfactory is nowhere explained, but the probable reason is that it suggests modern English "reckless," a word felt to be quite too weak. And yet it should surely be remembered that many a modern word had a stronger and more comprehensive meaning in Old or Middle English, and this should at least suggest an adequate investigation of the original content and use. An examination of the meaning of "recchelees" in such examples as were easily accessible results as follows:

The first appearance of the O. E. word "receleas" ("recceleas") is in the Corpus Gloss, where it translates Lat. "praevaricator" (MS "praefaricator"), Sweet's *Oldest English Texts*, p. 89. In this case we must remember that praevaricator means "one who violates his duty, a transgressor," from which we

---

[12] The suggestion of "rewleles" was made by Professor Koch of Berlin, some twenty years ago *(Anglia* V. *Anzeiger,* p. 128), and again by E. Kruisinga in London *Athenæum* of November 29, 1902. "Recetles" was proposed by Professor Ten Brink, but neither emendation has been adopted by editors.

may also infer the meanings of corresponding medieval words as given by Du Cange, "pravus, perversus, corruptus, immutatus." "Receleas" is used in a similar sense in the Alfredian *Boethius*, v, 3:

> Þu wendest þæt steorlease men and recelease wæron gesællige — translating Latin "nequam homines atque nefarios felices arbitraris."

Upon this passage Lye bases his entry, "receleas i. q. recceleas. Item nefarius, dissolutus." Benson had already preceded Lye with the definitions "negligens, dissolutus." The Alfredian *Bede* (iii, 13) uses the word in the following passage:

> Ymb þa gymene his ecre hælo he wæs to sæne and to receleas — translating the Latin "erga curam perpetuae suae salvationis nihil omnino studii et industriae gerens."

In Ælfric's *Homilies* (ed. of Thorpe, I, 320, 18) the following use of the word again indicates a far more serious neglect and disregard of duty than modern English "reckless" would imply:

> Ac se þe on þam ærran tocyme liþegode, þam synfullum to gecyrrednysse, se demþ stiþne dom þam receleasum æt þam æfteran tocyme.

> But he that at the former advent was mild, for the conversion of the sinful, shall judge a harsh doom to the "recchelees" [to use Chaucer's word] at the later coming.

The same serious sense is carried by the O. E.

nouns "receliest" and "receleasness," though I will not take space to illustrate them.

The Old English uses of the word "receleas" carry the sense of responsible and inexcusable neglect of duty, especially religious duty or regulation. In other examples, not relating to religious affairs, the sense of inexcusable neglect is often apparent, as when King Alfred arraigns the ignorance of his time in the Preface to the *Pastoral Care:*

> Hie [ure ieldran] ne wendon þætte æfre menn sceolden swæ reccelease weorðan, ond sio lar swæ oðfeallan.

The Middle English uses of the word "reccheles" ("recchelees") bear out those of the older language. A number of passages are at hand, but I select only a few. In *Old English Homilies* (First Series, p. 245) we find,

> For alle hit beoð untohene ant rechelese hinen, bute ȝef he ham rihte;
>
> For all these are untoward and "recchelees" servants, unless he directs them,

referring to the senses, which lead the soul to its destruction. So in *Piers Plowman* (B, Passus xviii, 2 f.), the writer speaks of himself

> As a reccheles ranke þat of no wo reccheth,
>
> And yede forth lyke a lorel al my lyftyme,

in which the reference is clearly to neglect of the soul's salvation. Several passages in Chaucer's own

writings might be cited, but I naturally refrain from
using any examples which are not conclusive as to
the stronger meaning of the word. One in which the
corresponding noun is employed may be noted:

> Now, certes, this foule sinne Accidie is eek a
> ful greet enemy to the lyflode of the body; for
> it ne hath no purveaunce agayn temporel neces-
> sitee, for it forsleweth and forsluggeth and
> destroyeth alle goodes temporeles by recchelees-
> nesse.—*The Parson's Tale* (l. 610).

But conclusive proof that Chaucer's "recchelees"
is used in a sense that would be especially applicable
to the Monk, as a prelate, is found in two other passages. The first is in *Old English Homilies* (Second
Series, p. 39), describing the good and bad parson.
Of the latter it says,

> Iners pastor aut sedet in ignorancia aut accu-
> bitat in negligencia, aut jacet in voluntate. Þe
> unwreste herde sit on unwisdomnesse, for he
> ne can is orf gemen; oðer hloneð and slepeð;
> and synegeð on gemeleste alse he þat is recheles
> and non eige ne stand of loverde; oðer lið on
> liþere wille and feste slepeð on his synne.

> The slothful shepherd sitteth in ignorance,
> for he knows not how to guard his flock; or
> lounges about and sinneth in negligence, as he
> that is "recchelees" and standeth in no awe of

his lord; or lieth in evil desire and sleepeth fast in his sins.

The second occurs in the treatise 'Of Confession' in the *Cursor Mundi*. I quote first from the directions given to a priest as to confessing the inmate of a religious house (ll. 27, 232 f.) :

> Þe preist agh spere al wit resun
> O men es in religion,
> Namli hu þai lede þamself
> Anentes þe abusiones tuelf;
> Þe formast, reccles prelat es.
>
> —Cotton MS.

The Fairfax MS is even more direct:

> Þe prest agh spere in gode resun
> Of men þat ar in religioun,
> Quelk reccheles prelatis is.

I may add from another part of *Cursor Mundi* (ll. 28, 238 f) a typical confession, part of which at any rate relates to a priest:

> I ha bene reckeles on many wys
> Anentis Crist and his servise . . . .
>
> *   *   *   *
>
> Mi childer als and my menȝe
> A reckeles ledar þai fand me.
>
> *   *   *   *
>
> Quare I was scheperd, hade sauls to kepe,
> To reckelesly I geit my schepe;
> I chastyd þam noght als me bird,

Ne teched trouth als saul hyrd;
Over slaw I was for þam to ris,
Reckeles to do þam þair servise.
I ha ben bath reckeles and suere
To helpe nedy in þair mistere.

In the first of the above quotations from *Cursor
Mundi* the allusion to 'Þe abusiones tuelf' is especially significant, since it leads us to the treatise
De Duodecim Abusionum Gradibus attributed to
Cyprian or Augustine (Migne IV, 847, or XL, 1079).
In this the tenth is called "Episcopus negligens"—
the "recceles prelat" of *Cursor Mundi,* and ample
explanation of Chaucer's "monk whan he is recche-
less."[13]

The question will still arise why did Chaucer explain the expression "reccheles" by reference to the
"monk out of his cloystre." This, I believe, is not
a serious objection to retaining the MS. reading,
after a proper appreciation of the meaning of
"reccheles." A "reccheles" monk, neglectful of all
the duties and requirements of the monastic life, was
felt to be as anomalous, compared with the true
observer of that life, as a fish out of water. Then
remembering, perhaps, that the latter expression

---

[13] Compare the 'Ten Abuses' in two versions as printed by
Morris in *An Old English Miscellany (Early English Text
Society,* XLIX, 184) ; one of these is:
"Preost þat is wilde,
Biscop slouh."

had been used in special connection with the idea of a monk out of his cloister, one in the fullest sense neglectful of rule, Chaucer adds the explanatory phrase. Besides, a "reccheles" monk and one out of his cloister were regarded as practically the same in medieval conception. The Benedictine Rule takes account of four classes of monks. The first and second are monks and nuns of the regular sort, a third the Sarabaites, an eastern class, and a fourth the wandering monks.[14] With the latter, the bane of the monastic order, were associated all forms of evil, as shown by many references, so that it is not at all strange that Chaucer should have used these two expressions as practically equivalent. In brief, then, the content and use of the word "reccheles," as shown by Old and Middle English examples, prove that it is entirely adequate to the line in which Chaucer uses it; and that there is no real conflict between the expressions "reccheles" and "out of his cloistre" in the following line.

In further exposition of the lines on the monk it may not be out of place to recall the number of specific precepts of the Benedictine Rule and the canons which Chaucer's monk was guilty of disobeying.

---

[14] Quartum vero genus est monachorum quod nominatur gyrovagum; qui tota vita sua per diversas provincias ternis aut quaternis diebus per diversorum cellas hospitantur, semper vagi et numquam stabiles. Et propriis voluptatibus et gule illecebris servientes et per omnia deteriores Sarabaitis. —Benedictine Rule, chap. i.

He disregarded, as we have seen, the canons against hunting (ll. 166, 177–82, 189–92). His fine horses and dogs were equally opposed to the vow of poverty taken by the monks. His fine clothes (ll. 193, 197, 203) were in direct contravention of the Benedictine requirement of the simplest and coarsest clothing. He paid no attention to the rule of study and of labor with the hands "as Austin bit" (ll. 184–7) ; in short, he was utterly neglectful of any part of the Rule he had solemnly sworn to observe, whenever it interfered with his interests in "the newe world" (ll. 173–6).

THE SUITORS IN CHAUCER'S PARLEMENT OF FOULES*

Ever since Professor John Koch of Berlin suggested the relation of Chaucer's *Parlement of Foules* to the betrothal and marriage of Richard II and Anne of Bohemia, his conclusions have been almost universally accepted.[1] They were felt to give a definite occasion and a fairly definite dating[2] to one of the most important of the minor poems. So fully have Professor Koch's conclusions been accepted that, in general, they have not been reviewed except in an entirely favorable manner.[3] Nor do I now

---

* *Mod. Phil.* Vol. VIII, pp. 45–62 (1910).

[1] 'Ein Beitrag zur Kritik Chaucers,' *Englische Studien*, I, 288; the same (enlarged) with title, 'On an Original Version of the Knight's Tale,' *Essays on Chaucer*, Chaucer Soc., p. 408.

[2] It is true that Professor Koch first suggested, in the essay above noted, St. Valentine's Day, 1381, as the date of writing, after which he assumed 1380, in his translation of the *Minor Poems* (1880), and then 1382, in the *Chronology of Chaucer's Writings* (Chaucer Soc., p. 37). The last dates were on the basis of the allusion to the planet Venus in ll. 117 f.

[3] The fullest restatements of the facts have been made by Bilderbeck, in *Selections from Chaucer's Minor Poems* (1897), and Professor J. S. P. Tatlock, in *Development and Chronology of Chaucer's Works* (Chaucer Soc., 1907). The latter has used Theo. Lindner, *Geschichte des deutschen Reiches unter König Wenzel* (1875), und C. Höfler, 'Anna von Luxemburg,' in *Denkschriften d. Wiener Akad., Phil.-Hist. Classe*, XX, in addition to Pelzel, *Lebensgeschichte des Königs Wenzeslaus* (1788), used by Koch. One or two points in Tatlock's treatment may be mentioned, lest they should seem to oppose my own statements in this article. "In June, 1380, commis-

propose to attempt any considerable alteration of
such important results in Chaucer study. Yet a
recent study of the subject has suggested a further
consideration of some points in connection with the
wooing of Anne. Especially do I wish to note the
discovery of a suitor for her hand, hitherto unmen-
tioned in any discussion of the poem.

Regarding the suitors of Anne Professor Koch
says:[4]

And at p. 110, he [Pelzel, whom he has just
quoted in regard to Richard's proposal for her
hand] relates that Anne was engaged as early
as 1371 to a Prince of Bavaria; and in 1373,
when she was seven years of age, to a Mar-

---

sioners were appointed to treat of a marriage between Richard and Anne, Wenceslas' sister," should read "between Richard and Katherine, daughter of Ludwig, recently emperor of
the Romans" (Rymer's *Fœdera*, VII, 257). So also, "and
December 20, Richard announced that he had chosen her,"
based on Höfler's somewhat rhetorical statement (129), should
be "December 26," as to date, probably a misprint merely.
The last part of the statement, however, seems to me to give
a wrong idea of the progress of the negotiations. I have examined the whole series of documents in a paper called 'A
New Note on the Date of Chaucer's Knight's Tale,' in *Studies
in Language and Literature*, a volume commemorating Professor J. M. Hart's seventieth birthday [cf. below, pp. 123–73].
Here may be added only that, in the commission of December
26, Richard merely says, since he had directed the eyes of his
consideration *(oculos nostrae considerationis)* toward the
lady Anne, it had pleased him to make beginning of a compact of matrimony *(placuit nobis . . . Fœdus inire Conjugii
Conjugalis)*, and on this account he had appointed certain
ambassadors to bring it to conclusion *(pro Negotii hujusmodi
Conclusione)*. Anne was to be received, not "on Michaelmas
next," but about that time *(circa Festum Sancti Michaelis
proximo futurum)* (Rymer, VII, 301).

[4] *Essays on Chaucer*, 407–8.

grave of Misnia . . . . In King Richard and the two German princes we may recognize [the] three eagles wooing the formel.

It is true Professor Koch does notice the strangeness of Chaucer's including the Prince of Bavaria, and he explains it by saying:[5]

People most likely had not a very clear notion as to the state of affairs in Germany . . . For, in fact, the Prince of Bavaria was no longer a competitor with King Richard, since his match had already been broken off for years.

Yet even this implies that Chaucer knew of the two German suitors and includes them both in his poem, without perhaps knowing that the first was no longer a rival.

Professor A. W. Ward, who accepts Professor Koch's identification of the suitors in his *Chaucer,* says:[6]

Anne of Bohemia, daughter of the Emperor Charles IV and sister of King Wenceslas, had been successively betrothed to a Bavarian prince and to the Margrave of Meissen, before —after negotiations which, according to Froissart, lasted a year—her hand was given to the young King Richard II of England. This suf-

---

[5] *Ibid*, 408.

[6] 'English Men of Letters' series, chap. ii, 57.

ficiently explains the general scope of the *Assembly of Fowls.*

Professor Skeat quotes Professor Ward as above and adds a footnote as follows:[7]

> The royal tercel is, then, Richard II; the formel eagle is Anne; the other two tercel eagles were her other two suitors.

Taken in connection with what is said in the text, this means the Bavarian prince and the Margrave of Meissen, to whom Anne had been at different times betrothed. In the Globe edition of *Chaucer* Mr. H. F. Heath puts the matter with even greater definiteness:[8]

> Anne is represented in the poem by the formel (i. e. female) eagle and Richard by the royal eagle, while the two tercels (i. e., males) "of lower kind," who plead for her love, are the Prince of Bavaria and the Margrave of Misnia, to each of whom Anne had been contracted.

It is to this explicit identification of the suitors that I wish to call special attention.

It must have occurred to others than Professor Koch that it was a strange procedure on Chaucer's part to introduce, as a rival suitor of Richard, one whose betrothal had been broken off as early as

---

[7] *The Works of Geoffrey Chaucer,* I, 75.

[8] *Introduction,* xxxix.

1373, at least seven, perhaps nine years, before the time of the poem.[9] Others may have wondered what reason we have to suppose that Chaucer even knew of such an engagement. Such news would surely not have had international circulation, nor would it have been freely communicated to those interested in this new match. At any rate, Chaucer would scarcely have been likely to use this long-past betrothal, if there had been a more active suitor in the field. As such a suitor may now be presented with confidence, we may safely dismiss William of Baiern-Holland, who was Anne's betrothed from 1371 to 1373, as not likely to have been in Chaucer's mind. This leaves but one of the two suitors usually mentioned, the son of Friedrich of Thüringen, who himself became Friedrich of Meissen in 1381.

This Friedrich of Meissen is a more important personage. Moreover, some significant details may be added to what has hitherto been connected with his betrothal. That betrothal had been arranged in 1373, as has been noted. That the match was considered a worthy one is clear from the terms Anne's father was willing to make. The sum of "10,000 Schock Groschen Prager Münze" was to be Anne's dower, and for it were pledged the two towns of

---

[9] Seven years, that is, if the poem was begun as early as 1380, the earliest possible date to which it could be assigned, either from the reference to Venus (l. 117), or from the beginning of negotiations for a German princess. It is nine years if the poem belongs to the summer of 1382.

Brüx and Laun, northwest of Prague.[10] We shall see
that this latter provision is of some importance in
the sequel. This second betrothal of Anne "had
been broken off," says Professor Koch, following
Pelzel, "on account of Mayence."[11] The affair "of
Mayence" to which Pelzel refers is the rivalry for
the archbishopric of Mainz at the death of Archbishop John on April 4, 1373.[12] The rival claimants
for the place were Adolf of Nassau and Bishop Ludwig of Bamberg, the latter uncle of Anne's betrothed
and favored by her father, the emperor Charles IV.
Adolf of Nassau obtained actual possession, and
Ludwig, in spite of recognition by the pope and the
emperor, had only pretensions to satisfy him.[13] In
June, 1377, also, owing to the loss of their chief
ally, the Thuringian house came to an agreement

---

[10] Horn, *Lebens- und Helden-Geschichte Friedrichs des
Streitbaren*, 80 f.: "Es hiess dieselbe nicht nach etlicher Vor-
geben Helena, sondern Anna, ... und solte vermöge der-
selben die leibliche Beylegung über 8 Jahr oder 1381 erfolgen,
auch der Keyserl. Tochter 10,000 Schock Groschen Prager
Münze zur Heimsteuer mitgegeben, oder aber, wenn die Zah-
lung binnen einen Jahr nach dem Beylager nicht geschähe,
davor Brüx Hauss und Stadt nebst der Stadt Luna [Laun]
pfandweise eingeräumet werden." The reference to "Helena"
instead of "Anne" is based on the fact that some of the
chroniclers give the former name as that of the daughter married to Richard II of England. One even says that Anne died
in 1379, and questions whether another may have replaced
her in the marriage. Horn sets the matter at rest by giving
the document of betrothal at p. 647.

[11] *Essays on Chaucer*, p. 407.

[12] Lindner, I, 23.

[13] *Ibid*, 63.

with its opponents, and the struggle between Ludwig and Adolf was at an end for the time.[14]

To follow this affair more fully, at the papal schism in 1378 Adolf of Nassau saw his opportunity. When Bishop Ludwig, supported by Wenceslaus, who had now succeeded his father, Charles IV, acted as Archbishop of Mainz in the Diet of 1379, Adolf at once became a Clementist, and received recognition of his claim to the archbishopric from the French pope.[15] But Mainz was too important to both Urban and Wenceslaus, and Adolf was found to be willing to return to the Urbanists, if the coveted archbishopric should be acknowledged by both pope and emperor. Urban saw the importance of a united Germany, and in January, 1381, Adolf was virtually recognized by Wenceslaus and the kingdom. Wenceslaus also looked after the disappointed Ludwig by making him archbishop of Magdeburg soon after.[16] There was no direct occasion, therefore, in the "affair of Mayence" for breaking the match with Anne. Pelzel must be in error in his statement of the breaking off of the betrothal for this reason. While rancor was engendered, perhaps, there is no evidence of a formal breaking of the engagement.

Meanwhile, the new alignment of the nations, re-

[14] *Ibid.*, 30, 63–64, 312–13.

[15] *Ibid.*, 103–4.

[16] *Ibid.*, 120–21, 133.

sulting from the papal schism, had brought new complications. Pope Urban was using every endeavor to win over the largest following, and bind the nations to himself with the closest bonds. On his part, Clement VII was doing his best to unite France and Germany.[17] If, therefore, Urban did not suggest the marriage of Richard II and Anne of Bohemia, he used all his influence to further that match, and so make impossible any terms between Wenceslaus and France, the latter now fully supporting the schismatic pope. As early as May 20, 1379, probably at the instigation of the papal nuncio, Cardinal Pileus de Prata, Wenceslaus had written to Richard proposing an alliance against schismatics.[18] This was the beginning of that more intimate relation between England and Bohemia which resulted in Anne's betrothal to the English king.

Such betrothal, and the marriage which followed, brought the virtual, though not the formal, abrogation of the engagement of Anne and Friedrich of Meissen. The latter was still only one, though the eldest, son of Friedrich of Thuringia, and helpless we may assume to press his claim against the powerful brothers of Anne, Wenceslaus, king of Bohe-

[17] *Ibid.*, 118. Speaking of this Lindner says: "Denn man hatte in Rom besseres im Sinne. Die Pläne der Avignonesen, den deutschen König durch eine Familienverbindung mit Frankreich zu liieren, mussten durchkreuzt werden."

[18] Höfler, 127; Lindner, I, 95.

mia and emperor, and Sigmund, king of Hungary.[19]
His betrothal was therefore merely set aside for
the greater match, now placed within the power of
Wenceslaus and strongly urged by the pope. Nor is
there evidence of any arrangement for settling the
definite claim which, owing to the terms of the betrothal, Friedrich of Meissen still had upon the emperor.

The best evidence that the betrothal of Anne and
Friedrich was never formally abrogated is the atti-
tude of the Thuringian house in the later affairs of
the empire. Then the representatives of that house
did not forget the double slight placed upon them,
first by Wenceslaus's failure to support Bishop Ludwig of Bamberg for the archbishopric of Mainz, and
second by his disregard of the long-standing marriage contract.[20] At the death of Friedrich of Thuringia in 1381, Friedrich, the betrothed of Anne,
became Margrave of Meissen, and began that strenuous career which gave him the name of "der Streit-
bare," "the Warlike." More than once he opposed
the emperor Wenceslaus, until, in 1397, in connection with the struggle between Wenceslaus and Jobst
of Moravia, the old debt incurred at his betrothal to
Anne was wiped out. In that year the warlike Margrave took from Wenceslaus the two towns, Brüx

---

[19] The part of Sigmund of Hungary is vouched for in the
chronicles cited by Horn, 83.

[20] Lindner, I, 133; II, 190.

and Laun, which had been pledged for Anne's dower.[21]

Still later, in 1409, when Wenceslaus arbitrarily took from the Germans a large part of their authority at the University of Prague and the German students seceded, Friedrich helped to welcome them, and to found for their use the University of Leipsic.[22] Thus was the Emperor Wenceslaus doubly humbled for his disregard of the marriage contract between Anne and Friedrich of Meissen.   It is of incidental interest that Friedrich remained unmarried all these years, not taking a wife until 1402, when he married a daughter of Henry the "Mild."   He became, too, a notable prince.   In 1423 he won for himself the electorate of Saxony, a dignity which thus became permanently attached to his house.

If, then, the betrothal of Friedrich was never for-

[21] My attention was first called to this and the following circumstance by my friend Professor George L. Burr of Cornell University. The passage from Horn occurs on p. 351 f. Horn writes: "Es bekräfftiget mich hierinn eine Verschreibung, welche ihm der König auf Unterhandlung des Bischoffs zu Bamberg and Marggraff Wilhelms des ältern, seines Vettern zu der Zeit Donnerst. vor S. Galli pro redimenda vexa über Brüx und Lune gegeben, weiln die vormaln 1373 zwischen dessen Schwester Annen und ihm abgeredete Ehe-Pacten nicht in ihre Erfüllung gegangen, und gleichwohl man sich bey entstehender Vollziehung Königlicher seits eventualiter anheischig gemacht, die versprochene Heyraths-Gelder an 10,000 Schock nichts desto weniger zu bezahlen, als oben bereits mit mehrern referiret worden, auch Churfürst Friedrich die davon versessen Zinsen, so wohl aufgewandte Kosten, Schäden und Zehrung nicht länger darben wolte."   He quotes an annalist to the same effect on p. 128, under the year 1397.

[22] Horn, 301 f.

mally broken, but merely set aside by Anne's imperial brother, Friedrich may reasonably be regarded
as one of the rivals of Richard in the allegory of the
Parlement of Foules. Should we try to identify him
with one of the "tercel" suitors of the "formel egle,"
it would naturally be with the second mentioned in
the poem, "another tercel egle . . . of lower kinde."[23]
As compared with that of the "royal tercel," too, the
profession of this second suitor would also apply
with striking aptness:

I love hir bet than ye do, by Seynt John,

.   .   .   .

And lenger have served hir, in my degree;
And if she shulde have loved for long loving,
To me allone had been the guerdoning.[24]

Surely, if these lines have more than general significance, they describe one to whom Anne had been
betrothed for many years, and who, before the negotiations with England, had no reason to believe that
his long engagement would not be followed by marriage.

But Chaucer, as we know, introduces a third suit-
or for the "formel egle," or Anne of Bohemia. I
propose to show that there was such a suitor, entirely disregarded in any previous discussion of the
subject, but far more active than even Friedrich of

[23] Ll. 449–50.

[24] Ll. 45–55.

Meissen, and a far more worthy rival of Richard II himself.[25] Moreover, there can be no doubt that Chaucer knew of him, however little he may have known of Anne's engagements to the German princes. I shall hope to show, also, that the language used by the third suitor is appropriate to this new rival of the young Richard. The way in which he came to be suitor for the hand of Anne will be clearer from some elements of the history of the time.

When the papal schism occurred at the election of Clement VII in September, 1378, the rival popes began a vigorous campaign for supporters. Charles IV, king of Bohemia and emperor of the Romans, as he called himself, held firmly to the Roman pope. Perhaps he was partly led thereto by the relation of the pope to his imperial title.[26] Charles, however, did not outlive the year of the schism, dying less than three months after the election of Clement. His son Wenceslaus, brother of Anne and a youth of only seventeen when he succeeded his father, was likely to be more easily influenced. As a result each pope sent him his messenger. Clement dispatched Bishop John of Cambray November 5, 1378,[27] and in March,

---

[25] But see article "Richard II," *Dict. of Nat. Biog.*

[26] He had obtained the title "emperor of the Romans" in 1346, but had not been crowned at Rome until 1354, and then only after pledging Pope Innocent VI that he would leave the imperial city the same day. Now, however, he wished acknowledgment of his claim, and he was recognized as emperor by Urban on July 26, 1378.

[27] Lindner, I, 102, note.

1379, when returning from Frankfort, Wenceslaus
was met by Cardinal Pileus de Prata of Ravenna,[28]
who had been commissioned to him as papal nuncio.
Pileus made haste to impress upon the young emper-
or that to accept the schismatic Clement would be
to make his father a heretic.[29] On the other hand,
for Wenceslaus to support Urban meant severing
the long-standing alliance with France.[30] That alliance had been more recently strengthened by his
father. On January 9, 1378, upon a visit to Paris,
Charles IV had spoken out unmistakably for France
in her contention with England, and had pledged his
son, his other children, all his relatives, his allies
and friends, and his whole power to her support.[31]
In the latter relation of ally of France, Clement VII
saw an opportunity to influence Wenceslaus. He
therefore urged a union between Bohemia and
France, to be rendered firm by a marriage of the
Dauphin with Wenceslaus's sister Anne.

Charles V of France was also eager for such an
alliance on grounds of general advantage to his

---

[28] *Ibid.*, I, 94.

[29] Höfler, 130; Lindner, I, 113.

[30] Recall that the blind king of Bohemia, John of Luxem-
burg, had lost his life at Crécy in 1346, fighting as an ally of
France; that his sister, Maria of Luxemburg, was the wife of
Charles IV of France, while his daughter Bona became the
wife of King John "the Good," and so mother of Charles V.
Wenceslaus and Charles V of France were thus first cousins.

[31] Höfler, 126.

kingdom. He had already sent a commission to the
Diet of Frankfort in 1379, and a year later he still
had hopes of success in his efforts.[32] The subject of
the marriage, even, had been broached. Of it the
French historian Valois says:

> Durant un séjour de Wenceslas à Aix-la-
> Chapelle, on avait parlé d'un mariage entre le
> dauphin, fils du roi de France, et Anne de Lux-
> embourg, sœur du roi des Romains. Une
> entrevue devait avoir lieu entre Charles V et
> Wenceslas . . . . La cour d'Avignon comptait
> beaucoup sur le résultat de cette conférence.
> Entre autres personnages qui promettaient de
> s'y rendre, je citerai les envoyés du roi de Por-
> tugal et, à leur tête, l'évêque de Lisbonne, qui
> déjà préparait le discours avec lequel il devait
> convertir Wenceslas. Cette entrevue n'eut pas
> lieu: le roi des Romains, tournant le dos à
> Reims, reprit la route de Cologne. Il se fit, il
> est vrai, représenter à Paris par quatre ambas-
> sadeurs; mais l'acte, sans doute rédigé d'avance,
> dont ces derniers étaient porteurs ne traitait
> que du renouvellement des alliances entre les
> deux maisons, sans souffler mot de mariage du
> dauphin avec la bohémienne Anne.[33]

---

[32] Valois, *La France et le grand schisme d'occident*, I, 269.

[33] *Ibid.*, I, 300. As authorities for this statement Valois cites
a "Lettre du cardinal de Viviers aux cardinaux de Florence
et de Milan," Baluzius, II, 869; and his own edition of the

This journey of Wenceslaus to Aix-la-Chapelle was
after the Frankfort Diet of April, 1380.[34] As late as
that time, therefore, the emperor was still considering the possible betrothal of his sister Anne and the
heir of the French throne. Indeed, we must not
assume that at any time the young Wenceslaus was
distinctly hostile to his cousin, Charles V of France,
or the latter's son, the prince who became Charles VI
in September, 1380. As an evidence of the intimate relations between the two, Froissart tells us
that, when Charles V. of France was ill in the summer before his death, Wenceslaus sent his own physician, George of Prague, to treat him.[35] It was
rather the papal situation which finally caused the
severing of such relations of alliance as had long
existed between the two countries.

To defeat such an alliance of Wenceslaus and
France was now the chief purpose of Pope Urban.
England had already accepted him as pope in the
Gloucester parliament of October–November, 1378.
There was, perhaps, no fear of losing her allegiance.
If Germany was equally certain to remain loyal, it
was still important to bind together the nations sup-
porting Urban by a firmer league against the schis-

"Discours prononcé le 14 juillet 1380, en présence de
Charles V, par Martin l'évêque de Lisbonne," in the *Bibliothèque de l'École des Chartes*, LII, 495, 500.

[34] Lindner, I, 114, 116, 430.

[35] *Chronicles*, II, chap. lv; Johnes, I, 615.

matics.   It was probably at the suggestion of the
papal nuncio that Wenceslaus first proposed to Richard II, in May, 1379, an alliance in support of Urban.[36]   This was shortly after a Diet at Frankfort,
on February 27, 1379, in which a league of German
princes had been formed 1or the same purpose.   In
furtherance of union between Germany and England, it would seem, the same papal nuncio, Cardinal
Pileus de Prata, went to the latter country in 1380.[37]
Moreover, it was probably he who first suggested
the marriage of Richard with a German princess.[38]
At any rate, it was in the same June, 1380, that
Richard definitely turned his eyes to such a possible
alliance.[39] Peace with France having been found im-

---

[36] See p. 65.

[37] He was there at least as early as June, since on the seventh of that month he obtained from Richard II certain rights
to revenues in connection with Lichfield and Lincoln cathedrals; Rymer's *Fœdera*, VII, 256.

[38] An entry in *Issues of the Exchequer* (Devon, 224) of January 9, 1384, would imply that the marriage of Richard and
Anne was perhaps considered somewhat earlier than June,
1380.   I have dealt with that in another place [See p. 134 f.],
but, if the inferences from that entry are wholly true, they do
not materially affect this paper.

[39] Rymer, VIII, 257.   The person first named in the commission, as already noted, was "Katherine, daughter of Ludwig,
recently emperor of the Romans."   The Emperor Ludwig of
Bavaria, however, had died in 1347, so that his daughter
would have been more than twice the age of Richard.   No
adequate explanation has been given of this proposal, or of
the sudden change to Anne, the sister of Wenceslaus, a little
later.   Could it be that, as the king of France is known to
have wished Anne for his son, afterward Charles VI, Wenceslaus was hoping to ally himself with France by the marriage of his sister, and with England by the marriage of his

possible, the councilors of the young king wished him to marry abroad that he might obtain an ally in the long-drawn-out war with France.[40]

Meanwhile the king of France, probably urged on by Clement VII, was more active for a league with his old-time ally in Germany. In the summer of 1380 he learned of the English negotiations for a marriage of Richard II and Anne of Bohemia. Even though soon stricken with the disease which brought his death on September 16, his sagacity emphasized the importance of the German league. On his death-bed he said to his courtiers: "Seek out in Germany an alliance for my son, that our connections there may be strengthened. You have heard that our adversary is about to marry from thence to increase his alliance."[41]

There is also evidence that these negotiations were carried on after the death of Charles V and the accession of Charles VI. The marriage of Anne with Charles was urged by the Clementists as the only way of winning Wenceslaus and Germany to their side.[42] A letter from Cardinal Peter de Sor-

aunt? In any case an explanation is not necessary for our immediate purpose.

[40] Froissart, *Chronicles*, II, chap. xliii; Johnes, I, 592–93: "The English . . . wished the king to choose a queen from beyond sea, in order to gain stronger alliances."

[41] Froissart, *Chronicles*, II, chap. lv; Johnes, I, 616.

[42] Höfler, 130; Lindner, I, 113: "Die einzige Hoffnung, Wenzel zur Umkehr zu bewegen, läge in jetzt schwebenden Verhandlungen über die Ehe zwischen seiner Schwester und dem Könige von Frankreich."

tenac implies that actual negotiations were under way. He says:

> Nec est spes eum [Wenceslaus] pro nunc revocandi, nisi per tractatum matrimonii, qui pendet de sorore sua danda regi Francie, in quo tractatu speratur, quod possit informari de justitia domini nostri, et de praeservatione fame et honoris patris sui mortui, et per consequens reduci.[43]

We have also the testimony to the same effect of the English chronicler, Adam of Usk. Speaking of Cardinal Pileus de Prata, whose notary in London he was, Adam says: "After his departure the said Lady Anne was bought for a price by our lord the king, for she was much sought in marriage by the king of France."[44]

Even as late as the early part of 1381 Wenceslaus had sent an embassy to France, nominally to urge Charles VI to support Urban as the true pope. The French historian Valois suggests that, while this may have been prompted by zeal for the church, it

---

[43] Quoted by Höfler (130) from Baluzius, *Vitae Paparum Avenionensium*, II, 869. The last clause refers to the fear of Wenceslaus that, if he recognized Clement, it would make a heretic of his father, who had died in the full acceptance of Urban's election.

[44] *Chronicon Adae de Usk*, ed. by Thompson, 102. The original reads: "Post cujus recessum dicta domina Anna, per dominum regem magno precio redempta, quia a rege Francie in uxorem affectata."

was possibly also to further, by indirection, the marriage project with Richard.[45]   The ambassadors reached Paris March 10, and even if they did not discuss, so late as this, the possible marriage of Anne with the French king, the English may have feared as much and have therefore still considered the French king as the rival of Richard.

From the foregoing recital it is clear that the most active rival of Richard II for the hand of Anne of Bohemia was not a German prince at all, but the far more important heir to the French throne, and king of France before the negotiations were concluded.   Behind him, too, were the close ties of blood between the reigning monarchs of France and Bohemia, the traditional friendship of the two countries, the recently renewed league between the father of Wenceslaus and Charles V of France, and the power of Clement VII and of his supporters in the French church.   The strength of the French desire for an alliance with the emperor of the Romans may perhaps best be seen in the strength of French resentment, when the decision in favor of Richard had been made, and the young princess Anne was on her way to England.   It is Froissart who tells the story:

> The Lady Anne of Bohemia remained with her uncle and aunt at Brussels upwards of a month.   She was afraid of moving, for she had

---

[45] *La France et le grand schisme d' occident*, II, 274.

been informed there were twelve large armed
vessels, full of Normans, on the sea between
Calais and Holland, that seized and pillaged
all that fell into their hands, and it was indifferent to them who they were. The report was
current, that they cruised in those seas waiting
for the coming of this lady; and that the king
of France and his council were desirous of carrying her off, in order to break the match, for
they were very uneasy at this alliance of the
Germans and the English . . . . On account of
these suspicions and fears, the young lady remained at Brussels one whole month. The Duke
of Brabant, by advice of his council, sent to
France the Lords de Rousselans and de Bous-
quehois, to remonstrate on this subject with the
king and his uncles, who were also his nephews
[that is, nephews of Duke Wenceslaus of Bra-
bant], being his sister's sons.

The knights of Brabant managed so well with
the king and his council that their request was
complied with, and passports granted for the
lady and her attendants to travel through any
parts of France she might choose, as far as
Calais. The Normans were remanded into port.
This answer the knights carried to Brabant to
the Duke and Duchess. The king and his uncles
wrote to say, they had granted the favor to

their cousin, the Lady Anne, at their solicitation alone, and for no other reason whatever.[46]

The clause, "for they were very uneasy at this alliance of the Germans and the English," is full proof of the serious efforts the French had made to continue their friendly relations with Germany. The last expression, regarding the passports granted, shows the resentment of the young king and his royal uncles toward the successful suitor Richard.

Perhaps, too, the knowledge that his chief rival for the hand of Anne was his enemy, the French king, may have influenced Richard in so eagerly seeking the Bohemian alliance. Possibly this was the reason also why Wenceslaus could make such excellent terms with the English king, giving no dowry with the princess, but rather obtaining for himself an enormous loan.[47]   Again this eagerness,

[46] *Chronicles*, II, chap. lxxxvi; Johnes, I, 681.   C. G. Chamberlayne, *Die Heirat Richards II von England mit Anna von Luxemburg* (Halle, 1906), undertakes to discredit Froissart's account of Anne's delay in Brussels and his statement of the French king's designs.   The explicitness of the account, however, the number of details, especially the mission to the French king from Wenceslaus of Brabant, his great uncle, and the character of the answer, bear heavily for Froissart's accuracy, or, if the tale is manufactured, for needlessly clever mendacity.   For our purpose, even the report in England of such a train of circumstances would have been sufficient to support the idea of the French king's rivalry for the hand of Anne.   Besides, if the whole of Froissart's account be brushed aside as a tissue of falsehood, it would not affect the preceding line of reasoning.   The discussion of Chamberlayne, however, has not convinced me that Froissart had not good ground for his circumstantial statement.

[47] The documents are in Rymer, VII, 288 f.   Wenceslaus received 80,000 florins as a loan, 20,000 of which were not to be

and the vast sum which Wenceslaus secured, may explain the distinctly critical tone of several chroniclers in referring to the marriage. We have already noted Adam of Usk's expression, "the said Lady Anne was bought for a price." The *Chronicon Angliae* says:[48]

> Hanc [Anne] igitur magno pretio, multisque coemptam laboribus, habendam rex praeëlegerat, quamquam cum inaestimabili auri summa oblata fuisset et filia domini Mediolanensis Barnabonis.

The writer of the Continuation to the *Eulogium Historiarum* adds another criticism:[49]

> Hoc anno Rex Annam sororem Imperatoris, Regis scilicet Bohemiae, solutis pro ea 22 m[illia] marcis, sine consensu regni, desponsavit.

To these may be added two other notes. The *Chronicon Henrici Knighton*[50] has this to say:

---

returned, as covering the expenses of the negotiations for the marriage and of Anne in reaching England. Besides, there were enormous gifts to those assisting in the negotiations; see the paper to which I refer above on p. 58, footnote 3 [*A New Note on the Date of Chaucer's Knight's Tale*, p. 152 f., and footnote 57, below.]

[48] See p. 331; Rolls Series, 64, 331.

[49] Rolls Series, 9, III, 355. The matter seems to have been wholly arranged by Richard's council, without consulting parliament, until on December 13, 1381, Richard asked for a grant of money because of his approaching marriage with Anne *(Rotuli Parliamentorum*, III, 104*a)*. The result of the discussion attending this request of Richard was the appointment of Michael de la Pole and Richard Fitzalan, Earl of Arundel, as governors of the person of the king and constant counsellors *(Ibid.*, III, 104*b)*.

[50] *Ibid.*, 92, p. 150.

Eodem anno apud Westmonasterium rex Ricardus desponsavit Annam, filiam regis Boemi, Sororem Imperatoris, et dedit imperatori ut dicebatur pro maritagio decem mille libras praeter alias expensas in quaerendo eam et adducendo eam sumptibus suis propriis.

Finally, John Malvern, in his continuation of Higden's *Polychronicon*, adds the more biting comment:

De ista regina quidam scripsit metrice,
Digna frui manna datur Anglis nobilis Anna,
sed scrutantibus verum videbatur non dari, sed
potius emi. Nam non modica pecunia refundebat rex Angliae pro tentilla carnis portione.[51]

Thus, it is clear that some at least felt Richard had made a bad bargain. Nor can there be much doubt that, considering the results to the nation as a whole, England paid an enormous price for her queen and her rather profitless alliance.

If this new aspirant for the hand of Anne is to be considered, it is natural to ask how far the language of Chaucer's third suitor of the "formel egle" will fit the case. I recognize that we must not try to see too much, and the main point is made in emphasizing the rivalry of Charles VI and Richard II. Yet the third suitor may not unreasonably be identified with the young king of France. For example the words,

---

[51] Higden's *Polychronicon* (Rolls Series), IX, 12.

Of long servise avaunte I me no-thing,[52]

would be peculiarly applicable. As already shown, it was in the spring of 1380 that there had first been talk of a marriage of Anne and the Dauphin of France.[53] It was not until September that Charles could have been a suitor in his own right as king. Even the words,

A man may serven bet and more to pay
In half a yere, although hit were no more,[54]

could scarcely have been better chosen, if they had been definitely intended for the young Charles. Indeed, it was scarcely more than a half-year from the accession of Charles in September, 1380, to the signing of the marriage treaty in London, May 1, 1381. Or, it was but about half a year from June, 1380, when the English negotiations and the French activity in the matter began, until the betrothal to Richard was virtually decided upon.

Again, has Chaucer, with such circumstances in mind as I have noted, intended to reflect the hopelessness of Charles VI's wooing? Even the beginning of the speech is that of one who feels he has no chance:

---

[52] *Parlement of Foules*, l. 470.

[53] See above, p. 70.

[54] Ll. 474–75.

6

Now, sirs, ye seen the litel leyser here,

. . . .

And eek Nature hirself ne wol noght here,

For tarying here, noght half that I wolde seye.[55]

Nor could the poet have chosen more appropriate
words than those at the beginning of the last stanza:

I ne say this by me, for I ne can

Do no servyse that may my lady plese;

But I dar seyn I am hir trewest man

As to my dome, and feynest wolde hir ese.[56]

Whether these last suggestions are equally interpretative, it must be admitted that the notes of time
in the speeches of the last two suitors have significant parallelism in the long betrothal of Friedrich
of Meissen, and the short period during which
Charles VI was considered a suitor. Moreover, the
short period mentioned in the last speech would far
more aptly fit the case of Charles VI than the two-
year betrothal of William of Baiern-Holland, which
had been broken off seven years before, even if that
betrothal could have been in Chaucer's mind.

It might be objected to the identification of the
"thridde tercel egle" as Charles VI of France, that
he too should have been called "royal" as was the

---

[55] Ll. 464, 467–68.

[56] Ll. 477–80. The manners of a ruder age almost suggest
that there may be here a less elegant slight upon the prowess
of the young Charles, a boy little over eleven years of age in
May, 1380, when his marriage with Anne was first considered.

first tercel, representing Richard. Yet to this objection I believe there are several good answers. In
the first place it may be assumed, as Mr. Pollard at
least does [assume],[57] that all the eagles of this first
choice of a mate are royal. It is true, Chaucer says
of the birds as a whole in the garden,

>Ther mighte men the royal egle finde
>That with his sharpe look perceth the sonne;
>And other egles of a lower kinde.[58]

When, however, we come to the choice of mates, Nature says to all the birds:

>The tercel egle, as that ye knowen wel,
>The foul royal above yow in degree,
>
>. . . . .
>
>He shal first chese and speken in his gyse.
>
>And after him, by order shul ye chese
>After your kinde, everych as yow lyketh.[59]

Now the "tercel egle," "the foul royal," is here used
for a class, of which there are three representatives
in contest for "the formel." This must be clear, I
think, from the last two lines, which refer not to the
choice of the other two tercels, but to that of the
other kinds of birds. Nor would it have been at all
flattering to Anne, England's new queen, if two of
those who wooed her were not of royal or princely

[57] *Chaucer* ('Literature Primer') 89.

[58] Ll. 330–32.

[59] Ll. 393–94, 399–401.

rank.   Besides, the "formel egle" is herself not
called "royal," although we can hardly believe she is
not to be so regarded.[60]

But if this answer to the point is not sufficient, it
would be easy to propose others. It might be pointed
out that, in the case of this third eagle, Chaucer
makes no indication of rank whatever.   If he does
not designate him as of high rank, neither does he
call him "of lower kinde," as in the case of the second suitor, who was at least a German prince.
Again, while to us it would seem natural to elevate
Richard's rival, in order to make the choice of the
English king a greater honor, the jealousy of France
and the French king may easily have prevented it
at such a time.   Still further, to Englishmen since
Edward III's time, there had been but one "king of
France," that is, he who sat on their own throne,
king of England and of France, as he regularly
styled himself.   To have called the "thridde egle"
specifically royal might have seemed in some sense
to acknowledge the right of Charles VI to that realm
which the English king claimed as his by inheritance.[61]   Finally, there was some reason for not exalt-

----

[60] It might be said that the royal tercel's words,
          "Unto my sovereyn lady, and noght my fere,
          I chese,"
are intended to imply Anne's rank as sister of an emperor,
but these need be regarded as no more than the common flattery of the lover.

[61] As some indication of the importance attached to merely
verbal acknowledgment of the French king, it may be noted

ing the position of the French king in his exact status at this time. When he came to the throne in September, 1380, Charles VI was a boy of not quite twelve. At the death of his father his unscrupulous uncles, the dukes of Anjou, Berry, and Burgundy, virtually seized all power, as the first had also seized all the jewels of his dead brother, Charles V.[62] The young king was helpless in their hands, scarcely more than a figurehead in the kingdom. These circumstances, in themselves, would be sufficient to account for the reference to the third suitor as merely "the thridde tercel egle."[63]

There is one other phase of the whole situation

that such recognition was carefully avoided in the state documents of the time. The French king is usually referred to as "our adversary of France," as in the case of the commissioners appointed to treat for peace in 1379 and April, 1380 (De Tractando cum Adversario Franciae). Even more interesting is the expression in the case of the commissioners appointed August 16, 1382, to treat with Wenceslaus for an offensive league against France. The document is called De Tractando cum Rege Romanorum et Boemiae super Ligis et Amicitiis, and the alliance was to be "Specialiter, in specialibus, contra Karolum Modernum occupatorem Regni Franciae."—Rymer, VII, 365.

[62] Froissart, Chronicles, II, chap. lxxvii; Johnes, I, 617.

[63] It is interesting to note the youth of all the parties to this royal courtship and European alliance. In June, 1380, when the negotiations between England and Bohemia began, Wenceslaus, king of Bohemia and emperor of the Romans, was a little more than nineteen, having been born February 26, 1361. Richard was just beyond fourteen, if born April 13, 1366, or thirteen, if that event occurred January 6 or February 26, 1367. Anne was also fourteen, as she was born May 11, 1366, and Charles VI, youngest of all, was not born until December 3, 1368. Perhaps the extreme youth of all the persons makes doubly appropriate the allegory connecting the union of two of them with the mating of birds.

that may now receive a more interesting interpretation, it seems to me. In his valuable essays Professor Koch had emphasized a clause of Wenceslaus's bioggrapher Pelzel,[64] in its relation to the free choice which Nature granted to the "formel egle."[65]   That clause was "and as Princess Anne had already reached the age to choose herself a husband."   Professor Koch thinks this alludes to Anne's "coming of age," as he calls it, explained by his footnote, "That is, I suppose, 14."[66]   Pelzel has apparently based his remark on the fact that the documents of the marriage contract show Anne to have appointed ambassadors to treat with Richard.   While this is so, however, we must remember that Anne's mother, Elizabeth, gave her parental consent, her imperial brother appointed the same ambassadors, and Anne herself distinctly says she had acted by the advice of her brother and mother.[67]

Whether these facts detract from Professor Koch's interpretation or not, there is another and much broader sense in which Anne had now a free

---

[64] *Englische Studien*, I, 288; *Essays on Chaucer*, 407.

[65] Ll. 645 f.

[66] *Essays on Chaucer*, 408.

[67] Rymer, VII, 293: "Ad concilia, requisitiones, necnon inductiones Serenissimi Principis, Domini Wenceslai, Romanorum et Boemiae Regis, Domini et Fratris nostri pertinendi, necnon Serenissimae Principis, Dominae Elizabethae, Romanorum Imperatricis et Reginae Boemiae, Dominae et Matris nostrae carissimae."

choice, and on account of which she might make some demands in her own right. Not only was the notable prince who became Friedrich, first elector of Saxony, hers by betrothal, but two kings of two of the most powerful nations of western Europe were at her feet. Each wished her, not as queen only, but for the far-reaching alliance with her imperial brother which union with her would bring. Each was deserving in himself, Richard, the passionate lover, and Charles, soon to be known as the "well-beloved." It is little wonder that, with such opportunities the modest "formel egle," which had blushed her pleasure at the lover-like speech of the "royal tercel," should soon after pluck up courage to say:

> Almighty quene, unto this yeer be doon
> I aske respit for to avysen me,
> And after that to have my choys al free.[68]

It is this unusual freedom of choice now in Anne's power to which these last lines of the poem may well refer. At least, such interpretation dignifies what otherwise has often seemed a lame conclusion to this beautiful poem. Anne could well afford to take her time, as it is fairly clear that her imperial brother or his advisers intended to do, until she could satisfy herself as to the advantages of this English proposal. Indeed, I have shown in another paper that the duke of Tetschen visited England in 1380 to see

---

[68] Ll. 647–49.

that far-away country, as it must have seemed, and decide whether Anne could profitably unite her fortunes with those of the English king.[69]

Perhaps it is fair to add, also, that such deliberation as Anne showed and such delay as she requested before her final choice may well be symbolic of the long-continued and minutely careful negotiations attending the great alliance of which her marriage was a part. That alliance not only broke, for the first time in many years, the traditional friendship of Bohemia and France, but it was intimately connected with the widespread league of nations for the support of Pope Urban VI in the great schism, and was confidently looked upon by Englishmen as strengthening their country's hands against her long-time adversary, France. The delay of a year, too, which has usually been regarded as mere dilatoriness, is thus dignified by the many considerations entering into the formation of this far-reaching European alliance.

The foregoing study makes clear, it is hoped, that some considerable revision is necessary in the usual explanation of the suitors in the *Parlement of Foules*. It has been shown that the betrothal of Friedrich of Meissen with Anne of Bohemia was never formally broken; that, at her engagement to

---

[69] See the paper mentioned on p. 58, footnote 3, above; and pp. 137ff., 142ff. below.

Richard II of England, it was still in force, so far as any agreement to its abrogation is concerned; that on this account Friedrich may be regarded as an actual rival of the young English king; and that the words of the second suitor for the "formel egle" in the poem would especially well apply to his long courtship.   It has also been made clear that, after the papal schism, there was an attempt to bring about a betrothal of Anne of Bohemia and Charles, son of King Charles V of France; that this union was desired by the French king and urged by the schismatic pope, Clement VII; that, according to the English chronicler, Adam of Usk, the young Charles, when becoming king in 1380, was a more active suitor for the hand of Anne; and that the words of the third suitor in the poem have special aptness as applied to him.   The latter, therefore, of whom in such relation Chaucer would certainly have had knowledge, is far more likely to have been in his mind than that Prince of Bavaria whose betrothal to the future queen of England had been broken off in 1373.

THE SUITORS IN THE PARLEMENT OF FOULES AGAIN*

It is a pleasure to express my appreciation of the article by Mr. Samuel Moore of Harvard in the January number of the *Notes,* because his facts do, in some sense, re-enforce the case I presented in the July number of *Modern Philology.* I am pleased also, that he so fully accepts the conclusions of that paper. Yet I should like to correct one point in which Mr. Moore seems to do my paper something of injustice. It occurs in the following passage:

> Professor Emerson decides without hesitation that the second eagle represents Friedrich of Meissen. His chief reason for the decision is that it would be "a strange procedure on Chaucer's part to introduce, as a rival suitor of Richard, one whose betrothal had been broken off as early as 1373, at least seven, perhaps nine years before the time of the poem." He offers no evidence of the breaking off of the earlier match.

A reading of the original article[1] will show that in these sentences I am calling attention to Professor Koch's reference to "the strange procedure on Chau-

---

* *MLN,* Vol. XXVI, pp. 109–111 (1911).

[1] *Modern Philology,* VIII, 45–62, (1910).

cer's part," and his emphasis upon the possible lack of knowledge regarding affairs in Germany.[2]   My real argument begins with the next sentence, which Mr. Moore does not quote: "At any rate, Chaucer would scarcely have been likely to use this long-past betrothal, if there had been a more active suitor in the field."   I then present at length the extremely active three, Friedrich of Meissen, Charles of France, and Richard II.   My argument, then, is in the activity of these three, and their closer relation in time than any other suitor who has yet been named.   If accepted at all, the reasoning carries with it the exclusion of any fourth suitor, especially one in whose case no activity has yet been proved for almost ten years before Anne's marriage.

To put the matter in another way, in his poem Chaucer had limited the suitors of Anne to three. The three chronologically nearest her marriage were those I have just named.   They, also, are logically the only ones to be considered, because of their active relations in the matter extending up to the marriage of Anne, and in the case of Friedrich of Meissen far beyond.   By the limits of the problem, therefore, as well as on chronological and logical grounds, the serious consideration of any other than these three suitors seemed to me then, as it seems to me now, quite unnecessary.   To argue further for the

[2] *Essays on Chaucer*, 407–8.

exclusion of William of Baiern-Holland seemed a work of supererogation.

On the other hand if, in the future, any one should attempt to displace Friedrich of Meissen or one of the other suitors, and again introduce William of Baiern-Holland, he must reckon with the data Mr. Moore has brought forward. Or if any one should wish to show why Chaucer chose three rather than four suitors, he might find the reason in Mr. Moore's added facts. Until one of these courses is adopted, I cannot see that these facts are so necessary to my argument as Mr. Moore seems to think.

Another evidence of friendly relations between the reigning houses of England and Hainault might have been cited by Mr. Moore. It is earlier than the account of the visit of Anne to the Duke and Duchess of Brabant on her journey to England, and I have used it, together with Mr. Moore's second quotation from Froissart (p. 10), in the paper to which I referred in a footnote to my *Modern Philology* article, that on the date of the *Knight's Tale*.[3] That article has been in type since last summer, but is not yet published.[4] The additional reference is in Froissart's *Chronicles*, II, ch. xliii (Johnes, I, 593). It tells how, when Sir Simon Burley started for Germany to negotiate for the hand of Anne,—he was

---

[3] See below pp. 128ff.

[4] In January, when this was written. It has since appeared.

appointed June 12, 1380 (Rymer's *Fœdera*, VII, 257),—he visited the Duke and Duchess of Brabant at Brussels, and there met Duke Albert of Hainault and other lords who had gathered for a "great feast of tilts and tournaments." Sir Simon made known his errand, and

> The duke and duchess of Brabant . . . were much rejoiced on hearing the cause of his journey into Germany, and said it would be a good match between the king of England and their niece. They gave Sir Simon Burley, on his departure, special letters to the emperor, to assure him they approved very much of this marriage.

If Duke Albert of Hainault had wished to oppose the betrothal of Richard and Anne on account of his son, here was ample opportunity just as the negotiations were beginning. The absence of the slightest evidence connecting that son with Anne after 1373 shows how unnecessary it is even to consider William of Baiern-Holland, as compared with the indispensable Friedrich of Meissen.

Still, in either case, the conclusions are the same, and the further data regarding one of Anne's earlier suitors are interesting in themselves, whether essential or not. Let me add that before Mr. Moore's article appeared, I had come to consider less valuable the suggestion of Professor Koch,[5] quoted in my former article, that "people most likely had not a very clear notion as to affairs in Germany." Something like international exchange of news, to an extent we are likely to underestimate, must have been common even in the fourteenth century.

It is interesting to note, also, Mr. Moore's further interpretation of the last lines in the *Parlement of Foules*. Yet is he quite right in assuming that his interpretation is wholly new? In discussing the *Legend of Good Women*, Mr. R. K. Root[6] gives essentially the same suggestion, referring the desired favor to the relief from official duties in February, 1385. Even before that, Koch had interpreted the last lines as indicating "that Chaucer was searching for a new subject to work upon," though he does not note Chaucer's purpose in the expression "for to fare The bet."

I cannot let this note go to print without expressing my regret that the study of the suitors of Anne did not develop something more definite regarding the date of the *Parlement*. The astronomical reference in line 117, as interpreted by Professor Koch,[7] must refer that portion to the year 1380 or 1382. It seems impossible that the poem could have been written in the latter year without some more definite

---

[5] *Essays on Chaucer*, 407–8.
[6] *The Poetry of Chaucer*, p. 140; cf. also p. 64.
[7] *Chronology of Chaucer's Works* (Chaucer Soc.), p. 37 f.

reference to the marriage, or at least the accomplished betrothal of Richard and Anne. Yet the year 1380 is too early for at least the latter part of the poem, since the year's delay, symbolized in the request of Anne for "respit" "until this year be doon" could not have been foreseen.

One middle ground between these two assumptions has perhaps occurred to others, although I believe not before suggested. Perhaps Chaucer wrote the introduction, or proem, at the earlier date, with or without reference to the marriage of Richard and Anne, though the marriage with a Bohemian princess had been proposed as early as June, 1380. Indeed the translation of the *Dream of Scipio* may once have been independent of any relation to the later subject of the king's courtship. It has little connection with the later story of the "formel egle" and her suitors,[8] except to introduce the guide "African" who, although he grasps the poet's hand in lines 169–70, is never again mentioned. Does the poet forget his benefactor, or are we to assume that he here intends a subtle characteristic of the psychology of dreams?

---

[8] We might except, perhaps, the first two stanzas, which, however, are general, rather than specific, on the subject of love, and not unlike many other lines of the poet. So the invocation to Venus (ll. 113–19) is only loosely connected with the general story, and even breaks the natural continuity of lines 112 and 120. Yet I cannot go so far as Mr. Root in calling the *Dream of Scipio* "an unfortunate bit of introductory machinery" (*op. cit.*, p. 66).

Yet whether the *Dream of Scipio* was written as an introduction to the later story or not, if the single stanza invoking Citherea is accounted for as belonging to the summer of 1380, the rest of the poem may be assigned with some confidence to 1381.[9] In the latter case it would have preceded, instead of followed, the *Palamon and Arcite,* or the *Knight's Tale* as we know it.[10] This would fully account for the omission of reference to the marriage, and show why the poem considered the courtship only. Perhaps it was first publicly presented in welcoming the new queen.[11]

It may be, too, that the problem of the date of the

[9] It must be remembered also that, according to the terms of the betrothal made in May, 1381, Anne was expected in England "about the feast of St. Michael," or September 29. The poet might therefore have been completing his poem not later than the summer of 1381. Besides, as the formal betrothal is mentioned in the poem no more than the marriage, the year's delay may have applied to the time between the opening of negotiations in June, 1380, and the actual betrothal in May, 1381. The poem may have been completed any time after the latter event.

[10] Professor Lowes suggests this order in 'The Prologue to the Legend of Good Women,' etc., *Publications of the Mod. Lang. Ass'n,* XX. 861, footnote. With more confidence, he also places the *Parlement* before the *Palamon* in his article on 'The Date of Chaucer's Troilus and Criseyde,' *ibid.,* XXIII. 290. Professor Tatlock also prefers 1380 to 1382 for the *Parlement* in *Development and Chronology of Chaucer's Works,* p. 43.

[11] As a side light on the question of date, it is difficult to explain the description of the "parliament" itself (ll. 519–619), without feeling that it is a satire upon this form of government. If so, it could scarcely have had a fitter subject than the parliament of Northampton, which met in November, 1380. The fiasco which this parliament made in its poll-tax proposals, and the consequent troubles of the year 1381, may easily

Parlement will be finally worked out in the relations of its ampler description of the garden of love,[12] and the more concise description of the temple of Venus in the *Knight's Tale*,[13] both based in the main on Boccaccio's *Teseide*. While no proof has yet been brought forward that the longer description was written first, it seems to me that is more natural than the reverse order.[14] If that be so, and the *Parlement* preceded the *Palamon*, the latter would be the subject which Chaucer alludes to, by anticipation, at the close of the former poem. Led to use the *Teseide*, as he had in the *Parlement*, and continuing to read it more thoroughly, the poet saw how he could mold a larger portion of it into the *Palamon and Arcite*, and this became his next venture. In any case, I cannot but think that 1381 is a much better date for the former poem than 1382.

---

have led many Englishmen to feel that representative government lacked many of the elements of success. Even the "Good" parliament of 1376 could scarcely have borne that name among courtiers, while most of those which followed for several years were anti-Lancastrian, and this would have probably meant that they had little of Chaucer's sympathy. Perhaps on this account, he now directed his satire against the Commons. Later he was bold enough to speak out with even greater severity on political subjects in lines 939–52 (E. 995–1008) of the *Griselda* story, and in *Lack of Steadfastness*.

[12] Ll. 183–294.

[13] Ll. 1060–1108; A. 1918–66.

[14] I note that Professor Lowes, in his article on 'The Prologue to the Legend of Good Women' and the note cited above, thinks that on the score of precedence "honors are easy."

WHAT IS THE PARLEMENT OF FOULES?*

Professor Manly's article with the above title (Morsbach *Festschrift*, p. 278) is noteworthy, if for no other reason, as perhaps the strongest statement possible by a disbeliever in the historical basis for Chaucer's *Parlement of Foules*. Let us see what the most radical skepticism may say against Koch's theory. And first, putting aside for a time Professor Manly's objections to the accepted symbolism of the poem, what does he put in its place? He does not deny that the poem was written about the time usually assigned to it. He admits that the theory is more plausible in its present form than when originally proposed by Professor Koch. But, after emphasizing that the poem is of the vision type, with a love debate, or *demande d'amours,* and that the assembly of birds was held on Valentine's day, he proposes as his new theory that the poem was merely a Valentine day exercise for some possible Valentine society of the time.

Now it may be said at once that no one denies, or need deny the three points in Professor Manly's analysis of the poem. It is a vision poem, it is a love debate, and the time is Valentine's day. Not one of these things interferes with the interpretation of

* *JEGP.* Vol. XIII, pp. 566–82 (1914).

the poem now so long and so generally accepted.
Professor Manly has missed the point, or at least has
not met it so far. It is the coincidence in time and
many particulars between Chaucer's poem and the
incidents of the royal courtship itself, which makes
for the interpretation of Professor Koch. This striking coincidence Professor Manly has not explained
away.

Yet there is, apparently, an implication in the suggestion of Chaucer's using well-known conventions,
that he could not have used them for a particular purpose. Now the practice of pointing out the conventional in a work, as if it were a complete explanation
of that work, has been ridden very hard of late
years. It has too often been assumed that the use
of a conventional form precluded any origination on
the part of the poet, or even adaptation to a particular end. This is neither logical nor complete criticism. There is much that is conventional in all poetry, even that of late times. But that we have completely eliminated the personality of the poet as anything more than a mere imitator, by the process of
finding some indebtedness to others is far from true.
Or that, if Chaucer in this particular case used a
conventional form, he could not have applied it to a
particular purpose or occasion is of course in the
last degree untenable.

Indeed, if Chaucer had been specifically planning

a poem on the royal courtship, he would naturally have used some form with which he had previously become acquainted. The vision form he had already used in another poem of occasion, the *Book of the Duchess*. He had also used the Valentine day setting in the *Complaint of Mars*, as Professor Manly points out here, referring to his article in *Harvard Studies and Notes* V, 107.[1]

Again, if Chaucer had been planning a poem on the royal courtship he would naturally have used the love-debate, since that was inherent in the subject itself. The use of one or more of these forms, therefore, does not prove that Chaucer may not have used them for a particular purpose, as in shadowing forth an important event in English court life. Again I emphasize the real point, the use of these conventions at such a time and with so many similarities of incident, that they suggest to us, as they presumably suggested to hearers of the poem in Chaucer's time, a relation to the courtship of Richard and Anne. The most effective way in which to overthrow the pres-

---

[1] Yet the language of Professor Manly in the *Festschrift* seems to imply too much. "That Chaucer himself took part in the literary features of such social entertainments is indicated by his *Complaint of Mars*," begs the question. Until we have further proof that there were such literary and social entertainments, they cannot be used for purposes of argument. Professor Manly uses the language of one who has won his case. All we know of the *Complaint of Mars*, so far as this point is concerned, is that Chaucer used the Valentine day setting for his poem, but nothing regarding the occasion of its delivery.

ent theory would be to show that the *Parlement of Foules* was made at some different time, and for some different set of circumstances than those usually supposed to be indicated.

Professor Manly makes no attempt to indicate a different time for the composition of the poem, as was earlier done by Tyrwhitt, followed by Godwin, who thought it applied to the marriage of John of Gaunt in 1359,[2] or by a writer in the *Saturday Review* of April 15, 1871, who applied it to the marriage of Lord De Coucy in 1364.[3] If such a time can be successfully brought forward, we must all give up the accepted theory. Nor does Professor Manly propose a different set of circumstances to which the incidents of the poem may be in some sense parallel. He merely opposes altogether any such parallelism. On the other hand, he does propose an occasion which, he thinks, sufficiently accounts for the poem, without connecting its incidents with contemporary life.

Yet it must be noted that, if Professor Manly could prove there were literary entertainments in England in honor of Saint Valentine as early as 1380

---

[2] Tyrwhitt's note is in *Appendix* to his *Preface*, C, note e. Godwin discusses the subject in his *Life of Chaucer*, ch. xxi (Vol. II, p. 68).

[3] See Furnivall's *Trial Forewords*, p. 70. That Tyrwhitt, as early as the late seventies of the eighteenth century, first connected the *Parlement of Foules* with an important marriage in England is significant indication of the appeal made by the poem's symbolism.

or 1382, he would not yet have overthrown the theory of Koch, as he seems to think. There is no reason why, if Chaucer had been planning to write such a Valentine poem about that time, he should not have chosen as subject the royal courtship, then in everybody's mind. That is, Professor Manly has proposed in his hypothesis only a new occasion for the delivery of such a poem. In so doing, however, he has not provided any new interpretation of the poem which precludes its reference to the circumstances usually supposed to be symbolized. In a similar way the *Complaint of Mars* may have been intended as a literary feature of such a social entertainment as Professor Manly thinks possible some score of years before it is known to have been in existence. Yet this would not prevent its reference to some incident of court life, as that to which Shirley refers in his manuscript note.

But Professor Manly has not furnished anything like adequate proof of the occasion which he proposes. This vital suggestion of his paper remains at best an unsupported conjecture. He would have us believe that the *Parlement of Foules* was written as a mere imitative exercise for a society, of which none is known to have been in existence for twenty years, and then only in a country which certainly did not usually adopt its social or literary customs from England. The hypothesis would suit admirably if its author could prove that the *Parlement of Foules* was written after 1400, when the French society of the Valentine cult was in existence,—and Chaucer was in his grave. As it stands, Professor Manly's extraordinary skepticism in the one case, and far more extraordinary faith in a society to suit his purpose seem somewhat at variance.

I say this, too, without any special prejudice in favor of Koch's theory. Professor Manly admits its greater plausibility with the modification it was my good fortune to make.[4] Yet if there be a better explanation of the poem than Professor Koch proposed, no matter how it conflicts with previous views, it is the part of common sense to adopt it. The new hypothesis, however, must not place a greater strain upon belief than the one which it displaces.

But Professor Manly urges some special objections to Koch's theory which must be examined. "To

---

[4] It is not uninteresting, I think, and not undeserving of record that two others had already made the discovery of Charles of France as one of the suitors in the poem, by the time my article was published in *Modern Philology* VIII, 45. These are Dr. Samuel Moore, now of the University of Wisconsin, and Dr. T. S. Graves of Trinity College, North Carolina. I presume they will have no objection to my referring to statements made to me in conversation some years ago. Besides, I noticed only recently that Coulton in *Chaucer and His England* refers to Charles and his wish to make Anne his wife, without, however, suggesting the relation to the *Parlement of Foules*. On p. 204 he speaks of "how Richard offered an immense sum for her [Anne of Bohemia] in order to outbid his royal brother of France." This statement I did not see until some time after printing my article.

whom," he asks, "was the poem intended as a compliment? To Richard, or Anne, or both? The critics are in general not specific on this point." He then argues that, if written after Anne's arrival in England, the poem was not complimentary to her. If written before, it was not complimentary to Richard. These objections seem to me greatly magnified, if indeed they have any foundation. Frankly, I take it the critics have not been "specific on this point" because they have not thought it necessary. Nor can it be regarded as necessary except by great emphasis on extremely minor details.

In fact, Professor Manly's premise that the poem is uncomplimentary in its present form to either or both of the royal personages rests, it seems to me, on no solid basis. That Chaucer might have made it more flattering to either or both is doubtless true. Why he did not do this we shall perhaps never know. But that these young people, not quite "children" in any real sense, would not have enjoyed this beautiful poem, as others must have enjoyed it, seems to me impossible. Neither Richard nor Anne was likely to find fault with such consummate artistry. Neither would have thought of dissecting it minutely, to see whether it sufficiently fitted his particular case.

But Professor Manly thinks Anne would have been offended that she is represented as "undecided in her choice," or "unable to decide." Such expressions, however, are quite too strong for the case. The formel eagle is represented as asking what all young ladies were supposed to desire, or what they were conventionally supposed to demand, the year of "respite for to avysen me." The best evidence that this could not have been derogatory to Anne is found when we compare the situation here with that in another of Chaucer's poems. In the *Book of the Duchess*, Blanche of Lancaster is represented as putting off her princely lover for a similar period. The first offer of marriage by a prince of the realm was quite as desirable for the daughter of Henry of Lancaster, as was that of Richard for Anne, considering the latter's other offers at the time. Yet it was only when John of Gaunt renewed his proposal "another yere" (l. 1258) that Blanche gave him "the noble yift of hir mercy." The parallel is even more favorable to Anne. The "man in blak" tells the story of an absolute rejection. The formel eagle merely asks time to reflect.[5]

Again, in his development of a supposed dilemma, Professor Manly thinks that, if the poem had been written before Anne's arrival in England, it must have been intended as a compliment to Richard.[6] In

---

[5] It matters little whether the allusion in the *Book of the Duchess* is based on fact or not. The use of it by Chaucer made it public property, and the reference to it in the poem by the lover himself shows that he did not regard it as a slight.

[6] To one statement of Professor Manly a footnote seems sufficient. He says: "If the poem was written before Anne's

this he believes it fails because the young king was
not immediately preferred to his rivals. This rivalry Professor Manly minimizes by calling Friedrich
an "insignificant princeling," and the young Charles
"nostre adversaire" instead of heir to the French
throne. However, no one will be misled by this clever
use of names. Friedrich of Meissen was originally
considered a worthy match for Anne of Bohemia,[7]
and the heir to the French throne was certainly so.
In any case, the rivalry was a real one for Richard,
and it was only a combination of circumstances,
political and religious, which finally turned the scale
in his favor.[8] Besides, Richard must by this time
have become somewhat accustomed to meeting ob-
stacles to his marriage. Negotiations for a marriage

---

arrival in England, in December 1381, it is difficult to see how
it can have been intended for her. She could not have known
of it unless Chaucer had sent it to her in Bohemia, and this,
while possible, is highly improbable." Is it impossible that
the poem could have been written in anticipation of Anne's
coming, and have been read or recited on her arrival in England? Compare the similar situation in the writing of Dunbar's *Thissel and Rose*, to which I later call attention.

[7] In a footnote to p. 280 Professor Manly seems to imply
that I had made too much of Friedrich's after-greatness.
That was not my intention, but the implied slight to the
young prince as a suitor may be easily answered. He was
thought worthy of Anne, not as an "insignificant princeling,"
but as heir to an important German principality, and as what
he was likely to become. The kinsmen of Anne could not
have been entirely blind to their own or her advantage.

[8] This has been made plain, I think, in my two articles,
with their numerous references to documents of the time: *A
New Note on the Date of the Knight's Tale*, Hart anniversary volume, p. 203; and the *Suitors in Chaucer's Parlement
of Foules*, already referred to. [See previous essay, pp. 59–76,
especially and below, pp. 127–169, particularly 132f.]

with Princess Mary of France had twice come to
nought,[9] and at least two other matches for him had
been proposed and put aside for various reasons.[10]
It is inconceivable that Richard should not have
known of these things, and certainly they were
known to the courtiers who heard the poem read or
recited. Had Chaucer, therefore, tried to minimize
the rivalry, in order to flatter Richard, he would not
only have been untrue to the facts, but would have
been in danger of rendering his effort at sycophancy
ridiculous.

Even if this were not so, does not Professor Manly
greatly magnify the young Richard's feelings? The
marriage of a prince is a conventional matter at
best. Richard especially was too young to take the
maturer interest of a man deeply in love, and must
have looked on the various stages of the negotiations
with curious rather than passionate eyes. When,
too, the young bride did arrive, he was quite too
much pleased and satisfied, to care whether a pretty
poem that seems to refer to his affairs had put
everything exactly to his liking.

But apart from these suggestions in refutation of
Professor Manly's objections, is the poem uncomplimentary to either of the royal personages? I put

---

[9] Froissart, *Chroniques* (De Lettenhove), VIII, 383, 385;
Longman, *Life and Times of Edward Third*, II, 271 f.; Skeat's
Chaucer, I, xxvii.

[100] Froissart, *Chroniques*, IX, 212.

aside for the present the question why Chaucer did not represent the successful conclusion of the courtship. Taking into account only what was attempted on the accepted theory, why is the poem uncomplimentary to either Richard or Anne?

As to Richard, the "royal tercel" of the usual interpretation, he is given the first choice of a mate; he is affectionately called "my sone" by the presiding goddess Nature, who specifically asks him to make his choice; his is the only speech to make any recognized impression on the "formel egle"; he is indicated to the latter in no uncertain terms by the "tercelet of the faucon," after the suitors had misunderstood the proposal of "batayle" for supremacy; and finally, as clearly foreshadowing the conclusion of the matter, Dame Nature advises the formel eagle in the most explicit language, "I counseyle yow the royal tercel take." Would not these several and favorable allusions be sufficiently flattering to the young king? Would he have been better pleased with more abject adulation?

Or could Anne fail to feel complimented by the allusions in the poem to her? She could scarcely have been praised more highly when the formel eagle is first introduced (ll. 372–78). She could not have been treated more kindly than when Nature covers her confusion at the professions of her young lover, and gently soothes her with "Doghter, drede

yow noght, I yow assure" (l. 447). She was given
the special privilege of choice (l. 409), a privilege
unknown to bird life and none too common among
marriageable women of the time. This privilege, too,
Nature emphasized a second time (ll. 626–7), although she immediately after gave advice that was
intended to settle the formel eagle's choice upon the
royal tercel. She was at last allowed to have her own
way—what more pleasing to a woman—in the choice
of a period for deliberation,

> And after that to have my choys al free.

This period she asks for herself alone:

> I wol noght serven Venus ne Cupyde
> For soothe as yet.

She is not one to play with her lover's affection, or
send him on a useless and dangerous quest, for like
Blanche of Lancaster in the *Book of the Duchess*
(ll. 1015–33),

> She ne used no suche knakkes smale.

Finally, her decision is received by Nature, and the
bird parliament has an entirely fitting ending of the
love debate.

Surely this did not indicate that Anne was "unable to decide," but rather that she thought it un-
maidenly and unconventional to make her choice so
quickly. Especially the fact that Nature and the
whole bird family take the conclusion as entirely
right—it was utterly at variance with what could

happen in bird life—must indicate that it was not
intended in any sense to show a vacillating character
in Anne of Bohemia. It is Professor Manly only, so
far as I now remember, who feels any dissatisfac-
tion for the formel eagle, or any doubt as to what
she really wished to do—at the proper time.[11]

I would press this last matter one point further.
If the bird parliament is nothing more, as Professor
Manly supposes, why this introduction of a convention—the putting off of the lover for a time—never
known in the realm of animal life, but characteristic
of human marriage arrangements in the period of
Chaucer's *Parlement of Foules?* What is the meaning on Professor Manly's hypothesis of this vital
element of the poem? Indeed, is not the conclusion
on his basis far more lame than he thinks it on the
accepted theory?

Another objection is urged by Professor Manly in
these words:

> Some stress has been laid upon the accuracy
> with which the descriptions of the suitors in
> the poem fit the three candidates. This appear-
> ance of accuracy is obtained by emphasizing
> certain phases of the situation and disregard-

---

[11] Even the late Henry Morley accepted the symbolic character of the poem, though he preferred to go back to Tyrwhitt's long discarded hypothesis as to the occasion intended.
Von Westenholz *(Anglia, Beiblatt* XII, 167) can hardly be
classed here, though as early as 1901 he suggested a mild
skepticism regarding Koch's theory.

ing others. If the poem be taken not seriously,
as an intended compliment to Richard and
Anne, but as a bit of merriment intended to
amuse the adults at the expense of these royal
children, the descriptions fit well enough. But
if this is the case, the poem is not a compliment
to Richard and Anne, but makes sport of them.

It will be seen from this second use of it that Professor Manly is fond of the logical dilemma. Nor
will anyone object to his putting the best face possible on the case. Granting the premises on which he
rests the dilemma argument, the case is his. But
are the premises sound?

Now I have tried to show—I purposely avoid the
special pleader's "I have shown," too much used of
late[12] — that Professor Manly has taken quite too

---

[12] It may be permissible in this connection to call attention
to Professor Manly's use of this expression in the Kittredge
Anniversary Papers. In his article 'What is Chaucer's House
of Fame,' he says: "Neither the *Boke of the Duchesse* nor the
Legend of Good Women has the slightest claim to be regarded
as allegorical; and the *Parlement of Foules*, as I have recently shown (Morsbach *Festschrift*) is a Valentine poem,
presenting a *demande d'amours* in the setting of a bird parliament."
I agree entirely that allegory and allegorical are often too
loosely used. But they are so used by very good critics—see
Legouis's chapter on the Allegorical Poems of Chaucer—and
Professor Manly's statement is far too strong. Besides, if
he also means by his sentence that he "has shown" the *Parlement of Foules* is not allegorical in the accepted sense, more
accurately a poem of occasion, he is himself using language
somewhat unwarrantedly, it seems to me. I have in mind
the words of Professor Kittredge in his 'Chaucer's Alceste'
(Mod. Phil. VI, 435) that "when a particular suggestion of
this kind has been put into type, it becomes a kind of dogma."

seriously the first horn of his argument. I cannot believe that the poem can be reasonably regarded as uncomplimentary to the royal lovers of 1380 and 1381. Yet has the other horn of the dilemma—a mixed figure seems absolutely necessary—any firmer foundation? It largely rests on a misconstruction of a part of my paper on the *Suitors in the Parlement of Foules*. When the discovery was made that another suitor might better take the place of the Prince of Bavaria in Koch's earlier interpretation, it was natural to see whether the new claimant would fit into the speeches assigned by Chaucer to the three tercel eagles. If no fit place had been found for him there, it would have been argument against admitting Charles of France as one of the suitors. It was with some pleasure, I admit, that I found the parallelism between the speeches and certain known facts to be more considerable than they had been in the older form of the theory. Yet I cannot believe that these coincidences were too much magnified in this conservative statement:

"It must be admitted that the notes of time in the speeches of the last two suitors have significant parallelism in the long betrothal of Friedrich of Meissen, and the short period during which Charles VI was considered a suitor."[13]

---

[13] *Mod. Phil.*, VIII, 58; [see above, p. 82].

But Professor Manly charges that the parallelism "is obtained by emphasizing certain phases of the situation and disregarding others." The specific instance to which he points (see his footnote 1 to p. 281) is due to an entire misunderstanding of one of my footnotes to the "Suitors" article.[14] I had thought the suggestion there put had sufficient clearness not to be wholly missed, and sufficient delicacy not to offend. It amounts to nothing in the argument, was not stressed as a part of it, and may be wholly disregarded without injuring the case. That Professor Manly has so completely misunderstood its import almost makes me regret using it. But he should hardly have assumed that I knew so little of fourteenth century history as to believe Richard was considerably more important in the affairs of England, than Charles VI in those of France, or any less "helpless in the hands of his uncles." I referred to a quite different kind of "prowess."

Again, Professor Manly seems to criticise my reference to what he calls "two equally good explanations of the 'half a yere' of line 475." His criticism might be justified, perhaps, if I had asserted that the "half a yere" must apply to one or the other of these periods. Even that might be possible if we knew to a day the time of Chaucer's writing the

---

[14] *Ibid.*, VIII, 58, footnote 3; [cf. p. 82, footnote 56, above.]

8

poem. But I had no idea of anything so minute, and I have prefaced the discussion of the speech of the third tercel eagle by the sentence: "I recognize that we must not try to see too much, and the main point is made in emphasizing the rivalry of Charles VI and Richard II." Further, the discussion is closed, not by stressing these matters, but by again resting the case on the aptness of the parallelism in the time references of the last two speeches.

Professor Manly objects also to applying certain lines of the poem (548–51) to Richard, since he was too young to be "worthieste of knighthode" and so "sittingest for hir." It is difficult to be serious with this sort of objection. Even though the critic admits that "allegories need not go on all fours," he here presses the matter as if we must not only find the "all fours" of the allegory, but also the hair and teeth. On such a basis how much of symbolic poetry would be left? How absurd, for example, for Spenser to picture Sidney as killed by a wild boar when everyone knew he was wounded in a fair fight with his enemies! Or how ridiculous for Milton to picture his dead friend, who probably knew nothing about sheep, as a shepherd of so little judgment in his sheep-tending as somehow to get mixed up with the sea; and how unthinkable that the poet should have introduced in this inappropriate imagery of a bygone age an historical allusion to the church of

England,[15] especially under such an impossible meta-
phor as "blind mouths." Or still again, how ludi-
crous, as good Doctor Johnson pointed out, for Gray
to ask Father Thames to tell him the names of the
youngsters who sported on his banks at Eton. As
the wise critic said, Father Thames had "no better

---

[15] Professor Manly's skepticism regarding the historical
basis of the *Parlement of Foules* also extends to my article on
the *Date of the Knight's Tale* in the J. M. Hart anniversary
volume. [See below, pp. 123–173]. Now I cannot expect to convince all of such a conjectural interpretation. Everyone who
proposes such an explanation of a few lines knows that its
final acceptance or rejection rests not with himself, but with
others. Still Professor Manly should not dismiss the article
with the statement he has seemed to think sufficient. Nor
need it have been implied that Professor Lowes, with whose
article on l. 26 of the *Knight's Tale* he couples mine, or myself had "diligently sought" to discover something that might
be tortured into a reference to a contemporary event. Such a
remark, to say the least, is not an answer to a reasoned case.
Yet let me meet directly Professor Manly's specific objection to my article. More than once in his contribution to
the Morsbach *Festschrift* he reiterates his reference to Anne
and her suitors as "children." The term is too strong for
two who were regarded as old enough to marry, and whose
training as princes would surely have given them greater
maturity of mind than usually accompanies such ages as
theirs. In combating my other article, however, he implies
a maturity of feeling regarding his kingly prerogative quite
unlikely in Richard, a boy of thirteen or fourteen, especially
if, as he rightly says in another place, "Richard was almost
as helpless in the hands of his uncles as Charles was in the
hands of his." Under such conditions of helplessness, and
the outstanding importance of John of Gaunt as English
prince and claimant of the Spanish throne, it is doubtful
whether the boy Richard could have felt any lack of consideration in the possible allusion to him as a "kinges brother
sone." In other words, Professor Manly should not reason
in the one case that the princes were younger than the facts
would warrant, and in the other that Richard would have
had the feelings of a man, ruling in person a great kingdom.
Besides, instead of refuting my main argument, Professor
Manly has again chosen to oppose a quite minor point in my
article.

means of knowing than himself." If Professor Manly presses so hard the allusion to Richard II in the *Parlement of Foules,* he must have great difficulty with many passages in English poetry.

But the main difficulty with Chaucer's *Parlement of Foules* as a poem of historical reference, a difficulty which all must feel at times, is its conclusion. This is really at the basis of Professor Manly's contentions. Why did not Chaucer carry the royal courtship to what would seem to us a more satisfactory close in the full acceptance of Richard by Anne, or even, if he wrote so late, in a description of the royal marriage?[16] I do not flatter myself that I can answer the question satisfactorily, but I may point out its relation to the controversy. That Chaucer did not complete the poem as we should have supposed he would, or might have done, does not invalidate the many resemblances between it and actual events of the time. We may wonder that he did not go a step further, but that need not take from our admiration that he went so far.

On the basis of such criticism as Professor Manly's, we might make difficulties with a good many

---

[16] Professor Lounsbury *(Studies in Chaucer* III, 321) is satisfied with attributing the conclusion as it stands to imperfect art. Coupling the poem with the *Book of the Duchess,* he says: "There is a sense of incompleteness about the two poems which detracts from their perfection as works of art." Later (p. 431), he speaks of them as terminating "so abruptly as well as so tamely that it can be fairly said of them that they are broken off rather than ended."

other poems. Who can explain, for example, why Chaucer chose to write a poem on the death of Blanche of Lancaster, rather than on Queen Philippa who died a month before and was so much more important to England? On most if not all grounds Chaucer, a squire in the household of the king, a man looking for advancement through personal favor — the only means of advancement in his time — would certainly have seen the greater opportunity. Yet it would be foolish to deny that the *Book of the Duchess* does refer to Blanche of Lancaster, because a sensible poet would have preferred Queen Philippa as a subject for his elegy. Or would it be reasonable to deny that the "man in blak" can be John of Gaunt, because he could not have been pleased with a proclamation to the world that Blanche of Lancaster, merely a subject of his royal father, had refused his proffers as a lover for a full year? Similar examples might be found in every period of our literature.

Such analogies merely point the possibility of Chaucer's having a reason that seemed good to him, for doing what seems not wholly clear to us. On the other hand, might it not be contended with much force that the close of the *Parlement of Foules* was not unsatisfactory for the time. The year of respite asked by the formel eagle, and thought by Professor Manly to be derogatory to Richard, was common

enough. If it was more commonly a sending of
the lover on some expedition to prove his worth, as
described by Gower in the *Confessio Amantis* (IV,
1620f.),[17] it is to Anne's credit that she required no
such sacrifice. But that such putting off of the lover
could not have been regarded as a slight, should be
clear from Chaucer's use of it in the *Book of the
Duchess*, already mentioned. Besides, we have a
parallel to the maidenly modesty of Anne in the
maidenly modesty of Emelye of the *Knight's Tale*,
as she prays in the temple of Diana.

Moreover, the conclusion was accepted without a
murmur by all the characters of the poem. The tercel eagles who were only too willing to engage in
combat for their love, as shown by one of the most
dramatic bits of the poem (l. 540), have no word of
complaint. As already noted, this is inconceivable in
the conduct of birds, if birds only are meant. Yet
the eagles, who have been so passionate in their first
speeches, receive the decision without objection, and
seem wholly content with Nature's

A yeer is not so longe to endure.

In the same way the other birds, who had been
only too ready to jangle and waste their time in
profitless discussion when given a chance—how delightfully Chaucer makes it give us pleasure as we
hear them—

---

[17] See the references given by Skeat, *Chaucer's Works*, I, 485.

Assented were to this conclusion.

Now I submit that what is represented as so wholly satisfactory to the characters of the poem, so wholly satisfactory to the poet himself we must assume, could not have been wholly unsatisfactory to hearers or readers at the time. We must not condemn the conclusion of a work, otherwise so charming, simply because we cannot wholly understand its relation to the plot. Moreover, if the poem otherwise suits so admirably a symbolic representation of the royal courtship, we may not deny its symbolism in other respects because we cannot fully appreciate the relation of its conclusion to the series of historical circumstances. Indeed, the full acceptance of the conclusion by all most intimately concerned strengthens, rather than weakens, the symbolic interpretation which so long has been placed on this beautiful poem.

One word further may be added. It is well known that Dunbar wrote his *Thissel and the Rose* in imitation of Chaucer's *Parlement of Foules*. In it Dame Nature presides over beasts, birds, and flowers, and appoints the lion, eagle, and thistle as king of each class of living things. Then she crowns the Rose as Thistle's queen. The occasion of the poem is known to have been the marriage, August 8, 1503, of James IV with Margaret, eldest daughter of Henry VII of England. But Dunbar wrote in the preceding May, as he tells us in the last line of the poem, and the imagery is wholly of that period. Now I do not mean to suggest that Dunbar must have imitated Chaucer's poem because he had heard it had been written for a similar occasion, though there may be something even in that. Chaucerian imitation in Scotland began within a quarter century of Chaucer's death, and Chaucerian tradition may have been accurately preserved in that country for a century. What I do wish to suggest is a certain parallelism between the poems in other respects.

As already noted, Dunbar chose to write his poem three months before the marriage of the king. He thus chose, as perhaps Chaucer did, not to describe the marriage itself, the greater occasion one would have thought. All he does, therefore, is to picture Nature as crowning the Rose as the most beautiful of the flowers, and to represent the birds as singing her praises. Does Professor Manly think this would have been sufficiently complimentary to the daughter of Henry VII of England? To be crowned queen of the May was a yearly occurrence in every village. Could Margaret have thought it worthy of her new position as queen of Scotland? Or would James IV have been any better pleased with the poem? Lines 134 to 140 give him some advice on his none too virtuous life, and he is asked in no uncertain terms to "lat no nettell vyle and full of vyce" and "no wyld

weid" take the place in his affections of "the fresche
Rose." Would the king be pleased with such allusion to him as a light of love? Or would the queen
enjoy this public reflection upon the character of the
prince she was marrying? Have we not here another of Professor Manly's dilemmas—with this difference, that we know the subject of Dunbar's poem,
know when it was written to a day, and know also
that he suffered no loss of favor because of what
Professor Manly would certainly think slighting references to Scotland's king and queen.

To return to the main question, there is no inherent reason why Chaucer should not have written a
poem upon the courtship of Richard and Anne.
Except for the lyrist Minot, whose small body of
verse was wholly in praise of his king, Chaucer more
than any poet up to his time or long after dealt with
contemporaries or contemporary life. The *Book of
the Duchess* is accepted by all as a poem of a particular occasion. The *Complaint of Mars* may have
had some basis in facts of the time. The *Legend of
Good Women* was written for Queen Anne, since
lines 496–97 of the *B. Prologue,* now generally believed to have been the first written, are a virtual
dedication of the poem to her. The envoy to *Fortune* is addressed to the English princes, probably the
uncles of the king, whatever be the interpretation
of "the beste frend" of that poem. *Lack of Stead-*

fastness is directed to a prince, usually supposed to have been Richard himself, at some crisis of his affairs. The poems *To Scogan, To Bukton* are to friends of the poet, the first playful, the second bearing upon court influence which Chaucer hoped might be exerted in his behalf. The envoy to the *Complaint of Venus* is directed to a princess at least, perhaps Isabel of York, and it also mentions by name a contemporary French poet known and honored in England. The *Complaint to his Purse* is an appeal to the new king of England, who heeded the witty request of the aged poet and bestowed a fitting reward. Even Adam Scriveyn is embalmed to an immortality he would doubtless have preferred to escape. And just the other day it seems to have been shown that Chaucer's incomparable *Truth* is not of mere general nature, but was dedicated in its envoy to a nobleman of England, who must also have been Chaucer's friend.

What more reasonable, therefore, as following a practice characteristic of the great poet, than that the *Parlement of Foules* should have had its occasion in one of the most interesting incidents in the life of Chaucer's king and queen.

A NEW NOTE ON THE DATE OF CHAUCER'S KNIGHT'S TALE*

In recent years the great question in connection
with *The Knight's Tale* has been its essential identity, in its present form, with the *Palamon and
Arcite* mentioned in the *Prologue* to *The Legend of
Good Women*.[1] The acceptance of that identity, which
is now usual, presupposes an earlier composition of
The Knight's Tale than was formerly thought possible, a date at least earlier than that of the *Legend*.
As to this point, Mr. F. J. Mather, in his *Introduction* to *Chaucer's Prologue, The Knight's Tale, and
The Nun's Priest's Tale* (1894), not only asserted
his belief in the essential identity of the *Palamon
and Arcite* with *The Knight's Tale*, but dated them
as of "about 1381."[2] This date Dr. Mather further
emphasized in his article, 'On the Date of the
Knight's Tale,' contributed to *An English Miscellany* (1901).[3] There, he made some use of Professor
Skeat's computation of the years when May 5 was
Sunday, and when the incidents of *The Knight's Tale*

---

* *Studies in Language and Literature: A Volume Commemorating the Seventieth Birthday of Professor James
Morgan Hart*, 1910, pp. 203–54.

[1] The *Prologue*, A, 408; B. 420.

[2] *Introduction*, p. xvii, and footnote.

[3] See p. 310.

might correspond with the dates of an actual year. This computation had been printed by Professor Skeat as early as 1868, though he chose the year 1387 as the more likely one in Chaucer's mind.[4] Dr. Mather, arguing for the identity of *The Knight's Tale* and the *Palamon and Arcite*, prefers 1381 to 1387, and his argument certainly makes good the preference.

Some confirmation of the earlier date was offered by Professor John L. Lowes in his article on 'The Tempest at hir Hoom cominge,' *Modern Language Notes*, XIX, 240–43. He there suggests that the "tempest," which has no counterpart in Chaucer's source, Boccaccio's *Teseide*, probably refers to an event of December 18, 1381, when Anne came to England to become Richard Second's queen.[5] The coming of Queen Hippolyta to Athens suggested, as he thinks, the current event of greatest importance to London,

---

[4] *Notes and Queries*, Fourth Series, II, 243. The note was later embodied in the *Temporary Preface to the Canterbury Tales*, p. 103, and still later in Skeat's *Chaucer* (1897 f).

[5] Froissart says that Anne sailed from Calais on Wednesday, landing in England the same day (see *Chronicles*, II, ch. lxxxvi). On the basis of Professor Skeat's calculation that May 5, 1381, was Sunday, this Wednesday in December would be the eighteenth. As Lowes notes, chroniclers vary a little in the date, and C. Oman *(Political History of England,* IV. 66) says December 21. In discussing 'The Prologue to the Legend of Good Women Considered in its Chronological Relations' *(Publ. Mod. Lang. Ass'n,* XX, 843), Lowes refers to his former article in *Mod. Lang. Notes*, and regarding Professor Skeat's computation, mentions "the very probable relation of the series in which it [the third of May] stands to the calendar of the current year." In other words, he seems to approve the use made of that computation.

the coming of her who was soon to be known as the
Good Queen Anne. It was but a step in the association of ideas to allude to what must have impressed Chaucer and his contemporaries as a singular instance of supernatural power.[6]

Beyond this, so far as I have seen, there has been
no further attempt to confirm so early a date for
The Knight's Tale. Professor John S. P. Tatlock, in
his *Development and Chronology of Chaucer's
Works,*[7] argues for 1384-6, and Mr. A. W. Pollard, in
his *Introduction* to *The Knight's Tale* (1903), assumes a similar period. Neither accepts the conclusions of Mather and Lowes, Tatlock arguing against
them in detail. Yet further confirmation of the 1381
is possible, I believe, from a passage which occurs
near the close of the *Tale,* when Theseus is about to
propose the marriage of Palamon and Emily. We
may begin with line 2967 of Group A (l. 2109 of
the *Tale* proper), and continue through 2974, though
not all the lines are equally important for our purpose:

> By processe and by lengthe of certeyn yeres,
> Al stynted is the moornynge and the teres
> Of Grekes, by oon general assent.
> Thanne semed me there was a parlement
> At Athenes, upon certain poynts and caas;

---

[6] See the quotations from the chroniclers given in the article
mentioned.

[7] *Chaucer Society,* Second Series (1907), p. 70.

> Among the whiche poynts y-spoken was,
> To have with certein contrees alliaunce,
> And have fully of Thebans obeissaunce.

To the first part of this passage there is a rough correspondence in *Teseide* xii, st. 3:

> Dappoichè furon più giorni passati
> Dopo lo sventurato avvenimento,
> Con Teseo essendo gli Greci adunati,
> Parve di general consentimento, etc.

But for the last four lines there is nothing in the original, as Professor Lounsbury early pointed out in his *Studies in Chaucer*, I, 46:

> The Italian work mentions days as passed and not years. It has no allusion to the summoning of a parliament for the purpose of considering questions of peace and war. These are the alterations and additions made by the English poet.

Professor Lounsbury did not further explain the passage, and special attention has been called to it but rarely. Professor Skeat merely adds, on lines 2967–86, "Cf. the *Teseide*, xii, 3–5." Mr. Pollard has an interesting note on "Thanne semed me," in his edition of *The Knight's Tale:*

> This strange phrase may be a reminiscence of Boccaccio's "parve" in the lines "Con Teseo essendo gli Greci adunati, Parve di general con-

sentimento Ch' i' tristi pianti omai fosser las-
ciati"—it seemed good to the Greeks in council
to give over mourning. Otherwise we can only
explain Chaucer's "semed me" as a relic of the
dream form in which he cast several of his earlier poems. Cf. "saugh I" of l. 1137.

Even the first part of this note is not very con-
vincing, while surely Mr. Pollard's free translation
of the Italian, especially his "in council," seems to
imply a closer resemblance to the English than
actually exists.

Only Mr. H. B. Hinckley, in his *Notes on Chaucer*,
has attempted to explain the last four lines of the
passage. Of these he says: "Chaucer had probably
heard something of the actual political union of
Athens and Thebes (see p. 54), which he is here trying to recall." On the page cited he refers to "the
establishment of the so-called Latin Empire of Con-
stantinople (A.D. 1204), to which the Duchy of
Athens was soon added as a fief." Some other details are given, but none that convince me Chaucer
had in mind facts so remote in time and place.

Far simpler and more reasonable than any of
these explanations, it seems to me, is it to connect
these lines with events that must have been in every
courtier's mind, if not in that of every Englishman,
during a considerable part of the year 1381 and the
early part of 1382. I refer especially to that alli-

ance of England and Bohemia which accompanied
the marriage of Anne and the young Richard II. If
emphasis be placed on Chaucer's "contrees" of line
2973, we may remember that the alliance of Bohemia and England was but part of a great European
league for the support of Pope Urban VI against
Clement VII, the schismatic. Of these the Bohemian
alliance is more important for England. That accom-
paniment of the marriage contract has been little
considered in the biographies of Chaucer, and perhaps on this account its relation to these lines has
not been fully appreciated. Yet it was highly important in its day, as it will be easy to show. Indeed,
while alliances of a minor sort were rather frequent,
especially during the reign of Edward III, there was
no such alliance of independent states accompanied
by a royal marriage to which the lines of Chaucer
could refer, except this of the years 1381–2. Besides,
it was just such an event as would have impressed
the mind of the poet, himself more than once engaged in similar foreign relations of his country.

To show at once that the alliance of England with
a foreign state and the marriage of the young king
were regarded as important, we need only note the
language of Froissart. I quote from the translation
of Johnes:

About this same season, there were many
councils held in England, by the uncles of the

king, the prelates, and barons, relative to marrying the young king Richard. The English
would have preferred a princess of Hainault
out of love for that good lady queen Philippa,
who had been so virtuous, liberal, and honorable,
and who had come from Hainault; but Duke
Albert, at that time, had not any daughters
marriageable. The Duke of Lancaster would
willingly have seen the king, his nephew, married to his daughter, whom he had had by the
lady Blanch of Lancaster, but the people would
not have consented to this for two reasons: that
the lady was his cousin-german, and too nearly
related; and that they wished the king to choose
a queen from beyond sea, in order to gain
stronger alliances. The sister of the king of
Bohemia and of Germany, daughter of the lately
deceased emperor, was then proposed and the
whole council assented to it.[8]

Yet even the language of Froissart, explicit as it
is regarding the wish for a foreign alliance, does not
emphasize the importance of this league between

---

[8] *Chronicles* II, ch. xliii: Johnes, I, 592–3. It will be noticed
that Froissart, after mentioning the interest in the marriage,
hastens to that choice which finally became the match. He
places this interest in the king's marriage just after the
death of Charles IV of Bohemia, November 29, 1378. The
rest of his account refers to later events. But Froissart also
mentions earlier negotiations for the marriage of the Prince
Richard, as we shall see.

England and Bohemia. To understand it fully, we must have in mind the more exact situation of England in this period. We must remember, that the war with France had already been carried on intermittently for forty years when Richard came to the throne; that the glories of Sluys, Crécy, and Poitiers had been more than clouded by the later failures of the Black Prince and the great Edward; that the command of the sea had been lost, and large portions of the French possessions wrested from the empire in the early seventies; and that at the death of Edward III every port was closed, lest the news should place England at the mercy of her hereditary foe.[9] All these were reasons why England was in need as never before, and why Pope Gregory XI, in the exercise of his power as mediator, had tried to bring the warring nations together by the marriage of the young Richard, even while still heir to the throne, with a princess of France.[10]

The failure of the efforts to bring England and

---

[9] Froissart's *Chronicles*, I. ch. 327; Johnes, I, 510.

[10] In these negotiations regarding the marriage of the young prince, Chaucer was at least twice engaged. See the discussion in Skeat's *Chaucer* I, xxvii f.; Longman, *The Life and Times of Edward* III, II, 271 f; Froissart's *Chronicles* I, ch. cccxxvi, where Chaucer is mentioned as one of the negotiators. It may be noted also that the marriage of Richard did not become an important consideration until after he had been acknowledged heir to the throne, just after the Black Prince died in 1376. Then the "Good" Parliament, in the very month of the Black Prince's death, had Richard brought before it and proclaimed by the archbishop of Canterbury as "the true heir apparent of the throne"; Longman, II, 256.

France together in 1376-7 and the early part of 1378 was soon followed by an event quite as great in European history as the Hundred Years War. Richard II had been on the throne scarcely more than a year when Gregory XI died (March, 1378), Urban VI was elected, and before many months Christendom was torn asunder by the great schism of the papacy. This breaking of long-established religious relations had the most far-reaching consequences. The nations were now compelled to decide between rival popes, and the decisions brought a new alignment in western Europe. France naturally espoused the cause of Clement, the French pope. England received the representatives of both popes at the Gloucester parliament of October-November, 1378, and decided to hold with Urban. Under these circumstances there was no papal mediator to urge a close of the disastrous French war, or a union of the two countries on the basis of a royal marriage. It was thus inevitable that England should look elsewhere for a queen, and for such alliances as she should thereafter form.

We need not consider all the various suggestions of a bride for the young king, some of them noted from Froissart. Most interesting is the proposal of Katherine, daughter of that Bernabò Visconti to whom Chaucer had gone as ambassador in 1378, perhaps partly in connection with this same business of

his young master's marriage.[11]   The appointment of
negotiators with Bernabò was made March 18, 1379,
Michael de la Pole, Sir John Burley, and Dr. John
Sheppey being named.[12]   Of more importance are
the negotiations which resulted in the marriage of
Richard and Anne of Bohemia in 1382.   I shall therefore undertake to present them in some detail, and
emphasize some elements that have not hitherto been
noted.

To understand the negotiations between England
and Bohemia we must keep in mind the important
relations of the papal schism.   That rupture not only
made a new alignment of the nations in spiritual
affairs, but separated, for the first time in many
years, the traditional allies Bohemia and France. We
need but remember that John of Luxemburg, the
blind king of Bohemia, had fought and given his
life as an ally of France at Crécy in 1346.   It is no
less significant of the strange changes which time
brings that the Black Prince, father of the Richard

---

[11] The conjecture is made by Professor Tatlock in *The Development and Chronology of Chaucer's Works*, p. 41.   It is
interesting to note that this match was highly considered by
some, at least.   The *Chronicon Angliae* (Rolls Series 64,
331), speaking of the marriage of Anne, says: "Hanc igitur
magno pretio, multisque coemptam laboribus, habendam rex
praeëlegerat, quamquam cum inaestimabili auri summa oblata
fuisset et filia domini Mediolanensis Barnabonis."   Perhaps
the hostility of the writer to John of Gaunt may have had
something to do with his apparent disapprobation of the
marriage with Anne, perhaps only his belief that a bad bargain had been made.

[12] Rymer's *Fœdera*, VII, 213.

who was soon to marry the granddaughter of that same blind king, won his first victory at Crécy, and there, is sometimes said to have adopted the insignia of the dead Bohemian monarch, the three black ostrich plumes and the motto "ich dien." Charles IV of Bohemia, John's son, and father of Anne, continued the French alliance. Yet he was fully in sympathy with the election of Urban VI as pope, and there is little probability that he would have changed his allegiance, had he lived to consider the claims of the schismatic pope. He died two months and nine days after the election of Clement, or November 29, 1378.

Before Charles Fourth's death, or on November 5, 1378, Clement had sent to the Bohemian court Bishop John of Cambray,[13] but early in the following year Urban dispatched, as papal nuncio, his efficient legate Pileus de Prata, Cardinal of Ravenna.[14] Pileus reached the court of Wenceslaus in March, 1379, and urged him to hold with Urban, as Ludwig of Hungary was doing. He emphasized, as an effective argument with the young emperor then only eighteen, that to support Clement would make a heretic of Wenceslaus's father, only a few months dead.[15]

---

[13] Lindner, *Geschichte des deutschen Reiches unter König Wenzel*, I, 102, footnote.

[14] Lindner, I. 94.

[15] Höfler, *Anna von Luxemburg, Denkschriften d. Wiener Akad., Phil.-Hist. Classe*, XX, 130; Lindner, I, 113.

For this and other reasons Wenceslaus remained firm, and even vigorously supported Urban. In connection with this support, he wrote a letter to Richard II of England, as early as May 20, 1379, suggesting an alliance against the schismatic Clement.[16] Curiously enough, at this very time English commissioners may have been at the court of Wenceslaus, perhaps to discuss the question of a marriage between Richard and Anne. Six days after the commissioners had been appointed to visit Bernabò Visconti, or on March 24, 1379, two of them, Michael de la Pole and Gerard de Lisle, were granted letters of safe conduct as about to go to the Roman court (versus Curiam Romanam).[17] From Rome, perhaps at the suggestion of the pope, they went to Germany, where they were unfortunately imprisoned, to be released only after another commission had been sent from England with a ransom.[18] But for this, the negotiations for a marriage of Richard and Anne might possibly have been hastened.[19]

[16] Höfler, 127. Lindner, I, 95, gives a rhetorical extract from this letter, in which Wenceslaus professes that he is willing to shed his blood for the church.

[17] Rymer, new ed. IV, 60.

[18] Rymer, VII, 232; this commission is dated January 20, 1380.

[19] I say possibly, because the question as to whether these commissioners were to propose such a marriage rests upon the interpretation of a record in the *Issues of the Exchequer* (Devon, p. 224) of January 9, 1384: "To Sir Michael de la Pole, Chancellor of England, lately sent from England to Milan, and from thence to the court of Rome to the King of the Romans and Bohemia as a King's messenger, to enter

In this letter of Wenceslaus to Richard there was no mention of binding the alliance by a royal marriage. On the side of Wenceslaus, it was perhaps not thought of at this time. On the part of Richard's councilors, the idea of a peace with France, cemented by the marriage of Richard with a French princess, was still in mind. The latter is certainly shown by the appointment, on September 26, 1379, of ambassadors to treat with "those of France" (cum illis de Francia).[20] The extent of the powers granted may be inferred from these words:

Et ensement de Tretir, Ordenir, et Accorder ovesque nostre dit Adversaire, ou sez Procu-

into a treaty for marriage to be had between the said Lord the King and Anne Queen of England, taken prisoner in those parts under the safe conduct of the same King of the Romans, upon [his] return from the parts aforesaid." If this record is correct, the marriage of Richard and Anne was proposed somewhat earlier than has usually been supposed. The Exchequer record is followed by the writer of the article on Pole in the *Dictionary of National Biography*, which, however, is certainly wrong in some of its statements, as pointed out by C. G. Chamberlayne in *Die Heirat Richards II von England mit Anna von Luxemburg* (Halle, 1906). On the other hand the latter assumes that "Curiam Romanam" above means the court of Wenceslaus, though admitting that its usual meaning is the papal court. This seems to me wholly untenable. Indeed, it is hard to believe that marriage negotiations with Bohemia were seriously considered in England during the winter of 1379–80. Twice while Pole was abroad (see above), commissions were appointed to treat with France and arrange for a marriage with a French princess. Perhaps, as the Exchequer entry is of January 9, 1384, nearly two years after the marriage of Richard and Anne, Pole's later connection with the marriage arrangements was confused with this earlier mission to Italy and Rome. In any case, negotiations with Bohemia were taken up anew in June, 1380.

[20] Rymer, VII, 229.

reres, sur Alliances, Confederacies, et Amities, soit il par Mariage et Contracte de Matrimoigne de nostre Persone de meisme, ou par autre voie quelque soit, en general, ou en especiale, come vous semblera bon.

Again on April 1, 1380, other ambassadors were appointed *De Tractando cum Adversario Franciae*,[21] with powers expressed in practically the same words. On the same day also, safe conduct was granted ambassadors of France to enter the English possessions and consider such treaty and marriage.

For some reason the negotiations were fruitless, as they had been so many times before. Possibly they were not carried out in entire good faith, for, on the first of March, 1380, an offensive and defensive alliance was entered into with Brittany.[22] Perhaps the explanation of the failure was in the influence of John of Gaunt and his anger against the alliance of France and Spain.[23] At least, on the twenty-third of May, power was given by the king to treat with the king and queen of Portugal,[24] and

[21] Rymer, VII, 248.

[22] Rymer, VII, 236. *Liga Offensiva et Defensiva, conclusa per quattuor Commissarios Regis et Septem Commissarios Ducis Britanniae.*

[23] Cf. C. Oman, *op. cit.*, IV, 19. Such influence of the Duke of Lancaster might also explain the apparent preference of the anti-Lancastrian chronicler of the *Chronicon Angliae* for the marriage with the daughter of Bernabò Visconti. See footnote 11, p. 132.

[24] Rymer, VII, 253.

on the fifth day of July a treaty with them was made.[25] On the first of June, provision was made for invading France under the command of Thomas, Earl of Buckingham.[26] On June 24 the king sent to every bishop of England a recital of the treachery and bad faith of the French king in negotiating, the purpose to proceed with the war, and a request for the prayers of the clergy for the success of the expedition.[27] With such preparations the Earl of Buckingham set out, and from July 20 to October marched quite around Paris, finally reaching Rennes in Brittany. That his expedition was of little avail to England does not concern us here.[28] Under such circumstances, either peace with France, or marriage with a French princess, was equally impossible. Nor did Richard again consider such an alliance with his long-time enemy until 1396, when Anne had been in her grave more than two years.

It was when these efforts at peace with France were a failure that an opportunity presented itself for a royal marriage and alliance with the house then representing all that was left of the empire of the Romans. The suggestion doubtless came from abroad. We have already noted that Wenceslaus had

---

[25] Rymer, VII, 262 f.

[26] Rymer, VII, 256.

[27] Rymer, VII, 260.

[28] Froissart, *Chronicles*, II, ch. 1 f; Johnes, I, 406; and Oman, *op. cit.*, IV, 19–20.

written to Richard in May, 1379,[29] suggesting an
alliance against schismatics. That letter was doubtless inspired by Cardinal Pileus, the papal nuncio to
Bohemia, who was doing all in his power to bring the
nations to the support of Urban.[30] Before another
year had passed, through his efforts, all Germany,
except the Duke of Brabant and the cities of Metz
and Mainz, had bound themselves to the support of
the Roman pope.[31] To further the same cause Cardinal
Pileus went to England in the spring or early summer of 1380. This we know first of all from Froissart.
He says:

> The Cardinal of Ravenna was at that time
> [the summer of 1380] in England and, being
> an Urbanist, was converting the English to the
> same way of thinking.[32]

Froissart was not wholly right that the cardinal of
Ravenna was, at just this time, "converting the
English," for Urban had been fully accepted at the
parliament of Gloucester (October 20 to November
16, 1378) when legates from both popes pressed
their rival claims. But there is other evidence that
Pileus de Prata, the Ravennese cardinal, had come to

[29] See p. 134.

[30] Lindner, I, 94.

[31] Lindner, I, 105: "Schon ehe der Reichstag zusammentrat,
konnte Pileus an Urban guten Bericht senden. Ganz Deutsch-
land bis auf drei, . . hangen dem wahren Papste an."

[32] *Chronicles*, II, ch. 1; Johnes, I, 606.

England in the year 1380. On June 7 Richard granted to the cardinal certain rights in offices connected with Lichfield and Lincoln cathedrals, "on account of the good affection which we have for the person of the reverend father in Christ, the cardinal of Ravenna, and for the good will and wish which he has shown us and our kingdom beforetime, and is showing at present."[33]

It was doubtless Cardinal Pileus of Ravenna who, to strengthen the cause of Urban, first suggested to the English, or at least now urged upon them, an alliance of their country with Bohemia and the marriage of Richard with a German princess. This becomes more evident, as we see the full relations of the marriage to the politics of the papal schism. Pope Urban, as we have seen, had secured the allegiance of Wenceslaus. But Clement still hoped to bring him over to his side, or at least to weaken his support of Urban, by persuading him to continue the long-existing alliance with France. This last he hoped to accomplish by the marriage of Anne of Bohemia, sister of Wenceslaus, and the son of Charles V of France, who was soon to become Charles VI. There had even been talk of this marriage of Anne and the Dauphin during a visit of

---

[33] Pro bona Affectione, quam erga Personam, Reverendi in Christo Patris, Cardinalis de Ravenna habemus, et pro bona Voluntate et Delectione, quas ipse Nobis et Regno nostro hactenus monstravit, et indies monstrat." Rymer, VII, 256.

Wenceslaus to Aix-la-Chapelle.[34] This visit was made
after the Diet of Frankfort, in April, 1380.[35] Besides,
the sagacious Charles V of France did not take kindly to the severing of relations with Germany, likely
to result from the papal schism. Even on his death-
bed, in the early autumn of 1380, he said to his
courtiers:

> Seek out in Germany an alliance for my son
> that our connections there may be strengthened.
> You have heard that our adversary is about to
> marry from thence to increase his allies.[36]

[34] Valois says, in *La France et le grand schisme d'occident*,
I, 300: "Durant un séjour de Wenceslas à Aix-la-Chapelle, on
avait parlé d'un mariage entre le dauphin, fils du roi de
France, et Anne de Luxembourg, sœur du roi des Romains.
Une entrevue devait avoir lieu entre Charles V et Wenceslas
. . . . La cour d'Avignon comptait beaucoup sur le résultat
de cette conférence. Entre autres personnages qui promet-
taient de s'y rendre, je citerai les envoyés du roi de Portugal
et, à leur tête, l'évêque de Lisbonne, qui déjà préparait le
discours avec lequel il devait convertir Wenceslas. Cette
entrevue n'eut pas lieu: le roi des Romains, tournant le dos
à Reims, reprit la route de Cologne. Il se fit, il est vrai,
représenter à Paris par quatre ambassadeurs, mais l'acte,
sans doute rédigé d'avance, dont ces derniers étaient porteurs
ne traitait que du renouvellement des alliances entre les deux
maisons, sans souffler mot de mariage du dauphin avec la
bohémienne Anne." I am indebted for pointing this out, to
my friend Professor G. L. Burr of Cornell University. As
authorities for this statement Valois cites, 'Lettre du cardinal
de Viviers aux cardinaux de Florence et de Milan,' Baluzius,
II, 869; and his own edition of the *Discours prononcé le 14
juillet 1380, en présence de Charles V par Martin l'évêque
de Lisbonne*, in the *Bibliothèque de l'École des Chartes*, lii,
495, 500.

[35] Lindner, I, 114, 116, 430.

[36] *Chronicles*, II, ch. lv; Johnes, I, 616. Charles V died September 16, 1380, and the passage shows that Richard's idea of
a marriage with a German princess was known in France at
this time.

Such a marriage with Anne of Bohemia was also urged when Charles VI had come to the throne. The Clementists saw in it their only hope of winning Wenceslaus and Germany.[37] This is fully implied in a letter of Cardinal Peter de Sortenac, quoted by Höfler. He writes:

> Nec est spes eum [Wenceslaus] pro nunc revocandi nisi per tractatum matrimonii, qui pendet de sorore sua danda regi Francie, in qua tractatu speratur, quod possit informari de justitia domini nostri et de praeservatione fame et honoris patris sui mortui et per consequens reduci.[38]

We have also the testimony of the English chronicler Adam of Usk. Speaking of the Cardinal of Ravenna, whose notary he was while the former was in London, Adam says:

> And after his departure, the said Lady Anne was bought for a price by our lord the king, for she was much sought in marriage by the king of France.[39]

---

[37] Lindner, I, 113: "Die einzige Hoffnung, Wenzel zur Umkehr zu bewegen, läge in jetzt schwebenden Verhandlungen über die Ehe zwischen seiner Schwester und dem Könige von Frankreich."

[38] Höfler, 130, footnote: from Baluzius, *Vitae Paparum Avenionensium*, II, 869. The last clause refers to the fear of Wenceslaus that, to recognize Clement, would make a heretic of his dead father; see p. 133.

[39] *Chronicon Adae de Usk*, ed. by Thompson, p. 102–3. The original reads: "post ejus recessum, dicta domina Anna, per dominum regem magno precio redempta, quia a rege Francie

The attempt of Clement to draw Bohemia and
France together through the marriage of Anne' perhaps accounts for the renewed efforts of Urban to
prevent that alliance. Thus, doubtless, Cardinal
Pileus came to England to urge the league between
Bohemia and England, France's enemy, perhaps also
a marriage of Richard II with a German princess.
Nor was such a suggestion of Pileus de Prata likely
to be without great weight. Made bishop of Ravenna
in 1370, he had long been engaged, as representative of the pope, in trying to bring peace between
England and France. In connection with this duty
he was given letters of safe conduct by Edward III
as early as June 8, 1374.[40] He was papal legate at
Bruges in the negotiations between England and
France in 1375, and he appears frequently thereafter in English records.[41] Coming at this time as
representative of both the pope and the emperor, it
is not strange that he should have been readily heard
by Richard's council.

The suggestion of an alliance between England
and Bohemia together with a royal marriage, was

in uxorem affectata," p. 2–3. One cannot fail to notice that
this rivalry of the king of France for the hand of Anne of
Bohemia has direct relations to the interpretation of the
Parlement of Foules. With that I have dealt in an article,
'The Suitors in Chaucer's Parlement of Foules,' *Modern
Philology*, VIII, 45. [See above, pp. 58–89.]

[40] Rymer, VII, 39.

[41] Rymer, VII, 51, 53, 56, 58, 61, 68, etc.

immediately taken up, it would seem. In this ready
response the councilors of Richard were doubtless
influenced by two motives. They desired a queen
for their young king, and they strongly hoped to
gain assistance against their old adversary, France.
Besides, France and Spain had joined in a newly-
formed league against the claims of John of Gaunt
to the Spanish throne, and this added a new reason
for desiring aid from abroad. As a result, on June
12, 1380, commissioners were appointed to treat for
a marriage of Richard with Katherine, daughter of
Ludwig, "recently emperor of the Romans."[42]

The commissioners were Sir Simon Burley, Sir
Richard Braybrook, and Bernard Van Sedles, the
first of whom had been appointed on the same day
tutor to the king, then two months more than fourteen years old; that is, if born April 13, 1366; or a

---

[42] Rymer, VII, 257: *De Tractando super Matrimonio inter
Regem et Filiam Ludovici, nuper Imperatoris.* In the commission the daughter is called "Dominam Katerinam Filiam,
celebris memoriae, Ludowici, nuper Romanorum Imperatoris."
The commissioners were accredited, however, "tam Serenissimi Principis Domini Wensalai Romanorum et Bohemiae
Regis, Fratris nostri carissimi, quam ejusdem Dominae Kate-
rinae et Amicorum suorum." This first choice of a German
bride for the boy king seems peculiar to say the least. The
only Ludwig "recently emperor of the Romans" was Ludwig
of Bavaria, who had died in 1347. His daughter, therefore,
could not have been less than twice as old as Richard. But
perhaps, at the beginning of these negotiations with a far-
away country, a mistake was made, and Anne, daughter of
Charles IV, king of Bohemia and emperor of the Romans
until his death in 1378, was from the first intended. At least
the choice was soon changed, and the negotiations for the
hand of Anne begun. Chamberlayne (p. 34) assumes a
scribal error.

little more than thirteen if born January 6, or February 26, 1367.

It was in connection with this appointment that Froissart says:

> Sir Simon Burley, a sage and valiant knight, who had been the king's tutor and much beloved by the prince his father, was nominated to go to Germany, to treat of this marriage, as a wise and able negotiator.[43] Every necessary preparation was ordered, as well for his expenses as otherwise. He set out from England magnificently equipped and arrived at Calais; from thence he went to Gravelines and continued his journey until he came to Brussels, where he met Duke Wenceslaus of Brabant, the Duke Albert, the Count de Blois, the Count de St. Pol, Sir William de Maulny, and numbers of knights from Brabant, Hainault, and other parts, partaking of a great feast of tilts and tournaments; and it was on this occasion all these lords were there assembled. The Duke and Duchess of Brabant, from the love they bore the king of England, received his knight most courteously. They were much rejoiced on hearing the cause

---

[43] *Chronicles*, II, ch. xliii; translation of Johnes, I, 593. Froissart's previous paragraph speaks of the "sister of the king of Bohemia and Germany," and just before mentions the death of Charles IV of Bohemia, which occurred November 29, 1378. From this he runs on to the later years, as everything else shows this to have been the first mission of Burley.

of his journey into Germany, and said it would be a good match between the king of England and their niece.[44]   They gave to Sir Simon Burley on his departure, special letters to the emperor, to assure him they approved very much of this marriage.   The knight set out from Brussels, and took the road through Louvain to Cologne.

There is also further evidence in Froissart that the negotiation proceeded rapidly in the summer of 1380.   In speaking of the invasion of France by the Earl of Buckingham, who left Calais on July 20, he says:[45]

> The English passed Terouenne without attempting anything, for the lords de Saimpi and de Fransures were within it.   They marched on towards Bethune, where they halted for a day; and I will tell you the reason.   You have heard how King Richard, by the advice of his uncles and council, had sent into Germany Sir Simon Burley to the emperor, to demand his sister in marriage.   This knight so well managed the business that the emperor, by the advice of his council and the great lords of his court, complied with the request, but he had sent with

------

[44] This would be Anne, not Katherine daughter of Ludwig of Bavaria.   Froissart seems not to have known of the proposals for Katherine, or more likely, if a Katherine were ever really considered, the change to Anne had already been made.

[45] *Chronicles*, II, ch. 1; Johnes, I, 606.

10

Sir Simon Burley the Duke of Saxony, first to Luxemburg and then to England, to observe that kingdom, in order that his sister might have a just account of it, so that, if agreeable, the marriage might be concluded.

The Cardinal of Ravenna was at that time in England and, being an Urbanist, was converting the ·English to the same way of thinking; he was waiting also the arrival of the above-mentioned duke. At the entreaties of the emperor and the Duke of Brabant, he and all his company obtained liberty to pass through France to Calais. They therefore travelled by way of Tournay, Lille, and Bethune, from whence they came to visit the Earl of Buckingham and his barons, who received the Duke of Saxony and his suite honourably. The Germans continued their journey through Aire and St. Omer, and from thence to Calais.

This very explicit statement makes clear that Sir Simon Burley was on his way back from Bohemia, with the Duke of Tetschen, or Saxony, by the latter part of July or the first of August, 1380, when the Earl of Buckingham was as yet a little distance from Calais. There is also in one manuscript of Froissart further record regarding this visit of the Duke of Tetschen. It reads:[46]

---

[46] *Chronicles*, II, at close of ch. lviii; Johnes, I, 622.

You have heard how Sir Simon Burley, that gallant knight, attached to the household of King Richard of England, had been sent with proposals to the emperor in Germany respecting the marriage of the Lady Anne, his sister, with the king of England. He had transacted the business with ability, so that the emperor and his council consented; but he had brought with him, on his return, the Duke of Saxony, one of the council of the emperor, for him to observe the state of England, and to make inquiries concerning the dower, and how it was to be settled on the queen. . . . .

The Duke of Saxony was much pleased with what he saw and heard, particularly respecting the dower; he was well satisfied with the king and his two uncles of Lancaster and Cambridge, for the other was in France, and also with the Earl of Salisbury, the Earl of Warwick, the Earl of Northumberland, and the other lords about the person of the king. When the Duke had remained some time in England, and finished the business he had come upon, he took leave of the king, promising to persevere in the marriage to the conclusion. At his departure, he received handsome presents of jewels for himself, for those attendant on the person of the emperor, and also for the ladies who had the management of the young lady, Anne of Bohemia, the intended future queen of England. The duke returned, well pleased, to his own country; but this business was not immediately concluded, for the damsel was young, and the councils of each party had many things to arrange; add to this, there shortly happened in England great misery and great tribulation, as you will hear recounted in this history.

In this passage the words "for the other was in France," following the mention of "his two uncles of Lancaster and Cambridge," refer to Thomas, Earl of Buckingham, whom the Duke of Tetschen had already met on the Continent.[47] But there is still further proof that this visit of the Duke of Tetschen was in 1380 and not the next year, for in June, 1381, the Earl of Cambridge was sent to Portugal.[48] He therefore could not have met the Bohemian ambassador in the summer of that year, and the visit of the Duke of Tetschen must have been in the preceding summer, as indicated by the other facts.

But there is further evidence that the negotiations for the Bohemian alliance were far advanced in the year 1380. On December 12 of that year, another com-

---

[47] See the preceding quotation.

[48] The orders for the impressment of ships for the Earl of Cambridge are dated May 12, 1380, in Rymer (VII, 305), as noted by Armitage-Smith in his *John of Gaunt*, 263, footnote.

mission was appointed to treat of the marriage.[49]
That this commission refers to the time after the
first visit of the Duke of Tetschen is clear from the
following words:

> Unde, cum, post aliquos Tractatus super hoc
> habitos, Nobiles et Illustres Viri, Domini,
> Przimislaus Dux Teschinensis, Conradus Krey-
> ger Magister Curiae, et Petrus de Wartemberg
> Magister Camerae ipsius Serenissimi Fratris
> nostri, ad nostram Praesentiam Londiniae de-
> clinarent, de dicta Parentela contrahenda, ac de
> certis aliis Ligarum, Amicitiarum, seu Confoe-
> derationum Articulis extitit ibidem mutuo Con-
> cordatum.

With the exception of Walter Skirlawe, who was
also named commissioner, those appointed at this
time were the same as on June 12. It seems but an
extension of the powers originally granted, though
after the Duke of Tetschen had spied out the land.
The change of name from Katherine, daughter of
Ludwig, to Anne, sister of the emperor, had also
been made.

These later negotiations were so far successful that
it was decided to continue them in Flanders, the commissioners to assemble on the feast of the Epiphany

---

[49] *De Potestate contrahendi Sponsalia et Matrimonium cum
Sorore Regis Romanorum*, Rymer, VII, 305. This document
occurs, not in its chronological place in the *Fœdera*, but
among the documents dated in May, 1381, when the articles
of agreement were finally signed in London.

(January 6).[50] Somewhat greater power was now given for the settling of the details of the marriage contract, and for this purpose Thomas, Duke of Kent, Hugo Segrave, and the indefatigable Sir Simon Burley were appointed. This latter paper was dated the twenty-sixth of December, and on January 12 safe conduct was granted to the commissioners of Anne to come to Calais.[51]

The negotiations now proceeded rapidly. On January 23 Anne appointed the Duke of Tetschen, Conrad Kreyger, and Peter de Wartemberg to act for her.[52] On the last day of January Elizabeth, mother of Anne, named the same ambassadors to consent on her part, and on the first of February Wenceslaus, king of Bohemia and Roman emperor, gave them

---

[50] This paper was headed *De Tractando, super Matrimonio inter Regem et Annam Sororem Imperatoris*, Rymer, VII, 280. In it occur these words: "Unde, cum, post aliquos Tractatus, super hoc habitos, pro Negotii hujusmodi Conclusione, quaedam Diaeta in Flandria fuerit assignata, pro cujus observatione Ambassatores solempnes, tam pro parte ipsius Dominae Annae, et Amicorum suorum, quam nostra, debebant, juxta Conducta ibidem, in Feste Epiphaniae Domini proximo convenire." This document says Anne was chosen "nedum propter ipsius Nobilitatem, set [sic] propter Famam celebrem bonitatis ipsius." Gairdner *(Dict. Nat. Biog.*, Anne) is unkind enough to suggest that this may have been because of Anne's probable lack of beauty, but the language of a serious state document surely does not justify this interpretation.

[51] The later date than that first mentioned would seem to imply that the commissioners did not meet as early as intended, but such delay may be explained by many another similar one of the time.

[52] Rymer, VII, 282: *Litera Procuratoria Annae Filiae Caroli Imperatoris et Regis Boemiae, ad Tractandum de Matrimonio contrahendo;* it is dated "x kalend. Februarii."

authority to make an alliance with England.[53] The
decree of Wenceslaus gives,

> Potestatem Tractandi, Contrahendi, Iniendi,
> Faciendi et Consummandi, pro Nobis et haere-
> dibus nostris Boemiae Regibus, Amicitias,
> Uniones, et Ligas Fraternales, et etiam Colligan-
> tias, Statum et Honorem Sacrosanctae Romanae
> Ecclesiae, et Sanctissimi in Christo Patris et
> Domini, Domini Urbani Papae Sexti, concernen-
> tes, ad Exterminium Scismaticorum nunc Vi-
> gentium et Rebellium, praesentium et futuro-
> rum, ipsius Domini Urbani Papae praedicti, et
> Successorum suorum Canonice intrantium, et
> per Collegium Cardinalium, dicto Domino
> Urbano adhaerens, eligendorum, cum Serenis-
> simo Principe, Domino Ricardo Rege Angliae
> Illustri, Fratre nostro carissimo pro se, et suis
> Haeredibus Angliae Regibus, etc.

The negotiations in Flanders being successful and
confirmed in Bohemia and England, on March 29,
1381, power was given to Edmund, Earl of Cambridge, Hugo Segrave, and Albert de Vere for con-
cluding the treaty on the part of England.[54] For the

---

[53] Rymer, VII, 283: *Commissio Imperatoris ad Tractandum
de Amicitiis et de Liga contra Scismaticos.* It was dated at
Nuremberg, and it may be seen to be carefully guarded from
any other intent than the support of the pope.

[54] This paper occurs in Rymer only at VII, 294, with other
papers of the treaty signed in duplicate for the rulers of the
two kingdoms. It is not in its chronological place. One

same purpose the Duke of Tetschen and his colleagues were received in England May 1, 1381, and
the treaty of marriage and alliance was signed on
the second of that month.[55] This document consists
of first, the treaty itself, *Tractatus de Matrimonio
Regis cum Anna Sorore Imperatoris;* next a recitation of the powers of the ambassadors, *Tenores vero
Procuratoriorum, de quibus superius fit mentio,
sequuntur sub hac Forma.* The latter are first from
Wenceslaus himself as to the alliance, then Anne
assenting to the negotiations; Wenceslaus again as
to the marriage of his sister; Elizabeth, mother of
Anne, giving her consent; and finally Richard assenting and appointing his ambassadors. These documents fill five and a half of Rymer's folio pages.

Even these are not all the records connected with
this royal marriage alliance. Several others fill subsequent pages of Rymer.[56] First is an *Obligatio Imperatoris pro 20 Millibus Florenorum,* for the sum
to be applied on the expenses in connection with the
negotiations for the marriage; the *Obligatio Am-
bassiatorum* [sic] *de Summa Regi Romanorum mu-*

---

point in the document is worthy of note as perhaps implying
England's great interest in the alliance. While in the commission of December 26, 1380, the points to be considered by
the contracting parties are first, the marriage and second, the
alliance; they are here reversed and the subject of the alliance considerably extended.

[55] Rymer, VII, 290-1.

[56] Rymer, VII, 295 f.

tuata; De Obligatione facta Regi Romanorum, by
which Richard agreed to loan (mutuare) Wenceslaus 80,000 florins when Anne was safely conducted
to Calais; a document *De quietantia certarum sum-
marum super Traductione Annae, Sororis Imperatoris,* in satisfaction of the former pledge of the emperor as to the 20,000 florins;[57] and finally a further
paper *De Potestate tractandi cum Principibus
Alemanniae, super Ligis,* this last dated the tenth of
May.

These numerous documents give some idea of the
elaborate negotiations of Richard and his advisers
with the king of Bohemia and emperor of the
Romans. Yet there is further evidence of the extent
to which the business was carried. In the first place,
the pope had been influential in bringing England
and Bohemia together, largely, it is very clear, for

---

[57] The exact agreement was that the emperor Wenceslaus
should advance 20,000 florins for the expenses of the negotiations and the journey of Anne; that, on her safe recep-
tion in England, he should receive a loan of 80,000 florins,
20,000 of which should not be returned as recompensing him
for the expenses incurred. Still further, on receiving the
Duke of Tetschen in May, 1381, Richard at once settled upon
him 500 marks sterling for the term of his natural life. This
was, in the language of the decree, "de Gratia nostra speciali,
et pro eo quod, Magnificum Virum, Przimislaum Ducem
Teschinensem penes Nos et de Concilio nostro retinuimus, ad
Terminum vitae suae moraturum, ac etiam pro bono Servitio
suo Nobis, impenso et in futurum impendendo." Similar
amounts were also granted to Petrus de Wartemberg and
Conrad Crayer, while sums of 500 gold florins were given to
Borzewey de Swyner, 200 each to Sifridus Foster and Conrad
di Ridberg, and fifty marks sterling to Lupoldus de Crayer,
son of Conrad. Rymer, VII, 288; I have preserved the spelling of the names as they appear in the decree.

the support which Urban VI thus obtained against his rival Clement VII. As already noted,[58] the cardinal of Ravenna had been in England a considerable time in direct representation of the pope. The result was that the alliance was accompanied with even more intimate relations of England and the papacy. These relations are indicated by a series of documents which show how fully the pope and his artful legate[59] looked to their own interests. First,

---

[58] See p. 138.

[59] The extent of Cardinal de Prata's personal rewards from his sojourn in England may be best inferred from the words of the *Chronicon Angliae* (Rolls Series 64, 283): "Pileus, tituli Sanctae Praxedis, presbyter cardinalis, per istud tempus venit in Angliam . . . et regem Anglorum, et regnum de inaestimabile summa pecuniae vacuaturus. Nam, ut asseruit, potestatem afferens inauditam, in brevi totum regnum ad ipsum confluere fecit pro diversis gratiis impetrandis. Revera diversa diversis beneficia contulit; indulgentias quas dominus papa concedere solummodo consuevit, et ipse concessit; biennales, triennales, confessionales literas quibuslibet solventibus gratanter indulsit. Ad capellanatum domini papae tam possessionatos quam mendicantes admisit, nec aurum eorum respuit, qui notarii publici effici precabantur. Altaria quoque portatilia nulli pecuniam offerenti negavit. Nec quadraginta libras, cum aliis donis Cisterciensium, repulit, quin gratiose concederet eis licentiam generalem vescendi carnibus extra monasterium indifferenter, ut in monasterio edere consueverunt. Excommunicatis gratiam absolutionis impendit. Vota perigrinationis ad Apostolorum limina, ad Terram Sanctam, ad Sanctum Jacobum, non prius remisit, quam tantam pecuniam recepisset, quantam, juxta veram aestimationem, in eisdem perigrinationibus expendere debuissent. Et ut cuncta concludam brevibus, nihil omnino petendum erat, quod non censuit, intercedente pecunia, concedendum. Interrogatus autem in qua poteste haec faceret, cum summa indignatione respondit, se Romae, si scire vellent ejus potestatem, omnibus responsurum. Jamque adeo referti erant argento ejus sacculi, ut advenientibus ejus ministri respondere dedignarentur, nisi aurum efferent, dicentes, 'Afferte nobis aurum; argento namque vestro pleni sumus.' Reces-

is one giving the papal legate certain substantial rewards, *De Fructibus Decanatus Eborum liberandis Cardinali Ravennas,* dated May 3, 1381, the day after the signing of the treaty of marriage.[60] Then come the documents *De Procedendo contra Scismaticos,* and *De Potestate Tractandi cum Papa, de Ligis,* both on May 5, and both appointing Sir John Hawkwood, Nicholas Dagworth, and Walter Skirlawe to negotiate with the pope.[61] These are followed by papal bulls from Urban VI to Richard, dated October 27, 1380, and March 18, 1381, and recorded on May 6. Then come the pecuniary rewards to the pope in

---

surus autem, aurum post se nequaquam relinquere voluit; sed secum super summarios deferri fecit, ad tantam quidem summam, quantam nunquam Anglia in taxa vel tallagio semel pendere consuevit." Adam of Usk *(Chronicon,* p. 2–3) is no less severe: "Ineundo cardinalis iste, false se fingens legatum a latere esse ac potestatem pape habere, vices papales tunc exercuit; me inter cetera notarium tunc, licet inutiliter, in domo fratrum predicacionis Londonie, ubi tunc morabitur, creavit. Infinitam pecuniam sic collegit, et ab Anglia cum eadem pecunia, eodem tractatu matrimonii expedito, ad sui recessit dampnationem; credens tamen, licet in vanum, facta sua hujusmodi per papam ratificari." Chaucer may well have had this prelate in mind when pointing some of his satire against the plundering clergy, as in the picture of the Pardoner, "His walet . . . Bretful of pardoun come from Rome al hoot."

[60] Rymer, VII, 296. Also the archdeaconate of Durham on July 11, 1381; Rymer, VII, 320.

[61] It will be remembered, from the discussion of the dates of the incidents in *The Knight's Tale,* that this May 5, 1381, was Sunday. Numerous other important acts of the year are dated on Sunday, as those of June 23 and 30 in connection with the Peasant Revolt, and that for conducting Anne to the king's presence, December 1. The ratification of the treaty of alliance by Wenceslaus was also on a Sunday, September 1.

a decree, *De Fructibus Archidiaconatuum et Prae-
bendarum, per Cardinales Rebelles occupatorum,
Papae Concessis*, May 8. Finally, there is associated
with these a delegation of power to Sir John Hawkwood, Nicholas Dagworth, and Walter Skirlawe, *De
Potestate Tractandi cum Ducibus et Dominis de Par-
tibus Italiae super Ligis et Amicitiis*. The alliance of
England, that is, though usually thought of as with
Bohemia only, included the papal states and Italy.
These show the relations of both alliances to the support of the pope. As already noted (p. 128), it is
possible that these further treaties with the papal
states and Italy account for Chaucer's use of the
plural "contrees" in l.2973. Except for France and
Spain, England was now united with most of the
countries of western Europe in the support of
Urban, though more especially with Bohemia by
reason of the marriage alliance.

The treaty with the king of Bohemia, signed by
commissioners of the two countries on May 2, 1381,
was formally ratified by Wenceslaus at Prague on
September 1 of that year. A letter to that effect is
given in Rymer VII, 331, under the caption *Ligarum,
cum Rege, Ratificatio Imperatoris*. This has bearing
on one point connected with the coming of Anne to
England. It is often said that she was to have been
received before Michaelmas (September 29) 1381,
and that she was delayed by the Rebellion of Wat

Tyler.[62] This idea is not fully justified by the original treaty which specifies "circa Festum Sancti Michaelis proximo futurum" as the time when Anne should be brought "in Regnum nostrum Angliae, vel saltem ad villam nostram Calesii, per praedictos Amicos et Parentes ipsius, et eorum expensis."[63] Besides, the late ratification of the treaty by Wenceslaus also makes such a supposition unlikely, if not impossible. Indeed, safe conduct was not given to one of Anne's attendants, John Eutermynel de Luk, until October 28.[64] The Commissioners to receive the princess were also not appointed until December 1.[65] Moreover, Froissart tells us that Anne was detained in Brussels "more than the space of a month" for fear of Norman pirates, rather than because of the troubles in England, of which in this place he gives no hint.[66] It is true that, in another passage,[67] he

---

[62] Bilderbeck, *Selections from Chaucer's Minor Poems*, p. 72; Tatlock, *Development and Chronology of Chaucer's Works*, p. 42.

[63] Rymer, VII, 301; cf. the *Obligatio Imperatoris pro 20 Millibus Florenorum.*

[64] Rymer, VII, 335, *Pro comitiva Annae futurae Consortis Regis.*

[65] Rymer, VII, 336, *De Domina Anna, Regina Futura, ad Praesentiam Regis ducenda.*

[66] *Chronicles*, II, ch. lxxxvi; Johnes, I, 681: "The Lady Anne of Bohemia remained with her uncle and aunt at Brussels upwards of a month. She was afraid of moving, for she had been informed there were twelve large armed vessels, full of Normans, on the sea between Calais and Holland, that seized and pillaged all that fell into their hands, and it was indifferent to them who they were. The report was current

sums up all the reasons for delay as follows: "For the damsel was young, and the councils of each party had many things to arrange; add to this there shortly afterward happened in England great misery and great tribulation." The latter clause probably refers to the Peasant Revolt. Yet the delay seems fully accounted for in other ways, and in any case that Revolt seems to have been but one of several causes tending to put off the marriage.

The account of this alliance has been given at length to show, from the time consumed in the negotiations and the number of details and documents, how important it must have seemed to the people of the fourteenth century. In the first flush of its accomplishment, it must have made a particularly strong impression on the English court and the English people. No such far-reaching treaty had been made in that generation. By it the traditional ally of France had been brought over to the English side, and great results were expected in the French war. Speaking of the attempts to find Richard a suitable bride, C. Oman says:

But a more splendid alliance was finally con-

---

that they cruised in those seas waiting for the coming of this lady; and that the king of France and his council were desirous of carrying her off, in order to break the match, for they were very uneasy at this alliance of the Germans with the English . . . . On account of these suspicions and fears, the young lady remained in Brussels one whole month.

[67] See the quotation on p. 147.

cluded with the sister of the monarch who held
the highest titular dignity in Christendom,
Wenceslaus, King of Bohemia and emperor-
elect . . . . A connection with him was hailed
with joy by the whole realm.[68]

In his article on Richard II in *The Dictionary of
National Biography*, J. Tout says:

But the refusal of Wenceslaus of Bohemia,
the new king of the Romans, to follow his relative and traditional ally, the King of France, in
his support of Clement placed a much more brilliant match within Richard's reach. The opportunity of drawing central Europe into his alliance against France was not to be missed, and
Richard knew Charles V to be seeking the hand
of Wenceslaus's sister Anne for his own son
(Valois, I, 300; Usk, 31). Urban used all his
influence in Richard's favour.[69]

Besides, we have the authority of Froissart that
the alliance was seriously regarded by England's

---

[68] *Op. cit.*, IV, 66.

[69] If I may hazard an opinion, after reading all the accessible documents rather carefully, the forms of both the above
statements give a wrong idea of the initiative in the alliance.
John of Gaunt and the council of the king may have hoped
for great assistance from it, but we can now see that the
main mover in the whole procedure was the pope. Moreover,
the pope and Wenceslaus were the only ones greatly benefited
by the alliance. The former gained support for his divided
kingdom, the latter a vast sum for his personal pleasures.
Though Anne made a good queen and was passionately loved
by Richard, England was mainly a pawn in the great game
of international politics.

greät rival. We have already noted the gravity with
which the dying Charles V of France sensed the
situation.[70]   Moreover, speaking of the Norman ships
in the channel when Anne was waiting in Brussels
to go over to England, Froissart says:

> The report was current that they cruised in
> those seas, waiting for the coming of this lady;
> and that the king of France and his council
> were desirous of carrying her off, in order to
> break the match, *for they were very anxious at
> this alliance of the Germans and the English.*[71]

Everything shows that this English-German league
made a profound impression in Europe as a whole.

The importance of such a foreign alliance may
well explain why it was in Chaucer's mind when, in
writing the *Palamon and Arcite*, he came to the marriage of Palamon and Emily, an almost royal union
between representatives of two independent states.
The likeness of the situation may easily have impressed him strongly, and the direct reference to
things English have slipped into the narrative of
things fictitious, to which the poet was giving a new
reality in his verse.   Such influence of things actual
would have been especially natural during the last
part of 1381, or the first part of 1382.   As we have

---

[70] See p. 140.

[71] Chamberlayne, in the dissertation already referred to,
undertakes to discredit this whole passage in Froissart, but
it seems to me on insufficient evidence.

seen, the Duke of Tetschen and his fellow commissioners arrived the first of May, 1381, though the treaty was not ratified until September 1, and Anne did not actually come to England until after the middle of December. Then came the royal wedding, for which parliament was halted in its deliberations, to assemble again on January 27. If Professor Lowes is correct in his explanation of "the tempest at hir hoom cominge,"[72] and his suggestion in the same paper that "the feste that was at hir weddynge" may be an allusion to the feasting at Anne's marriage, the further reference of the line,

To have with certein contrees alliaunce,
would seem to confirm such a date, if not to establish it with practical certainty.

There is perhaps even more confirmation of the point in the reference of the lines preceding those relating to an alliance:

Thanne semed me ther was a parlement
At Athenes upon certain poynts and caas.

These lines are also based on nothing in the original *Teseide,* but again have an unmistakable parallel in the events of the time in England. "Thanne semed me" is certainly Chaucer's own remark of the original *Palamon and Arcite,* unchanged when the story was given to the Knight of *The Canterbury Tales.*

---

[72] *Mod. Lang. Notes,* XIX, 240 f.
11

The "parlement" may as easily have been that which sat from November 13, 1381, for exactly a month, when it was adjourned for the holidays, the coming of the new queen, the marriage, and the festivities attending them. Owing to the latter events its sessions were not resumed until January 27, much to the dislike of its members, we are told. It continued to sit until February 25, and in both sessions had before it many weighty "poynts and caas" to be settled. The Peasant Revolt had made necessary various acts, as of indemnity for those who had put rebels to death without trial; annulment of the charters of freedom to villeins which the young king had granted to pacify the rebels; a general amnesty at the suggestion of Anne;[73] a change in the king's household, and the settlement of a quarrel between John of Gaunt and the Earl of Northumberland.[74] To this busy parliament, one which must have made a deep impression at the time, Richard applied for a grant of money because of his approaching marriage with Anne.[75]

---

[73] There are two of these in Rymer (VII, 337, 345), both addressed to the Count of Kent. The first is entitled *De Generali Pardonatione, ad Requisitionem Annae futurae Consortis Regis concessa, proclamanda,* and is dated December 13, 1381; the second *De Pardonationibus, ad Requisitionem Annae Reginae concessis, Proclamandis,* dated February 14, 1382 (N.S.). The first refers with some warmth to the "detestable insurrection" (detestabile insurrectione, nuper facta).

[74] *Chronicon Angliae,* p. 328; Oman, *op. cit.,* IV, 62–3.

[75] *Rotuli Parliamentorum,* III, p. 104a. The entry is in a paragraph relating what was done on Friday, December 13, and as Parliament also adjourned on that day for the holidays, it is clear that the application could not have been later.

While the treaty of alliance had already been entered into, the request for money would certainly have brought discussion of the whole matter. Not unlikely, supporters of the measure made much of the great alliance just formed, and the expected advantage to England. Such, at any rate, would fully account for the allusion by Chaucer. Both parts of the reference, therefore, would point to the year 1381, more especially the latter part when the alliance was to be consummated by the royal marriage.

It may be argued that the last line of the allusion,
    And have fully of Thebans obeissaunce,
interferes with the suggested interpretation. To this it may be said that, except for the one word "Thebans," this line is equally applicable to the circumstances of the time. Like "Athenes" in line 2971, the word was necessary to the story, even if Chaucer intended an indirect reference to English affairs. Beyond this, the idea is equally foreign to the *Teseide*, and equally appropriate to English conditions. The quotation from Froissart on p. 128f. is full proof that England wished such an alliance as would assist her in her long-standing quarrel with France. Especially John of Gaunt, the chief figure in the royal family, may well have desired an ally against France and Spain, now joined against his claim to the Spanish throne.[76] Perhaps this was the reason

[76] Cf. J. Armitage-Smith's *John of Gaunt*, p. 260 f.

also, why the offer of Bernabò Visconti's daughter with a "vast amount of gold"[77] had been rejected. At least, an active ally was felt to be important, and in the league with Wenceslaus the rulers of England thought they had secured such powerful aid against their enemies. To mention, therefore, the "obeissaunce" expected of Germany would doubtless be in keeping with what Chaucer was hearing on every hand.

It is not necessary for our purpose to point out that this great alliance finally proved of little advantage to England. Although the emperor Wenceslaus was willing to enter into an agreement against schismatics and for the support of Urban against Clement, he never seems to have had any intention of actively opposing the political enemies of England, especially France, to which he was bound by bonds of blood and friendship. This of course, did not become known until some time after Wenceslaus had consented to give his sister to Richard II for the considerable sum of 80,000 florins. Exactly when that sum was paid I do not know,[78] but presumably it was at least before the Duke of Tetschen left England in August, 1382.[79] Meanwhile England continued her efforts to make a

---

[77] "Cum inaestimabile auri summa," *Chronicon Angliae,* 331.

[78] It was to have been within fifteen days after Anne's arrival (infra quindecim dies) ; Rymer, VII, 301.

[79] Safe conduct was given him by the council of the realm on August 12; Rymer, VII, 364.

further treaty of league and friendship with the
emperor, and a further commission was appointed.[80]
The specific purpose of this league is clearly outlined
in the instructions.   It was to be established,

> Specialiter, in specialibus, contra Karolum
> Modernum occupatorem Regni Franciae, Ludo-
> wicum Comitem Valesii ipsius Germanum, Lu-
> dowicum Andegavensem, Johannem Buturicen-
> sem, et Philippum Burgundiae, Duces, praeten-
> sos, ipsius Karoli Patruos, necnon contra Jo-
> hannem olim nominantem se Regem Castellae et
> Legionis, adhuc Occupatorem dicti Regni Cas-
> tellae et Legionis, licet per Ecclesiam depositum
> et damnatum, et Robertum gerentem se pro
> Rege Scotiae, eorumque Haeredes, Valitores et
> Fautores.[81]

The commissioners probably accompanied the
Duke of Tetschen as he returned to Bohemia, but in
any case their efforts were unavailing. Wenceslaus
was more interested in his ease and personal pleasure than in fighting Richard's battles. He was willing only that some very mild agreement should be
entered into. Such an agreement between the two
kings may have been made. At least in March, 1383,[82]
a proclamation of Richard speaks of the "friendship

---

[80] *Ibid. De Tractando cum Rege Romanorum et Boemiae super Ligis et Amicitiis,* dated August 16, 1382.

[81] *Ibid.* 365.

[82] *Ibid.* 382.

and constancy" (sinceri amoris dulcedinem et inti-
mae dilectionis constantiam) between Wenceslaus
and himself, which "are known to thrive and to have
thriven" (vigere ac etiam viguisse noscuntur) "lon-
gis retroactis temporibus ac etiam ex nova pridem
affinitate contracta." The proclamation goes on to
speak of "certain treaties, confederations or com-
pacts we have entered into" (quasdam ligas, con-
foederationes, sive pacta duximus inienda), and adds
that we shall be now and in future true, loyal, and
perfect brothers and friends (quod exnunc et in
antea, temporibus perpetuis affuturis, veri, legales,
ac perfecti fratres erimus et amici). As this was far
from an offensive and defensive alliance, we may perhaps surmise it was merely intended to strengthen
the hopes of that crusade against the schismatic
pope, Clement VII, which Urban VI had proclaimed,
and for which England sent to Flanders a disastrous
expedition under the fighting Bishop of Norwich.

Yet the failure of the alliance of England and
Bohemia, at least so far as assisting England against
her enemies, could not be foreseen in the glamor of
its first publication. Besides, Chaucer would be only
too likely to reflect the optimism of the court circle,
when he made allusion to it in his new poem. The
ultimate failure of the league, therefore, is no bar
to the interpretation of the passage under discussion.

The question may naturally arise whether, if these
allusions bear so closely upon the events of the time,
there may not be other passages which relate to similar circumstances. On the other hand, the value of
such allusions is in their wholly incidental character,
their almost unconscious inclusion in the author's
work. We should not expect many such, in any poem
not distinctly allegorical. Yet an examination of
other parts of *The Knight's Tale* with this in view
has revealed one slight allusion that, in connection
with the more significant passage above, may have
relation to the year 1381. It will be remembered that
Palamon and Arcite are said to be,

of the blood royal

Of Thebes, and of sustren two y-born (ll.1018–19).
This royal relationship is again referred to in Arcite's
speech, ll.1545–51:

> Allas, y-broght is to confusioun
> The blood royal of Cadme and Amphioun;
> Of Cadmus, which that was the firste man
> That Thebes bulte, or first the toun began,
> And of the citee first was crouned king,
> Of his linage am I, and his of-spring
> By verray ligne, as of the stok royal.

Further than this the relation of the brothers to
royalty is not explained by Chaucer, nor, so far as I
find, in the *Teseide*. Yet when praising Palamon to

Emily in 1.3084 Theseus makes the very distinctive statement,

He is a kinges brother sone, pardee.

This quite exact description of relationship is in a passage to which there is no counterpart in the *Teseide,* according to the comparison made by Mr. H. S. Ward.[83]   As we have been already told by Chaucer that the two lovers are children of two sisters (1.1019), we must now assume that they are, at the same time, sons of two brothers. This is no impossible condition, of course, but it seems strange that, if it were of importance enough to chronicle, it should not have been mentioned in the first, or an early reference to their relationship.   Moreover, though the "blood royal" has been mentioned, we are nowhere told that either is a king's son, except in the general sense of lines 1545–50. If this were a possibility in Chaucer's mind, why should he not have made the praise of Palamon greater by calling him a king's son at once?   On the contrary, we are now virtually informed that Arcite's father was a king, and Palamon's was not. This is the more surprising, also, since the passage is apparently one of praise for Palamon, though really detracting from the rank of the hero, as compared with that of his dead cousin.   All things considered, therefore, the

---

[83] See the side notes to the Six-text edition of *The Canterbury Tales* (Chaucer Society Publ.), Cambridge and Lansdowne MSS., and the reprints of the latter.

expression warrants some explanation, and a not unnatural one may be found in another indirect allu sion to the young king.

We have seen how Chaucer associated the marriage of Palamon and Emily with that of Richard and Anne, at least so far as to refer to circumstances of the latter's coming to England in lines 2967f. The situation perhaps had another parallel in his mind when he made Theseus address Emily as "suster" in line 3075, and Chaucer refers to her as such in lines 1833 and 2818. Theseus thus stands in the same relation to her as did the emperor Wenceslaus to the future wife of Richard. Even if this element in the parallelism of situation did not influence the poet, he had still used it sufficiently so that, in praising the bridegroom Palamon, he may easily have turned in thought to the royal Richard, and used language exactly applicable to him. Not a king's son himself, Richard was the son of a brother of one who, for a decade, had been accepted by the English as the rightful king of Spain. The young Richard II was actually, therefore, that which it would seem Palamon could scarcely have been, a "kinges brother sone."[84]

---

[84] Although making no mention of this passage or possible allusion to Richard II in Chaucer's *Knight's Tale*, Höfler does call special attention to just this peculiarity of the situation: "Es war eine schwerwiegende Thatsache: Richards Oheime waren Königssöhne, aber nicht er, der König." *Anna von Luxemburg*, p. 121.

This relationship, so understood of Richard, is one which we might easily miss. We give little attention to the claim of John of Gaunt to the throne of Spain, because we know how completely he failed to make it good.[85] It is needless to say that the England of Richard's time thought differently. Not only was John of Gaunt the richest and most powerful noble, but he was by all odds the greatest figure in England during the last years of Edward the Third's reign and most of Richard's. His claim to the throne of Spain was fully allowed. He was regularly called King of Castile in the royal degrees and commissions of the time.[86] There was every reason, therefore, why an English poet of the last quarter of the fourteenth century should have thought it an honor to speak of him as king. Moreover, to recognize this relation was real praise to the young Richard. He was but a boy of fourteen or fifteen. Except for his dramatic appearance before the revolting peasants in the summer of 1381, he had been no real influence in active affairs. He was still to remain in leading strings for five years more. Though a king in

[85] That is, in his own case. But by the treaty of 1388 with Juan I of Castile, John of Gaunt's daughter Katherine married the Infante Enrique, and as his wife became queen of Castile in 1390. The arrangement was a virtual acknowledgment of John of Gaunt's claim to the throne, at least in the person of his heir.

[86] See the documents in Rymer's *Fœdera* after 1371. In these he is regularly called John, King of Castile, or Castile and Leon, before he is named Duke of Lancaster.

name, he was still best known to his people as son
of the Black Prince, and nephew of his royal uncle
of Lancaster. Besides, to refer to him as "kinges
brother sone" was not only true to the facts, but at
the same time, a delicate compliment to the powerful Duke.

Here, then, is another allusion which could scarcely
refer to a time much later than Richard's marriage
in January, 1382, and would more likely be thought
of by the poet when the marriage was in every one's
mind.   It would still further strengthen the suggestion that *The Knight's Tale* was written about the
time of Anne's coming to England, or at least not
long after the marriage.[87]

To sum up the discussion in relation to the dating
of *The Knight's Tale*.   If the reference in the line,

---

[87] One might almost question whether the tale, to which
Chaucer gives the title 'Palamon and Emelye' in the next to
the last line, may not have been one of his contributions to
the court festivities at the marriage of Richard and Anne.
At least the lines

> Betwixen hem was maad anon the bond
> That highte matrimoigne or mariage,
> By al the conseil and the baronage,

based only in a general way upon the *Teseide*, would also describe English conditions.   Such a supposition as to the use
of the *Tale* might give special point to the supplication, placed
in the present tense as if more than a device for vividness,

> And God, that al this wyden world hath wroght,
> Sende him his love, that hath it dere aboght.

May there not have been, even here, some lurking suggestion
of the long series of negotiations, and the long waiting, since
the marriage with Anne had been first proposed?   Of course
this latter point should not be pressed, and would be of no
value without the more important lines already noted.

To have with certain contrees alliaunce,

can be applied to the alliance of England and Bohemia, or to that and the other alliances connected
with it, as I think has been sufficiently shown to be
in the highest degree probable, the date of the poem
must have been after May 1, 1381, and more probably after September 1, when the alliance was ratified by the king of Bohemia. If, too, the allusion,

Thanne semed me ther was a parlement

At Athenes, upon certein poynts and caas,

refers to the parliament of which Richard asked a
grant of money, on account of his approaching marriage with Anne of Bohemia, the date of this part of
The Knight's Tale must be between November 13,
1381, and February 27, 1381-2. The latter part of
this time, or more especially that after December 18,
would exactly suit the time of the allusion in the
line,

And of the tempest at hir hoom cominge,

if Professor Lowes is right in referring that line to
the storm, or tidal disturbance at Anne's arrival in
December. If, as he also thinks, the line immediately
preceding,

And of the feste that was at hir weddynge,

may refer to the feast at the marriage of Richard
and Anne, the time need not be carried forward beyond the latter part of January, or the month of February. There is, also, perhaps, some confirmation of

the date in the description of Palamon in language
that would be certainly true of Richard,

He is a kinges brother sone, pardee.

In other words, all these allusions would fall within
the current year 1381, as the year was then reckoned. They would also help to confirm the apparent
reference in another part of the poem to May of
that year, as shown to be possible by Professor Skeat
many years ago.

Perhaps, from the discussion, it will not seem
wrong to go one step further. Even if the computation of Professor Skeat is not accepted, or there
be hesitancy in agreeing with the conclusions of
Professor Lowes, the more significant allusion to the
great English-German alliance and the parliament
in which it was surely discussed is sufficient to establish the last part of 1381, or the first months of 1382,
as the certain date for the composition of Chaucer's
Knight's Tale.

A NEW CHAUCER ITEM*

Every detail in the life or work of one of our older authors is so important, so necessary in building a structure that can never be too complete, that we all wish to know as early as possible any new discovery. It is pleasant, therefore, to call attention to a new ray of light on the life of Chaucer, first seen by a worker in another field. In the scholarly and ample *Histoire de Charles V* by R. Delachenal, the first two volumes of which appeared in 1909, the author notes that Chaucer acted as confidential messenger to Edward III in connection with the peace negotiations at Calais in 1360. The record, though brief, is more than suggestive of larger things. In the Exchequer Accounts preserved in the Public Record Office, Bundle 314, no. 1, M. Delachenal found this slight entry:[1]

> Datum Galfrido Chaucer, per perceptum domini, eundo cum litteris in Angliam iii real.
> [. . .]x s.

---

* *MLN*, Vol. XXVI, pp. 19–21 (1911).

[1] *Histoire de Charles V*, II, 241, footnote. In reviewing M. Delachenal *(Eng. Hist. Review, January,* 1910, p. 160), J. F. Tout mentions the latter's note on Chaucer thus: "M. Delachenal (II, 241) quotes from an Exchequer Account evidence that Geoffrey Chaucer, already ransomed from his short captivity, was a humble participant in the negotiations of October, 1360, at Calais, being sent thence by royal precept with letters to England." From this, however, one would scarcely gather the importance of this new note.

To understand the relations of this brief entry it is necessary to bear in mind the events of this important time. In the spring of 1359 the truce of Bordeaux had expired, together with its extensions to St. John's day, June 24. During the summer the English king made extraordinary preparations for an army to crush France once for all.[2] With this army, too, Chaucer, then a young man of nineteen or twenty, entered upon his first military experience. At the last of October the grand army of Edward left England, and early in November marched from Calais, its objective the holy city of Reims where French kings had been crowned for centuries. There it was Edward's purpose to take the French crown, which he claimed as his by right of inheritance. Then he would conquer the country he already considered his own. But the campaign went badly for the great commander, as it went badly for his less exalted subject, the young esquire. Reims would not surrender herself even to the great Edward, and the young Chaucer, probably in some too-bold foraging expedition, fell into the hands of the enemy.

After the unsuccessful siege of Reims for some weeks, Edward salved his wounded vanity by marching still further into the heart of France in January, 1360. On March first of that year he also ransomed his young retainer, the poet, perhaps with money he

---

[2] Froissart's *Chronicles*, I, ch. ccvi; Johnes's trans., I, 269.

had too easily extorted from the Duke of Burgundy for immunity from invasion of his lands. When the English king finally reached Paris, things went little better than they had done at Reims. The crafty Duke of Normandy would not accept Edward's challenge to fight, and famine forced the king to march off toward Brittany. In May, however, while at Brétigny near Chartres, the English king was persuaded to accept terms of peace. These terms, roughly sketched at the little village which gives its name to the treaty, were to be worked out in detail at Calais during the following months.

Immediately after the peace preliminaries at Brétigny, Edward III and the four sons who had accompanied him[3] in the campaign returned to England.[4] Edward, and doubtless his sons, sailed from Honfleur, landing at Rye on the evening of the 18th of May. Then, too, if the usually reliable *Fœdera*[5] is to be followed, the king mounted his horse at once and reached London by nine o'clock the next morning. That the Black Prince, the Prince of Wales, was also in England soon after is evident from another fact. In July, with the Duke of Lancaster, he

[3] Froissart's *Chron.*, I, ch. ccvii; Johnes, I, 269.

[4] Thomas Gray's *Scalacronica*, p. 196.

[5] Rymer's *Fœdera*, VI, 196. It is a tall tale, since Rye is fifty-five miles from London as the crow flies. But sometimes distances, like nice customs, "curtsy to great kings"; or better still, such a journey was not impossible to strenuous Edward, not yet forty-eight years old.

escorted the captive king, John of France, to Dover, perhaps to Calais, on the return of the prisoner to his native country. The company rode by way of Canterbury, made the same halts for the night as Chaucer's Pilgrims are generally believed to have done, that is at Dartford, Rochester, and Ospringe,[6] and like them reached Canterbury on the fourth day. As Chaucer was in the household of Lionel, or of his Countess wife, we must suppose that he too returned to England in May, 1360.

In August Edward sent the Prince of Wales over to Calais, to continue the negotiations begun at Brétigny and elaborate in detail the terms of peace. He left London August 24 and remained at Calais until November 6, when he was again in London. This exact statement of time is based upon another Exchequer record found by M. Delachenal. It shows that the Prince was paid a pound a day for seventy-five days, or from August 24 to November 6 inclusive.[7] The treaty itself was signed October 24.

It was during these negotiations that Chaucer was a bearer of letters to England. So far as we know, Lionel, Earl of Ulster, to whose household Chaucer was attached, had not gone over to Calais with the

---

[6] Furnivall, *Temporary Preface to the Canterbury Tales*, p. 129; based on *Comptes de l'Argenterie*, published for the Société de l'histoire de France by L. Douet-d'Arcq.

[7] *Op. cit.*, II, 241; Exchequer Accounts, Bundle 314, no. 2.

12

Prince of Wales. This would seem to show that
Chaucer must have been detached, temporarily at
least, from Lionel's household, and have been more
directly in the king's, or at least the prince's employ.
While both Lionel and Edmund, as well as the Prince
of Wales, were with their father, the king, in the
final ratification of the treaty, there is no reason to
believe that they preceded him to Calais. Edward
himself did not go until October. On the other hand,
we do know that Chaucer had ridden the campaign
in France with the division of the Prince of Wales,
to which the other sons of Edward were attached,
and possibly at this time the future poet had attracted the attention of the Black Prince.[8] In any
case, the payment for Chaucer's services on this
occasion, by order of the king himself, throws new
light upon the poet's detachment from the service of
Lionel.

The record gives no further hint of the character
of Chaucer's services. The "letters" doubtless related
to the peace negotiations themselves, probably to difficult points upon which the Prince of Wales wished
special advice from the king. Perhaps they referred
to a most vital point then being pressed by the

[8] Froissart's *Chron.*, I, chap. ccvii; Johnes, I, 269: "Next
marched the strong battalion of the prince of Wales; he was
accompanied by his brothers." I hope soon to print a study
of this campaign of 1359–60, with special reference to Chaucer, and shall then give more fully my authority for some of
these statements.   [See below, pp. 182ff.]

French representatives, the renunciation of the title
"king of France" made by Edward III at Brétigny.
This renunciation was now wholly omitted from the
terms of the treaty of Calais. It was a clever move
on the part of the French negotiators, for by this
omission the treaty appeared to disregard such claim
on the part of Edward. Whatever we conjecture,
the service itself speaks for the recognized trust-
worthiness of the young poet. It was a first, and
possibly not an unimportant, step toward the position in the king's household of a few years later, and
even toward the diplomatic positions which another
decade brought to him.

Further than this, the new fact regarding Chaucer
gives at least some definite data for a period hitherto
a blank in his life. After his ransom by the king,
March 1, 1360, we have had no record of him until
June 20, 1367, when the king granted him a pension
of twenty marks a year as "our chosen valet."[9] It
is true that a pension of ten marks a year to Philippa
Chaucer, on September 12, 1366,[10] is usually supposed to be indirectly connected with her marriage
to the poet about that time. But direct reference to
Chaucer himself does not occur until the following
year.

We now know, however, that as early as the be-

---

[9] *Life Records of Chaucer*, p. 160.

[10] *Ibid.*, p. 158.

ginning of the period 1360–67 Chaucer had been
selected for a mission of trust by the king, or by the
highest in authority next to the king, the Prince of
Wales. There is thus more ground than has generally been supposed for believing Chaucer may have
had, even so early, some connection with the king's
service. Some years ago Professor Skeat conjectured this with assurance. He says: "He [Chaucer]
must have been attached to the royal household not
long after the return of the English army from
France."[11] Mr. Kirk, also, in *Forewords* to *Life Records* (1901) argues for the same idea, on the ground
that the annuity granted Chaucer in 1367 must have
been for service extending over some considerable
time.[12]

One further note of interpretation may be ven-
tured. Apparently the record above was made at
Calais, since it refers to bearing letters to England
[in Angliam] rather than from France. This would
also account for the reckoning of the compensation
in French reals, followed by the statement in English
shillings. At least, such a supposition would explain
the last part of the entry, even though the MS. is
illegible, as shown by the brackets. Exactly the same
reckoning in French and English money occurs in the

---

[11] *Works of Geoffrey Chaucer*, I, xx (1894).

[12] "He was in the king's service during the greater part of
that period [1360-67], as he received an annuity at the end
of it." *Life Records of Chaucer*, p. xv.

expense accounts[13] of King John's return to France, already mentioned as taking place in this same year. We there learn also the value of the real, three times mentioned as equivalent to three shillings.[14] We may thus infer that the completed Exchequer record would probably read, "iii real [s, some word for 'valued at', i]x s."

The French historian adds no comment on the record he has discovered, except to say that he does not know whether it has been found by Chaucer's biographers. Nor does he suggest the possibility of other information regarding Chaucer in the unpublished Exchequer accounts. It would seem not unlikely that something more may yet be found, in spite of the fairly thorough search which has been made. Yet even if this should not prove true, every Chaucer student will be grateful to M. Delachenal for this single gleaning regarding the poet's life.

---

[13] *Ibid.*, Appendix II, p. 129.

[14] Compare, "Le Roy, offerande a la messe, a Eltan [Eltham], 1 royaul, 3s." *Ibid.*, p. 129. "Monseigneur Philippe, pour semblable, en ce lieu, 16 royaux, 3s. piece, valent, par mons. de Jargny, 48s." *Ibid.*, p. 131. "Mons. Philippe, pour semblable, 1 royau, 3s." *Ibid.* p. 132.

CHAUCER'S FIRST MILITARY SERVICE— A STUDY OF EDWARD THIRD'S INVASION OF FRANCE IN 1359–60*

I

Chaucer's first military service, at the age of twenty or thereabouts, has special significance as his earliest entry into something like public life. The French invasion of 1359–60, in which the young poet to be then took part, was also one of unusual experiences. In this expedition, it will be remembered, he was taken prisoner, to be ransomed after some weeks by King Edward as we know from well-established record. The importance, therefore, of this first knightly adventure, or misadventure, in the life of the young Chaucer makes it worthy of a more extended notice than it has yet received. Besides, the bare facts which we have hitherto known have not been as fully illustrated as is possible from the historical materials of the time.

To understand the conditions of this episode in Chaucer's life, we must bear in mind the extraordinary successes of Edward III in the early part of the Hundred Years' War. The mastery of the sea had been gained by the great naval victory of Sluys,

---

* *Romanic Review*, Vol. III, pp. 321–61 (1912).

June 24, 1340, probably the year of Chaucer's birth, and the scarcely less celebrated overthrow of the Spanish fleet off Winchelsea, August 29, 1350. The fortunate victory of Crécy had been won in August, 1346, and the famous battle of Poitiers almost exactly a decade later, or in September, 1356. In this splendid victory of the Black Prince, King John of France had been captured, and a truce for two years was arranged March 23, 1357. Two months later the captured king of France graced a Roman triumph in the streets of London.

The boy Chaucer, probably born in the year of the victory at Sluys, must certainly have remembered something of the great fight of Crécy. Surely, as he grew older, he would have heard how the English king had barely escaped at the perilous passage of the Somme, and how the overwhelming numbers of the French king had then been beaten by the military genius of the great Edward. Perhaps, also, in these early years the boy was fired with youthful ardor as he heard of the Ordinance of Normandy, newly discovered at Caen just before the battle of Crécy, and the terrible purpose of the French "to annihilate the English nation and language."[1] At least, Edward cleverly used that famous document

---

[1] Longman, *Life and Times of Edward III*, I, 246; *Rolls of Parliament*, II, 216–17. In the latter the purpose is expressed in the words "a destruire et anientier tote la nation et la lange Engleys." Edward ordered the Ordinance read to the London people by the Archbishop of Canterbury.

to inspire hatred of its makers and incidentally en-
large his own armies. Nor is it unlikely that Chaucer
would have heard the well-known story of the siege
and fall of Calais when he was a boy of seven, and
the saving of her haltered burgesses by the chivalry
of Sir Walter Manny and the humanity of the queen.

When, just ten years later, Crécy was followed by
Poitiers, Chaucer, a youth of sixteen, was old enough
to observe personally the preparations of Henry,
Duke of Lancaster, for the new invasion of France,
and to follow the fortunes of the Black Prince as
tidings were brought to England. Nor can there be
reasonable doubt that the future poet, on a May
morning of 1357, saw the captive King John of
France, mounted on a finely caparisoned white
charger, pass London bridge and make his slow way,
through countless throngs, to Westminster palace
some time after midday.[2] What London youth of
spirit could have been absent from such a spectacle!
Besides, that Chaucer was in London at this time is
practically certain. Already in the service of Elizabeth, Countess of Ulster, wife of Edward III's son
Lionel, he was provided with clothes as a member of

---

[2] *Oeuvres de Froissart,* ed. by Kervyn de Lettenhove,
Chroniques, VI, 13. The day is uncertain, though Walsingham *(Historia Anglicana,* I, 283) says May 24, the date also
given by Villani. Froissart's account gives no date, but
emphasizes the great preparations ordered by the English
king, the gilds appearing in their regalia. Beside the French
king rode the Black Prince on a little black hackney.

the Countess's household not only in April, but as late as May 20, 1357,[3] perhaps for this very occasion of King John's unwilling entrance to the capital of his conqueror.

Two years later, when the truce of Bordeaux was about to expire, it was extended first into April and then to June 24, in vain hopes of peace being made permanent. Even in January, 1358, urged by Pope Innocent VI as mediator, preliminaries for such a peace were prepared, but were rejected at Paris. Though the States General met, the influence of Charles of Navarre, who himself wished to be king of France, prevented the acceptance of the terms proposed.[4] A year later the English king, with slight regard for the helpless position of his royal captive, opened negotiations with King John himself. On the very day that the original truce would have expired, March 24, 1359, the captive monarch and the English king signed a treaty in London.[5] It was a shameless treaty for France. Though Edward renounced his claim to the French throne, he was to have most of northern France either directly or as suzerain. In addition 4,000,000 golden crowns were

---

[3] *Life Records of Chaucer* (Chaucer Soc.), II, 152.

[4] At first, there was much hope of a peace which might have altered the history of Europe for a century. Knighton records the rejoicing of the pope: "Interim redeunt nuncii de curia papae dicentes papam et totam curiam laetam fore de concordia et suum assensum praebuisse."—*Chronicon*, II, 103.

[5] For the terms see Walsingham, *Historia Anglicana*, I, 286.

to be paid for King John's redemption, the princes of the blood being hostages for the ransom.

Such a treaty, dismembering their country as they felt, was abhorrent to the French people. A storm of indignation followed. The anger of the French showed itself in harsh treatment, even murder of English merchants in France and Flanders.[6] The States General, again assembled to consider these new conditions, preferred to endure their hard estate rather than lose so large a part of their country, even for the person of their king. Such an answer was therefore sent to England by the regent of France, Charles, Duke of Normandy, and Edward on his part then resolved on war. "He would enter France with a most powerful army," he said, "and remain there until there was an end of the war by an honorable and satisfactory peace."[7]

------

[6] Knighton, *Chronicon*, II, 105.

[7] Froissart, *Chron.*, VI, 184: "Il entreroit si puissamment ou royaumme de Franche et y demourroit tant qu'il aroit fin de guerre ou bonne pès à son plaisir et à son honneur." In this part of the *Chronicles* Froissart is largely dependent upon *Les vrayes chroniques* of Jehan le Bel. For example, this account of Edward III's purpose in the war and the gathering of the forces is based upon chap. civ of le Bel (Vol. II, p. 245, in ed. of Polain). The same chapter includes the account of the gathering of the continental auxiliaries, an account which Froissart follows almost word for word. On the other hand, for the whole campaign Froissart gives much more material than Le Bel. I have therefore followed the former, noting such differences of the latter as seemed important.

II. *Edward's Preparations for War*

Edward immediately set on foot extraordinary preparations for this new invasion of France. "He began making more splendid preparations than he had ever done before," are the words of Froissart.[8] Nor was the enthusiasm less considerable among the people. The former victories were to be repeated or perhaps eclipsed. Men flocked to the standard with unparalleled enthusiasm. Froissart's description has been often quoted:

> Chacuns s'apareilla au mieux qu'il peut, et n'y demora nuls escuiers, ne chevaliers, ne homs d'onneur qui fust haitiés, de l'aage de entre xx ans à lx ans, en Engleterre, qui ne fuist honteux de demorer ou pays, . . . siques priès tout li conte, li baron, li chevalier et li escuier dou pays d'Engleterre vinrent à Douvres[9] à grant vollenté apriès leur seigneur, si richement montés et appareilliés qu'il peurent, excepté chiaux que

---

[8] *Chron.* VI, 184: "Si fist commencier à faire le plus grant appareil que on euist oncques veu faire en celui pays pour guerrier." Cf. also VI, 202: "Vous avés bien chy-dessus oy compter quel appareil li roys englès faisoit pour venir en France, et estoit si grans et si gros que oncques devant, ne apriès, on ne vit le pareil en Engleterre."

[9] Thomas Gray's *Scalacronica* (p. 86), the continuator of Higden's *Polychronicon* (Appendix to vol. VIII, 409), and Walsingham *(Hist. Anglicana,* I, 287) say Sandwich, some ten miles away, but the inconsistency is only apparent. Higden also says the gathering of the army was as early as August 15, the feast of the Assumption.

li roys et ses conssaux avoient ordonné et estau-
bli pour garder ses castiaux et ses baliages,
ses mairies, ses offisses et ses pors de mer."[10]

Some idea of the magnitude of the preparations
may be gained from their effect upon the continental
peoples. Edward's military genius was acknowledged
in all Europe. One proof of this is the offer to him
of the imperial crown soon after the battle of Crécy.
Now the fame of his new project spread rapidly in
foreign countries, and as a result soldiers of fortune
and adventurous knights of many lands assembled
at Calais. Froissart is again our informant that

Pluiseurs baron et chevalier de l'empire
d'Alemagne, qui aultrefois l'avoient servi,
s'avencièrent grandement pour estre en celle
armée, et se pourveirent bien estofféement de
chevaus et de harnas, cescuns dou mieuls qu'il
peut selonch son estat, et s'en vinrent, dou plus
tost qu'il peurent, par les costières de Flandres,
devers Calais.[11]

Knighton adds to this that Sir Walter Manny of
Hainault had brought with him from Germany,
Hungary, and other places 1,500 well-armed men.[12]
Thomas Gray also speaks in particular of the

---

[10] *Chron.*, VI, 216–17.

[11] *Chron.*, VI, 203, the second redaction, but only slightly
more explicit than the first.

[12] *Chron.*, II, 105.

Marquis of Meissen, with a great number of Germans who had come to aid the king.[13]

It was more natural that people of nearer countries should seek to follow the English king. With these neighbors on the continent England had most intimate relations. From Hainault Edward had married his queen. The Flemings and Brabanters were bound to the English by close commercial interests. From these countries, therefore, it was especially likely that many should offer themselves for the war, and what war always meant in those days, boundless opportunity for plunder and passion.

The eagerness with which foreign adventurers sought service under Edward may be judged from their haste to join the expedition. As already noted, the truce of Bordeaux had been extended to the feast of St. John, or June 24.[14] It was not until August 12 that the king, in a letter to the archbishops of

---

[13] *Scalacronica,* p. 187: "Le markeis de Mise ove tout plein des Allemaunz qi illoeques estoint venuz en eide du dit roi." It is interesting to remember in this connection that in 1373 Friedrich, later Margrave or Marquis of Meissen, became betrothed to Anne of Bohemia, who finally married Richard II, Edward III's grandson. [Cf. above, pp. 58–89.]

[14] Here may be noted another probable incident in Chaucer's life. On Sunday, May 19 of this year 1359, the young John of Gaunt, Earl of Richmond, married Blanche, daughter of Henry, Duke of Lancaster. The marriage took place at Reading, but it seems impossible that Chaucer should not have been present in the retinue of the Countess of Ulster. There, too, the young poet must have seen the three days of jousting celebratng the event. Even if Chaucer were not at Reading to see the marriage of the two who were to be the subject of his first poem which can be accurately dated, he sure-

Canterbury and York, proclaimed the failure of peace negotiations, and asked for the prayers of the church for the success of the new war.[15] Yet so eager were the foreign adventurers to fight under Edward that by the first of August "tout chil seigneur alemant, missenaire, hasbegnon, braibenchon, haynuyer et flamencq, povres et riches"[16] reached Calais to meet the English king.

So numerous were these soldiers of fortune that they soon became troublesome in the English-French city.[17] The trouble was partly due to the delay of Edward himself, and the consequent expense which these strangers were incurring. How serious affairs became is indicated by Knighton, in telling of the coming of Sir Walter Manny and his company:

> Venerunt ad Calesiam et cum introissent villam, tractaverunt villam ad suum placitum. Acceperunt hospitia et ejecerunt Anglos et quos-

---

ly saw the London tournament in honor of the marriage. That also lasted three days and there, according to tradition, the king himself, his four sons, and nineteen of the principal nobles of England, wearing the city's cognizance, held the field against all comers. So at any rate it proved when, to the joy of all London, the supposed mayor, sheriffs and aldermen revealed themselves as the sovereign and his company. This tradition is given in Armitage-Smith's *John of Gaunt* (p. 15), based on Barnes's *History of Edward III.*

[15] "Novit Deus," he says of the failure, "delusi fuimus inaniter et vexati." Rymer's *Fœdera*, VI, 134.

[16] Froissart, *Chron.*, VI, 203.

[17] *Ibid.* VI, 204: "Se li rois d'Engleterre fust adont venus, ne arrivés à Calais, il ne se seuist où herbergier, ne ses gens, fors ou chastiel, car li corps de le ville estoit tout pris."

dam occiderunt, et ultra mensuram multa magistralia exercuerunt.[18]

The result was that about October first[19] it was necessary to send over to Calais Duke Henry of Lancaster to keep the adventurers in order.

The plan by which the Duke of Lancaster brought peace to much distressed Calais was simplicity itself. The adventurers from many lands had been attracted by no exalted motive. They had gathered for but one purpose, hope of plunder and such satisfaction of the baser passions as war in the Middle Ages made easily possible. Knowing this the Duke of Lancaster offered them such opportunity as they had hoped for on a larger scale with the English king. He told them that he intended "making an excursion into France to see what he could find,"[20] and he made it easy for them to pay the debts they had already contracted by lending each a sum of money. As a result, there marched out of Calais with the Duke "about one thousand men with armor, without counting the archers or footmen." The latter probably exceeded the men at arms several times, so that we may well believe Froissart's remaining

[18] *Chron.*, II, 105.

[19] Froissart, *Chron.*, VI, 205, gives the date as "environ le feste Saint-Remy," that is October 1. Higden *(Continuation of Polychronicon)* says "circa festum Sancti Michaelis," while Knighton *(Chronicon)* says "post festum Sancti Michaelis."

[20] Froissart, *Chron.*, VI, 205: "Il volloit chevauchier en Franche pour veoir qu'il y trouveroit."

bit of description: "They set out from Calais in a magnificent train."[21] So numerous were the adventure loving soldiers of Europe who flocked to the standard of Edward in his invasion of France.

The Duke of Lancaster led the foreign host by St. Omer, past Bethune, and came to Mont St. Eloy, a monastic foundation two leagues from Arras. There they remained four days "to refresh themselves." The character of their refreshment, doubtless typical of all their war-making, appears from the next significant sentence of Froissart: "il euissent desrobet et gastet villes et villettes sans fermeté."[22] Thus the Duke of Lancaster accomplished a two-fold purpose, to satisfy his too troublesome foreign friends and injure France as much as possible. Thus, too, he continued through the month of October, when, on November first, across the Somme from Cérisy,[23] the Duke learned that King Edward was already at Calais and wished his immediate presence.

Froissart makes no mention of any movement from England to France between that of the Duke

---

[21] *Loc. cit.:* "Puis se partirent de Callais à grant noblèce, . . . et pooient bien estre mille armures de fier, sans les archiers et les gens de piet." The sec. red. reads "II^m armeures," etc.

[22] *Ibid.* 206. Froissart's first version, more favorable to France, emphasizes the hardships (maintes grandes mésaises) of the English because of lack of forage.

[23] Now Cérisy-Gailly, on the south side of the river and about half way from Bray-sur-Somme to Corbie. There they found bread and wine in abundance.

of Lancaster and that of the main army under Edward. Thomas Gray, however, says that Roger Mortimer, Earl of March, passed the sea six days before the king, that is on October 23.[24] He also made a raid, as the Duke of Lancaster had done, taking the coast road to Boulogne and, after burning Étaples at the mouth of the Canche, returned to Calais. This expedition helped to make secure to the English the country in the neighborhood of the English-French port.

III. Edward's Army at Calais

The expedition of Edward had gathered at Dover or Sandwich between the middle of August and October.[25] Already there had been collected at that place 1,100 ships for the transportation of the army and stores. The king was attended by his four sons, Edward the Black Prince, Prince of Wales, Lionel, Earl of Ulster, John of Gaunt, Earl of Richmond, and Edmund, soon to be made Earl of Cambridge.[26] With

[24] *Scalacronica*, p. 187: "Le count de la Marche, qi passe estoit la mere vj jours devaunt le dit roi, fist un chevauche outre Bologne, ardy Lestapelis et repaira."

[25] The *Continuation* of Higden's *Polychronicon*, VIII, 409: "Hoc anno, circa festum Assumptionis beatae Mariae, Edwardus rex Angliae et ejus primogenitus princeps Walliae, dux Lancastriae, et omnes fere proceres Angliae cum exercitu equitum et sagittariorum, congregatis circa mille curribus, apud portum de Sandwich aliquandiu sunt morati."

[26] Froissart, *Chron.*, VI, 219. Other chroniclers confirm Froissart. Le Bel says the king had with him "le prince de Galles et ses deux freres" (*Chroniques*, II, 254). *Les grandes*

13

Lionel, too, must have been the young Chaucer who, for at least two years, had been attached to the household of the Countess of Ulster. He must have been present, therefore, at the great gathering of the army near Dover when Edward proclaimed his purpose in the war and passionately asserted that "he would die rather than not accomplish his object." He must have heard, too, the answering shouts of approval from the assembled host, and the cries of "God and Saint George" as the English embarked for the continent.[27] It was a wonderful experience for a young man on the threshold of the twenties to be thrown into one of the great international conflicts of the age, especially as he was surrounded by all the glamour of war for one connected with the court.

Edward reached Calais in the last week of October. According to Gray it was Monday,[28] which was

---

chroniques de France (chap. cxix) say, "le prince de Galles, son ainsne fils, et autres de ses fils," while the Chronique des quatre premiers Valois (p. 100) enumerates "le prince de Galles, duc de Lenquastre, et les enfans du dit roy d'Angleterre." There was still one son, Thomas of Woodstock, then five years of age, to be left as nominal guardian of the kingdom.

[27] Ibid. 217.

[28] Scalacronica, p. 187. The continuator of Higden says "about the feast of All Saints"; Walsingham (Hist. Angl., I, 287), October 27. The Eulogium Historiarum (III, 228) agrees with Gray. In chap. cv of the Chroniques (II, 254) Le Bel says Edward reached Calais "deux ou trois jours devant Toussains," but in chap. cviii (II, 267) he puts it "trois jours ou quatre."

the twenty-eighth of the month. According to Froissart it was "two days before the feast of All Saints,"
or October 30.[29] Perhaps the slight differences in the
chroniclers merely cover the differences in time between the arrival of the king and the rest of the
army, which would certainly not have crossed and
disembarked in a single day.

King Edward remained but a few days in Calais,[30]
"for he was desirous of marching after his cousin
the Duke of Lancaster," says Froissart. The language of the chronicler might have been much
stronger. Even eight days could hardly have been
more than sufficient for unloading the immense
stores of baggage and equipment brought from England. The occasion for these extraordinary stores
was the condition of the French kingdom:

> Si estoit le pays, de grant temps avoit, si
> apovris et si essilliés, et meismement il faisoit
> si chier temps parmi le royaulme de France et
> si grant famine y couroit, pour le cause de ce
> que on n'avoit iii ans en devant riens ahané sus
> le plat pays, que, se blés et avainnes ne leur
> venissent de Haynaut et de Cambresis, les gens
> morussent de faim en Artois, en Vermendois et
> en l'évesquiet de Laon et de Rains. Et pour ce

---

[29] *Chron.*, VI, 217.

[30] Froissart (*ibid.* 219) makes it "four or five days" in the
first version, "four" in the second; the *Scalacronica* (p. 187)
says "eight days."

que li rois d'Engleterre, ançois que il partesist
de son pays, avoit oy parler de le famine et de
le povreté de France, estoit-il ensi venus bien
pourveus, et cascuns sires ossi selonch son
estat.[31]

The detail to which these preparations extended
may be seen from another of Froissart's statements
which reveal much and suggest so much more. In
addition to all the usual equipment, there had been
taken

toutes pourvéances pour l'ost et ostieus dont
on n'avoit point veu user en devant de mener
avoecques gens d'armes, sicom moulins à le main,
fours pour cuire et aultres coses pluiseurs
nécessaires.[32]

Such articles are even more fully enumerated in a
later account:

Vous devés savoir que li seigneur d'Engleterre et li riche homme menoient sus leur chars
tentes, pavillons, forges, moullins et fours pour
forgier fiers de chevaux et autre cose, pour
mieure bled et pain quire, s'il trouvaissent les
forges, les moullins et les fours brisiés . . . et
avoient sus ces kars pluisseurs nacelles et bate-
lès fais si soutielment de quir boulit, que troy
homme se pooient bien dedens aidier et nagier

---

[31] Froissart, *Chron.*, VI, 224–5, sec. red.

[32] *Ibid.* 223, sec. red.

> parmy un escault ou un vivier, con grant qu'il
> fuist, et celi peschier et laissier hors, si lor plai-
> soit.[33]

·Nor were the lordly pleasures forgotten. In addition to this abundant preparation for war,

> li roys avoit bien pour lui xxx fauconniers
> à cheval, chargiés d'oisiaux, et bien lx couples
> de fors kiens et otant de lévriers, dont il alloit
> chacun jour ou en cache ou en rivière, enssi
> qu'il li plaisoit. Et si y avoit pluisseurs des
> seigneurs et des rices hommes qui avoient lors
> chiens et lors oisiaux ossi bien comme li roys.[34]

When Edward did move out from Calais on Mon-
· day morning, November 4, it was "with the largest
army and the best appointed train of baggage-wagons
that had ever quitted England."[35]   Even Henry
of Lancaster, returning from his preliminary raid,
and meeting the king four leagues from Calais, was
surprised at the host.   There was

---

[33] Froissart, *op. cit.*, VI, 256.

[34] *Ibid.* VI, 256–7. Edward III's extreme fondness for hunting is well known. An historic instance occurred when the
captive King John of France was being brought to London.
Edward was hunting when the royal prisoner passed by and,
with "boorish bonhomie," as Longman says (*Life and Times
of Edward III*, I, 399, based on Villani, *Cronica*, III, 295),
invited him to enjoy the same sport, he himself continuing
when King John declined. Besides, one of Chaucer's most
spirited pictures of the *Book of the Duchess* (ll.348f.) concerns the hunting of the "emperor Octovien," certainly intended for Edward III, as Professor Skeat has pointed out in
his note to the passage.

[35] *Ibid.* 220.

si grant multitude de gens d'armes que tous
li pays en estoit couvers, et si richement armés
et parés que c'estoit merveilles et grans déduis
à regarder lors armes luisans, lors bannières
ventellans, lors conrois parordenés."[36]

Perhaps at this time Chaucer first saw the sight
which suggested the description of Duke Theseus's
army in the *Knight's Tale* (ll.117–19) ;

The rede statue of Mars, with spere and targe,
So shyneth in his whyte baner large,
That alle the feeldes gliteren up and doun.

At least, though Chaucer may have seen more than
one army in the splendor of its entrance upon a
great expedition, he was never again to see such
extensive preparations as had been made at this
time. Indeed, there was to be a decided falling away
in the fortunes of Edward III after this campaign
of 1359. No great victory like Sluys or Crécy or
Poitiers was to be won by the English until, more
than half a century after, Henry V fought the
French at Agincourt.

Edward's army moved from Calais in three great
divisions. These were, in addition to the vanguard,
"five hundred knights, well armed, and a thousand

---

[36] Froissart, *ibid.* 210. As illustrating the closeness with
which Froissart follows Le Bel, I may quote the latter's words
at this point (chap. civ, II, 249) : "si grande compaignie que
toute la terre estoit couverte de gens; et estoit grand plaisir
de regarder le noblenesse, armes reluire, banieres voler, cla-
rins et trombettes sonner."

archers," under the command of Roger Mortimer, Earl of March, whom Edward appointed his constable as he left the city.[37] The three divisions of the main army were commanded by the Duke of Lancaster, after he had rejoined the army, Edward the Black Prince, and the king himself.[38]

The size of Edward's army is variously estimated by the chroniclers. Matteo Villani, the Italian, places it at 100,000 including the 21,500 under the Duke of Lancaster.[39] Froissart is much more conservative in this case and doubtless nearer the truth. He says the king's battalion, or division, was "composed of three thousand men at arms and five thousand archers."[40] The division of the Prince of Wales "was composed of twenty-five hundred men at arms most excellently mounted and richly dressed." He fails to mention the archers, though their presence is proved by the next sentence: "Both the men at arms and the archers marched in close order." Fortunately Le Bel says "four thousand archers and as many

---

[37] Froissart, *ibid.* 220; compare also VI, 253: "ses connestables . . qui toudis avoit le première bataille (li contes de la Marche)." The Earl of March, whom Gray calls "le plus secre du dit roy," died of fever at Guillon, February 24, 1360, during the march on Paris *(Scalacronica,* p. 187).

[38] Le Bel says *(Chron.,* II, 255) : "le prince de Galles et le conte de Richemont son frere, qui nouvellement estoit marie a le fille dou duc de Lencastre."

[39] *Chronica,* bk. IX, chap. liii.

[40] *Chron.,* VI, 220. So also next two quotations.

foot-soldiers,"[41] in addition to the men at arms. Nor does Froissart give the number of men commanded by the Duke of Lancaster, but it may be assumed to have been something like as many as under the Prince of Wales. If, now, there were as many foot-soldiers as archers in the king's division, the whole army would have included about thirty thousand fighting men, besides laborers and camp followers. Even this was a large army for the time, especially large considering the fighting condition of the French kingdom.[42]

Some confirmation of the great size of the army of Edward may be gained from the immense baggage-train which extended, according to Froissart, "two leagues in length."[43] This seems not unreasonable, considering the known preparations of Edward. Yet when Froissart adds that "it consisted of upwards of five thousand carriages," we may suppose that there

---

[41] *Chron.*, II, 255: "quatre mille archiers et autant de brigans faisans l'arriere garde."

[42] The difficulty in computing the size of the army is naturally the extreme meagerness of information on the part of the chroniclers, or even their inexactness. It is Walsingham who tells most definitely that the king's division was the largest: "Et fortissimam [turmam] retinuit penes ipsum" *(Hist. Angl.*, I, 287). Froissart implies the same in one or two places, as *Chron.*, VI, 220 and 257. Mackinnon *(History of Edward III,* p. 455), without giving authority but doubtless with Le Bel in mind, reckons the Prince's division as including 8,000 besides the men at arms, and the whole army as above.

[43] *Op. cit.* 220, following Le Bel *(Chron.,* II, 255) "deux legues Franchoises."

must be some exaggeration. Walsingham gives the number as "almost one thousand,"[44] a number much more in keeping with the army in other respects.

Not only was the invading army in orderly divisions, but it was also from its first advance prepared for battle at any moment. This "arrangement the foreign lords viewed with delight" when they met the English army on their return from their raid with the Duke of Lancaster. They saw that the English "marched slowly in close order, as if they were about to engage in battle."[45] Again in the next chapter, Froissart repeats the same general fact with slight additions:

> toutes ces gens d'armes et cil arcier rengiet et sieret ensi que pour tantost combatre se mestier euist esté. En chevauçant ensi il ne laissassent mies un garçon derrière euls qu'il ne l'attendesissent, et ne pooient aler bonnement non plus que iii lièwes le jour.[46]

IV. *The March Through France to Reims*

When King Edward left Calais he advanced on the same route that the Duke of Lancaster had taken

---

[44] *Hist Angl.* I, 287. Froissart says "eight thousand" in *Chron.*, VI, 256. In the latter place he adds of the "chars," "tous atellés de iiii fors cevaux qu'il avoient mis hors d'Engleterre." A little computation makes clear that the number of carts mentioned could not have been placed in the space indicated, to say nothing of room for movement.

[45] Froissart, *Chron.*, VI, 211.

[46] *Chron.*, VI, 223, slightly altered from the first version, though without essential change.

a month before.[47] Nor does this chronicler at any
time imply that the great army did not march as
one body to Reims itself. Other writers make clear,
however, that the three divisions of Froissart were
three columns taking different routes. Walsingham
perhaps suggests this when he says that the army
was divided into three divisions (turmae) on account
of forage, since this might mean an arrangement in
columns some distance apart so as not to interfere
with each other in obtaining supplies.[48] Fortunately
Thomas Gray, who himself made the march, is still
more explicit. Not only did the divisions take different routes, but he traces with considerable exactness those of the king and the Prince of Wales, adding that the route of the Duke of Lancaster was between the other two.[49]

[47] Froissart, *Chron.*, VI, 219. Le Bel and the other French
chroniclers are no more explicit with regard to the route of
Edward.

[48] *Hist. Angl.*, I, 287: "Diviso exercitu suo in tres turmas
propter victualia: unam turmam fortem Henrico Lancastriae
duci commisit; Edwardo vero principi turmam aliam for-
tiorem; et fortissimam retinuit penes ipsum." Knighton
(*Chronicon*, II, 106) gives the same testimony: "Et tunc
supervenit rex Edwardus cum omnibus aliis magnatibus, et
diviserunt se in tres turmas et acies, et abinvicem se divi-
dentes singulae acies ceperunt iter suum."
    So far as I have found, Mackinnon is the only English
writer who has mentioned these three columns of Edward's
army, and he only in a footnote to p. 456 of his *History of
Edward Third*.

[49] *Scalacronica*, p. 187–8: "Les iij hostes alerent divers
chemins . . . Le duk de Lancastre tint le chemyn entre le
roi et soun fitz." As a side light upon these divisions of
Edward's army and the separate routes, it may be noted that

All divisions of the army followed the broad valley, or plain which begins on the northern coast of France between Calais and the mouth of the Somme. This open plain about forty miles wide extends southward, following the Somme to the neighborhood of St. Quentin, when it divides into two branches. The one bends eastward, following the valley of the Sambre. The other makes a half circle by Laon, Reims, Épernay, Sézannes to the valley of the Seine. It forms a broad highway into the heart of France, and now served the English king, as it was to serve his son, John of Gaunt, in 1373.

The more exact route of Edward's division is a fairly definite one, whether we follow Gray, or Froissart who mentions no other. Passing by St. Omer the king made a halt at Béthune, and next at the monastery of Mont St. Eloy, two leagues from Arras. Chaucer was not with this division of the invaders, as we shall see later. Yet he was near enough to this monastery so that he may have learned for the first time the story of its patron saint. If so, he was to this fact indebted for the oath which he later associated with two such different personages as the

_____

when John of Gaunt, in 1373, led an army through France to Bordeaux, an early "march to the sea," the two columns took different routes until they reached the valley of the Aisne. From Calais the eastern column marched by St. Omer, St. Pol, and Arras, while the western took the course by Thérouanne, Hesdin, and Corbie. Twice afterwards, also, the army separated into two columns for different routes. See the map in Armitage-Smith's *John of Gaunt*, p. 106.

gentle prioress and the carter in the *Friar's Tale.*
At Mont St. Eloy, too, the Duke of Lancaster and the
troublesome foreign lords had halted four days "to
refresh themselves," while in all his march through
France the English king was to show special preference for the rich ecclesiastical houses.[50]

Passing by Arras, which was strongly fortified
and held by the Count de St. Pol, Edward proceeded
almost directly south to the strong town of Bapaume
in Artois. It is a temptation to tarry with the army
in this region and hear from Froissart of the pleasant adventure which here befell the German knight,
Sir Reginald de Boullant, and M. Galahaut de Ribemont; how the former, on a morning raid, met the
latter on his way to the defense of Péronne; how Sir
Reginald was cleverly deceived by the Frenchmen,
who said they were Germans and kept their visors
down to prevent detection; how, in the fight which
followed, the unsuspecting Sir Reginald lost most of
his men, though M. Galahaut—with true poetic justice—also received a "furious stroke" from which
he died soon after. I give a bare outline of what the
chronicler tells with delightful detail through most
of this chapter, before he too says, "We will now
return to the king of England."[51]

---

[50] The voluminous work of Denifle, *La désolation des églises,
monastères, et hôpitaux en France pendant la guerre de cent
ans,* shows what terrible losses were sustained by these religious houses of all kinds. For this campaign see Vol. II, 336 f.

[51] *Chron.,* VI, 225, sec. red.

From the region of Bapaume Edward made a long
detour to the east, following the eastern arm of the
plain already mentioned into Cambresis. There he
made his headquarters at Beaumetz, slightly northeast of Bapaume toward Cambray and some twenty-
five miles northwest of St. Quentin. The halt of the
English was for four days "to refresh themselves and
their horses,"[52] and the refreshment was, as usual,
at the expense of the people of the plains. They had
felt themselves secure because they were a depend-
ency of the Empire, and not a part of the French
kingdom. They had, therefore, made no attempt to
store their provisions in fortresses, and the English
king found everything in abundance. When they
saw the invader overrunning the greater part of
their country, Bishop Peter of Cambray and the
lords of the various towns sent to "inquire the cause
of the war." Yet the only answer received from
King Edward was that they had formed alliances
with the French, and had aided them with provisions. "The Cambresians," as the chronicler says in
dismissing the incident, "were therefore obliged to
put up with their losses and grievances as well as
they could."

This journey into Cambresis was far from the
direct route to Reims. The inference is unavoidable
that necessity already compelled the English king to

---

[52] Froissart, *Chron.*, VI, 231.

consider the provisioning of his army. The raid of
the Duke of Lancaster had already devastated the
valley of the Somme as far as Cérisy. Besides, the
invasion of Edward being known in advance, the
French had stored their provisions in fortified towns
and garrisoned these as strongly as possible. Still
further, as Froissart tells us,

> Avoech tout ce li temps estoit si crus et si
> plouvieus que ce leur faisoit trop de meschief et
> à leurs chevaus; car priesque toutes les nuis
> plouvoit-il à randon sans cesser, et tant pleut en
> ce wain que li vin de celle vendenge ne vallirent
> rien en celle saison.[53]

In spite of the great stores with which Edward's
army set out, there was now something like want.
It was a case of the commissariat determining the
course of the army.

From Beaumetz Edward marched still further
eastward into Thiérache, making his headquarters
at the abbey of Femy (Fesmy), not far from Le
Nouvion and near the borders of Hainault.[54] It was
another well-chosen halting place, for at Femy also
"they found great plenty of provisions for them-

---

[53] *Chron.*, VI, 225, sec. red.

[54] Froissart, *Chronicles*, as translated by Lord Berners
(Tudor Trans., II, 44), and by Johnes (Book I, chap. ccviii).
This place is not mentioned in the text of de Lettenhove, al-
though the second redaction mentions Thiérache (Tierasse),
Chron., VI, 234. That Edward passed from Cambresis into
Thiérache is also confirmed by Gray; see footnote 56 below.

selves and their horses." Yet the supplies of the
abbey did not wholly suffice for the host of the
English. As usual,

> Ses gens couroient par tout à destre et à senes-
> tre, et prendoient vivres et prisonniers là où il
> les pooient avoir.[55]

It was the fertile valley of the Oise where food and
forage were in abundance.

Leaving the abbey of Femy, Edward marched al-
most directly south toward Reims. Gray mentions
the march through the districts of "Loignes" and
Champagne, the first apparently in the region of
Vervins and Aubenton, south and a little east of
Femy.[56]

Froissart adds further that the English king
crossed

> le rivière de Somme, le rivière d'Oise et le
> rivière d'Esne sans contredit, les unes à gués et
> l'autre (l'Esne) passa-il au Pont-à-Vaire.[57]

The place at which the Aisne was crossed, now

---

[55] Froissart, *Chron.*, VI, 234, sec. red.

[56] *Scalacronica*, p. 187. The whole route of the king is given
as follows: "Le dit roy tient le chemyn de seint Thomers
[St. Omer] pres de Arraz, et delee Cambresi, par Terrages
[Thiérache], par Loignes, par Chaumpein, a devaunt de
Reyns." Loignes I do not find, but places in the vicinity of
Vervins and Aubenton have the prefix Logny, as Logny-les-
Chaumont, Logny-les-Aubenton, and are doubtless in the
region meant.

[57] *Chron.*, VI, 231. Froissart includes the Somme among the
rivers crossed, but this is impossible, unless it be some small
tributary near its very source.

Pontavert, is in the canton of Neufchatel, about twelve miles almost directly north of Reims. Meanwhile, more by accident than by design, the columns of the divided army had come together in Champagne some ten leagues from the city toward which they were all moving.[58] How this happened we shall best see from tracing the route of the Black Prince after leaving the king's forces not far from Calais.

The Black Prince, with his division, left the king's army early in the march from Calais, perhaps near the abbey of Licques. There Edward met the Duke of Lancaster who, returning from his raid, took his place as commander of a division. It is more than likely that the columns separated about this time. With the Prince's division, also, is our special interest, for with it rode the brothers of the Black Prince, and with Lionel, Duke of Ulster, would be the young Chaucer.[59] Fortunately we know the exact route of this division from the personal narrative of Thomas Gray in the *Scalacronica* already mentioned.[60] Ac-

[58] Knighton, *Chronicon*, II, 106: "Nesciebat una acies de caetero ubi altera devenit usque in diem Jovis ante festum sancti Andreae [Thursday, November 28]. Quo casualiter duae acies transeuntes occurrerunt regi ad unam villulam ad x leucas de Reynes in Campania." It is naturally impossible to identify this village, but it should be in the neighborhood of Clermont, if the distance from Reims can be relied upon.

[59] The matter is not one of conjecture. Froissart distinctly says *(Chron.,* VI, 220): "Apriès venoit li forte bataille dou prinche de Galles et de ses frères." See also the quotations from other chroniclers in footnote 26.

[60] That Gray actually made the march with the Black Prince is vouched for by the *French Roll* of Edward III under date

cording to this account the Black Prince first halted
at Montreuil some thirty miles southwest of St. Omer.
This, then, gave Chaucer his first sight of a place
which he was again to visit at least twice, some
twenty years later, on unsuccessful missions of peace
and a marriage for Richard II with a princess of
France.[61]

From Montreuil the Prince led his army in a
southeasterly course direct for Reims. His next important halt was at Hesdin, like Montreuil in the valley of the river Canche. Advancing further south
through Picardy he crossed the Somme, perhaps not
far from Amiens.[62] Then the army proceeded by
Nesle and Ham in Vermandois, and around the bend
of the river Somme toward St. Quentin. From the
neighborhood of the latter place the Black Prince

of August 20, 1359, which reads: "Thomas de Grey, miles,
qui in obsequium Regis in comitiva Edwardi, principis Wallie,
ad partes transmarinas profecturus est." This is quoted by
Delachenal, *Histoire de Charles* V, II, 152, footnote.

[61] See the discussion in Skeat, *Works of Chaucer*, I, xxviif.
The first of these occasions was in the early part of 1377,
when Richard was still the Prince; the second in 1378 after
he had assumed the crown. To these we may probably add
a third visit to the same place even earlier, since Chaucer
accompanied John of Gaunt on his expedition into France in
1369, and Gaunt's army also visited Montreuil. See Armitage-
Smith's *John of Gaunt*, p. 72, and map facing p. 106.

[62] The western column of John of Gaunt's army, ten years
later, passed through Hesdin and crossed the Somme at Corbie,
while the eastern column crossed at Bray-sur-Somme. Either
would suit the route of the Black Prince, the first less than
ten miles east of Amiens, the second about twenty miles away.
See the map mentioned in preceding footnote.

14

marched to the Oise, crossing it southeast of St. Quentin it would seem.[63] There Chaucer had his first sight of a river, the name of which was again remembered when, in writing a passage of the *House of Fame*, he wished a convenient rime for "noise." He was describing the volume of sound which issued from every opening of the temple of Fame and he adds,

> And ther-out com so greet a noise,
> That, had hit [the temple] stonden upon Oise,
> Men mighte hit han herde esely
> To Rome, I trowe sikerly.[64]

Besides, it may not be impossible that the figure which next came into Chaucer's mind was suggested by recollections of the military expedition with which he crossed this same river. In a second description of the "noise" Chaucer says:

> And the noyse which that I herde,
> For al the world right so hit ferde,
> As doth the routing of the stoon
> That from the engyn is laten goon.[65]

---

[63]Professor Skeat in his life of Chaucer *(Works,* I, xviii), following Froissart's account of Edward III's march, assumes too confidently that the army "must . . . have crossed the Oise somewhere near Chauny and La Fère." But, since Chaucer was with the Black Prince and his route was farther to the east, the crossing was more probably nearer Séry (now Séry-les-Mézières) or Ribemont, as shown by the later march of this division.

[64] *House of Fame,* l. 1927 f. (Book III, 837 f.)

[65] *Ibid.* l. 1913f.

This would be the sound of the projectile from the mouth of the small cannon of Chaucer's time, a sound which he perhaps heard for the first time when with this expedition, certainly the first time in war itself.[66]

After crossing the Oise, according to Gray, the Prince led his army by "Retieris," or Rhétel, which the enemy burned to delay the march of the English. The latter, however, gained a passage of the Aisne at Château-Porcein, a little west of Rhétel. "Retieris," or Rhétel, is somewhat east of the natural route of the Prince, but the exactness of the record seems to be fully confirmed by the mention of Château-Porcien less than ten miles away.[67]

The mention of "Retieris" by Gray is also one of the most suggestive bits of his narrative, because of its relation to the poet Chaucer. It will be remembered that in 1386 Chaucer was called as a witness in an heraldic suit between Richard, Lord Scrope, and Sir Robert Grosvenor. In his testimony the

[66] Such suggestion seems more likely if we remember how recent was the use of cannon by the English, the first time, it is said, at the battle of Crécy in 1346.

[67] Gray's account of the Prince's route is as follows: "Le prince, le fitz du dit roi, tient le chemyn de Monstrol [Montreuil], de Hedyn, par Pountive et Pikardy, outre leau de Soumme par Neel [Nesle], par Haan [Ham] en Vermandas . . . Le prince tient soun avaunt dit chemyn par Seint Quyntin et par Retieris, ou lez enemys meismes arderoint lour vile pur destourber lour passage; lez gentz de qi prince conquistrent passage au chastel Purcien, ou passa par Champain, et approcha lost soun pier a devaunt de Reyns." *Scalacronica*, pp. 187–8.

poet gave most valuable data for reckoning his age, that he was "forty years old and more," and that he had borne arms "twenty-seven years." The latter statement, sufficiently definite and impersonal to be relied upon, carries us back to 1359 and this first military expedition in which Chaucer was engaged. More important still, his testimony mentions the very place "Retters" of Gray's account. He tells us that he had seen Sir Richard and Sir Henry Scrope bearing the disputed arms "before the town of Retters, and so during the whole expedition until the said Geoffrey was taken [prisoner]."[68]

The language of Chaucer does not specify, it is true, that he was speaking of this particular appear-

[68] *Life Records of Chaucer*, p. 264f.; Sir H. Nicolas, *The Scrope and Grosvenor Controversy*, II, 405; Skeat's *Works of Chaucer*, I, xxxv. Sir H. Nicolas had assumed that Retters of Chaucer's testimony was Retters near Rennes in Brittany; see Skeat as above. This led Professor Lounsbury to point out *(Studies in Chaucer*, I, 56–57) that Retters in Brittany was some two hundred miles from the operations of Edward's army at this time, and quite impossible. In the Appendix to the same work (III, 452f) he suggested Rhétel, quoting Froissart's form of the name, as Reters, Retiers, Rethiers. To this we may now add Gray's use of the form Retieris under the more interesting circumstances of Chaucer's own visit to the place with the column of the Black Prince.

Nicolas is perhaps responsible for the oft-repeated statement that Chaucer was taken prisoner at Rhétel. In the *Scrope and Grosvenor Controversy* he makes the statement: "Lord Scrope [Henry] served as banneret in the retinue of John of Gaunt, then Earl of Richmond, and was at Retters when Geoffrey Chaucer was taken prisoner by the French" (II, 114–15). "He [Chaucer] was, he says, made prisoner by the French near the town of Retters, during that expedition which terminated with the peace of Chartres in May, 1360" (II, 409).

ance before Rhétel. As we shall see, the region was
later visited by the foraging bands of Edward's
army. Yet there are several good reasons for believing that Chaucer had this very occasion in mind
when, nearly thirty years after, he was testifying
in the Scrope and Grosvenor suit. First, it was the
poet's earliest sight of the town, the only one of
which we have definite record. As shown by Gray,
a demonstration was made against this place by the
army to which Chaucer and, as I shall show, the
above mentioned Scrope belonged. Again, the added
expression in the testimony of Chaucer, "and so during the whole expedition," would seem to imply that
the army was still on the march, that is, had not yet
reached its goal at Reims. Finally, to these reasons
we may add another important fact, amply supported by evidence and seemingly sufficient to clinch
the argument.

From the testimony in the Scrope and Grosvenor
trial we learn that both Sir Richard and Sir Henry
Scrope, whom Chaucer testified to having seen "before the town of Retters," belonged to the retinue of
the Earl of Richmond, John of Gaunt.[69] The latter,

---

[69] Depositions to this effect were given by Sir Ralph Cheney
(Nicolas, *The Scrope and Grosvenor Controversy*, I, 77: II,
260) ; by Sir Gerard Grymston (I, 105; II, 292) ; Sir John
Constable (I, 108; II, 296); Sir William Chaucy (I, 112;
II, 304) ; John Rither, Esq. (I, 144; II, 351), and a number
of others. I take as an example the deposition of Sir Gilbert
Talbot (I, 174) : "Mons. Gilbert Talbot del age de xl ans,
armeez par xxv ans, ... dist qil ad veu le dit Mons.

it has already been shown from Froissart, was with
the division of the Prince of Wales in its march
toward Reims.[70] On the other hand, when the army
of Edward settled down before the city, the Earl of
Richmond, as we know on the best authority, was
detached from the division of the Black Prince and,
with the Earl of Northampton, held St. Thierry.[71]
As there is no mention of the detachment of Earl
Lionel, presumably he and Chaucer who served him
remained with the division of the Prince. In this case
he would have been less likely to have seen Sir Richard
and Sir Henry Scrope at all, and certainly not before
Rhétel, even if the latter had been visited in some
later raid. It is practically certain, therefore, that
in his testimony of 1386 Chaucer had in mind his
first sight of Rhétel and the demonstration before it
of the division of the Prince of Wales on his march
to Reims.

Of the Black Prince's further march to Reims

Richard Lescrope estre armeez en mesme lez armez dazure
ove en bend dor en le compaignie de Mons. de Lancastre,
qestoit adount le count de Richemond, en le viage de Roy qe
mort est devant Parys, et Mons. Henri Lescrope armeez en
mesmes lez armez ove un label blanc." The "devant Parys,"
as is clear from other depositions, is used merely for the end
of the whole campaign of 1359-60. Chaucer alone mentions
"Retters." No less than three others of the Scrope family
were also in the army of Edward, as Sir William Scrope in
the retinue of the Prince of Wales, and Sir Geoffrey who followed Henry, Duke of Lancaster.

[70] See footnote 59.

[71] See the account by Rogier and the testimony of *Les
grandes chroniques de France*, quoted in footnote 85.

Gray gives no account except that "the people of the Prince gained a passage [of the Aisne] at Château-Porcien, when he passed through Champagne and approached the army of his father in front of Reims."[72] Of the Duke of Lancaster's column, also, Gray makes no further record than that it marched between the routes of the other two.[73] Yet one incident seems to be connected with this division of the army and gives a hint of one stage of Lancaster's journey. This is the capture of Baldwin d'Annequin, master of the crossbows of France and at this time governor of St. Quentin. Sir Bartholomew Burghersh, whom Gray calls a chieftain in the Duke's division, while on a foraging expedition in the direction of St. Quentin, accidentally came upon Mons. Baldwin and his company. An engagement took place and

> y eut grant hustin et pluiseurs reversés d'un lés et d'aultre. Finablement li Englès obtinrent le place, et fu pris li dis messires Bauduins et prisonniers à monsigneur Biertremieu de Bruwes à qui il l'avoit esté aultre fois de le bataille de Poitiers.[74]

It was a notable capture and both Froissart and Gray record it.

One event in the march of Edward's three armies

---

[72] See footnote 67.

[73] See quotation in footnote 49.

[74] Froissart, *Chron.*, VI, 234; Gray, *Scalacronica*, p. 187.

has still to be mentioned. According to Knighton, in the last days of November, the three columns had come together in Champagne, some ten leagues from Reims. Such a meeting, unintentional though it is said to have been, was by no means unlikely from the routes of the different divisions. The king had marched almost directly south from Thiérache. The Black Prince had moved southeast from St. Quentin, across the route of the king, and a meeting was inevitable. The Duke of Lancaster, advancing between them, was forced to the common point at which the eastern and western armies came together. Where the meeting was we can but conjecture, yet Knighton's account would seem to place it before the crossing of the Aisne. The distance of the Aisne from Reims would scarcely have allowed such a meeting ten leagues from the latter city. The coming together of the forces was followed by a great council with the Duke of Lancaster and the other leaders on St. Andrew's day (November 29) and the day following,[75] after which the three columns again separated on their journey to Reims. It was at this time, doubtless, that the Black Prince led his army against Rhétel in hope of plunder perhaps, while the

---

[75] Knighton, *Chronicon*, II, p. 106: "Quo casualiter duae acies transeuntes occurrerunt regi ad unam villulam ad x leucas de Reynes in Campania, ubi rex tenuit unum magnum concilium cum duce Lancastriae et aliis magnatibus suis in vigilia sancti Andreae et die sequenti; et exinde ceperunt iter suum versus Reynes in tribus aciebus sicut prius fecerant, ita tamen quod singuli possent scire ubi essent."

king and the Duke of Lancaster proceeded more directly toward Reims by different routes. This would explain Gray's statement of the Black Prince's "approaching the army of his father in front of Reims.[76]

As to the time of reaching Reims the chroniclers differ. The English writers name the thirteenth or eighteenth of December.[77] On the other hand, Froissart says the twenty-ninth of November, St. Andrew's day.[78] The *Mémoires* of Rogier, who risked his life to carry messages to the Duke of Normandy, Regent of France, names Wednesday the fourth of December.[79] Perhaps all these differences may be reconciled by the confusion of the first approach of the vanguard with the complete investment of the city which doubtless took some days. Or perhaps Froissart, who gives the earlier date, has confused the early accidental meeting of the three armies with that about Reims itself.

---

[76] Footnote 67.

[77] Walsingham *(Hist. Angl.,* I, 287) gives the first, "in feste sanctae Luciae." Knighton *(Chronicon,* II, 107) says "xviii die Decembris."

[78] As usual Froissart is following Le Bel, who says of the English king: "[il] demoura en celluy pays de la feste Saint-Andryeu jusques a sinq septmaines aprez Noel." *Chron.,* chap. cv, II, 255.

[79] "Le roy d'Angleterre arryva avec son armée devant le ville de Reims au commencement du mois de décembre, le mercredy iiiie dudict mois de décembre, mil trois cens cincquante neuf." Varin, *Arch. admin. de la ville de Reims,* III, 156, n. i. *(Mémoires de Rogier,* fol. 109), quoted by Delachenal, *op. cit.* II, 154.

At any rate, not far from the first of December
the English king reached the goal he had set for
himself on leaving England.   It was Edward's purpose to capture the city where French kings had
been crowned for centuries, and there assume the
crown of France which he claimed as his by right
of inheritance.   Then, as he seems to have thought,
all would be easy in the further conquest of his continental possessions.   But even at this time the prospects were none too bright.   The unusually rainy
season had been against him.   His extensive provisions for supplying the army had been long since exhausted.   The poverty stricken condition of the country made foraging difficult.   The policy of withdraw-
ing into the fortified towns and refusing to fight
made impossible any offensive operations except a
regular siege.   Above all, the rains continued, followed by approaching winter, and the lot of the
greatest military commander of the age was per-
plexing, if not dangerous.[80]

---

[80] It is Froissart who emphasizes the difficulties of Edward's
position.   Speaking of the king and his chiefs about Reims,
Froissart says (Chron., VI, 235): "Si n'avoient pas leurs
aises, ne le temps à leur volonté; car il estoient là venu ou
coer de l'ivier, environ le Saint-Andrieu, que il faisoit froit,
lait et pluvieus, et estoient leur cheval mal logiet et mal livret,
car li pays, ii ans ou iii en devant, avoit estet toutdis si
guerryés que nuls n'avoit labouret les terres; pour quoi on
n'avoit nuls fourages, blés, ne avainnes en garbes, ne en
estrains, et convenoit les pluiseurs aler fourer x ou xii liewes
loing."

Gray's brief account makes no mention of such difficulties.
Knighton (Chronicon, II, 107) presents the matter far more

V. *Edward Before Reims*

When Edward reached Reims, he disposed his
army in the villages round about, covering especially
the main avenues of communication. His purpose
was to block all entrance of provisions to the inhabitants, and trust to hunger to bring the city to sub-
mission. The king himself, as both English and
French chronicles attest, took up his quarters at
St. Basle beyond Reims.[81] St. Basle was a monastic
house on the highest point of land in the neighborhood, the "montagne de Reims" just back of the little
village of Verzy, some ten miles away on the road to
Chalons. The monastery had been founded in the fifth
century, says tradition, by Basolus who, coming to
pray at the tomb of St. Remy, had here placed his
hermitage.[82] From this position Edward was now
able to overlook the whole field of operations, while
he could there also best protect his army from attack
by the Regent of France, the Duke of Normandy.
The Prince of Wales, says Rogier, was stationed at

favorably: "Et notandum quod in toto illo viagio non periit
quisquam nostrorum nec damnum sustinuit praeter quod dominus Thomas de Morreus percussus est medio de una gunna."

[81] Froissart, *Chron.*, VI, 234–5; Rogier, quoted by Varin,
Archives administratives de la ville de Reims, III, 156–8, in
Collection de documents inédits: "Le roy d'Angleterre . . .
loga sa personne en l'abbaye de St. Basle."

[82] A life of St. Ba⸱¹ is in Migne *(Patrologia,* Vol. CXXXVII,
p. 643), *Vita S⸱ ⸱ Basoli Confessoris, Auctore Adsone,* together with ar ⸱ccount of his translation, by the same author.

Ville-Domange about five miles southwest of Reims.[83]
It is about half-way between the road to Dormans
on the west, and that leading almost directly south
from Reims to Épernay. These two roads were thus
guarded by the prince's division, while this arrangement also placed the king and three of his sons near
each other.

Froissart gives no further account of the disposition of Edward's army. He merely says that, after
the king and the Prince of Wales, the Duke of
Lancaster "tenoit en apriès le plus grant logeis," and
"li Conte, li baron et li aultre chevalier logiet ens ès
villages entour Rains."[84] Rogier is more explicit and
is confirmed by *Les grandes chroniques de France*.
The Duke of Lancaster was at Brimont, on the road
directly north from Reims and about eight miles
away. Between him and the king, at Béthany and
Cernay-les-Reims on either side of the road to
Rhétel, were Roger Mortimer, Earl of March and
Edward's constable, with Sir John Beauchamps. Both
villages are about five miles northeast and east of

-----

[83] Following Le Bel, Froissart says St. Thierry where, according to Rogier, was the Earl of Richmond, John of Gaunt,
with the Earl of Northampton. On the other hand, when
Froissart mentions that the Prince and his brothers were
together, we have confirmation of his previous statement that
they belonged to the same division. Presumably, then, Lionel,
Earl of Ulster, remained with the Prince, and with Lionel
would be Chaucer also. Froissart's words are: "Li rois fist
son logeis à Saint-Bale oultre Reims, et li princes de Galles
et si frère à Saint-Thiéri." *Chron.*, VI, 234–5.

[84] *Chron.*, VI, 235.

the besieged city.[85]   To the west of the Duke of
Lancaster's quarters, at St. Thierry, were the Earls
of Richmond and Northampton, guarding the road to
Laon.   Near by, slightly northwest of St. Thierry,
was Villers-Franqueux also held by the English.   On
the Vesle, directly west of Villers-Franqueux and
about twelve or fifteen miles northwest of Reims
itself, was Courlandon in the direction of Soissons.
This position prevented access to the besieged city
from that side and completed the environment.   So
closely were the lines drawn that Rogier says no one
could enter the city either on horse or foot.[86]

Except for encircling the city in this way Edward
made no attempt at a regular siege.   This was partly
because of the fortifications, which had been ren-

---

[85] Rogier says: "Le roy d'Angleterre . . . loga pour sa personne en l'abbaye de St. Basle; le prince de Galles, son filz,
estoit loge a Villedamange; le conte de Richemont, et celuy de
Norentonne a Sainct Thiery; le duc de Lenclastre a Brimont;
le mareschal d'Angleterre et messire Jehan de Beauchamps a
Bethany." Varin, III, p. 156–8, a quotation for which I am
indebted to Professor G. L. Burr, of Cornell University.
Les grandes chroniques (chap. cxix) states the matter
thus: "Et fu le roy d'Angleterre logie a Saint-Baale, a quatre
lieues de Rains ou environ. Le prince de Galles, son ainsne
fils, estoit logie a Ville-Dommange, a deux lieues de Rains;
le conte de Richemont et celuy de Norentonne a St. Thierri,
a deux lieues de Rains; le duc de Lenclastre a Brimont, assez
pres de Rains; le mareschal d'Angleterre et monseigneur
Jehan de Biauchamps estoient a Bretigny [Bethany], a lieue
de Rains."

[86] "Et chevauchoient les gens susdictes tous les jours environ
la dicte ville en telle maniere que aucun n'y pouvoit entrer
n'y a pied ne a cheval." Varin, III, p. 156. Yet Rogier, or
Rogier de Bourich, succeeded in carrying a message to the
regent of France at Paris, and returning to Reims with an
answer dated December 26.

dered doubly strong in the months since war had
been in prospect. Efforts to fortify the city had
begun as early as 1357 and had continued through
the two following years.[87] In December, 1358, the
neighboring castles had been put in a state of defense, or destroyed if they were likely to be dangerous to the city in case of seizure by an attacking
force. In February, 1359, the Benedictine abbey of
St. Thierry had been leveled lest it should afford protection to the enemy, and the same was true of a
number of other religious houses in the vicinity. On
July 10 the regent of France had notified the governor, Gauchier de Chatillon, of the approaching invasion, and again on October 22 of the raid of the Duke
of Lancaster. Even at this time, however, the city
was prepared for a long siege.

For these reasons, when Edward settled down before the sacred city, he found a very different state
of affairs from what he had expected. The earlier
successes of himself and the Black Prince had made
them overconfident. Both expected to meet the enemy
in the field and crush them as they had done at
Crécy and Poitiers. Miscalculating, too, the preparations of the inhabitants of Reims, Edward hoped
for a speedy surrender of the city without the losses
an assault would entail. Perhaps the quiet with

---

[87] Denifle, *La désolation des églises*, etc., 341f.; Delachenal,
op. cit. II, 154f.

which the English were received was in itself decep-
tive. Knighton tells us that they took their places
about the city in peace, no one offering resistance,
and each lord feasting the others, as if all had been
in their native land.[88]

As there was no regular siege, there was no attempt to prepare siege engines, to batter the walls,
or to assault the city, unless possibly for a day or
two at the very last. But there was still much for
the besiegers to do. The army must be supplied with
food, and forage was not easy to be had in the country round. The rains still continued incessant. The
result was a necessary scouring of the country for
miles, even leagues about. These foraging parties
often met with the enemy, sometimes being victo-
rious, sometimes meeting defeat.[89] Such expeditions
concern us especially from the probable relation
of one of them to Chaucer himself. Fortunately
Froissart, Gray, and Knighton are more explicit regarding some of the minor engagements than some
of the larger operations. Perhaps these were more
often recounted by returning soldiers when the hardships of the campaign were forgotten or suppressed.

---

[88] *Chron.*, II, 107: "xviij° die Decembris venit rex cum omnibus suis ad villam de Reynes et recipiebant se hospitio ex
omni parte villae, et quieverunt pacifice nulli malum aut mo-
lestiam inferentes. Et fecerunt convivia unusquisque dominus
cum alio acsi in proprio solo fuissent in Anglia."

[89] Froissart, *Chron.*, VI, 235: "Si estoient souvent rencontré
des garnisons françoises, par quoi il y avoit hustins et mes-
lées; une heure perdoient li Englés, et l'aultre gaegnoient."

It is natural that these minor engagements should not be given in chronological order, and Froissart makes no attempt to do so. Gray is more definite as to the time of one or two, and Knighton gives dates for others. For example. Gray tells us that the successful attack upon "Attigny in Champagne" was "at the time of the coming of the king before Reims."[90] Froissart gives the name of the captor as Eustace D'Auberchicourt. This daring leader and knightly lover of Isabelle de Juliers, Countess of Kent, had been taken prisoner in an engagement on June 24, 1359, after the expiration of the truce. His friends had ransomed him, however, for 22,000 livres,[91] and he again carried on an extremely profitable warfare by exacting ransom for the "towns, castles, vineyards and private houses" he captured. Attigny, which he now seized, is on the Aisne about ten miles east of Rhétel. In this place Sir Eustace

> avoit trouvet dedans grant fuisson de pourvéanches, et espécialement plus de vii cens piéches de vin, dont il en départi les ii quars et plus au roy et à tous les seigneurs, chacuns seloncq se qualité.[92]

---

[90] *Scalacronica*, p. 188: "Autres rou:es estoient dez Englois, ascuns dez queux eschalleroint la vile de Attinye en Chaumpayn en le jour du venu du dit roi devaunt Reyns."

[91] Froissart, *Chron.*, VI, 153, 163f, 189f.

[92] Froissart, *Chron.*, VI, 232. In the second redaction this plunder is magnified to "iiim tonniaus de vins," and it is sent "au roy d' Angleterre . . . et à ses enfans, dont il li sceurent grant gret."

Sir Eustace hoped to be made Count of Champagne by Edward,[93] and he remained an unusually helpful ally in levying contributions upon the country during the siege of Reims.

Froissart also tells us that companies from the army overran the whole "county" of Rhétel, special mention being made of Warcq, Mézières, Donchery, and Mouzon. These places are in the valley of the Meuse, from forty-five to fifty miles from Reims in a straight line, and considerably farther by ordinary routes of travel. They show the distance traversed for forage and adventure by Edward's roving bands.[94]

Another raid was made to the east and southeast of Reims by the Duke of Lancaster, the Earls of Richmond and March, and Sir John Chandos.[95] It was the

---

[93] Froissart, *Chron.*, VI, 169.

[94] The passage in Le Bel *(Chron.*, II, 256) reads: "En le conte de Rethes, jusques a Warck, a Mesieres, a Donchery, a Moison." This is the only mention of Rhétel in any of the chronicles, except the "Retieris" of Gray's *Scalacronica*. This reference, too, is not to the village but the district of Rhétel which went by the same name. All the towns mentioned are at least twenty miles from Rhétel the village.

[95] Gray says *(Scalacronica*, p. 188) : "Hors de lost le roy, le duk de Lancastre, lez countis de Richemound et de la Marche." Knighton *(Chron.*, II, 107) adds "dominus Johannes Chandos." Froissart *(Chron.*, VI, 236 mentions "messires Jehans Camdos [Chandos], messires James d' Audelée, li sires de Muchident et messires Richars de Pont-Cardon et leurs routtes." As we have seen, the Earl of Richmond was now no longer with the Black Prince, but at St. Thierry with the Earl of Northampton (See p. 40). Nor is mention made of any immediate retainer of the Black Prince in this raid.

15

night of the feast of St. Thomas of Canterbury
(December 29), as Knighton tells us, that they proceeded by forced marches toward Cernay-les-Dormoy.
This Cernay is a small town something more than
thirty miles directly east of Reims on the Dormois, a
tributary of the Aisne.[96] It was strongly fortified with
a double foss and a great wall full to towers.   Its
defenders were "ii bons chevaliers," one being "Guy
de Caples."[97]   Both Froissart and Knighton give a
detailed account of the attack, which the former says
was "fortement et radement."   According to the latter
the English were seen as they approached in the
early morning, a surprise failing, but they continued
to advance.   When they neared the walls the Duke
and the others dismounted to examine the moat.   On
being received with taunts and insults, they immediately crossed the fosses and with great labor
ascended the walls.   Finally, gaining these, they entered the town and put to death those of the inhabitants who did not escape, the latter dying in the
water and marsh of the moat.   The castle at once
surrendered to the Duke of Lancaster, and the town
was given to the flames.

After burning Cernay on the last day of the year

[96] Following the part of the sentence quoted in the last note,
the *Scalacronica* adds that they "gaignerent dieus viles,
marches enforcez, Otry [Autry] et Sernay [Cernay], sure
leau de Ayne et la marche de Lorrein."

[97] Knighton, *Chronicon*, II, 107; Froissart, *Chron.*, VI, 236.

1359, on the first day of the new year the Duke and
his company took their way to Autry, another town
of Dormois on the Aisne three leagues northeast of
Cernay and more strongly fortified. From this town,
however, the villagers had already fled in fear, and
the English, turning back toward Reims, came to
Manre some fifteen miles west of Autry. This place
had also been forsaken by its inhabitants, but was
burned by the raiders. Then they returned to
Edward's army and, as they had come back safe and
sound, Knighton devoutly adds "let God be praised."
Perhaps the pious wish was colored by Knighton's
evident partiality for the Lancastrian house.

If the English were successful in these raids, so
fully given by Froissart, Knighton, and Gray, it was
not always to be so. The first of these chroniclers
gives at even greater length the failure of the "lord of
Gommegnie" and his followers to the number of about
three hundred, in their attempt to join Edward's
army at Reims. This lord of Hainault had returned
to Queen Philippa in England when Edward had
reached Calais and banished all strangers from the
city. Yet, desirous to advance himself, he recrossed
to Calais with some Gascon and English squires,
enlisted further followers in Hainault, and set out
from Maubeuge for the besieging army. They passed
into Thiérache, through Avesnes and Trélon to the
village of Harcigny. There they stopped to refresh

themselves. But de Gommegnie and six of his followers, not satisfied with what Harcigny afforded
them for breakfast, rode out of the village and into
an ambuscade which had been arranged with great
secrecy by the lord of Roye and his men. They had
been following de Gommegnie's company the preceding day and night, awaiting a favorable chance,
which was now afforded them by the enemy himself.
The fight was a short one, though told with all the
realism and detail of Froissart at his best. Fighting
valiantly at great disadvantage de Gommegnie and
three of his squires were forced to yield. The others
of the party were slain, all except the valets who, not
waiting to see whether their masters were heroes,
put spurs to their horses and saved themselves by
flight.

Then the lord of Roye and his men galloped into
the town of Harcigny, demanding the surrender of
the remaining followers of de Gommegnie. Surprised
and unarmed as they were, they were easily taken,
except a small band which retreated to a fortified
house surrounded by a moat, and thought to hold
out until the English king could send succor. But
the lord of Roye was not to be withstood. Threat-
ening death if an assault were made necessary, he
succeeded in inducing surrender, and the prisoners
were marched off to the castle of Coucy and other
places. It was about Christmas, 1359, and when

informed of it, the king of England "was mightily enraged."[98]

Meanwhile, the English gained a great success to the northeast of Reims. On Wednesday the twentieth of December, Sir Bartholomew Burghersh, with many from the followers of the Prince of Wales and the Earl of Richmond, had made an attack on the village of Cormicy near which Sir Bartholomew had been stationed. The village is situated some ten miles from Reims on the road to Laon, and contained at this time a "very handsome castle belonging to the Archbishop of Reims," defended by Sir Henry de Vaulx.[99] Notwithstanding that the village was surrounded by a double foss and a good wall, it was taken by the English in a night attack. The castle still held out, however, and as this was impregnable to assault, Sir Bartholomew set his men to undermining the tower, promising a handsome reward for quick results. Thus stimulated, the miners worked night and day until on Monday, the sixth of January, the tower was no longer supported by solid foundations, but by props of wood ready to be burned.

At this point Knighton fails us in all but a single point. The lord of Clermont, he tells us, now surrendered with the soldiers and burgesses, and by the eighth of January the tower had fallen and the city

---

[98] Froissart, *Chron.*, VI, 239–42.

[99] Knighton, *Chronicon*, II, 108; Froissart, *Chron.*, VI, 247f.

had been burnt to the ground. Fortunately this bald account is extended in Froissart by a narration of one of those chivalrous episodes which, sometimes at least, relieved the brutality of medieval war. When the mines were ready to be fired, Sir Bartholomew asked for a parley and demanded immediate surrender of the enemy. As Sir Henry laughed at the demand, the good Sir Bartholomew, with true knightly courtesy, offered to explain the reason for his assurance of success. On Sir Henry's accepting safe conduct, he was shown the mine and the tower supported only by wooden props. This satisfied the French knight, who thanked Sir Bartholomew for his courtesy and surrendered at discretion. When the fires were lighted and the great tower came down with a crash, Sir Henry again thanked his English conqueror:

> car li Jaque-Bonhomme, qui jà resgnèrent en ce
> pays, s'il euissent enssi esté de nous au deseure
> que vous estiés orains, il ne nous euissent mies
> fait la cause pareille.[100]

How long Edward remained before Reims we do not certainly know, since the chroniclers differ

---

[100] Froissart, *Chron.*, VI, 250. Gray *(Scalacronica*, p. 188) makes brief mention of the episode: "Hors de lost du dit prince fust la vile de Curmousse [Cormicy] eschale et le chastel gaigne, la toure rue a terre par myne par lez gentz du prince."

Under Bartholomew Burghersh the *Dict. of Nat. Biog.* refers to the "castle of Sourmussy in Gascony," the writer never having looked beyond the form in some corrupt text.

among themselves. The *Chronique des quatre premiers Valois* says "during the winter,"[101] Froissart
gives the period as "bien le tierme de vii sepmaines,[102]
and Knighton agrees in this particular.[103] The
Grandes chroniques de France calls it "forty days."[104]
At any rate, the best testimony indicates that on
January 11, 1360, Edward acknowledged the failure
of his ambition to be crowned in the sacred city, and
stole away in something of defeat and chagrin. It
was Saturday night of St. Hilary's day.[105]

---

[101] "Et par toute la saison de l'hyver maintint le roy d'Angleterre le siege devant la cite de Rains." Quoted by Delachenal,
op. cit. II, 159.

[102] Froissart, *Chron.*, VI, 253.

[103] Knighton, *Chronicon*, II, 110.

[104] *Grandes Chron.*, VI, 167: "Le dymanche xi jour de jan-
vier, environ mienuit, le roy d'Angleterre et tout son host,
apres ce que il et demoure en son siege devant Reims par xl
jours, se desloga," etc.; quoted by Delachenal, *Hist. de
Charles V*, II, 161.

[105] Walsingham (*Hist. Angl.*, I, 287) refers to Edward's stay
at Reims "ubi moram traxerunt usque in diem Sancti Hilarii."
Most chroniclers do not mention an assault on the city. Froissart distinctly denies such procedure. He says (*Chron.*, VI, 32):
"Ossi, le siége durant, oncques li Englès n'aprochièrent pour
assaillir, car li roys l'avoit enssi deffendu et ordonné parce
qu'il ne volloit mies ses gens travillier, navrer, ne blechier."
And again (*Chron.*, VI, 253): "Ensi se tint li roys englès
devant Reims bien le tierme de vii sepmainnes, mès oncques
n'y fist assaillir, ne point, ne petit, car il euist perdu se
painne." Le Bel has this general statement (*Chron.*, chap.
cvi, p. 257f.) : "Ne oncques ne volut consentir que nul s'apro-
chast de ville ne de fortresse pour assaillir, car il ne veoit pas
voulentiers ses gens perdre ne mettre leur corps en si evi-
dente aventure."
On the other hand the *Chronique des quatre premiers Valois*
(p. 105f.) mentions an assault lasting for a day. It tells
how engines were prepared for battering the walls; how two

VI. *The Campaign to the Peace of Brétigny*

From Reims Edward led his army south to Chalons, Bar-sur-Aube, Troyes, Saint Florentin, Tonnerre, Montreal, and Guillon, the last of which he reached on February 18, a little more than a month after leaving Reims. It was Ash-Wednesday, and at Guillon the army remained until mid-lent, as Froissart says, or about March 15.[106] There, also, Edward made his treaty with the Duke of Burgundy, by which the latter bought immunity from English invasion for three years on payment of 200,000 florins.[107] There, too, on March 1, 1360, the keeper of the wardrobe of the king's household paid for the ransom of Geoffrey

attacks were made, one on the side of the Paris gate, and one on the opposite side; how the assault was in three divisions while a fourth was held in reserve; how the "battles" were led by the Prince of Wales, the Duke of Lancaster, and the Earl of Richmond with Sir Thomas Holland and "mons. d'Ansellee" [Annesley?]; how the assault began in the morning and how, when the Prince's men had filled the moats with wood, it was burned by the defenders; how the king encouraged the English attack, and how it continued to the close of the day. So much detail would seem to indicate something of fact, yet Delachenal (*op. cit.* II, 159) seems to discredit the account. In any case it is unnecessary for our purpose.

[106] *Chron.*, VI, 254. Six days later, "die sancti Mathei," as Knighton marks it, the French showed the one evidence of martial spirit in this campaign. They had gathered a fleet in Normandy and now attacked Winchelsea, committing various depredations, though finally repulsed. The attack was well conceived in order to bring about the return of Edward to England. The movement was unsuccessful, however, the English rising with enthusiasm to protect their country. See Knighton, *Chron.*, II, 109f.; Walsingham, *Hist. Angl.*, I, 288f.

[107] Gray, *Scalacronica*, p. 189; Knighton, *Chron.*, II, 110; Froissart, *Chron.*, VI, 258. In a note De Lettenhove gives the date as March 10.

Chaucer the sum of sixteen pounds, equal to about
$1,200 today.[108] When or where Chaucer had been
taken prisoner we do not know, but some light may
be thrown on the subject by the circumstances of the
campaign.

We have noted that in 1386 Chaucer testified to
having seen Sir Richard and Sir Henry Scrope before the town of Rhétel, and we have shown that the
army of the Prince of Wales, with which Chaucer
marched, threatened that town not long before
reaching Reims. The remainder of Chaucer's testimony, that he saw the Scropes so armed "during
all the expedition until he was taken prisoner,"[109]
would certainly imply that his capture was some time
after the appearance before Rhétel. As there is no
evidence of any engagement before the English army
reached Reims, the capture must have been after
December 4. It is equally unlikely that the event
took place after the army left Reims on January 11.
The chroniclers make no mention of conflicts with
the enemy on the march to Guillon, nor of special
difficulties as to forage. The army was passing

---

[108] *Life Records of Chaucer*, II, 154. We must not forget the
pleasantry of Dr. Furnivall, that the ransom of the poet did
not quite reach the amount paid for Sir Robert de Clynton's
war-horse. Ward (*Life of Chaucer*, English Men of Letters
Series, p. 51) assumes that Chaucer's imprisonment lasted
until the peace, but there is not the slightest reason for this
conjecture.

[109] *Life Records*, p. 265: "Par tout le dit viage tanqe le dit
Geffrey estoit pris." See the discussion on p. 211f.

through a fairly rich country which had not before been overrun. The most natural, almost inevitable conclusion is that Chaucer was made a captive between December 4, 1359, and January 11, 1360.

The occasion for such a misadventure was also more likely to have occurred while the English were before Reims. The army was then inactive except for the necessities of forage. But such necessities were great, and these, together with the spirit of adventure naturally fostered by the monotony of the siege, would have led to hazardous and sometimes unsuccessful expeditions. Indeed, it is during this time only that Froissart hints at losses to the English,[110] while from several chroniclers we know that in at least one of these expeditions for forage some belonging to the prince of Wales's division took part.[111] It is more than a matter of conjecture, therefore, that in some foraging raid while the army was besieging Reims, by accident or by reason of some unsuccessful deed of daring, the young Chaucer fell into the hands of the enemy.[112]

[110] See p. 223 and footnote 89.

[111] See pp. 224ff., especially p. 229.

[112] It is impossible not to associate with Chaucer in this whole campaign, and perhaps in this particular adventure, the description of the squire in the *Prologue* to the *Canterbury Tales*. He, also, at the same age, made a "chivachye"
"In Flaundres, in Artois, and Picardye."
See note to line 86 in Mather's edition of *The Prologue*, etc., p. 5. Nor is it impossible that, like the squire, Chaucer was

Where Chaucer was kept a prisoner for the two months or two months and a half of his captivity, we have no means of knowing. Yet the courtesy accorded prisoners of rank or station, as shown by many a record of Froissart, would indicate that his captivity need not have been a hard one. Even the kings of France and Scotland while in Edward's power were given large liberty under parole. Moreover, King John's return to his English captivity in 1363 is the best evidence that such parole was not usually forgotten by a gentleman.[113] Chaucer, therefore, may easily have passed a not unpleasant sojourn with some wealthy French nobleman, and have been treated with courtesy and kindness because of his relation to the English royal house. Left largely to himself within the bounds of his parole, we can scarcely think of the future poet as not interesting himself in books. Did he here, in the country of Machaut and Deschamps, each of whom was born

---

already a "lovyere," and had already looked with ardent eyes upon that Philippa "pantaria" who is joined with him in the earliest record of his life. Cf. *Life Records*, p. 152, Household accounts of the Countess of Ulster, April to December, 1357.

[113] Such parole was broken, it will be remembered, by the Duke of Anjou, son of King John and hostage for the payment of the latter's ransom. Fearing that the ransom might never be paid, he obtained permission to travel four days' distance from Calais, and then took what may be appropriately called "French" leave. Yet the estimation in which this dishonorable action was held is clear from the return of the French king himself to English captivity, a captivity from which he was released only by death.

not more than thirty miles from Reims,[114] first learn
to appreciate the poetry of the former, and thus early gain some inspiration for his own? Even the conjecture has a certain fascination.

When Chaucer was ransomed, March 1, 1360, he
must have joined the army of Edward and have followed it in the campaign against Paris. The English
had marched into the heart of France, with no

---

[114] The village of Machaut is slightly northeast of the city;
Vertus, where Deschamps was born, directly south, a little
southeast of Chalons. Far more interesting is it that both
Machaut and Deschamps were in Reims during the siege.
The first had long been a resident canon there; cf. the *Introduction* to his *Works* by E. Hoepffner, *Société des anciens
textes français*, I, p. xxiii. According to the latter editor,
too, Machaut was writing in this very year his *Complainte à
Henri*, in which he mentions the troubles which had come
upon him, and especially, as confirming the time, "dit on que
li rois d'Angleterre vient li seurplus de ma substance querre."
That Deschamps was present in Reims at the time of the
siege, depends upon a passage in the *Miroir de Mariage*. Into
that poem he incorporated an account of the whole campaign,
said to be based upon the *Grandes chroniques de France;*
cf. lines 11,660f., and especially for Deschamps's presence in
the city, ll. 11,850f. See also the *Vie de Deschamps* by Gaston Raynaud in Deschamps, *Oeuvres complètes*, XI, 12.
Thus, while Chaucer was to be a captive of the French, two
French poets who most influenced him in later years were suf-
fering hardship at the hands of Chaucer's king. Why may
we not go one step further? Romance, if not history, would
certainly bring the three more closely together under these
unusual circumstances. At any rate, in his captivity Chaucer
may well have met and read, among other works of that poet,
Machaut's *Dit du Lion*, written in 1342, and perhaps the basis
for Chaucer's lost *Book of the Lion*, as Tyrwhitt long ago
suggested. More recently *(Mod. Phil.*, VII, 465) Professor
Kittredge has shown Chaucer's indebtedness in the *Book of
the Duchess* to another of Machaut's works, *Le Jugement dou
Roy de Behaingne*, written in 1346. This, therefore, as well
as its companion piece, *Le Jugement dou Roy de Navarre*,
written in 1349, may have come to Chaucer's knowledge at
this time.

thought of keeping open any communication with their base in the modern fashion. Chaucer could scarcely have returned to England if he had wished, and must therefore have continued with the invading host until the peace of Brétigny. With this part of the campaign there is no need to deal at length, since it had no special relation to the poet's life. Yet it must have been full of activity to him as to the whole army. Gray, who is here more explicit, gives many a detail of adventurous expeditions and of their varying results. It is he, for example, who tells us that, after the death of the Earl of March, Edward's constable, the Black Prince led the vanguard, so that possibly Chaucer was with that division.[115]

From the ranks of the besiegers Chaucer saw the walls of Paris, probably for the only time in his life. He was there, too, when on the Monday after Easter, April 6, Edward challenged the city in three lines of battle, the Duke of Lancaster and the Earls of Northampton and Salisbury leading the first, King Edward the second, and the Black Prince the third.[116] Later Chaucer marched with the army toward Brittany, though, as Edward did not reach that province, we need not assume that the poet then learned the Breton lay from which he later made the

---

[115] *Scalacronica*, p. 193.

[116] Knighton, *Chronicon*, II, iii.

Franklin's Tale.[117] With the army, too, he experienced the terrible storm of that Black Monday, as the *Chronicle of London* calls it, when

> chéi dou chiel en l'ost le roy uns effoudres, uns
> tempestes, ungs orraiges, uns esclistres, uns
> vens, ungs grésils si grans, si mervilleux et si
> oribles qu'il sambloit que li chiels deuist s'en
> partir, et li tierre ouvrir et tout engloutir; et
> chéoient les pierres si grandes et si grosses que
> elles tuoient hommes et chevaux, et n'y avoit si
> hardi qui ne fuist tous esbahis.[118]

---

[117] Edward had been compelled to march toward Brittany in order to secure provisions for the army. To the devastated condition of the country we have the unique testimony of Petrarch who, in the latter part of 1360, bore the congratulations of Galeazzo Visconti of Milan to King John of France on his return to Paris. I quote the translation of Hallam (*Europe during the Middle Ages*, p. 90) : "I could not believe that this was the same kingdom which I had once seen so rich and flourishing. Nothing presented itself to my eyes but the fearful solitude, an extreme poverty, lands uncultivated, houses in ruins. Even the neighborhood of Paris manifested everywhere marks of destruction and conflagration. The streets are deserted; the roads overgrown with weeds; the whole is a vast solitude." *Mémoire de Pétrarque*, III, 541.

[118] Froissart, *Chron.*, VI, 273. Knighton (*Chron.*, II, 112) : "Nam in eorum reditu de civitate Parisiensi versus partes de Orlions in Bevosina, subito supervenit horribilis tempestas tonitrui fulguris deinde grandinis, et occidit gentes absque numero et plusquam vj millia equorum, ita quod cariagium exercitus defecit fere in toto, et oportuit necessario redire versus Angliam, sed Deus transtulit miseriam necessitatis in honorem regiae majestatis."

Chronicle of London (Nicolas), p. 64: "The same yere . . the xiiii day of Aprill, thanne beynge the morwe after Ester day, Kyng Edward with hys oost lay aboughte Paris; which day was a foul derk day of mist and of hayl, and so bitter cold that manye men deyde for cold; wherfore unto this day manye men calen it the blake Moneday." Delachenal who

This terrible storm, the chroniclers tell us, more than the wise counsel of the Duke of Lancaster, determined Edward to accept terms of peace. At any rate, the army got no farther than the little village of Brétigny near Chartres, when it found its labors suddenly ended. Negotiations resulted in a truce for a year, during which a more permanent peace was concluded. The truce, or peace of Brétigny as it is called, was made May 8, 1360. It was later confirmed at Paris by the Duke of Normandy, Regent of France, when he bound the oath with a gift to the Prince of Wales of reliques from the holy cross, spines from the crown of thorns, and valuable jewels. The Prince of Wales took the oath on the part of the English in the great church of Louviers, northwest of Paris,

---

quotes this rightly changes xiiii to xiii, as the Monday after Easter was April 13 in 1360.

The *Scalacronica* (p. 193–4) puts the storm on Sunday, but gives the correct date, April 13: "Le dymange le xiij jour davrille, pur defaute de feur as cheveaux covenoit faire un tresgrandisme journe devers Beaux. Le temps estoit si tresmervaillous mauveis de plu, de greil, et de neggie, ove tiel freidour qe plusours feblis vadlets et cheveaux periroint mortz as chaumps, enlasserent plusours chariotis et somaille com en un fortune du pier temps de froid, vent, et de moil, qe en cel cesoun avoit este vieu de memoir." Can it be that Chaucer remembered this black Monday when, in the *Miller's Tale*, he made Nicolas predict (330–2):

"That now, a Monday next at quarter-night,
  Shal falle a reyn and that so wilde and wood,
  That half so greet was never Noes flood."

This Black Monday made a profound impression on England, and figures largely in the most important reference to this French campaign in English poetry of the period. See *Piers Plowman*, passus III, l. 188f., and the note by Professor Skeat. The passage is found in the first form of the poem, supposed to be of the year 1362.

on May 15.[119]   This accomplished, King Edward and
his sons at once left for England,[120] arriving at Rye
on May 18 and reaching London as soon as possible.[121]   Without doubt, therefore, Chaucer also returned to England at this time.

One further fact is necessary to this account of
the campaign of 1359–60 in its relation to Chaucer.
The peace of Brétigny was rather a convention leading to a treaty.   The treaty itself was worked out in
detail at Calais.   Meanwhile, there was much to do
in executing the preliminaries already agreed upon.
To assist in carrying these out, in July the captive
King John was allowed to go to Calais under escort,
at least to Dover, of the Duke of Lancaster and the

---

[119] Gray *(Scalacronica,* p. 195–6) gives these details in language of more than usual seriousness and nobility: "Le duk
de Normande et regent de France, qe maladez estoit den-
postym, le jura a Parys en presence de vaillaunz chevaleres
Englois pur ceo y envoyes par queux le dit regent tramist au
dit prince de Galis tresnoblis precious reliqes du seintisme
croice, de la coroune des espines de quoi Dieux fust corone
en la croice, ove autres noblis jueaux, en signifiaunce qe sure
la croice, la dit coroune a test, nostre Seigneur fist pees, salut,
et tranquillite pardurable au lygne humain.   Le dit prince de
Galis fist meisme le serement en le grant moustier de Loviers,
le xv jour de Maij, lan susdit, en presence dez noblis cheva-
leris Fraunceis pur la cause y envoiez."

[120] Gray *(Scalacronica,* p. 196) : "Le dit roy Dengleter prist
soun chemyn devers Huniflu ou se mist sure mere devers
Engleter, sez fitz et plusours seignours ove ly."

[121] Rymer's *Fœdera* (VI, 196) makes Edward reach Westminster the next day: "Memorandum, quod die Lunae Decimo
octavo die Maii . . . Dominus Rex . . . ad Regnum suum
Angliae veniens, in Portu de la Rye, circiter horam Vesper-
tinam, applicuit: Et, exinde statim equitando, in Crastino
apud Palatium suum Westmonasteriense, quasi bassa Hora
Nona, accessit."

Prince of Wales.[122] In the latter part of August the Prince of Wales, the Duke of Lancaster, and others passed over to Calais in order to complete the treaty. This is known from a record discovered by M. Delachenal, which shows that the Prince of Wales was paid for his services at this time ten pounds a day for the seventy-five days between August 24 and November 6 inclusive.[123] The English king did not go over until October, and the treaty was not signed until October 24.[124]

---

[122] The continuator of Higden's *Polychronicon* (Appendix to Vol. VIII, p. 410) tells of the escort to Calais, and Knighton *(Chron.,* II, 113) gives the time: "Circa translationem sancti Thomae," or about July 7. M. Delachenal *(op. cit.* II, 240) infers from a letter of King John dated Canterbury, July 5, 1360, that the Prince of Wales went only to Dover: "Scavoir vous faisons que apres nostre depart de Londres . . . nostre nepveu le prince [de Galles]nous a tenu compagnie, et tendra jusques a Douvres."

[123] "Idem computat in vadiis suis capiendo x.l.per diem a xxviiii[o] die augusti dicto anno xxxiiii[to], quo die iter suum arripuit cum familia sua de hospicio suo infra London, versus Caleys pro tractatu pacis ibidem habito inter reges Angliae et Francie, ibidem morando et exinde redeundo usque vi diem novembris proximo sequentem, quo die venit ad London, cum familia sua ad hospicium suum predicto, per lxxv dies, primo die et ultimo computatis, DCCL l, capiendo per diem x l., sicut supra continetur." Exchequer Accounts, Bundle 314, no. 2, as quoted by M. Delachenal, *op. cit.* II, 241.

[124] According to Rymer's *Fœdera* (VI, 214–15), Edward signed documents in London on September 30, and in Calais on October 16. Longman *(op. cit.* II, 58) says the English king landed at Boulogne October 9. The long delay in signing the treaty had been partly due to the difficulty the French had in raising the enormous ransom of King John. As is well known, Galeazzo Visconti, Lord of Milan, furnished the 600,000 florins necessary, on condition that Isabella, third daughter of King John of France, should be given in marriage to Galeazzo's son Gian. Villani says the marriage took place about the eighth of October.

16

The importance of these details lies in the fact that,
in connection with them, we get one more glimpse of
Chaucer, another discovery of M. Delachenal.   In
the expense account of Lionel, Earl of Ulster, as
preserved in the Exchequer Accounts of the Public
Record Office, London, is one item which reads:

> Datum Galfrido Chaucer, per preceptum do-
> mini, eundo cum litteris in Angliam, iii roiales
> precii ix s.[125]

---

[125] Quoted, except for parts of the last four words, by
R. Delachenal, *op. cit.* II, 241, and first called to my attention
by Professor G. L. Burr of Cornell University when sending
me the *Histoire* for the investigations of this paper.   That the
record occurs in the expense account of Earl Lionel is clear
from the heading of the MS. (No. 1 of Bundle 314): "Expense domini comitis Ultonie apud Caleys, existentis ibidem
ad tractatum, et redeundo in Angliam, facte per manus
Andree de Budeston, anno xxxiiij to."   This last fact, however,
was not given by M. Delachenal, and I learned it only when
writing to him after my article 'A New Chaucer Item,' had
been printed in *Mod. Lang. Notes*, XXVI, 19 (January, 1911).
M. Delachenal had also referred to Chaucer as "clerc du roi,"
and had assumed that he had played a minor part in the
peace negotiations at Calais ("participa . . . aux négocia-
tions à Calais").   Basing my article on these statements, I
was too liberal in my conjecture that Chaucer was perhaps
detached from the service of Lionel and more directly in that
of the king or Prince of Wales.   Yet I should add that
M. Delachenal in his letter (of April, 1911) questioned my
interpretattion of "domini" as if it were "domini regis," saying he had himself been in doubt whether the reference was to
the king or to Lionel.   I at once wrote to Mr. A. W. Pollard,
of the British Museum, asking him to have the record examined as to Chaucer and the interpretation of "domini."   He
placed the matter in the hands of Mr. R. L. Steele, who sent
me the Chaucer record above (May 17, 1911), confirming the
conjectural restoration of the last part (see my article in
Mod. Lang. Notes above).   He also answered that an examination of the whole record showed that the "domini" of the
Chaucer item was Roger Beauchamp, captain of Calais Castle, by whose order many of the other payments were made.

Such a record may mean more than at first appears. What were these letters which Chaucer bore to England at this important time? Were they of merely private nature, or were they connected with the peace negotiations? We shall probably never know with certainty, but M. Delachenal's conjecture seems more than likely, that they were connected with the chief business in hand.

Whether Chaucer returned to Calais after bearing messages to England can not be known. Yet it is reasonable to believe that he bore answers back to his master Lionel. If so, he was doubtless an onlooker at that "most magnificent and grand supper in the castle of Calais"[126] which the king of England gave to the king of France. "It was well arranged," says the chronicler, "and the children of the king, and the Duke of Lancaster, with the greatest barons

---

In this Mr. Steele, on whom I supposed I could rely, was in error, as shown by the fuller transcript of the account published by Mr. Moore in *Mod. Lang. Notes* XXVII, 79. In either case, I had known since the letters of M. Delachenal and Mr. Steele that Chaucer was still in the employ of Lionel, Earl of Ulster, and had already embodied it in this paper. That I did not publish this fact at once was owing to my intention to deal further with the whole subject, sufficiently expressed, I had supposed, in footnote 8 of my article, 'A New Chaucer Item,' in the above named periodical.

The Chaucer item seems to read: Datum Galfrido Chaucer per preceptum domini eundo cum litteris in Angliam iij roiales precii ix s.

[See *Romanic Rev.*, Vol. III, facing p. 359, for a facsimile of the MS. The small page of the present volume as compared with the original has made it impracticable to reproduce the facsimile here.]

[126] Froissart, *Chron.*, VI, 320.

of England, waited bareheaded." Besides, as Professor Skeat has conjectured,[127] he was probably with his master Lionel when the latter, together with the Prince of Wales and his brother Edmund, accompanied the king of France "in pilgrimage to Our Lady of Boulogne." One can not do better than allow Froissart to describe the picturesque event:

> Et ensi vinrent-il tout de piet et devant disner jusques à Boulongne où il furent receu à moult grant joie, et là estoit li dus de Normendie qui les attendoit. Si vinrent li dessus dit signeur tout à piet en l'église Nostre-Dame de Boulongne, et fisent leurs offrandes moult dévotement, et puis retournèrent en l'abbeye de laiens qui estoit apparillie pour le roy recevoir et les enfans dou roy d'Engleterre.[128]

Then, when all these ceremonies were over, the English princes and nobles, with the noble hostages of France, finally closed the campaign of 1359–60 and the attendant peace negotiations by returning to England. It was "the vigil of All Saints," says Froissart, and Chaucer's first experience in war and public service had lasted almost a year and a day.

VII. *Results*

For our purpose, it is unnecessary to summarize the purely historical results from this detailed study

---

[127] *Works of Chaucer*, I, xix.

[128] Froissart, *Chron.*, VI, 320, sec. red.

of Edward III's campaign of 1359-60. What has
been added on that side will be evident from comparison with previous accounts. As indicated by the
title, the study has been undertaken with special reference to the life of the young Chaucer. How noteworthy the year to him, how broadening by travel,
adventure, hardship of camp life, imprisonment, em-
ployment as trusted messenger, experience of every
sort, it is impossible to estimate. Besides, some new
light has been thrown on the man himself through
this more minute relation of the doings of the army
with which he was connected.

We now know that Chaucer marched with a division of the army led by the Black Prince, rather than
with that led by the king or Henry of Lancaster.
With this division, too, the poet made his first visit
to Montreuil, the scene of later diplomatic business
during the year 1377, in which he was a more important factor. We know also the more exact course
through France of the Prince's division, and therefore of Chaucer's journey. Again we know, from
Thomas Gray's contemporary account, that the division with which Chaucer moved appeared before
Rhétel previous to reaching Reims. It seems certain
that it was of this event Chaucer testified in the heraldic trial of Scrope and Grosvenor in 1386. Further,
Chaucer's capture by the French has been shown to
have been probably between the fourth of December,

1359, and January 11, 1360, when Edward left Reims. The poet's imprisonment, therefore, lasted at most for some two months or two months and a half. On being ransomed, Chaucer must have rejoined the army at Guillon in Burgundy, since reaching England at this time from the heart of France would have been practically impossible. With the army, too, he must have continued until the peace of Brétigny when, with the king and his sons, on May 18, he sailed for England. Later in the same year, Chaucer again went over to Calais, probably with his master Lionel in October, and by him was sent as a bearer of letters from Calais to England. The inference seems justified that this service was on business connected with the peace negotiations. On his return to Calais—and such return seems probable—Chaucer doubtless saw something of the royal feast in Calais of the kings of England and France, and as Professor Skeat has suggested, was probably present on the pilgrimage of his master Lionel to Boulogne in the last week of October. He finally returned to England on November 1, after a series of unusually varied experiences lasting almost exactly a year.

CHAUCER'S TESTIMONY AS TO HIS AGE*

Some years ago, when first seeing in the volumes of the *Scrope and Grosvenor Controversy* the suggestion of Sir Harris Nicolas that discredit or inconclusiveness belongs to Chaucer's testimony regarding his age in 1386, it occurred to me that the reasoning had little to commend it. Now that the suggestion of Sir Harris has been urged with apparently greater force by Mr. Samuel Moore in *Anglia*, XXV, 1–8, it seems worth examining more carefully. The reasoning of Sir Harris Nicolas may be baldly stated in syllogistic form. Some men who testified in the Scrope and Grosvenor heraldic trial were, let us not say members of an early Ananias club, but at least too careless of exactness. Chaucer was a man who testified in the aforesaid trial. Therefore Chaucer's testimony cannot be trusted.

Placed in this form the fallacy of the reasoning appears at once. Nor is the argument essentially better in the form now stated by Mr. Moore. Twenty-three of those who testified in the Scrope and Grosvenor trial varied from their true ages, as ascertained from other documents, by from three to seventeen years. Fourteen others varied from their true ages, as otherwise ascertained, either one or two years. Chaucer testified in the trial aforesaid, though

* *Mod. Phil.*, Vol. XI, pp. 117–125 (1913).

247

we have no independent testimony as to his inaccuracy. Still we may not trust Chaucer's testimony,
because some of his fellow-witnesses were inaccurate, and he may have been so.[1]

It is evident that this reasoning does not much
assist us in the main point, the interpretation of
Chaucer's testimony. It will be clear to all, I think,
that the faulty memories or deliberate deceptions of
any number of Chaucer's fellow-witnesses do not
really reflect upon his integrity. If it suggests a
possibility of error, that error must be proved by
independent evidence in Chaucer's individual case.
It cannot be logically inferred from the testimony of
others regarding themselves. Even if a conspiracy
to conceal the truth could be proved against them, it
would not involve Chaucer without independent evidence that he was a conspirator.

---

[1] I have no desire to cavil at Mr. Moore's reasoning. Yet it
may be pointed out, that he assumes inaccuracy of four of the
twenty-three witnesses on the Scrope side, by the statement
of their ages when called in behalf of Grosvenor. This is
scarcely independent evidence of a sufficient sort. If these
four cannot be depended upon when called on the one side,
their statements cannot be assumed to be correct when called
on the other. These witnesses should rather be thrown out
altogether, or at least wholly discredited. That would leave,
of the twenty-three cited by Mr. Moore, nineteen who show
considerable inaccuracy in the statement of their ages, besides
fourteen who come within two years of their exact age. I
refer to those mentioned by name in the above article. Moreover, so far as I can determine from Mr. Moore's statements,
these four are the only ones who overstated their ages, a procedure quite at variance with the general practice in such
cases, as we shall see. There is thus another reason for dis-
trusting their testimony in one place or the other.

Nor does Mr. Moore's conjecture, that the age of
the witness may have been the guess of some recording clerk, seem to be necessary, as I shall presently
show. Before doing so, let me call attention to its im-
probability in Chaucer's case. If the age of Chaucer,
as given in the Scrope and Grosvenor trial, were
the guess of a clerk, we must assume the same explanation for the next statement attributed to the
poet. When giving his age he also asserted that he
had "borne arms twenty-seven years."[2] Now, this
twenty-seven years leads us back exactly to the year
1359, when we know that Chaucer was with the
army of Edward III in France.

Besides, the words of Chaucer are even more exact
than the round number twenty-seven implies. His
testimony in the Scrope and Grosvenor trial was
given on December 15, 1386. In 1359 the truce of
Bordeaux had been extended to St. John's Day, June
24. The failure of the peace negotiations was proclaimed by the king on August 12, though Edward
and his sons did not leave England until the last of
October.[3] If, therefore, Chaucer's arming had been
as early as August, 1359, it was in December 1386,
at most twenty-seven years and four months that he
had "borne arms." This significant part of Chaucer's

---

[2] "Armeez par xxvii ans," *Life Records of Chaucer,* p. 265.

[3] See my article on Chaucer's 'First Military Service,'
Romanic Review, III, 325f.; cf. above, pp. 182–246.

testimony — for I shall assume it to be Chaucer's until further proof is forthcoming—is therefore accurate to a nicety.[4] May we not infer that the witness who was so exact in the one fact was not far wrong in the other statement, that he was "of the age of forty years and more?"[5] What interpretation, then, may reasonably belong to the latter expression?

The phrase "of the age of forty years and more" does not, at first sight, lend itself to extreme exactness. Let us see, however. And first Mr. Moore also notes, in his careful examination of the testimony in the Scrope and Grosvenor trial, that a large number of the witnesses gave their ages as forty, fifty, or sixty years, with or without the "and more" *(et plus)*. He comments: "It is certainly an extraordinary fact that, among about 140 persons between the ages of thirty-five and sixty-four years of age, there should be more than 75 persons who are said to be either forty, fifty, or sixty years of age." In a footnote he explains that he has disregarded the *et plus* in this computation. Yet, before we assume intentional or other inaccuracy here, let us ask what

---

[4] In a brief sketch of the poet's life for a recent edition of *Poems of Chaucer*, I have based the most important inference as to the poet's age upon this part of the testimony. If, as Froissart says, "there was not knight, squire, or man of honor, from the age of twenty to sixty years, that did not go," the first age would just include a youth born in 1340, as the last-mentioned age just included Henry, Duke of Lancaster, and under Edward the most important military leader.

[5] "Del age de xl ans et plus," *Life Records*, p. 265.

these figures mean in the light of the best modern interpretation of statistics.

It is well known to statisticians of the census that returns of ages always contain a certain element of error. For example, on a priori grounds it must be assumed that the number of persons of different ages living at one time should vary by a definite arithmetical progression. Thus, as the death-rate is a fairly constant factor, increasing from year to year, there will be fewer persons of the age of twenty-one than of twenty, of twenty-two than of twenty-one, and so on in a regular series. The actual census returns, however, do not show this regular decrease in the number reporting at different ages. In the first place, as a statistical authority states, "More persons return themselves as younger than they are, than as older than they are."[6] Again, "Concentration is greater on years which are multiples of ten, than on years which are multiples of five and not of ten."[7]

To correct such recognized inaccuracies, statisticians are accustomed to modify census reports as to ages by various methods. The methods need not

---

[6] Allyn A. Young, 'Comparative Accuracy of Different Forms of Quinquennial Age Groups,' *Publications of the American Statistical Association*, VII, 27, p. 38. Professor Young also wrote the article called 'Age' in the *Supplementary Analysis of the Twelfth Census*, p. 130.

[7] *Ibid.*, p. 27. This concentration of returns on certain years is well illustrated by a chart in *Vital Statistics* (A. Newsholme), p. 3.

concern us here. The character of the discrepancies between the reported ages and the corrected tables are more to the point. Thus, to illustrate the statement above, that more people give their ages as too low than too high, note these figures.[8] In the United States census of 1890, 1,359,566 persons reported themselves as thirty years of age, while only 891,222 reported twenty-nine years, and only 729,771 reported the age thirty-one. The correct figures, according to Professor Young, should have been 984,000 for twenty-nine years, 969,057 for thirty years, 942,977 for thirty-one years. Thus 390,509 more persons reported the age of thirty than were of that age. That is, roughly, more than every fourth person reporting the age of thirty was inaccurate. The exact proportion is 1 to every 3.7 persons.

Moreover, as Professor Young also points out, those persons who were inaccurate in reporting the age of thirty, were more probably in excess of thirty rather than below thirty years old. For while, according to his corrected tables, 92,778 fewer than should have done so reported the age of twenty-nine, 213,206 fewer than should have done so reported the age of thirty-one. That is, more than one-fifth of those who were thirty-one understated their age by at least one year, and thus helped to make up the

[8] Allyn A. Young, 'The Adjustment of Census Age Returns,' *Western Reserve University Bulletin*, V, 79f.; table on p. 101.

unusually large report for the age of thirty. On the other hand, less than one-tenth of those reporting the age of twenty-nine were inaccurate, and probably few of them reported the age of thirty. Clearly, more people in 1890 gave their ages as too low than too high. Besides, such facts are not peculiar to one census, or to one country. So far as census tables show, they represent a tendency common to all peoples and to all periods.

Again, to illustrate the statement above, that age returns in a census today show concentration on multiples of ten, note these figures from Professor Young's table. The actual reports for the years forty, fifty, sixty—to take the ages Mr. Moore uses —were 1,037,336, 776,333, 502,788, respectively. The corrected numbers are, in the same order, 682,948, 516,573, 321,397. Thus, the reports in excess of the facts were 354,388 for forty years; 259,598 for fifty years; 181,391 for sixty years. For forty and fifty years the exact proportion of inaccuracy is 1 person in 2.9, for sixty years 1 person in 2.8. At least every third person who reported an even number forty, fifty, or sixty was reporting inaccurately.

The relation of these figures to the testimony as to age by witnesses in the Scrope and Grosvenor trial will be evident. In our own country, in 1890, at least every third person who gave the age of forty, fifty, or sixty reported himself as somewhat younger than

he was. Contrary to Mr. Moore's idea, therefore, it
is no matter of surprise that five centuries before,
almost to the year, something like the same thing
should have taken place. Of the 75 persons out of
about 140 between the ages of thirty-five and sixty-
four who testified that they were forty, fifty, or sixty
years of age, with or without the addition "and
more," one-third may be at once assumed to have
understated their ages. This leaves 50 out of 140 to
be accounted for. If all these added the phrase "and
more" to the year given, as Chaucer did, we may suppose they belonged in the groups of years forty to
forty-four, fifty to fifty-four, sixty to sixty-four.
That is, these are the years to which belong those
who wrongly concentrate on forty, fifty, or sixty by
understating their ages. Now these groups include
in all, fifteen years, or one-half the period Mr. Moore
takes for his basis of comparison. It would be
natural enough if 50 out of 140, or a little more than
one-third, had been of ages falling in one-half of the
time specified, the period between the ages of thirty-
five and sixty-four. Indeed, if the whole 75, only
slightly more than one-half the 140, should be included in the fifteen years cited above, it would be
quite within reason. As I have not access at present
to the volumes of Sir Harris Nicolas on the *Scrope
and Grosvenor Controversy*, I do not know exactly
how many witnesses added the phrase *et plus* to the

year of age given.[9] Nor is this necessary. Even if
only a part did, the general tendency in such cases
to concentrate on multiples of ten, probably stronger
five centuries ago than today, would fairly account
for the facts. It is, therefore, wholly unnecessary to
suppose, as Mr. Moore does, that the ages attributed
to the witnesses were the guess of a recording clerk.

Let there be no misunderstanding of this argument. It is not my purpose to prove the accuracy of
the witnesses in the Scrope and Grosvenor trial, and
hence reason for Chaucer's accuracy as well. To do
that would be but to repeat, in another form, the
fallacious reasoning of Sir Harris Nicolas. I have
tried to show that the inaccuracies of the witnesses
are not so remarkable as they have been supposed
to be; that they are not so different from similar
inaccuracies under circumstances not wholly dissim-
ilar today. Yet our main interest is with the testimony of a single individual, the poet Chaucer, whose
appearance in this trial makes one more definite fact
of his life.

Can we, then, in the light of modern statistics,
make a more exact interpretation of Chaucer's refer-

---

[9] Fortunately Chaucer was one of these. We must infer
that he was not content with the general concentration on a
multiple of ten, and this "and more" must therefore be reckoned with in his particular case. Even in the case of other
witnesses, Mr. Moore is scarcely justified in disregarding this
"*et plus*" as practically meaningless. The phrase may have
meant different things to different individuals, but at least
has some significance.

ence to his age as "forty years and more."[10] Let us begin with another conclusion of Professor Young regarding the census statistics of 1890. He says:

It would appear that the four years below forty (thirty-six to thirty-nine) are excessively large as compared with the years above forty (forty-one to forty-four). This is probably chargeable in part to a peculiar tendency on the part of those whose ages are greater than forty to return themselves as less than forty. It would seem, also, that the concentration on the year forty is drawn in but very slight degree from years less than forty.[11]

This means, as applied to the testimony in the Scrope and Grosvenor trial, that those who testified they were forty years of age were certainly as old as that, and perhaps a little more. That is, understatement, not overstatement, of age is the rule. If then, Chaucer had acknowledged forty years only in 1386, we might reasonably infer he could not have been less than that age. Mr. Moore is quite incorrect, therefore, in assuming from the inaccuracies of other witnesses that Chaucer may have been "only thirty-six or thirty-eight years old."[12] Overstatement of age can-

---

[10] It is some years since I purposed to make the application of modern age statistics to this problem. Mr. Moore's article merely gives the occasion.

[11] Allyn A. Young, 'Comparative Accuracy,' etc., as above, pp. 36–37.

[12] See p. 6 of *Anglia* article cited above.

not be assumed as likely, and cannot be argued in
a case for which we have no independent testimony.
Besides, if there is a tendency in the present age to
hesitate in acknowledging forty years, it was probably much stronger at a time when the age of forty
was regarded as "old," or approaching old age.[13]

Can we go one step farther? What light do modern statistics throw upon the further acknowledgment of Chaucer in his "forty years and more"? The
authority of Professor Young has already been
quoted to show that the concentration in the census
reports upon the year forty is drawn mainly from
the years forty-one, forty-two, forty-three, forty-
four. Thus, the 354,388 who wrongly reported their
age as forty in the census of 1890 are assumed by
Professor Young to belong to the years forty-one,
forty-two, forty-three, forty-four in the sums 171,-
239, 5,225, 81,078, and 96,846, respectively. Arranged in the order of frequency given, the years of
these inaccurate reports are forty-one, forty-four,
forty-three, forty-two. We cannot know which if
any of these numbers represent Chaucer's "forty
years and more." We may consider the probabilities
in relation to other facts of his life. The age of
forty-one in 1386 is wholly improbable for Chaucer,

---

[13] Compare Chaucer's own allusion to his old age in the
Envoy to Scogan, probably written when he was at most fifty-
three years old, and Skeat's comment, with other examples,
in *Works of Chaucer,* I, xvi.

17

since his birth year would then have been 1345, and
he would have been only fourteen when arming for
the campaign of 1359, and only fifteen when he bore
letters from Calais to England, as discovered by
M. Delachenal.[14] The age of forty-four, the next in
general probability, is also to be preferred to forty-
three or forty-two on all grounds. It is more reasonable to believe Chaucer was at least seventeen when
arming for the campaign of 1359, than that he was
fifteen or sixteen.

But may Chaucer have been older than forty-four
in 1386? It has already been implied, in the first
quotation from Professor Young, that modern census
tables show a concentration on multiples of five as
well as multiples of ten, though the concentration is
much more frequent in the latter than in the former
case. In the census of 1890, 354,388 in excess of the
correct number concentrated upon forty years of
age, while a little more than half as many in excess
of the correct number, or 204,800, concentrated upon
forty-five.[15] Perhaps little is to be inferred from
these figures directly. Yet if Chaucer had been forty-
four years or under in 1386, the probabilities are
great that he would have been satisfied with the

---

[14] *Histoire de Charles V*, II, 241.

[15] In the same census the concentration on thirty was more
than twice as great as on thirty-five, that on fifty more than
three times as great as on fifty-five. The figures in excess of
the corrected ones for thirty and thirty-five are 390,509 and
181,114; for fifty and fifty-five, 359,598 and 73,824.

acknowledgment of forty years of age. If in 1890, as has been shown above, every third man who was forty-one, forty-two, forty-three, or forty-four reported forty years, it would not be strange if Chaucer, five centuries ago, should have been willing to do the same. His testimony to "forty years and more" is not proof that he was more than forty-four years of age. It does lend color to the idea that he may have been forty-five or a little more, and yet have reported as he did. If he were forty-four in 1386, he would have been born in 1342. If his testimony to more than forty years means anything in the light of modern statistics, he may easily have been born in 1341 or even in 1340.[16]

For practical purposes it is not necessary to support the validity of Chaucer's testimony. To say that he was born about 1340 is ordinarily sufficient. Yet to see in the testimony to his age in 1386 a fairly valid statement of fact is pleasant, because the impression left by Chaucer's works and what we know of his life is that of a more than usually accurate

---

[16] In the interest of extreme exactness, it should be noted that Chaucer may have been only forty-five when testifying in the Scrope and Grosvenor trial of 1386, and yet have been born in 1340, as he reckoned it. This would have been true if the date of his birth had fallen between December 15, 1340, and March 25, 1341. Or, if he had been born in the latter half of December, he would have still been only forty-five in 1386 and have been born in 1340, as we reckon it. Either of these possibilities would make it easy to interpret his "forty years and more" as a fairly exact statement of his age.

man, even of an exact man for his time.[17]   His em-
ployment on many and important missions of diplo-
macy lends color to this idea.   In the article above
mentioned, Mr. Moore has added valuable proof of
the poet's business ability, as shown by his long tenure of the controllership of customs, compared with
the terms of other incumbents.[18]   Even his works
give evidence of the accuracy of the man in more
ways than one.   He twice recorded, in a manner we
can hardly suppose accidental, the particular day of
the month when he had the vision of the *House of
Fame*.   The *Lines to Adam Scriveyn* indicate his in-
sistence on exactness in recording his verses.   His
references to his sources, when understood as he intended, are usually correct, as my colleague Professor
Hulme suggests.   His exactness in referring to the
appearance of the planet Venus in the *Parliament of
Birds* has been fruitful in dating the work.   The
similarly exact allusions to time in the *Canterbury
Tales* are of unusual value for the same purpose.   The
whole of the *Astrolabe* gives proof of an exact mind,
a mind inquisitive and acquisitive of what we should
call science today.

In one case, it is true, we might apparently accuse

---

[17] I do not forget Professor Lounsbury's criticism of Chaucer
for certain minor inaccuracies in his works; see *Studies in
Chaucer*, II, 177–88, 416–26.   Yet the number mentioned is
small compared with the many allusions in his work as a
whole.

[18] See pp. 14–19, and especially p. 18.

Chaucer of error in a fact about which he must have
had some accurate knowledge. Curiously enough
this concerns the age of a prominent man with whom
the poet was more or less intimately associated. In
the *Book of the Duchess* (l. 455) Chaucer gives the
age of John of Gaunt as "four and twenty" instead
of nine and twenty, as it should have been. This has
been explained, it is true, as a possible error of xxiiij
for xxviiij by the loss of v in copying.[19] Yet such
explanation has always seemed to me less likely than
that Chaucer was purposely flattering the young
prince by an understatement of his age. In either
case, however, we have good reason for not assuming a mere inaccuracy on Chaucer's part. Still, if
Chaucer's understatement of John of Gaunt's age
was for purposes of flattery, we have something akin
to the understatement of ages by witnesses in the
Scrope and Grosvenor trial. It may indicate a common tendency of the time. If, then, Chaucer's emphasis of forty was an understatement of his own
age as much as he understated that of John of Gaunt
in the *Book of the Duchess,* we should again reach
the conclusion that he was about forty-five years old
in 1386.

Yet it is better to arrive at this conclusion through
such interpretation of Chaucer's testimony as I have
made in the body of this paper. That interpretation

---

[19] Mr. Brock's suggestion, noted by Professor Skeat.

assumes Chaucer's statement to have been intended as accurate, since we have no evidence to the contrary. It then explains his testimony as to his age in the light, not of statements by a few others of his own time who may or may not have given their own ages correctly, but of general tendencies among people of all nations today, tendencies likely to have been more, rather than less, pronounced five centuries ago.

"SEITH TROPHEE"*

Professor Tupper, in his article on Chaucer's
Trophee in the January number of the current volume of this journal, has forestalled me in publishing
a paper on the same subject, already in final form
and submitted to two or three friends within the last
two months. To Professor Tupper's article, with its
new support of Mr. G. L. Hamilton's suggestion, may
I add one or two notes.

Although Chaucer speaks of "Guido eek de Columpnis" in the *House of Fame,* 1469, he probably
also knew that manuscripts of the *Historia Trojana*
often gave the name with the singular cognomen.
This may be seen, to go no further, from Ward's
Catalogue of Romances in the British Museum. Of
the two earliest there described, both written about
1350, the second gives the singular of the name—"de
Columpna"—in the Prologue, although the plural "de
Columpnis" occurs in the Epilogue. With this the
third, fourth, and ninth manuscripts also agree, while
the seventh has the singular form of the name in the
Epilogue. The thirteenth, a French translation of
1380, has "Guy de la coulompne" in the rubric. Other
manuscripts are imperfect, or Ward does not describe them as to the name, but enough has been

---

* *MLN.* Vol. XXXI, pp. 142–6 (1916).

given to show that in English manuscripts the singular of the cognomen is about as common as the plural.

In French the name has remained as "de Colonna" or "Columna," indicating a long established French usage. In English, Lydgate's use of the singular form is well known, *Troy Book*, 360:

And of Columpne Guido was his name.

Printed editions of the *Historia* in the fifteenth century, so far as the British Museum catalogue shows, use the singular. For Italian, Tiraboschi seems to have known only the singular form of the name, as in his *Storia della Litteratura Italiana*, IV, 326.

That Guido himself used the "de columnis," as has been made probable, is not here in question. We are interested in what was known and thought to be true in the time of Chaucer. Although Chaucer wrote "de Columpnis" in the *House of Fame*, therefore, there was no reason why he should not have used the singular descriptive title in another place when needing another kind of rime. While, too, as Mr. Hamilton suggested, *Trophee* may be a translation of the plural *columnis*, it more naturally translates the singular which could scarcely have been unknown to Chaucer.

Now it is easy to miss, owing to its considerable change of meaning, that *trophee* in Chaucer's time meant primarily "a column." The classical word,

Greek τροπαῖον, Latin *tropaeum,* signifying at first
the turning point of the battle leading to defeat of
the enemy, had been transferred to denote the sign
of victory,—not yet captured armor as today, but
the trunk of a tree. The tree-trunk then gave way
to a stone pillar, as the former decayed perhaps, or
was carried away by relic hunters. The natural de-
scendant of medieval Latin *trophaea (trophea),* Old
French *trophee,* is of infrequent occurrence. Considerable search reveals only the single example in
Godefroy, and that later than one would wish, but
clearly implying the parallelism *trophee—column.*
It is from LeMaire's *Illustrations des Gaules et Sin-
gularitez de Troye* (1510–12) : "les colonnes qui illec
estoient plantees pour trophees et enseignes de vic-
toire."

English works later than Chaucer and than Lydgate's *Trophe* show the word in this early sense.
That Chaucer's use of the word as a proper name did
not establish the common noun in the language is
not strange. If reintroduced in the sixteenth century, the parallelism of meaning still holds. Thus
the *NED.* quotes, as of 1550, T. Nicoll's *Thucydides*
I, 36 : "The Athenians did make and set up their
trophe or signe of victorye, pretending to have had
the better." Here the word translates Greek τροπαῖον,
although the reference is apparently to *Thucydides*
I, 63, not 36. Spenser uses the word at least seven

times, six times in the exact form of Chaucer, once
as *trophe*.[1]   Five times also he has the classical idiom
of rearing a *trophee*, that is, erecting a pillar or monument, and a sixth time implies it in the "immortal
moniment" of his verse.   A still better example is
in Ben Jonson's *Prince Henry's Barriers*, 61–62:

> And trophies, reared of spoiled enemies,
> Whose tops pierced through the clouds and hit
>   the skies.

Examples from Shakespeare might also be cited in
which the word means column or monument of similar sort, rather than that which is placed upon the
column, the trophy of today. Compare the "trophies,
statues, tombs," of *Venus and Adonis* 1013, and

> That these great towers, trophies, and schools
>   should fall

of *Timon* V, iv, 25.

To return to Chaucer, why did he not use *column*
rather than *trophee* for Guido's title?   The question
seems reasonable today, but so far as records show,
column was not a part of the English language in
Chaucer's time, and was not to be for fifty years.
The first example is from the *Promptorium Parvu-
lorum* of 1440, and then only for the column of a

---

[1] *Visions of Bellay*, Van der Noodt's *Theatre*, sonet V, and
revised form; *Virgil's Gnat*, 126–7; *Faerie Queene* VII, vii,
56; *Colin Clout*, 951; *Amoretti*, LXIX.   In his translation of
Du Bellay, Spenser merely took over the French word from
the *Songe ou Vision sur Rome* (1558).

book. To Chaucer, therefore, the introduction of the
new word *column* was no more natural than the
use of *trophee* for the first time. Besides, in his
Hercules story Chaucer was completing an eight-line
stanza, and wished a fourth rime with long close *e*.
Guido, column, pillar were equally impossible, even
if he had not the latter *(piler)* already in mind for
his next line. Rather than recast his stanza, or perhaps by a happy thought rendered unhappy only by
our obtuseness, he hit upon *Trophee* for Guido and
his stanza was complete.[2]

In answer to Professor Kittredge's difficulty regarding the eastern pillars,[3] Professor Tupper has
sufficiently emphasized the minor character of this
inaccuracy. It may be noted, however, that Chaucer,
when writing what we know as the *Monk's Tale*, also
knew the Alexander story and his journey to "the
worldes ende," as shown by lines 641 to 648.[4] If this
did not include a knowledge of the eastern pillars,
Gower's double reference to them would indicate

[2] The quality of the vowel is right, since Greek *ai*, Latin *ae*,
in an open syllable appears as close *ē* in Chaucer. Compare
Machabee riming with *magestee, he, prosperitee* in this same
Monk's Tale, 589, and with *contree* in 665. So also *Ptholo-
mee (Ptholome)* riming with *be* in the *Wife of Bath's Prologue*, 182, 324, and with *subtiltee* in the *Summoner's Tale*,
581–2. The "selten" of Ten Brink's *Chaucers Sprache und
Verskunst*, § 67, applies to the number of examples.

[3] "The Pillars of Hercules and Chaucer's 'Trophee' " in the
Putnam Anniversary Volume, 545f.

[4] The last two lines look very much like part of the Alexander passage in Guido's *Historia*.

that they were not unknown to reading men. Compare also the allusion in the *Parliament of the Three Ages,* 334, to take only one other example. Perhaps Chaucer's association of Alexander and Hercules in a single line of the *House of Fame* (1413) may indicate some special relation of the two in his mind. At any rate, he needed no corrupt text for knowledge of the eastern pillars of Hercules.

Regarding Chaucer's "at bothe the worldes endes," it matters little whether we accept the idea of mere inaccuracy of memory, or the explanation of the phrase by Professor Skeat (*Chaucer's Works* II, liv). One might even venture a combination of the two. Perhaps Chaucer intended at first only a mention, based on Guido, of the western pillars. The expression in the last line of the stanza, "he a piler sette," looks as if he had only the one story in mind. Then, remembering the eastern pillars and changing a word and an ending, he left "at bothe the worldes endes" as we know it. Yet he did not think best to alter the apt rime word *Trophee,* or the last line in which "a piler" still stands, at variance with all statements, though not seriously affecting the brief narrative. Besides, the association of the eastern and western pillars in Chaucer's mind, as Mr. Hamilton pointed out, may have been due to Guido's mention of Alexander's visit and naturally suggestive of Alexander's eastern journey.

Finally, I would add to Professor Tupper's contention that Chaucer's *Trophee,* especially as it is in
rime, must have been deliberate and must be associated with the pillars of Hercules story. The only
known author, giving any account of any pillars
that can be associated with the name *Trophee,* is the
Guido usually known as "delle Colonne," but long
known equally well as "de Colonna" or "Columna."
Nor is it sufficiently inconsistent that Chaucer used
"de Columpnis" in rime in one place and a translation of "de Columna" in another requiring a different rime-word. Moreover, of the two difficulties in
the passage of the *Monk's Tale,* the explanation of
the name is more vital than the explanation of one
detail in the story of the pillars.

On the other hand, Professor Kittredge's conjecture implies too many steps not yet taken by any one,
too many corrupt texts of which we have not a single example. It also requires us to assume, not only
that Chaucer put into rime the name of an author
of whom he knew nothing,[5] but also that he could
not recognize in the word *trophea,* the Old French
trophee, Latin *tropea* "pillar," and so naturally connected with the Hercules story. Lastly, it suggests,
if not assumes, that Chaucer, not knowing the eulo-
gist of Hercules, offered a gloss upon his own igno-

---

[5] The case of "Lollius" is not quite in point it seems to me,
since the relations of that name may not yet have been made
out.

rance by jotting down on the manuscript for the
mystification of posterity, "Ille vates Chaldeorum
Tropheus.[6]

---

[6] Thanks to Professor Tupper, that mystification seems now
a thing of the past. It is not necessary to dwell on the use
by Chaucer, as by others of course, of either part of a name
for the person or author intended. Examples in Chaucer's
works are *Ovid* or *Naso*, *Judas* or *Scariot*, *Scipoun (Scipio)*
or *African*, *Julius* or *Caesar*, *Achilles* or *Eacides*, *Tytus* or
Tytus Livius. Nor is it of much importance, perhaps, that
he uses in other places expressions analogous to what we are
discussing. Thus *seith Machabee* occurs in rime in this
Monk's Tale (l. 665), and *seith Dante* similarly in the *Legend
of Good Women* (l. 336), while *seith Ovyde* is also found in
the latter at line 1683. Yet both these facts show Chaucer
would have been following no uncommon practice if he used
seith Trophee for the Guido "of the column."

ENGLISH OR FRENCH IN THE TIME
OF EDWARD III*

The position of the English language after the Norman Conquest has been variously stated. To early writers English was entirely displaced except among the lowest orders of society. Later writers assumed that the native tongue must early have begun to be rehabilitated as the language of the whole people, and interpreted the few direct references accordingly. Hume, in his early presentation of the first view,[1] might be pardoned for following the forger Ingulf, and his countryman Scott for popularizing Hume in the first chapter of *Ivanhoe*. Such pardon, however, should scarcely extend to a serious historian or writer of much later time. Palgrave seems to have been the first to protest the view of Hume a century before,[2] but Freeman,[3] who did so

---

* *Rom. Rev.* Vol. VII, pp. 127–143 (April—June, 1916).

[1] *History of England* (1754–61), I, 200: "William had even entertained the difficult project of totally abolishing the English language; and for that purpose he ordered that in all schools throughout the kingdom the youth should be instructed in the French tongue; a practice which was continued from custom till after the reign of Edward III, and was never indeed totally discontinued in England. . . . No other tongue [than French] was used at court: it became the language of all fashionable company; and the English themselves, ashamed of their own country, affected to excel in that foreign dialect." Ingulf is distinctly mentioned by Hume in a footnote to the same page.

[2] *History of Normandy and of England* (1851–64), III, ch. xv, and especially p. 627f.

[3] *The Norman Conquest* (1867–76), ch. xxv, and appendices

271

much to show the true continuity of English history from pre-Norman times, made the first elaborate and painstaking examination of the evidence for the case.

The first serious historian to convey the same impressions as Scott's romance, itself an exaggeration of Hume, was Augustin Thierry in his *Histoire de la Conquête de l'Angleterre par les Normands* (1825). This, too, was made more accessible to Englishmen and doubtless more influential by Hazlitt's translation in 1837. Thierry's indebtedness to Scott for his general notion of English-Norman history has been long recognized, but his romantic view still colors the conception of many writers. How close the French historian is to the English novelist may be seen from two quotations. Contrasting the English language in England and Scotland, Thierry says:

Cette langue, que sa ressemblance avec celle des Anglo-Saxons faisait nommer *anglisc* ou anglaise, avait un sort bien différent en Écosse et en Angleterre. Dans ce dernier pays, elle

to Vol. V. Freeman recognized his indebtedness to Stubbs *(Constitutional History of England* 1874–78), for some facts, and alludes to Palgrave. Otherwise his treatment of the subject is original and far reaching, in spite of some errors on purely linguistic matters. He particularly combats Hume's statement above, in the opening sentence of his twenty-fifth chapter: "Of all the dreams which have affected the history of the times on which we are engaged, none has led to more error than the notion that William the Conqueror set to work with a fixed purpose to root out the use of the English tongue."

était l'idiome des serfs, des gens de métier, des
gardeurs de troupeaux, et les poëtes, qui chan-
taient pour les hautes classes, ne composaient
qu'en pur normand; mais au nord de la Tweed,
l'anglais était la langue favorite des ménestrels
attachés à la cour; il était poli, travaillé, gra-
cieux, recherché même, tandis que de l'autre
côté du même fleuve, il devenait rude et sans
grâce comme les malheureux qui le parlaient.[4]
And again of the French language in England:

Il y remplaça insensiblement la langue sax-
onne, qui, n'étant plus parlée que par la partie
de la nation la plus pauvre et la plus grossière,
tomba autant au-dessous du nouvel idiome anglo-
normand, que celui-ci était au-dessous du français, langage de la cour, du baronnage et de
quiconque prétendait au bon ton et aux belles
manières.[5]

The idea that English remained entirely in the
background for more than three centuries after the
Conquest is often reflected in what is said of the language in the time of Edward III. Thus Pauli, in his
Bilder aus Alt-England (1st ed., 1860) has this definite pronouncement:

Wir haben keinen genügenden Beweis, dass
nur einer der drei ersten Edwards geläufig

---

[4] *Op. cit.*, p. 5.
[5] II, 378.
18

englisch gesprochen habe; dem dritten unter ihnen noch soll es schwer geworden sein, bei einer öffentlichen Gelegenheit drei Worte in der · Volkssprache hinter einander hervorzubringen.[6]

Pauli's statement led Longman (*Life and Times of Edward the Third,* II, 72) to say:

King Edward the Third was barely able even to speak English, always wrote his dispatches in French, and his proclamations were often made in that language.[7]

Pauli, as already noted, gives no authority for his statement regarding King Edward's English. Long-

---

[6] The quotation is from the edition of 1876, pp. 194–5. Pauli gives no authority for the statement, and Freeman, who quotes it *(Norman Conquest,* V, 597), says he knows of none. Nor is there any authority given in Pauli's continuation of Lappenberg's *Geschichte von England,* pp. 307–504, relating to the reign of Edward III. It is Freeman, also, who mentions the Roman manuscript of Froissart, used below, but who did not consider it in detail, as the period of Edward III was beyond that he was treating.

[7] Longman's footnote to the above quotes the translation of Pauli made in 1861. We get some idea of the modernity of Pauli by his giving 1328 as the year of Chaucer's birth; and of Longman by his quoting as Chaucer's, on the same page with the above sentence, Thomas Usk's *Testament of Love.* Pauli and Longman are perhaps responsible for such a remark as that of Professor Kittredge, in his admirable *Chaucer and his Poetry,* p. 37:
"King Edward had but slight acquaintance with the English language, and no interest at all in English literature."
Over against these unsupported assertions of Pauli and Longman might be placed that of the oldest biographer of Edward III, Joshua Barnes, who says in his *History of Edward III* (1688), p. 912: "He understood Latine, French, Spanish, Italian, and High and Low Dutch, besides his Native Language." Barnes's *History,* too, is said by J. F. Tout to be still "in some ways" "less unsatisfactory" than the Longman or Mackinnon Lives of the same monarch.

man has added what is perhaps the main reason for
Pauli's language: Edward's use of French in dispatches and sometimes in proclamations. But the
writing of dispatches in French, and the use of
French or Latin in proclamations do not indicate
that English may not also have been known and used
by both king and secretary. In the use of French
for public documents the scribes were merely following a long established custom, going back to the time
of Richard I, the first king after the Conquest of
whose reign no English public document is preserved.
One may compare Cromwell's use of Latin in foreign
dispatches, or Frederick the Great's use of French in
more modern times. On the other hand, as early as
1258, when Henry III wished to reach the people of
all England, he sent out the Provisions of Oxford in
English as well as in Latin and French.

Besides, ignorance of English on the part of
English kings, even if it were based on incontestable
proofs, does not support the conceptions of Thierry
and Scott regarding the language in the country as a
whole. The first two Georges in the eighteenth century could not speak English, and the second George
also used French in his correspondence.[8] Yet this
does not argue even a decadence of the English lan-

---

[8] Palgrave, *History of Normandy and England*, III, 635–6,
used this later parallel, and noted that "the correspondence
between George II and the Prince of Wales, as laid before
Parliament during their unhappy discussions, is wholly in
the French language."

guage among their subjects. That kings of Norman and Angevin birth did not use English freely, does not prove that English was not in general well understood by their courtiers, or even by themselves. Moreover, that great nobles and churchmen used Norman or Angevin French does not necessarily argue that English was not also known and used by most of them.

But are there facts to oppose such contentions as those of Pauli and Longman regarding Edward Third's asserted ignorance of English? I shall consider specifically the status of the language in the time of Edward III, and his own use of it, because he is often brought forward so prominently in discussions of the subject. This is the more surprising, too, since his reign fell in the century of the great victory of English as a national language. Of this we have more than incidental allusions. Before half of Edward's reign had ended, the reaction against French in the schools had been begun by John Cornwall, as we know from John of Trevisa's translation of Higden's *Polychronicon* (Bk. I, ch. lix), a passage which has often been printed. Seven or eight years before Chaucer wrote the *Book of the Duchess*, that is in 1362, the Commons had been granted their petition that pleadings in the law courts might be in English. The next year parliament was opened by a declaration of the summons in the native tongue.

Soon English petitions to parliament, English wills, letters, and gild statutes appear. Side by side with these more incidental allusions, a new and abundant literature is the open evidence of the new place the English language was already holding in Britain.

Yet besides these there are contemporary allusions to the growing use of English which have not been fully appreciated. The Roman manuscript of Froissart, barely referred to by Freeman, was discovered by Baron Kervyn de Lettenhove as late as 1860. It was then found that the medieval chronicler had prepared a fourth redaction of parts of his great history, with considerably more of detail in certain particulars than he had earlier used. Among them are significant references to the use of English in the time of Edward III,—references numerous enough to confirm each other, and more weighty because of their wholly incidental character.

The first relates to an incident of Edward Third's first year on the throne, when he was a boy of fourteen. After the defiance of Edward by Robert, King of Scotland, the English king asked Sir John of Hainaut to assist him against the Scots, and the latter responded with a great company. The young king, to feast the Hainauters, held a great court at the House of the Minor Friars in London on Trinity Sunday (June 11), 1327. There a fight broke out between the English archers and the grooms of the visitors. In the parley which followed, the king addressed Sir John, and the latter answered him in a defensive plea. At this, perhaps so as not to be understood by the Hainauters, Sir Thomas Wake spoke in English to the king. The passage reads:

> Donc respondi messire Thomas Wage [Wake], marescal dou roi, et dist au roi en son langage: "Sire, il parole sagement, et peut estre tout ce qu'il dist."[9]

Whether this was so that the Hainauters might not perceive the drift of the remark, as seems reasonable, we are at least told a little later that they could not understand English:

> Et disoient bien li auqun baron et chevalier d'Engleterre as chevaliers de Hainnau, qui point n'entendoient le langage des Englois, et liquel ne haioient point les Hainnuiers, mais le disoient pour euls aviser, à la fin que il fuissent le mieuls sus lor garde: "Chil archier de Lincole, et moult d'aultres communs, pour l'amour d'euls, vous ont quelliet en grant haine; et se il n'estoient brisiet de par le roi, il le vous mousteroient et de fait."[10]

This incident, slight as it is, shows that Edward III as a young king must have understood English. Besides, it must have been no unusual thing to ad-

---

[9] Froissart's *Chroniques*, Luce ed., I, 266; De Lettenhove's ed., V, 127.

[10] Froissart (Luce), I, 267; (De Lettenhove), V, 128.

dress him in that language. Otherwise his marshal would not have presumed to use the native speech in such a way.

Some confirmation of the fact that the monarchs of England at this time were addressed in English is furnished by another incident. When Edward II was in the hands of his enemies, after his deposition and the election of his son to the kingship, he was treated with great indignity. One circumstance in the *Vita et Mors Edwardi Secundi* is reported as follows:

> Duxerunt etiam exemplar patientiae per grangias castri Bristollii, ubi de foeno factam coronam capiti, jamdudum oleo sancto consecrato, imposuit nefarius ille de Gorney, ausus contingere Christum Dei: cui illudentes ironia nimis acerba milites dixerunt, "Fare forth, syr Kynge."[11]

[11] *Chronicles of Edward I and II* (Rolls Series), II, 316. The Latin quoted is based on an earlier French account, in which the words to the king read, "Avant, sire kinge." Even this might all be English, since French *avaunt* in this sense is recorded in English of not many years later, the English translation of the *Romance of the Rose*, 3959 and 4790. That English alone would have been used by the common soldiers seems the only probability. The Latin translator at least so understood them.

The incident was reported to Sir Thomas de la Moore, at whose suggestion it was recorded, by another Englishman who was present with the king and his guards when it occurred, a William Bishop (Gullielmus Bisschop). It was recorded in the French form within twenty years of the event. Bishop Stubbs, in his introductory discussion of the *Vita*, says: "I believe it to be in the main trustworthy."

Now such a terse record surely does not mean that once and once only some such expression was used to the deposed king. It must mean that the mock heroics were many, and frequently repeated in the several months during which every kind of ill-treatment was heaped upon him. It equally follows, also, that these expressions of ironical courtesy could have had no point, even to his brutal captors, if Edward II had not well understood English. The record seems reasonably good evidence that the father of Edward III, as the son, did understand the language of Englishman. Whether Edward III, with whom we have especially to do, could speak English depends on other passages which will be cited. Meanwhile, we have information regarding the use of English by the great nobles.

When Edward went to France in 1329 to pay homage to the king of France for the duchy of Guienne, he was accompanied to Amiens by a considerable body of high retainers. They included, as recited in the first of Froissart's paragraphs, the Bishops of London and Lincoln, perhaps the Bishop of Winchester; four earls,—Henry, Earl of Derby and son of Thomas Earl of Lancaster, together with the Earls of Salisbury, Warwick, and Hereford; six barons,— Lords Reginald Cobham, Thomas Wake, marshal of England, Richard Stanford, and Lords Percy, Manny, and Mowbray; more than forty other nobles and

knights.[12] The retainers were clearly representative
of the nobility of England, as of its intelligence and
knightly custom. But the homage of Edward was
not wholly satisfactory to the French king, and the
English king was not ready to proceed further until
he had consulted the records in his own country.

To explain this breaking off in the paying of homage, Froissart says, in the Roman manuscript:

> La nature des Englès est telle que tous jours
> il se crienment à estre decheu et repliquent tant
> apriès une cose que mervelles; et ce que il aue-
> ront en couvenant un jour, il le deliieront l'autre.
> Et à tout ce les encline à faire ce que il n'enten-
> dent point bien tous les termes dou langage de
> France; ne on ne lor scet conment bouter en la
> teste, se ce n'est tout dis à lor pourfit. Et en-
> corez en avint adonc ensi. Dont li signeur et li
> per de France, qui là estoient venu et asamblé
> pour celle matère, en furent trop fort esmervil-
> liet; et en parlèrent especiaument à mesire Jehan
> de Hainnau, et li remoustrèrent tous les poins et
> les articles dou dit honmage conment il se devoit
> faire.[13]

---

[12] The list of those who were to go to France is given in
more detail (Nomina illorum qui cum Rege transfretarunt)
in Rymer's *Fœdera*, IV, 387–8.

[13] Luce's *Froissart*, I, 306; De Lettenhove's V, 237. The
document finally signed by representatives of the French and
English kings is in Rymer's *Fœdera*, IV, 765.

Here, then, is admirable evidence that English was
not only the usual language of a large circle of prominent courtiers of Edward III, but that they could
not have been thoroughly acquainted with any other.
For surely there was not enough difference between
the French of England and the French of the Continent, so that men commonly using the one should
have failed to understand the other. But there is
further direct proof that English was the usual language of the great nobles, even in state affairs. Moreover, the next passage shows that Edward III must
not only have understood English, but have sanc-
tioned its use in a great council of the nation.

In 1337 Edward III, urged by Count Robert of
Artois to make war upon the king of France, placed
the matter before a council of the realm, or many
councils, as Froissart says in another place.[14] One of
these was a great gathering at London in the palace
of Westminster, "consisting of the prelates, the nobles, and the mayors of cities and towns of England."
The account goes on to tell how the king, in order to
be seen the more easily, was seated in royal state,
with the crown on his head and royal scepter in his
hand. Two steps below were the prelates, earls, and
barons, while below them were six hundred knights.
In the aisles were the men of the Cinque Ports, and
the mayors of cities and towns. When all were

---

[14] *Chroniques* (De Lettenhove), V, 321.

assembled and silence made, as Froissart goes on to say:

> Adonc se leva uns clers d'Engleterre, licensiiés en droit et en lois, et moult bien pourveus de trois langages, de latin, de françois et dou langage englès; et conmença à parler moult sagement. Et estoit messires Robers d'Artois dalés lui, liquels l'avoit enfourmé, trois ou quatre jours devant, de tout ce que il devoit dire. Si parla atempreement et remoustra tout en hault, et [en] englois, à la fin que il fust mieuls entendus de toutez gens, car tous jours sçut on mieuls ce que on voelt dire et proposer ens ou langage où on est d'enfance introduit qu'en un aultre, tous les poins et les articles desquels messires Robers d'Artois les avoit, le roi, le clerc et auquns signeurs, enfourmés; et con proçains li rois, lors sires, en quelle istance il estoient là venu et asamblé, estoit de l'iretage et de la couronne de France. Et qant il ot remoustré la parole tout au lonch, par grant avis et par bon loisir, tant que tout l'avoient volentierz oï, il demanda ens ou nom dou roi à avoir consel de toutes ces coses.[15]

After this presentation of the case, Earl Henry of Lancaster spoke at length, and the others "respondirent tout d'une vois: 'Il dist bien.' " The implication

---

[15] Luce's *Froissart*, I, 360; De Lettenhove, V. 326.

clearly is that Earl Henry spoke in English, and that the king understood if he did not reply in that language. That Henry of Lancaster knew English is attested by another and more dramatic incident. At the naval battle against the Spaniards (Espagnols sur Mer), August 29, 1350, we are told:

> Li dus de Lancastre, assés priès de là, se combatoit à Espangnols et oy criier en englois: "Rescouse, rescouse au prince de Gallas!" Si dist à ses chevaliers: "Alons deviers mon cousin le prince; je voi bien que il a à faire." Donc chil qui tenoient le gouvernal de sa nef, le fissent tourner à force, et li aultre estendirent lor single contrement; et tout combatant, vosissent ou non li Espagnol, il vinrent jusque à la nef du prinche que li Espagnol tenoient à dangier.[16]

It is not explicitly stated that the Duke's second command was in English, but nothing else can be believed for a moment. Commands in different languages at such a time are not to be thought of.

So far, proof appears in this Roman manuscript of Edward Third's full understanding of the English speech. It is also certain that he could and did use English on occasion. After Edward's great success against the Scotch at Halidon Hill the great nobles came out from Berwick to do homage, as their fa-

---

[16] Luce's *Froissart*, IV, 326; De Lettenhove, IV, 269.

thers had done homage to Edward's grandfather at the same place. The scene is described as follows:

> Tout li signeur d'Engleterre, qui là estoient en la presence dou roi, s'ouvrirent et laissièrent les Escoçois passer. Il enclinèrent le roi, et non plus avant. Li rois les requelli de une parole tant seullement, ce fu que il dist en son langage: "Bien venant." De trop petit se disfèrent li uns langage de l'autre.[17]

The passage shows somewhat more than the speaking of a single word. For one thing, it was not to be expected that the young king, even then only twenty, should have had much to say to rebellious nobles now returning to their allegiance. Nor was there need that he should have been conciliatory in any sense. Besides, too, we can hardly believe he had been taught like a parrot to pronounce a single vocable. Indeed, the last sentence indicates the king knew enough English to compare his Midland form with that of the North, and was interested in the comparison.

If, however, there was still any doubt of Edward's understanding the language of his people and speaking it to some extent, that doubt ought to be set at rest by another passage in the Roman manuscript which can not be explained away. It describes with somewhat greater detail than any other the well-

----

[17] Luce's *Froissart*, I, 324; De Lettenhove, V, 277.

known scene of the captive burgesses of Calais in 1347. We are told that Edward was in the hall of his lodging when it was announced Sir Walter Manny was come with the haltered prisoners. The king went out to receive them, followed by a great concourse. Then Froissart says:

En la place toutes gens se ouvrirent à l'encontre de li. Si passèrent oultre messires Gautiers et li siis bourgois, et s'en vint devant le roi et li dist en langage englois: "Très chiers sires, vechi la presentation de la ville de Calais à vostre ordenance." Li rois se taisi tous quois et regarda moult fellement sus euls, car moult les haioit et tous les habitans de Calais, pour les grans damages et contraires que dou temps passet li avoient fait.

Chil siis bourgois se missent tantos en genouls devant le roi, et dissent ensi en joindant lors mains: "Gentils sires et nobles rois, veés nous chi siis, qui avons esté d'ancesserie bourgois de Calais et grans marceans par mer et par terre, et vous aportons les clefs de la ville et dou chastiel de Calais, et les vous rendons à vostre plaisir, et nous mettons en tel point que vous nous veés en vostre pure volenté, pour sauver le demorant dou peuple de Calais qui souffert a moult de grietés. Si voelliés de nous avoir pité et merchi par vostre haute noblèce." Certes il

n'i ot adonc en la place, conte, baron, ne chevalier, ne vaillant honme qui se peuist astenir de
plorer de droite pité, ne qui peuist parler en
grant pièce. Li rois regarda sus euls très crueu-
sement, car il avoit le coer si dur et si enfelloniient
de grans courous, que il ne pot parler; et qant
il parla, il conmanda en langage englois que on
lor copast les testes tantos. Tout li baron et li
chevalier qui là estoient, en plorant prioient, si
acertes que faire pooient, au roi que il en vosist
avoir pité et merchi; mès il n' i voloit entendre.[18]

Upon this, Manny begged the king in the name of
his sovereign gentility and nobleness (souverainne
gentillece et noblece), to have pity on the men who
had offered their lives for others. But the king stops
him as follows:

Adonc se grigna li rois et dist: "Mauni, Mauni,
soufrés vous. Il ne sera aultrement." Mesires
Gautiers de Mauni [lacuna here] et n'osa plus
parler, car li rois dist moult ireusement: "On
fache venir là cope teste. Chil de Calais ont
fait morir tant de mes honmes que il couvient
ceuls morir aussi."

Then it is that the queen makes her pathetic plea
and the king grants the lives of the brave Frenchmen to her supplication. Nothing is said about the
language of these last speeches, but if English was

---

[18] Luce's *Froissart*, IV, 29; De Lettenhove, IV, 214.

used by Manny and the king in the first place so that the captives should not understand what was said, as is probable, then that language would have been continued to the end of the scene. In any case, as Freeman briefly mentions, there is no doubt of the use of English both by the king and by Manny.

It is difficult to see how these several passages can be gainsaid, or how they can be very differently interpreted from what has been here attempted. Of course, so far as the exact incidents are concerned, Froissart was at most reporting the statements of others. He himself could not have been present at these early events. But regarding the use of English by Edward III and his courtiers, Froissart was a wholly competent witness. As is well known, he had first visited England a score of years before Edward's death, and his opportunities for observing king and court were unlimited. Moreover, Froissart could have had no reason for deceiving contemporaries or posterity on such a point. If anything, we should have expected his sympathies to be with the use of French in England. When, therefore, he testifies to the use of the English language, his testimony must be regarded as doubly valuable.

But the question may be asked, why then, in this fourth and last redaction, did he thus add these significant references to the use of English when he had not mentioned the latter fact before? I suggest a possible explanation. The last half of the fourteenth century was one of growing consciousness regarding the English language, and its peculiar status in the land of its birth. Trevisa's additions to Higden, already noted,[19] are one evidence of this. Chaucer in his *Troilus* (V, 1793f.) had glanced at "so greet diversitee in English," especially "in wryting of our tonge," and begged that no one would "miswrite" and "mismetre" his poem, as he also begged "Adam Scriveyn" to be more careful in his copying. Thomas Usk in his *Testament of Love,* written about 1387, after according to "clerks" their Latin and to Frenchmen their French, adds: "And let us showe our fantasyes in suche wordes as we lerneden of our dames tonge." With such new consciousness regarding the status of English finding expression even in literature, it may be that Froissart became impressed with the new spirit, and thus came to note, as he had not thought of doing before, the use of English by one or another of his characters. At any rate, even if we can not fully account for them, we may not disregard these allusions to the use of the native tongue.

One thing further may be said of Edward Third's relation to the English language. When in 1346 he took the French city of Caen, he found there the Ordinance of Normandy, purporting to be an agreement between Philip of France and the Duke of Nor-

[19] [See above, p. 276f.]
19

mandy for a second Norman conquest of England.[20]
This document was at once used by Edward to inspire patriotism in his English subjects. Besides, it
is in point that the English king emphasized the purpose of the confederates "to destroy and wholly annihilate the English nation and language." The latter
idea is the noteworthy factor.

This reference to the English language occurs in
the Introduction to the Ordinance when laid before
parliament, as follows:

> Et sur ce fu moustre une Ordinance faite
> par le dit Adversaire, & ascuns Grants de
> France & de Normandie, a destruire & anientier
> tote la Nation & la Lange Engleys: Et de faire
> Execution de ceste l'Ordinance le dit Adversaire
> avoit ordeignez le Count de Eu, & le Chaumber-
> leyn de Tankerville, od grant Multitude des
> Gentz d'armes, Genevois & Gentz a pie de y estre
> alez. Mes sicome Dieu voleit, les ditz Count &
> Chaumberleyn furent pris a Caen, & plusours
> de lour Gentz tuez, & ascuns de eux pris, si q'ils

---

[20] Michelet, *Histoire de France*, IV, 323, was the first to
throw discredit upon this Ordinance, suggesting that it was a
forgery. More recently some doubt of its genuineness has been
expressed by an English historian, as by Sir. J. H. Ramsay
in his *Genesis of Lancaster* (I, 324), who speaks of it as
"a real or pretended compact." For the purpose of this discussion it makes no difference whether the Ordinance was
real or forged, since the use of it is the important thing· On
the other hand, surely Philip of Valois and John I of Normandy were quite as capable of entering into such an agreement as Edward III was of forging it.

ount faillez quant a ore de lour purpos, ent loez soit Dieux. De quele Ordinance le copie s'ensuyt, en la forme souzescrite.[21]

Now, the Ordinance itself does not mention the English language specifically, but does propose a new Norman Conquest which should be thoroughgoing. One passage will show this purpose:

> Item, Acordez est, que en cel cas que Dieu eidant le Roialme d'Engleterre par le dit Voiage se conquerra, le Conquest serra fait tut en noun & l'onur du dit Monsieur le Duc; et que tut ce que le Roi d'Engleterre y a, serra & demorra au dit Monsieur le Duc come Rois & Seigneurs, & as Droitz & as Honurs que le Roi d'Engleterre les tient.[22]

This Ordinance Edward III at once sent over to England, and the Archbishop of Canterbury preached upon it at St. Paul's, doubtless by the king's order.[23] How fully the Archbishop emphasized the

---

[21] *Rotuli Parliamentorum*, II, 158.

[22] The Ordinance closes with the words: "Ce feust fait au Boys de Vincenii, le xxiii jour de Marcz, l'an xxxviii'" [that is 1338].

[23] Robert of Avesbury, *De Gestis Regis Edwardi Tertii*, p. 363:

"In vigilia Assumptionis beatae Mariae, virginis gloriosae, anno Domini millesimo cccmoxlvito, reverendus pater dominus Johannes de Stratforde, Cantuariensis archiepiscopus, ante processionem generalem, pro pace et dicto rege Anglorum tunc, ut praemittitur, infra regnum Franciae militante, a clero et populo Londoniensi illo die solempniter faciendam, verbum Dei ipsis clero et populo ad crucem in cimiterio ecclesiae Sancti Pauli Londoniis praedicans et exponens, inter

destruction of the English language we do not know,
but presumably the same introduction which accompanied the parliamentary copy was in his hands and
that he made the most of it. This would seem to be
implied by another document which bears upon the
subject.

Not only did Edward lay the Ordinance of Normandy before parliament and have the highest func-
tionary of the English church expound it to the people of London, but he took pains to have it more
widely disseminated. A long communication, with
the title "De Causa Guerrae, contra Philippum de
Valesio, Clero & Populo exponenda," was sent to the

caetera publicavit quod nobilis comes Huntingdoniae, qui cum
dicto rege Anglorum in conflictu habito apud Cadamum fue-
rat febribus fatigatus, ad Angliam tunc reversus, literas
quasdam, inventas in Cadamo, continentes praesumptuosam
Normannorum confoederationem seu ordinationem ad sub-
versionem ipsius regis et regni Angliae, per consilium dicti
domini P[hilippi] de Valesio ordinatas et callide adinventas,
sibi tradidit vulgariter exponendas, ut per hoc excitaret cle-
rum et populum eo libentius preces fundere salutares pro
pace et dicto domino rege Anglorum et suis, qui ipsos Nor-
mannos, per medium ipsorum transeuntes, in suis propriis
laribus edocebant, ne ad infrascripta per ipsos dictis regi et
regno comminata mitterent manus suas."
Murimuth's *Continuatio Chronicarum* (Rolls Series), pp.
211–12, gives the account with even more of feeling: "Prae-
dictam ordinationem Gallicorum, licet nullum sortiebatur
effectum, publicavit archiepiscopus duodecimo die Augusti in
cimiterio Sancti Pauli Londoniis in sermone suo habito cum
processione solempni, ut per hoc excitaret populum regni, ut
eo ferventius diligerent regem et devotione pro prosperitate
et expeditione ipsius orarent, qui ipse populum suum a dictis
Gallicorum machinationibus conservavit indempnes, se ipsum
et suos, ut praemittitur, per terram et aquam multis periculis
exponendo."
Knighton, *Chronicon*, II, 431, also mentions the Ordinance
of Normandy and the intended invasion of England.

heads of both the Dominican (Preaching or Black) Friars and the Augustines, evidently that they might use it wherever they went.[24] This document, after reciting at length the case against Philip, proceeds:

> Set ipse, diu per Tractatus hujusmodi nos protrahens fallaciter sub incerto, & Expensis gravibus nos exponens, nichil nobis facere voluit in effectu; set semper, sub dictorum umbra Tractatuum, cumulavit peramplius Mala Malis, nos & nostros persequens hostiliter, tam in Terra, quam in Mari, & in subversionem Linguae Anglicanae cominans pro viribus & conspirans, etc., etc.

The emphasis, it will be seen, is again placed on the destruction of the English language.

Now it is unbelievable that the destruction of the English language would have been mentioned so prominently if there had not been hope of its appealing to the popular pride. It is true that appeal had first been made by Edward's grandfather, Edward I, who had laid before parliament in his summons of 1295 what he asserted was the purpose of the French king:

---

[24] Rymer's *Fœdera*, V, 496–8. This is the copy to the Dominicans, as shown by the beginning:

"Rex, dilecto sibi in Christo, Provinciali Ordinis Fratrum praedicatorum in Anglia, Salutem."

At the close, however, is the note, "Eodem modo mandatum est Priori & Conventui Sancti Augustini London, mutatis mutandis."

Linguam Anglicam, si conceptae iniquitatis proposito detestabili potestas correspondeat (quod Deus avertat) omnino de terra delere proponit.[25]

Now, however, a half century later, the third Edward carries the appeal directly to the people, as if the matter were at this later time one of greater popular interest. We can scarcely be wrong in supposing it was so.

The use made by Edward of the Ordinance of Normandy, together with the evidence of his own knowledge and use of English speech, are good reasons for believing that the victory of English over French as the language even of the court was complete sometime before the period usually set. The conservatism of the schools would have persisted considerably after the wish for English in teaching had been often expressed. John Cornwall was doubtless not the first to see the importance of the reform, though the first of the schoolmaster class to institute the change. The desire for English in the courts must have preceded, perhaps for a generation, the actual granting of the permission to use it. The wish for an English "summons" for parliament must have long antedated the actual petition of the Commons. Besides, it was no bolt out of a clear sky when in 1386 the Mercers

---

[25] Rymer's *Foedera*, II, 689. This copy of the summons is that sent to the Archbishop of Canterbury and the clergy; it is reproduced in Stubbs, *Select Charters*, 484.

of London presented in English their vigorous and picturesque petition to parliament. Such use of the mother tongue must have been only the expression of a popular wish that had long been growing among London tradesmen. That class would scarcely have risked its hope for a redress of serious grievances on the use of a despised tongue.

One may well go further. The quantity of literature in English during the whole of the fourteenth century, and especially the second half, can not be accounted for on the supposition that the English language was only beginning to make its way among the upper classes.[26] Besides, it seems scarcely pos-

---

[26] I can not forbear quoting two other examples of what seems to me a curious obscuring of facts. Legouis, in his excellent *Geoffrey Chaucer*, has this on the subject of language—I quote the translation:

"Whilst the use of English was steadily extending to all classes throughout the fourteenth century, and making its way into the schools, the law-courts, and the parliament, poets were still groping for a proper medium. John Gower, the contemporary and friend of Chaucer, bore witness to the uncertainty by writing the first of his three great poems in French, the second in Latin, and the third in English. But English was split up into dialects differing sufficiently from each other to hamper intercommunication; the differences in vocabulary and syntax were such as to render a man barely intelligible to those who did not speak his own dialect."

Here Legouis, in using Gower for his purpose, has neglected practically every other author of the time. There is no evidence that Minot, Chaucer, Trevisa, the poet of *Pearl*, or the authors of *Piers Plowman, Mandeville's Travels*, and the Wyclifite *Bible* were "groping after a medium." Legouis must have in mind his countryman Thierry, and the latter's view of English conditions. As to dialects, too, Legouis has apparently forgotten that Chaucer made his Reeve of the *Canterbury Tales* use the Northern dialect to some extent, while he also made the Parson say,

sible that Laurence Minot, between 1333 and 1352, could have composed his stirring national lyrics on Edward Third's Scottish victories without some hope of their appealing, not only to prominent Englishmen, but even to the king himself.[27] Nor is there evidence that Chaucer, squire and courtier and king's

---

> I am a Southren man,
> I can nat geste — rum, ram, ruf — by lettre,

showing that Chaucer at least knew the alliterative literature of the West and Northwest Midland. The difference between the dialects is often greatly exaggerated.

The latter exaggeration appears also in a statement by H. W. C. Davis, *England under the Normans and Angevins*, p. 183:

"For social purposes the tongue of Caedmon and Alfred was altogether inadmissible. It could hardly be otherwise, since the English tongue had differentiated into dialects so various that the Yorkshireman was unintelligible to a native of the western shires. The north and south communicated perforce through the medium of a foreign language."

Mr. Davis's remark on the dialects apparently rests on a rather violent interpretation of William of Malmesbury *(Gesta Pontificum Anglorum*, Bk. III, Prologue, Rolls Series, p. 209). One might find quite as prejudiced statements about Scotch of the eighteenth century, for example in the *Monthly Review* on Burns, December, 1786. But that "the north and south communicated perforce through the medium of a foreign language," that is, French, is delicious. Mr. Davis has forgotten that William the Conqueror used English and Latin, never French, in public documents, and that no French public document is known before 1215, a decade after England had lost Normandy, and a century and a half after the Conquest. In less than half a century, also, English was again resumed for public use, as in the proclamation of the Provisions of Oxford in the reign of Henry III.

[27] Miss Clara L. Thompson, in the *Cambridge History of English Literature*, I, 400, has carried conjecture considerably further: "Minot seems to have been a professional gleeman, who earned his living by following the camp and entertaining soldiers with the recitation of their own heroic deeds. It is possible, however, that his skill in versification may have led to his promotion to the post of minstrel to the king, and that he held some recognized office about the court."

man as he always was, could have been leading a revolt against courtly taste when he devoted his long literary life, beginning more than a decade before Edward III passed away, to practically exclusive use of the English speech. If Edward III and his court largely employed French to the exclusion of the native language, the young squire, dependent upon court favor for preferment as he was, would hardly have adopted the despised English. Has not too much been made of purely negative evidence, at least for the fourteenth century?[28]

In any case, the notion that Edward did not understand and speak English, and that it was not commonly known and used by the great nobles most intimately associated with him, would seem to be set at rest.

---

[28] Gower was a laggard in the use of English, it is true. But Gower was not dependent on the court, and seems never to have had any great popular purpose. He was a man of catholic tastes, with sufficient leisure and detachment to satisfy them in his own way.

THE OLD FRENCH DIPHTHONG EI (EY) AND MIDDLE ENGLISH METRICS*

I. *Seint, Seinte*

In §140 of the Introduction to my *Middle English Reader* (1905) I wrote:

"The OF. *seint* often appears as *seinte*, but not exclusively before feminines. It is probable that both forms were adopted without regard of the OF. distinction of gender, though *seinte* would naturally occur before certain feminines, as *Seinte Marie*." To this statement I was led by some fairly full examination of the matter in various texts. Moreover, in my *Selections from Chaucer* (1911), I discarded Professor Skeat's *sëynt*, printing *Seinte Loy* (Prol. 120), *Seinte Poules* (509), *Seinte Peter* (697). Dr. MacCracken did the same in his edition of *Chaucer* (1913). More recently Professor Tatlock has also rejected "Skeat's impossible *sëynt*" *(Mod. Lang. Notes,* XXXI, 139, footnote), and has given some further examples from Chaucer to support the use of *seinte (seynte)* before masculines. It seems desirable to bring together a larger number of examples to illustrate the statement above and perhaps add something to the discussion.

The examples may be classified as follows, refer-

* *Rom. Rev.* Vol. VIII, pp. 68–76 (1917).

ences being to Chaucer, unless otherwise specified. The predominance of masculine forms is of course due to the greater number of men saints. Vocatives are excluded, as not now under consideration, and no other strictly weak forms occur.

I. Seint (seynt) is monosyllabic and unstressed, (1) before names beginning with a vowel and accented on the first syllable, whether masculine or feminine: Seint Yve *(Ship. T.* 227; *Som. T.* 235); Seint Austin *(Ship. T.* 259); Seint Anne *(Man. of L. T.* 543); Seinte Anne *(Friar's T.* 315), where of course final *–e* was not pronounced; Seint Ambrose *(Sec. N's T.* 271); Seynt Idiot *(Troil.* I, 910).

(2) before a name beginning with a consonant and accented on the first syllable, whether masculine or feminine: Seint Julian *(Prol.* 340; Gower, *Conf. Amant. III,* 34); Seint Jame *(Prol.* 466; *Reeve's T.* 344; *W. of B's Prol.* 312; *Clerk's T.* 1098; *H. of F.* 885); Seint Joce (W. *of B's Prol.* 483); Seint Nicholas *(Prior.'s T.* 62); Seint Poules *(N. Pr. Prol.* 14); Seint Paul *(N. Pr. T.* 621); Seint Ronyan *(Host to Phys.* 24); Seint John *(Som. T.* 92, 544); Seint Gyle *(Can. Yeo. T.* 632; *H. of F.* 1183); Seynt Valentyne *(P. of F.* 309, 322, 386; *L. of G. W.* 145B, 131A; *Amor. Comp.* 85); Seynt Note *(Mil. T.* 585), if a nine-syllable line as is probable; Seint

Peter, Seint Poul (Gower, *Conf. Amant.* II, 3335) ; Seynt Venus *(L. of G. W.* 338B), if a nine-syllable line as seems certain; in the A text, however, *Seint* is monosyllabic with the name stressed on the last syllable (compare II, 1).

II. Seint (seynt) is monosyllabic and stressed before a name of two or more syllables accented on the second: Seint Beneit *(Prol.* 173) ; Seint Thomas *(Prol.* 826; *Mil. T.* 105, 239, 275; *W. of B's Prol.* 666; *Merch. Prol.* 18; *H. of F.* 1131) ; Seint Cutberd *(Reeve's T.* 207) ; Seint Denys *(Ship. T.* 59, 67, 151, 308, 326) ; Seint Martyn *(Ship. T.* 148) ; Seint Austin *(Prior Prol.* 7) ; Seint Edward *(M'k's Prol.* 82) ; Seint Kenelm *(N. Pr. T.* 290) ; Seint Ronyan *(Host to Phys.* 34) ; Seint Eleyne *(Pard. T.* 623) ; Seint Jerome *(W. of B's Prol.* 674) ; Seint Dunstan *(Friar's T.* 204) ; Seint Simoun *(Som.* T. 386) ; Seynt Johan *(B. of D.* 1319) ; Seint Cecilie *(Sec. N's T.* 85, 550) ; Seint Cecile *(Can. Yeo. Pr.* I) ; Seynt Cecyle *(L. of G. W.* 426B, 416A) ; Seint Venus *(L. of G. W.* 313A) ; Seint Gregoire (Gower, *Conf. Amant.* V, 1756).

III. Seinte (seynte) is dissyllabic and stressed, (1) before a name accented on the first syllable, whether masculine or feminine: Seinte Marie *(Host to Phys.* 22; *Pard. T.* 357; *Friar's T.* 306; *Merch. T.* 1174) ; Seynte Clare *(H. of F.*

1066) ; Seynt [e] Venus *(W. of B's T.* 604; possibly also *L. of G. W.* 388B, but compare I, 2) ;
Seinte Cecile *(Sec. N's T.* 274) at beginning of
line, though possibly either with the name accented on the second syllable (so coming under
II), or even with *Seinte* a monosyllable and the
name a trissyllable accented on the first;
Seynt[e] Loy *(Prol.* 120; *Friar's T.* 266) ;
Seynt[e] Poules *(Prol.* 509) ; Seynt[e] Peter
(Prol. 697) ; perhaps Seynt[e] Note *(Mil. T.*
585) or better under I, 2, as a nine-syllable
line.[1]

(2) before *charitee* and *trinitee* in dative
phrases: Seynte charitee *(Kt. T.* 863; N's Pr.
T. 500; *Som. T.* 411) ; per seinte charitee (Gower, *Conf. Amant.* IV, 964) ; seinte trinitee *(Som.
T.* 116).[2]

---

[1] The Globe Chaucer reads seinte Venus *(W. of B's Prol.*
604); seinte Loy *(Prol.* 120; *Friar's T.* 266); seinte Peter
(Prol. 697); seinte Note *(Mil. T.* 585), but sëint Poules *(Prol.*
509). Compare its hëynous with split diphthong in *Troilus*
II, 1617.

[2] For more completeness I note the following vocatives:
Seinte Marie *(Merch. T.* 93; *Sir Thop.* 73; *H. of F.* 573);
Seinte Frideswyde *(Mil. T.* 263); Seint Valentyne *(P. of F.*
683; *Comp. to Lodest.* 43). In *Merch. T.* 655 *Seinte Marie*
may best be read *Seint Marie* with accent on the last syllable, though possibly with *Seinte* dissyllabic and *Marie* accented on the first syllable. In *Mil. T.* 297, 300, the vocative
as well as the meter require *Seint[e]*, *Benedight, Seint[e]*
Petres soster, and I think there should be no hesitancy in so
reading; compare Ten Brink, *Chaucers Sprache,* §242. For
Seint Valentyne above, we must assume the occasional loss of
final –e in a vocative, as in *Troil.* I, 458; *Pard. Prol.* 24, 49.

In these examples one or two cases of doubt or difference in reading have already been considered. It may be added of *Seint Poules (N. Pr. Prol.* 14) that, while *Seint* may be monosyllabic with stress on the preceding *by*, it is also possible to read *Seinte, hoste* before the cesural pause then being a monosyllable, as it is in *Manc. Prol.* 56. In *Prol.* 173 a smoother line would be

The reule of Seinte Maure or Seint Beneit, and such reading might be justified, as we shall see. In no other case in Chaucer is *Seint* stressed when followed by a name usually accented on the first syllable, and for this reason I have not included it in the above lists.

Most of these examples need no special explanation. Even if written *Seinte* before a name beginning with a vowel or before a name accented on the second syllable, the final unstressed *–e* would not normally be pronounced. In such cases, therefore, there could be no distinction of gender expressed, even if intended. This accounts for all examples under I, 1 and II. An unstressed *seint*, or *seinte* if it should be so written, is monosyllabic in all cases, as under I, 2, and here again gender could not have been intended by the single form. There remain only the examples under III. In these *seinte (seynte)* can not be a feminine form, since it is quite as necessary to the meter before masculine names like *Loy*,[3] *Poules*, *Peter*, as before the feminine name *Venus* in *W. of B's Prol.* 604.   Besides, it also occurs regularly before *charitee*, *trinitee*, which could hardly have retained their Old French gender relations in English.   The idea that the forms *seint—seinte* represent Old French gender relations breaks down entirely.   Can the two forms be accounted for on grounds of English usage?

No one seems to have brought to this discussion a well-known variation between the forms of strictly English adjectives.   Ten Brink pointed out *(Chaucers Sprache,* §231) that final –e has been added to certain English adjectives by analogy of forms with that ending historically.   He mentions only the two forms *fayr—fayre,* while a considerable number of such double forms might be given, as for instance by Kittredge *(Language of Chaucer's Troilus,* §49).   Let us take for example *fayr—fayre, fresh—fresshe.* Both of these, too, in their longer forms with *–e* are common enough before feminine names, but the longer forms are not invariable before such names. In this respect, therefore, the use of the two forms in each case is practically parallel with that of *seint—seinte.*   In the examples I exclude weak forms

---

[3] Unless we restore in this word its OF. form *Eloy.* Doubtless, however, the shortened form was the more common in English.

of course, as well as those before nouns beginning with a vowel, and for the present all dative phrases.

Thus *fair (fayr)* appears, to quote only a few examples, in "a fair forheed" *(Prol.* 154) ; "a fair for the maistrye" *(Prol.* 165) ; "faire Custance," where *faire* must be a monosyllable *(M. of L's T.* 621) ; "so fair, so debonaire" *(L. of G. W.* 276B) ; "hit be not fair" *(L. of G. W.* 2548). The second form *faire (fayre)* is also frequent, as "faire Venus" *(Comp. of M.* 46; *Kt. T.* 1805) ; "faire Rewthelees" *(Comp. to his L.* 31) ; "fayre Cecilie" *(Sec. N. T.* 115).

Similar examples of *fresh—fresshe* may also be found. Of the first are "gay, fresh, ne jolif" *(R. of R.* 435) : "so fresh, so yong" *(Troil.* II, 636) ; "fresh was his hewe" *(L. of G. W.* 1761). The second form *fresshe* appears often, as "fresshe beautee" *(Pity* 39) ; "robe fresshe" *(R. of R.* 1187) ; "fresshe rede rose" *(P. of F.* 442) ; "fresshe brother Troilus" *(Troil.* II, 157) ; "This Diomede, as fresshe" *(Troil.* V, 844) ; "fresshe flour" *(L. of G. W.* 116B).

Examples of other adjectives of double form might also be cited, as *heigh (hey, hy) — heighe (heye, hye),* and the foreign derived *fals—false.* For the latter compare "fals report" *(Troil.* I, 593) ; "fals felicitee" *(Troil.* III, 814) ; "she is fals" *(Troil.* IV, 616) ; "false worldes brotelnesse" *(Troil.* V, 1832) ; "false Polyphete" *(Troil.* II, 1467), as most manuscripts read the passage.

It must be clear from these examples that the variation of *fair—faire, fresh—fresshe, heigh (hey, hy) —heighe (heye, hye), fals—false,* and we may now add *seint—seinte,* rests on no gender relation. I suggest that the second form with final unstressed *–e* is due to analogy of the large class of adjectives which have that ending for historical reasons. Middle English adjectives, like Middle English nouns, fall into two well-marked classes—those without final unstressed *–e* and those with that ending; cf. my *Mid. Eng. Reader,* §138–9. Some adjectives of the first class regularly assume an inorganic or unhistorical *–e.* Others, as those we are discussing, appear in both forms at different times. Such shifting from one form to another is exactly paralleled by a similar shifting of some nouns between the two similar classes of substantives. As influential, also, may perhaps be considered the constant shifting from strong to weak forms in adjectives capable of weak inflection, as well as the freedom with which an inflectional *–e* in the singular might be used or not for the meter at the pleasure of the poet; cf. Ten Brink *(Chaucers Sprache,* §236).

But another final unstressed *–e* has a bearing upon the subject. Adjectives like nouns sometimes retain such an *–e* in dative phrases. Such datives of nouns have long been recognized, as by Ten Brink, *op. cit.* §201. In *Mid. Eng. Reader,* §126, I have cited

20

for nouns the dative phrases as *on live* "alive," *to
bedde* "to bed," *to wedde* "for a pledge," *for fere* "for
fear," and in §139 (revised ed.) such adjective
phrases as "of *none* gode," "of *harde* grace." To these
may be added as examples from Chaucer "in *olde
tyme*" *(B. of D.* 53) ; "of *olde* tyme" *(Troil.* V, 470) ;
"on *alle* thing" *(B. of D.* 141; "in . . . *salte se*"
(Troil. III, 8) ; "of *ferne* yere" *(Troil.* V, 1176) ; "of
faire yonge fresshe Venus" *(Kt. T.* 1528). With such
examples multiplied as may easily be done, it is impossible not to believe in this occasional dative of the
adjective in dative phrases.[4] Not only, therefore,
may the final unstressed –e of certain adjectives be
due to analogy of adjectives which regularly have
such an ending, but in some cases it may be due to
this retention of final –e in dative phrases.

Enough has been said to show that a variation between *seint—seinte,* as in other such words, can be
accounted for on a wholly English basis. With such
variation established, too, must disappear Skeat's
sëynt forms with the diphthong broken into two syllables,—quite "impossible" in any case, as Professor
Tatlock has implied. Instead of *sëynt* we should read
seinte (seynte) without doubt. The latter form is

---

[4] This dative, not noted by Ten Brink, is occasionally recognized as such by Skeat in his *Glossary,* as also in his *Gram-
matical Outlines to Works of Chaucer,* VI, §78. Manly, *Language of the Legend of Good Women,* §49, has a mild suggestion that certain phrases may perpetuate an old dative con-
struction.

by general analogy of adjectives in final unstressed
–e, as in Seynte Peter *(Prol.* 697), a nominative case,
or more commonly a dative in a dative phrase. For
example, all the other instances in which *seinte
(seynte)* should be read before a masculine noun in
Chaucer, Seynte Loy *(Prol.* 120; *Friar's T.* 266),
Seynte Poules *(Prol.* 509), and possibly Seynte Note
(Mil. T. 585), occur in dative phrases, and may be
regarded as retention of a final unstressed –e from
an older case form. So also Chaucer's seynte charitee *(Kt. T.* 863; *N's Pr. T.* 500, *Som. T.* 411) and
seynte trinitee *(Som. T.* 116) are in dative phrases.[5]

One objection may be met. In Gower's *Confessio
Amantis* IV, 964, the Old French phrase occurs in
full, "per seinte charitee," and there can be no question that Chaucer, as Gower, may have had the French
expression in mind. On the other hand, in his considerable number of examples of *seint—seinte,* Chaucer
must have been reflecting English speech usage in
the case of other English adjectives, and we may
reasonably assume that the double forms of this
word were due to purely English analogy. Foreign
influence is not necessary, and probably did not make
itself felt.

Such general analogy of English adjectives end-

[5] It may be worth while noting that in all the examples of
seint-seinte so far given in this paper, 63 are in dative phrases,
compared with 23 nominatives, 9 vocatives, and 1 accusative,
all singulars in number.

ing in unstressed –e seems a much more adequate explanation of the facts than Ten Brink's suggestion of the "petrified vocative" (§235, note). The one example which Ten Brink quotes as certainly exemplifying his theory, "goode faire Whyte" of *B. of D.* 948, might seem to support it, but such a theory would not well explain the great number of examples, especially the frequent datives. To Ten Brink's idea Zupitza *(Deutsche Litteraturzeitung* 1885, col. 610) demurred, as Professor Tatlock also in the article above. Zupitza proposed that weak forms of adjectives, especially of *god (good)*, occur before proper names by analogy of such weak forms after demonstratives and possessives. Freudenberger *(Ueber das Fehlen des Auftakts in Chaucers heroischem Verse,* pp. 37–39) fell back on Ten Brink's theory of vocative influence, adding the possible influence of the weak form of the plural. Neither of these accounts for the many phrases which do not contain a proper name, and neither seems as adequate an explanation as the one here proposed. The influence of the vocative and other weak forms may have assisted the analogy I have pointed out, but they are scarcely sufficient in themselves for the majority of examples.

II. *Deynous Heynous*

Professor Skeat made the diphthong *ey* dissyllabic at least once in each of these words, and Professor

Kittredge *(Language of Troilus,* §140, 146) suggests such reading of the second in *Troilus* II, 1617, in order to make an otherwise nine-syllable line more regular. If, however, this diphthong may not be separated in this way, and I think I have shown it to be unnecessary in *seint—seinte,* what is to be said of these words? For the second, which occurs in the expression "so heynous" at the beginning of a line, the assumption of a nine-syllable line solves the difficulty at once, and is clearly better than the split diphthong.[6]

Skeat's *dëynous* occurs in the *Reeve's Tale,* 21,

His name was hoten deynous Simkin,

a line which is clearly imperfect without some modification. The Petworth MS. even reads *deynezous,* perhaps suggesting such a double form as occurs in ME. *pitous, piteous.* Chaucer, however, uses only the *deynous, pitous* forms, the first appearing as a dissylable in *Troilus* I, 290:

Which somdel deynous was, for she leet falle.

In accord with the latter, therefore, and instead of what I believe is the impossible dieresis in *deynous,* I suggest emending the line by reading *Simekin.*[7] Double forms of the same name are so common in Chaucer that *Simkin—Simekin,* even in the same

---

[6] The Globe *Chaucer* follows Skeat in splitting the diphthong here.

[7] The Globe *Chaucer* reads *Symekyn* here, in line 3941, but not in line 3945.

tale, would be no departure from his ordinary usage.
Such classical names as *Theseus, Perotheus, Alma-
chius,* appear with *eus (ius)* as one or two syllables
at the pleasure of the poet. A still better classical
example is *Cleopataras (L. of G. W.* 582), with extra
syllable for the meter, beside *Cleopatras (L. of G. W.*
604) and the more common *Cleopatre.*

A more exact parallel in a common name is
Jankin—Janekin. Besides the appearance of the first
in *Ship. Prol.* 10, *Som. T.* 580, 585, it occurs in *W. of
B's Prol.* 548, 628, 713. In the same *Prol.* 303, 383,
its variant *Janekin* is found, and should doubtless be
read at 595 also.[8] In his *Glossary* Skeat has suggested such a reading as possible "in some places,"
without indicating them specifically. So slight a
change, therefore, as *Simekin* for *Simkin* is not only
in keeping with the double forms *Jankin—Janekin*
in other places, but is unquestionably better than a
dissyllabic diphthong in *deynous.* Perhaps *Simekin*
should be read at line 35 also, the final *–e* of *hadde*
being elided before *hosen,* and certainly at line 39,
where *wolde* is better as a monosyllable. The form
Simekin is more necessary in the latter line, because
of the rime with *boydekin,* and Harleian MS. reads
Symekyn in this place, a reading adopted by the
Globe *Chaucer.*

---

[8] Mr. MacCracken so reads in his edition of *Chaucer.*

III. *Criseyda, Eneidos, Oenone*

It need scarcely be said that the dieresis marked
by Skeat in the first two of these words rests upon a
different basis from that in the words so far discussed. In both these cases classical forms of the
words fully account for the treatment of *ey (ei)* as
two syllables, compared with the usual treatment of
ey (ei) as a true diphthong in the first name when
derived from Old French. The third name, as used
by Chaucer, is a misunderstanding of a classical
form, certainly not a splitting of what was recognized as a true diphthong.

The purpose of this paper is not simply to discount
Professor Skeat's splitting of the Old French-Middle
English diphthong *ei (ey)* into two syllables for met-
rical purposes. More important, it is hoped, is the
suggestion of the true analogy for numerous double
forms of adjectives in Middle English, and the fuller
explanation of the adjectives with final unstressed
–*e* in dative phrases.

CHAUCER'S "OPIE OF THEBES FYN"*

Chaucer's considerable knowledge of medical matters is well known. Witness his description of the Doctor of Physic in the Prologue to the *Canterbury Tales;* the diagnosis of Arcite's condition after his fall from his horse in the *Knight's Tale* (A.2743f.) ; the specific mention of "signes of empoisoning" in the *Pardoner's Tale* (C.889f) ; the povre widwes" freedom from disease and the reason therefor in the *Nun's Priest's Tale* (B.4026f.) ; the fuller discourse of Pertelote on the probable cause of Chauntecleer's bad dreams; and the still more elaborate description of remedies (B.4111–57). More recently we have learned from Professor Lowes[1] that, in attributing to Palamon the "loveres maladye of Hereos" (A.1373–70), Chaucer was wiser in medieval medicine than his commentators for many a day.

Let me call attention to two instances, not adequately explained, in which Chaucer has introduced specific references to medieval medicines where there were no such references in his originals. In the tale of Hypermnestra *(Legend of Good Women,* 2668–70) Chaucer makes "Egestes" tell his daughter of the draught he gives her for her husband:

---

* *Mod. Phil.* Vol. XVII, pp. 287–91 (1919).

[1] *Mod. Phil.,* XI, 491.

312

> Yif him to drinke whan he goth to reste,
> And he shal slepe as longe as ever thee leste,
> The nercotiks and opies been so stronge.

For this specific mention of narcotics and opium Ovid[2] has only the most general allusion to a soporific in

> Quaeque tibi dederam vina, soporis erant.

In the second instance Chaucer's use of narcotics and opium is even more a departure from the original. Boccaccio in the *Teseide* has Palamon escape from prison by changing clothes with his physician Alimeto. Chaucer makes the escape depend upon a wholly different circumstance *(Kt. T., 612–16)*:

> For he had yive his gayler drinke so
> Of a clarree maad of a certeyn wyn,
> With nercotikes and opie of Thebes fyn,
> That al that night, thogh that men wolde him
>   shake,
> The gayler sleep, he mighte nat awake.[3]

Palamon himself had drugged the "gayler" with the finest opium in the world, "opie of Thebes," of which no adequate account has been given by Chaucer commentators.[4]

---

[2] *Heroides* xiv. 42.

[3] In the original *(Teseide, V, st. 24)* mention is made of wine which Panphilo had brought in, and he and the guard drink until they are *mezzo affatappiato*. Yet the wine is not said to be drugged, and plays a less essential part in Palamon's escape.

[4] Professor Skeat notes the occurrence of *Opium Thebaicum* in the margin of the Ellesmere and Harleian MSS. Beyond

I have neither time nor medieval medical books
sufficient to follow out minutely the sources of
Chaucer's knowledge of Thebaic opium and narcotics,
but some hints may be given. Thus, the ancients
knew two forms of opium, one a decoction of the
whole poppy plant called meconium (Gr. μηκώνειον),
as by Theophrastus (b. about 372 B.C.), the first botanist. The other was opium proper (Gk. ὀπός, ὄπιον)
from the seed-pod only, discussed by Dioscorides of
Anazarba (*ca.* 77 A.D.), who wrote the most important work of the ancients on medicinal plants. Both
these forms of opium continued to be known and used
through the middle ages, and both are mentioned, for
example, by Simon A. Cordo (Januensis), who died
some ten years before Chaucer was born. Chaucer's
plural "opies" of the *Legend of Good Women* may,
therefore, have been based on his knowledge of the
two kinds of opium[5] known in his time and long before. This, at any rate, seems probable, although it is
possible he merely refers to opium as grown in dif-

---

this he mentions merely that the term is found in Burton's
Anatomy of Melancholy. Others have ineffective notes.

[5] The word meconium has almost a place in Old English.
In the *Leechdoms*, I, 156, a remedy for sore eyes mentions the
"popig . . . þe Grecas mœcorias and Romane papaver album
nemnaþ and Engle hwit popig hataþ." The word *mœcorias,*
though not hitherto explained, I believe, must be a modification of Greek μηκώνειον or of Latin *meconium,* probably in
the plural form. I conjecture, also, that the OE. word had
œ, or æ for œ, corresponding to Greek η, to which we have
something like a parallel in Orm's use in early Middle English. The final *s* is paralleled by that in *lactucas* for *lactuca,* 'lettuce,' in *Leechdoms*, II, 212,12.

ferent localities. Thus the commercial opium of the middle ages to the twelfth century is said to have come from Asia Minor.

Thebaic opium requires a further note. Pliny in his *Natural History* refers the cultivation of opium to Asia Minor only. But a commentator on Pliny, Bk. XX, cap. lxxvi *(Excursus de Opio,* in the edition of the *Bibl. Clas. Latina)*, gives the significant statement:

> Arabes et officinae Thebaicum, seu quod in Egypto circa Thebas colligetur, opium prae caeteris commendarunt.

One of the most important of these Arabian physicians, the learned botanist and traveler Ibn Baithar (d. 1248), had this to say of opium and its origin in Egypt[6]:

> Il n'est réellement connu ni en Orient ni en Occident, mais seulement en Egypte et particulièrement dans le Saïd, au lieu appelé Boutidj [the name in Arabic follows]. C'est de là qu'il provient et qu'on l'expédie dans toutes les autres contrées.

Simon A. Cordo of Genoa (Januensis), who traveled widely to acquire knowledge of medicinal plants in their native haunts, is very explicit regarding opium Thebaicum in his *Clavis Sanationis.* As will be seen, he also distinguishes meconium:

---

[6] I quote from L. Leclerc's French version.

Opium ab opos que est lacrimus nomen extra-
hit. Opium verum que est melius fit scissis levi-
ter capitellis papaverum nigrorum adhuc veren-
tium terre ita ne scissura interiora penetret iteri
ora et lac que egreditur collectum in vasculis
desiccatur tale tebaicum vacatur. Sed quando
capita ipsa cui suis foliis contunduntur exprimi-
turque succus atque siccatur sit aliud opiumque
miconis dicitur que patet per dia. ca. de miconio
que est papaver.[7]

Let me add a modern confirmation of Chaucer
from *An Inquiry into the Nature and Properties of
Opium* by Dr. Samuel Crumpe, London, 1793, p. 12:

Egypt, and especially the country about
Thebes, was long famous for the quantity and
excellence of its Opium, and hence the term Thebaic still given to some of its preparations.

The term Thebaic, by the way, is still preserved
in Thebaine, one of the opium alkaloids discovered
by Thiboumery in 1835.

Of the narcotics Chaucer mentions both times in
connection with opium, he gives us no hint. But by

---

[7] From the Venice edition of 1486, which is without pagina-
tion. His fuller statement regarding meconium need not concern us here. The transcript was made for me at the Sur-
geon General's Library in Washington. [The correct form of
the name of the compiler of the "earliest modern Dictionary
of Drugs" (so called by Allbutt, *Greek Medicine in Rome*, 386)
seems to be Simone d. (or de) Cordo (Simon Januensis or
Genuensis). The forms "Simon Cordo," "Simon a Cordo,"
also occur. He was a native of Genoa, his dates 1270–1330.]

the fourteenth century, numerous narcotics were
known, with no such distinction of any one as in the
case of Thebaic opium. Thus Bernard Gordon, the
Bernard of Chaucer's Prologue to the *Canterbury
Tales* (1.434), who wrote his *Practica seu Lilium
Medicinae* in 1307, under the caption *De stupifacien-
tibus, somnum provocantibus, et de iis quae vomitum
provocant,* has lists for internal and for external application.

The former are:

Mitiora Sq. violaceus, syrupus de papavera;
succi: lactucae, sempervini, solatri, portulacae,
cicutae; conserva: violarum, nympheae.

For external use he mentions:

Oleum violacium, oleum mandragoris, un-
guentem populconis, decoctum corticis mandra-
go, semen hyoscyami, lac muliebre, semen papa-
veris, decoctum salicis, opium, anethum viride
in oleo coctum.[8]

These, then, or some of them, we may assume to
have been in Chaucer's mind when he added to his
originals the explicit references to narcotics.

To return to Palamon's escape. It is not necessary
for me to account for Palamon's manner of obtaining the drugs he used so effectively, though modern
realism would certainly have done so more fully
than by incidental allusion to the "helping of a

---

[8] *Lilium Medicinae,* ed. of 1550, p. 915.

freend" *(Kt. T.,* A 1468). I suggest, however, that if
Chaucer knew as much about the "loveres maladye of
hereos" as our modern scholars, he must have known
that "nercotiks" and even "opie of Thebes fyn" were
a proper remedy for love-melancholy. They should,
therefore, have been on the dressing table of an aris-
tocratic prisoner afflicted so grievously as Palamon—
and surely I need not account for the dressing table
in a prince's prison chamber. Some new fury of
jealousy against the more fortunate Arcite was all
that was necessary to suggest the new use of the
drugs. Compared, too, with Boccaccio's labored introduction of a physician who would risk death by
impersonating Palamon, this is only another evidence of Chaucer's cleverness. Of course the sympathetic "freend" may have persuaded the jailor that
Palamon's case of "hereos" required the remedies.

Professor Skeat did not make full use of the reference to opium Thebaicum in Burton's *Anatomy of
Melancholy.* It proves to be aptly in point, however.
Skeat refers it to Part III, Sec. ii, Mem. vi. Subsec.
ii, without note of the edition he used. After some
search I find it in Shilleto's edition, Part III, Sec. ii,
Mem. v, Subsec. i, the very place it should be to support my conjecture. The whole "Member" is on
Cure of Love-Melancholy, the "Heroical or Love-
Melancholy" of Part III, Sec. i, Mem. i, Subsec. i,
corresponding to Chaucer's "hereos," as Professor

Lowes showed. The subsection in which the reference to Thebaic opium appears just at the close, is devoted to the *Cure of Love-Melancholy by Labour, Diet, Physick, Fasting*, &c. The particular passage may as well be left in the Latin of Burton, but to make its aptness doubly sure, it also mentions various narcotics, as Hyoscyamus (henbane), cicuta (hemlock), lactuca (lettuce), portulaca (purslane), all mentioned by Bernard Gordon quoted above. For the cure of love-melancholy these were to be used in external application. Hence the "clarree" which Palamon mixed for the unsuspecting jailor.

CHAUCER AND MEDIEVAL HUNTING*

Too little attention has been paid to Chaucer's knowledge of hunting, and to those passages in which it appears in his works. For example, it will be easy to show that some words of specific relation to the pursuit of game have been misunderstood, or inadequately explained. Thus some passages in the poet may be more clearly elucidated. Again, Chaucer's knowledge of hunting is evidenced by the number of hunting terms used by him. The *New English Dictionary* cites Chaucer as the first to use the following words or expressions in specific hunting meanings: *alaunt, default, dog for the bow, emboss, forloyn* sb.; *foun* "fawn, young deer of first year";[1] *have a course at; lymer* "limmer, lime-hound"; *overshoot* "lose the scent"; *pricasour* "hunter on horseback"; *priking* "tracking the hare"; *rechase, ruse* vb., *slay with strength; sour* "sore, buck of fourth year"; *toret* "swivel." To these also the great dictionary might have added, as first appearing in Chaucer, *find* "discover game sought," and *relay*, besides the compounds *great hart, hart-hunting, master-hunt*, and probably *great horn*, which it does not give at

---

* *Rom. Rev.* Vol. XIII, pp. 115–150 (1922).

[1] In *Troilus and Criseyde* I, 46–8, Chaucer uses foun *(fown)* in the figurative sense of "new thought, emotion," a meaning not recorded by the *NED*.

all. In addition, Chaucer uses the hunting terms *form* "lair of a hare"; *hallow, hamel (hamble); moot (mote); strake forth; sue* "pursue as game"; *trist (tryst)* "hunting station."[2]

The need of further examination of Chaucer's language of hunting will be apparent from a consideration of the hunting scenes in the *Book of the Duchess,* passages believed to be peculiarly Chaucer's own.[3] These are especially lines 344–433 and 1311–23. The first begins with the preliminaries of the hunt, the hunter blowing "t' assay his horn," the "going up and doun" of "men, hors, houndes, and other thinge," the gossip of the hunting occasion by "al men."

Chaucer's "other thinge" may seem indefinite, but he probably felt he could not further use the elaborate preparations for a king's hunt. Some idea of what they were may be gained from Turbervile's

---

[2] It will be seen that most of the words here enumerated are of Old French origin, as the special forms of hunting to which they apply were derived from French hunting-practice. The phrases *dog for the bow* and *strake forth* are wholly English, while *course* in *have a course at* and *master* (Chaucer's *mayster*) in *master-hunt* are French. *With strength* in *slay with strength* is the English equivalent of OF. *à force.*

[3] M. Sandras, in *Étude sur Chaucer* (1859), pointed out some slight likeness to certain lines of a French poem in the *Collection Mouchet* II, 106, but offered little proof that Chaucer knew the poem. Skeat thinks the evidence of little value, and from Chaucer's independence of his source in other hunting scenes, I think we may here believe he was picturing things as he knew them personally.

chapter on "How an Assembly should be made in the Presence of a prince," which he precedes by seventy-two verses on the many details. For example, the Butler should bring with him

> Some wagons, cartes, some mules or jades yla-
> den till they sweate,
> With many a medcine made for common queynt
> diseases,
> As thirstie throates and typpling tongs, whome
> Bacchus pype appeases,

besides an astonishing array of viands of various sorts.[4] The Duke of York's *Master of Game* of about 1400 also tells of the sylvan feast accompanying the hunt in his chapter on "The Assembly" (ch. xxxiii. p. 163), and adds regarding details in ch. xxxvi that there must be "carts also to bring the deer that shall be slain to the place where the curées at hunting have been usually held."[5]   All these were doubtless the "other thinge" in Chaucer's mind.

----

[4] Reference is to chap. xxxv in the page for page reprint of George Turbervile's *Booke of Hunting* (1576) in the Tudor and Stuart Library. The quaint cut in Turbervile gives a good idea of the royal feast in the wood.   In the first edition Queen Elizabeth is the central figure with two ladies in waiting just behind her, while all about are evidences of a merry time.   When the edition of 1611 was issued, the same cut was retained, except that by a curious transformation King James then took the place of Elizabeth before the identical tree of the original, and the ladies in waiting were deftly changed into masculine retainers.   See the reproduction of the two cuts side by side in Strutt's *Sports and Pastimes.*

[5] In the absence of the promised reprint of the MSS. in *Palaestra,* I have used the edition of the Baillie-Grohmans

The first specific hunting expression used by Chaucer is in the boast of the men as they "speken of hunting,"

How they wolde slee the hert with strengthe.

"Slee the hert with strengthe," or "by strength" as sometimes in the *Master of Game,* means "to kill in regular chase with horses and hounds." *With strength* is the English equivalent of OF. *à force,* later rendered also by *at force,* as in Turbervile. The next expression with special hunting meaning, *embosed* in the further boast of the hunters, needs more extended comment, as I believe. The lines containing it are,

> And how the hert had, upon lengthe,
> So moche embosed, I not now what.

These lines, and especially the word *embosed,* seem to me to have been wholly misunderstood. Skeat explains *embosed* as

---

(Chatto & Windus, 1909). See also ch. xxvi. for the numerous preparations preceding the day of the hunt.

The *Master of Game (Maystre of the Game)* was made by Edward Third's grandson, Edward second Duke of York, about 1406–13. As is well known, the book was largely a translation of *Le Livre de Chasse* by Gaston de Foix, or Gaston Phoebus, as he was called from his great beauty. However, five chapters of the English book were original, those marked xxii, xxvi, xxxiv–vi in the Baillie-Grohman edition, while there were also in other chapters some changes and some additions by the English author. These are of special value in explaining English, as distinct from French, hunting practice. In quoting the *Master of Game,* for the purely illustrative purposes of this paper, it has seemed sufficient to use the modernized version of the Baillie-Grohman edition.

a technical term used in various senses, for
which see the New Eng. Dict. Here it means
"so far plunged into the thicket"; . . . In later
authors it came to mean "driven to extremity
like a hunted animal"; then "exhausted by running," and lastly "foaming at the mouth" as a
result of exhaustion.

Now, the meaning which Skeat gives to the word
embosed in this passage seems wholly insufficient for
the place, and, as I think, depends upon a misunderstanding of its origin and sense development. Skeat
admits that *upon lengthe* means "after a long run,"
but does not see that "plunged into a thicket after a
long run" would in no sense complete the boast of
the hunters, while "so much plunged into a thicket"
would scarcely be good English. The boast of the
hunters is properly concluded, however, if we assume Chaucer used *embosed* in its usual sense when
applied to the hunt.   They told "how they would slay
the hart with strength, and how the hart had, after
a long run, so much exhausted himself (become so
much exhausted), or so much foamed at the mouth,
and thus became flecked with foam in his weary exhaustion," that he had at last succumbed to their
long continued efforts.   In other words, this is the
specific hunting term *embosed (embost, embossed),*
here used for the first time in our literature.

Skeat's error is natural if we follow the *NED.* on

which he depended, for that excellent work links Chaucer's *embosed* in this passage with Milton's *embost* in *Samson Agonistes*, 1700, which it assumes to mean "plunged into the thicket" and to be an otherwise unknown variant of *emboskt*. The Milton passage, figuring the overthrow of his enemies by the blind and despised Samson, reads as follows:

So Virtue, given for lost,
Depressed and overthrown as seemed,
Like that self-begotten bird
In the Arabian woods embost,—
That no second knows nor third,
And lay erewhile a holocaust,—
From out her ashy womb now teemed,
Revives, reflourishes, then vigorous most
When most unactive deemed.

Now if Milton's *embost* means "plunged into the thicket," the great poet must not only have used a tautological repetition of the idea "in the Arabian woods," but also have omitted any similitude to the preceding "given for lost, Depressed and overthrown" of Virtue, and indirectly of Samson. On the other hand, if *embost* is taken to mean "worn out, exhausted," a meaning fully recognized by the *NED.* in other places, the parallelism with Virtue and Samson is complete. In addition, Milton is absolved from using *embost* when he meant *emboskt*, a word which he elsewhere uses, as we shall see, in its more correct form *imbosk*. The figure, that of an animal wearied out by the hunters and admirably adapted to the enslaved Samson, is here applied to the phoenix at the end of its long life. Such use of *embost* entirely agrees with the traditional accounts of the phoenix. After her long life in Arabia (sometimes India), in which she had wearied herself to exhaustion, she did not remain in her native land, but flew away to the city of the sun—a necessary part of the myth—where the "holocaust" of Milton took place, and the beginning of a new life. Even the Milton passage is more logical and more effective with the meaning now first proposed.

In other words, both the Chaucer and Milton examples belong with those quoted by the *NED.* from Skelton, Turbervile, Spenser, and others, in which there is no idea of "plunged into a wood," but rather some variation of "wearied, exhausted," developed from the idea of "foamed at the mouth, became covered with flecks or bosses of foam from hard running." To clinch our argument, Milton elsewhere used both *emboss (embossed)* "cover with bosses, be covered with bosses," and *imbosk* "hide in the wood, lie in ambush," probably from Italian *imboscare*. The first is found in *Par. Lost* xii, 180, and *Par. Regained* iv, 119. The second Milton used in the following sentence of *Reformation in England*, Bk. I, where he says of the adversaries of reform: "They seek the dark, the bushy, the tangled forest, they would im-bosk."[6] The poet knew both words and used each correctly.

The only other example quoted by the *NED.* with *emboss* in the supposed meaning "plunge into a wood" is this from Butler's *Elephant in the Moon* 125–30:

> An Elephant from one of those
> Two mighty armies is broke loose,
> And with the Horrour of the Fight
> Appears amaz'd, and in a Fright;
> Look quickly, lest the sight of us
> Should cause the startled Beast t' imboss.

The satirical skit of Butler is hardly one from which to reason regarding the exact meaning of a word, and had not the Milton passage been misunderstood, I doubt whether Butler's use of *imboss* would have been seriously considered. The preceding *quickly* would perhaps imply in *imboss* some such meaning as "hide, hide oneself," and if so, the word may be a retention of the ME. *enbussen* beside *enbuschen*, OF. *embussier* beside *embuscher* "hide in the wood, lie in ambush." For examples see Maetzner's glossary to the *Sprachproben.* The form in Butler may be due to confusion with *emboss,* although *imbuss* would improve the rime with *us.* The same etymology would also account for Spenser's *emboss* in *F.Q.I.*

[6] See p. 34 of W. T. Hale's edition in *Yale Studies in English.*

iii, 24; I, xi, 20; III, i, 64; VI, iv. 40, the etymology of which has been doubtful. The meaning "hide, conceal oneself" from "hide in wood" would fit all examples more satisfactorily than has been proposed heretofore. At the same time, "foam at the mouth, become flecked with foam," would not be wholly unsuitable in the Butler line, or Butler himself may have mistaken the meaning of this unusual word.[7]

The writer of the *NED.* article on *emboss v.* (2) "plunge into a thicket" was clearly puzzled by his own etymology—"perhaps from En+OF. *bos, bois* wood" — for three times he adds explanatory or half-apologetic notes. Of the etymology itself he says, "if so the word is ultimately identical with *imbosk v.* The development of sense, as suggested below, is strange, but appears to be in accordance with the existing evidence." Under meaning (2) the editor says, "The sense 'drive to a thicket,' required by the etymology suggested above, is not clearly evidenced." And still again, under meaning (3), "The sense 'foam at the mouth' is probably influenced by emboss *v.* (1), as if an 'embossed stag' were one 'studded' with bubbles of foam."[8] With the three examples which once seemed

---

[7] The *CtDict.* proposed for the Spenser passages OF. *emboister* "enclose, insert, fasten as in a box," but that does not seem to me a satisfactory explanation, especially when the earlier *enbussen* is actually recorded.

[8] The simpler etymology is to assume at once that *emboss* "foam at the mouth" is from the *NED.*'s *emboss v.* (1) meaning "swell, rise in bunches or bosses." The further sense development is "be covered with bunches or bosses of foam from

to support the *NED.*'s etymology otherwise explained, we may well assume that the Middle English hunting term *embosen (enbossen)* of Chaucer is the OF. *embocer (enbosser)* "to swell, rise in bunches or bosses," then of a deer in the chase "become exhausted," as I have pointed out above.

Further proof that "cover with foam (by hard running)" is the correct meaning of the hunting term is found in Turbervile, who says of the hart (p. 244) "When he is foamy at the mouth we say he is embost." The exact idea is clearer from the fact that Turbervile is enumerating expressions used at various progressive stages of the hunt, and "embost" stands next before "spent or done." Again, the meaning "wearied, exhausted" is clear from Cotgrave's use of *imbossed* in defining *malmené.* Under *mené* he defines the former as "ill-handled, abused, hardly used; sore layed to; wearied, tired, jaw fallen, *imbossed* or almost spent as a deer by hard pursuit." Finally, Chaucer himself again used *embossed (enbossed)* in *up-enbossed hye* of the ornamental bars on the red saddle of Dido *(Leg. of Good Women* 1200), while he also employed the root of OF. *embussier (embuscher),* ME. *embuscher,* in *embusshements* of the *Tale of Melibeus.* It is worth

---

the mouth"; "foam at the mouth and cover the body (of a hunted deer) with bunches or bosses of foam"; "be wearied or exhausted from long running, evidenced by such foaming at the mouth and covering of the body with bosses of foam."

noting that OF. *embocer (embosser)* is not recorded before the sixteenth century, but Chaucer's use of it twice is ample proof of its earlier existence.[9]

To return to the hunting scene in the *Book of the Duchess,* when Chaucer rode to the field he overtook, as he says,

> a gret route
> Of huntes and eek of foresteres.

Huntes is the earlier form of our word *hunters,* of course, but the *forester* of Chaucer's time was an official more largely connected with hunting than with the preservation of timber, as in more recent times. Thus Manwood tells us *(Lawes Forest* xxi, §4), "A forester is an officer of the King (or any other man) that is sworn to preserve the Vert and Venison of the forest, and attend upon the wild beasts within his Bailiwick." The name was applied first of all to the *master forester,* such as Chaucer himself was in 1398 at North Petherton Park, or to the "forester of the Baillie" in which was the forest to be hunted. He was an important character, for the *Master of Game* explains (ch. xxxvi) that "The master of game should be in accordance with the master forester or parker where it should be that

---

[9] Turbervile again uses *embost* on p. 103: "If peradventure it happen that the pricker on horsebacke, being at his relaye, should see an Hart of tenne passe by him, and yet heare not the other huntsmen nor their hornes, then let him looke wel whether the Hart be embost or not." The hunter would thus know whether the animal thus seen was the one hunted.

the King should hunt such a day." He should also show the master of game "the King's standing, if the King would stand with his bow, and where the remnant of the bows should stand." Finally, he must explain "what game the King would find within the set," that is, the part of the forest already set off by men and hounds for the hunt. Under him the master forester had numerous under-foresters, such as was the Knight's yeoman in the *Prologue to the Canterbury Tales,* or that forester of the *Physician's Tale (CT,* C 83), a former poacher who had given up

> His likerousnesse and al his olde [or theves] craft,

and for this reason,

> Can kepe a forest best of any man.

Thus *forester (forster),* as Chaucer used it, was nearly equivalent to modern *game-keeper,* and quite as important in the medieval hunt.

The hunt of which Chaucer dreamed was not in a park, in which case the procedure would have differed somewhat, as the *Master of Game* informs us in ch. xxxvi, but at a *forest-syde,* as we learn from line 372 (see also 363). The actual run for the hart was probably in the more open spaces, and possibly in the plains or *launds,* like that of Theseus in the *Knight's Tale* 833 *(CT,* A 1691). Moreover, the poet dreams explicitly of a King's hunt, such as he had doubtless witnessed many times as chosen valet of

Edward III, and later was often to observe in more
honorable position. The distinctive details of such
a hunt, which need not now concern us, take up chapters xxvi and xxxvi of the *Master of Game*—both
original with the English author, and so especially
applicable to English usage—and the xxxv and xxxvi
of Turbervile's *Booke of Hunting*. The particular
King of the poem, "the emperour Octovien" of 368,
"this king" of 1314, is reasonably believed to figure
Edward himself, who, at fifty-seven or fifty-eight,
was still vigorous enough to enjoy his favorite sport.

The next hunting term which Chaucer uses, and
was the first to use, although the *NED*. first cites the
Duke of York's *Master of Game* some thirty years
later, is *relay*, or the plural *relayes* of line 362. This
Skeat defines briefly as "a fresh set of dogs," but it is
properly, as the *NED*. puts it, "a set of fresh hounds
(and horses), posted to take up the chase of a deer
in place of those tired out." The last phrase, "in place
of those tired out," is scarcely justified, for the relay
hounds did not so much replace the others as take up
the hunt more vigorously.[10]

Turbervile, in chapter xxxviii, "How to set Relayes,"
gives an account of the preparations the night be-

---

[10] The editors of the *Master of Game* say also that the relay
was not let go until both hart and following hounds had
passed (see footnote to p. 169, and App. under "relays"), but
the text does not seem to me wholly to justify this interpretation, or Turbervile's chapter (xxxviii) on *Relayes*. Certainly not all the pursuing hounds were allowed to pass before the relay was unleashed.

fore and many details of place and action. The *Master of Game* (ch. xxxiv) emphasizes the assignment of relays—there were usually three at least—"by advice of them that know the country and the flight of the deer," "the readiest hunters and the best footers with the boldest hounds with them" being placed "where most danger is." From him also we know that at every relay there were "two couple of hounds, or three at the most." Thus the relay consisted primarily of men, with hounds in leash to be let go on occasion, but "if the deer be likely to fall among danger," that is, run among the herd or to another deer, "it were good to assign some of the horsemen among the relays, to help more readily the hounds if they fall upon the stynt," that is, lose the scent. "Danger" in the hunting sense was the difficulty arising from the hunted deer running among others of its kind, and so confusing the pursuing hounds.

Chaucer's *lymere* (362, 365), modern *limmer* or *lime-hound*, is rightly but not fully explained by Skeat as a "dog held in a *liam*, lime or leash." When he adds "to be let loose when required," Skeat has mistakenly confused the medieval lymer with the running hounds, while he seems otherwise ignorant of the special duty of this important animal. The lymer was the tracking hound, trained to scent out game for the hunt, to "move" or start it when hunted, and to regain the scent again if it were lost by the running hounds. He was most strictly required to avoid any other than game animals, and especially not to bark or bay when on duty. When tracking he was held by a leash "three fathoms and a half" in length, to give him some leeway—"be it ever so wise a limer it sufficeth"[11]—but was not otherwise let loose.[12]

The lymer was of no particular breed, but his training required early separation from the other hounds, intimate association with his master, and long exercise in his particular duties. His lime, or

---

[11] *Master of Game*, ch. xx, p. 126. Twici explains the use of the lymer more fully by having his questioner ask (Dryden's modernization of the Middle English text, p. 20): " 'Now I would wish to know how many of the beasts are dislodged by the lymer, and how many of the beasts are found by the braches.' Sir, all those which are chased are dislodged by the lymer; and all those which are hunted up are found by the braches." He has also told us just before that the hare "is chased" and the hart, wolf, and boar. So also the *Craft of Venery*, a MS. of about 1450 (A. Dryden, p. 105): " 'Syr, how many bestis ben there enchased?' iiij, the hert, the hare, the bere, the wolfe," where *bere* is probably an error for *bore* by the e—o confusion as often in MSS.

[12] See the same ch. xxxiv, p. 174: "For by right the lymer should never out of the rope, though he slip from ever so far." Indeed, the oldest hunting treatise in Old French, *La Chace dou Serf*, written about 1250, advises tying up the lymer, at least while blowing the call for the hounds. In Dryden's translation it reads: "Cross (or pass over) the lair until you have dislodged him [the hart], and then tie your hound [that is the lymer as shown by the preceding sentence] up to a branch, and then you shall blow the call, three long motes, to have your hounds." See a figure of the lymer in A. Dryden's Twici's *Le Art de Venerie* (p. 95) from a MS. of Gaston de Foix. On the other hand, Dryden says in his note 18 (p. 52 of the A. Dryden edition of *Twici*): "The lymer after the unharbouring, was frequently allowed to join in the pursuit when the pack came up with the huntsman," although I do not so find it in the early treatises.

leash, as distinct from the "couple" of a hound, was "made of leather of a horse skin well tawed," although for ornamental purposes it might be of white, or green and white silk, or of white leather.[13] It was attached to a collar which might be in later times—probably not for actual hunting—of white or crimson velvet, and even embroidered with pearls. The lime, or leash, was fastened to the collar by means of a swivel, or a *toret*, as Chaucer calls it in the *Knight's Tale (CT,* A 2152), and this was sometimes of silver.[14] This indicates that a good lymer was a choice dog, affectionately regarded by his master or mistress. Chaucer's use of the plural *lymeres* is also right in connection with medieval hunting. The lymer which started the game could not be in every place in which a tracking hound might be needed. While his master did follow the hunt as well as he could, other lymers were placed where they were likely to be needed. The *Master of Game* is explicit in ch. xxxiv. p. 166:

> And see that amid the relays, somewhat toward the hindermost relay, especially if it be in danger, that one of the lymerer's pages be there with one of the lymers. And the more danger, the older and the readier and the most tender nosed hound.

---

[13] *Mast. of Game,* App., under limer.

[14] Madden, *Privy Expenses of Princess Mary,* in App. to *Master of Game.*

When Chaucer says that "at the forest-syde"

> Every man did right anon
> As to hunting fil to doon,

he illustrates with several actions in entire accord
with hunting practice. He has, it is true, omitted
the usual use of the lymer in "moving" or starting
the game, perhaps because he had already mentioned
that important animal. Besides, the lymer was sometimes not used "if the deer be stirring in the quarter,
and have not waited for the moving of the lymer"
(Master of Game, ch. xxxiv, p. 167). And again in the
chapter "Of the Manner of Hunting when the King
will Hunt" (xxxvi), the action begins at once with
the blowing of "the three long motes for the uncoupling" by the master of game, Chaucer's *mayster-
hunte.* This, at any rate, is the practice in Chaucer's
king's hunt. Following immediately on the lines
quoted at the beginning of this paragraph, he adds:

> The mayster-hunte anoon, fot-hoot,
> With a gret horne blew three moot
> At the uncoupling of his houndes.

Perhaps the *fot-hoot* "hastily" of Chaucer is intended to indicate the more rapid beginning of the
king's hunt in this place, or perhaps the lymer's part
is included in the general *within a whyl* of the next
line (378).   Here, too, *master-hunte* "master-hunt"
is a technical term later displaced by *master of game*
or *master of the hunt,* but reappearing in the seven-

teenth century in the Earl of Monmouth's Boccalini's *Advertisements from Parnassus* (1656) : "Zenophon, Apollos master-hunt." This far earlier use by Chaucer is not recorded in the *NED*. Probably we should also consider *gret horn*, "great horn" in this place, a technical compound from allusions in the brief original chapter of the *Master of Game*, ch. xxii "How a Hunter's Horn should be Driven." There the Duke of York tells us,

> There are divers kinds of horns, that is to say bugles, great Abbot's, hunter's horns, ruets, small forester's horns, and meaner horns of two kinds. That one kind is waxed with green wax and greater of sound, and they be best for good hunters.

Just what were the "great abbots," as I judge the name should be written, is not clear, but the distinction between great and small horns is evident enough. The brief chapter closes with another reference to small horns:

> As for horns for fewterers and woodmen I speak not, for every small horn and other mean horn unwaxed be good enough for them.

It may be added that Gower also uses *grete hornes* in speaking of Actaeon's hunt *(Conf. Amant*, I, 343), the term having no source in the original Latin.

If there were space, it would be interesting to consider more exactly the difficult word *moot* (376),

22

usually defined as "a note upon a horn" (Skeat's glossary), without more specific and correct reference to hunting language.   At least, that *moot* is not wholly equivalent to a single note, seems indicated by Turbervile.   Among his several "measures for blowing," he pictures that of "the uncoupling of the coverte side" as a succession of four-four-four-two-one notes, "to be blowen with three windes," that is, repeated three times.   I wonder whether *moot (mot)* is not one or more notes blown with one breath, or wind, a more or less complicated blast of the horn, as would seem to be indicated by other of Turbervile's "Measures of blowing set downe in the notes for the more ease and ready help of such as are desirous to learne the same."[15]   One regrets that the Duke of York did not fulfil his promise to write "a chapter that shall be of all blowing," that is, of all kinds (see p. 170).   Of course there is always a possibility that the "measures" differed in different periods.   In any case, Chaucer is using the hunting term correctly, as well as the specific signal *three moot,* for the uncoupling of the running hounds in actual pursuit of the deer.   On the other hand, the earliest use of the term, as cited by the *NED.,* is by Chaucer's Northern contemporary, the author of *Sir Gawain and the Green Knight.*[16]

---

[15] See the plates at the close of the book·

[16] Chaucer is quite in accord with the Duke of York's direction *(Mast. of Game,* ch. xxxvi, p. 190) : "And when the king

"The uncoupling of the houndes" at the blowing of the "three moot" is followed by three actions indicated by three technical words, two of which occur in Chaucer for the first time, although the *NED.* gives him credit for the earliest use of one only. These actions are the *finding, hallowing,* and *rechasing* of the deer, indicated by Chaucer's *y-founde, y-halowed,* and *rechased.* The "finding" of the hart refers not to the starting of him by the lymer, but to the discovery by the hounds themselves after he has begun to run. For this purpose, certain hounds were especially set apart, as indicated by the *Master of Game* (ch. xxxiv, p. 167):

And always should the yeoman berner [the man in charge of the hounds], the which is ordained to be the finder, follow the lymer and be as nigh him as he might with the raches [the running hounds] that he leadeth for the finding.

And again in the same place:

But now to come again to the lymer, it is to wit that when the lymer hath moved him, if the lymerer shall see him he shall blow a mote and rechase, and if the deer be soule [that is, alone] the berners shall uncouple all the finders.[17]

is at his standing or at his tryste, whichever he prefers, and the master of game or his lieutenant have set the bows and assigned who shall lead the Queen to her tryste, then he shall blow the three long motes for the uncoupling."

[17] Turbervile does not explicitly mention the finder or finders, but explains the action in this way on p. 106: "Then

The *hallow (halloo)*, which is connected with the verb used by Chaucer, is not specifically treated by the Duke of York, although frequently mentioned. Turbervile, on the other hand, in chap. xiii, p. 31, tells us that the hounds must be taught "to know the Hallowe as well by the horne as by the mouth." Then follows a description of the manner of teaching them. The hallow was distinct from the hunting cries, or words of encouragement or caution, which are given here and there in both the *Master of Game* and Turbervile's *Booke of Hunting*.[18] The verb *hallow* in specific hunting meaning occurs first in *Cursor Mundi* (15,833), although there in a figurative sense; Chaucer seems to have first used it in an actual hunting scene. The first use of the noun *hallowing* in the same sense is in *Sir Gawain and the Green Knight*, probably composed a few years before the *Book of the Duchess*.[19] Chaucer's *y-halowed*, then, from OF. *haloer (halouer)*, means specifically "to set on the dogs with the hallow (halloo)" after the "finding."

when the Prince or Master of the game is come, and the houndes for the crie, all the horsemen must quickly cast abrode about the covert, to discover ye Harte when he rowzeth and goeth out of his hold, yt they may the better know him afterward by the cote and by his head." On the next page he has the expression, "Until ye Deare be descried and rightly marked."

[18] See the *Appendix* to the former under "Hunting Cries."

[19] It is noteworthy that the hunting cries given in the *Master of Game* are still in most cases in their Old French form, although Chaucer, thirty years earlier, used some of them in the English of his *Leg. of Good Wom.* 1213. In Turbervile the English terms are always used.

The third action of the hunt, following the uncoupling of the hounds, is indicated by Chaucer's *rechased,* on which Skeat has the following note: "Headed back. Men were posted at various places to keep the hart within bounds." Few of Skeat's notes are more misleading. Etymologically *rechase* did mean "chase back or again," but *rechased faste Longe tyme* can not mean "chased back a long time," but rather "chased, pursued, hunted fast a long time," the prefix *re-* having here no more force than in *receive, request.* It is true that, especially in contrast with *chase,* the word did have the meaning of "chase back or again," as shown by examples in the *NED.,* but not in this place or many others that might be cited, as often in the *Master of Game.* Again, in medieval hunting the word had the derivative meaning "to blow the measure indicating the chase or hunt, to rally and take up the hunt," and this, accompanied by the action of pursuit, is the meaning in the *Master of Game.* The call to *rechase (rechace)* was blown "when the lymer hath moved him" [the hart or other game] (p. 168); when the deer has passed a relay and the hounds of the relay take up the hunt (p. 169); when, after trying every device to escape, the deer finally stands at bay and the last onset is made (p. 173).

The *NED.* is wrong here, also, in giving the meaning to Chaucer's *rechase*—the first citation of the

word—"to chase (a deer) back into the forest." The
second quotation, one from Caxton's *Jason (EETS
p. 23)*, should have shown *rechased* was used in the
simple sense of "pursued." There, *rechased his
enmyes unto nyghe by the ooste* means no more than
chaced hem unto the grete ooste of the preceding
paragraph. In the *Craft of Venery*, also, (MS. of
about 1450 in A. Dryden's *Twici*, p. 107) we have:
"When he (the hare in this case) is stert, thou schalt
rechase apon the houndez iij times;" that is, give the
call of rechase (rechace) to urge on the hounds.

It should be noted that *rechase* has the same meaning and use in hunting as Norman French *recheat*,
which from "take back or again" had come to mean
"take to oneself, assemble, rally," with disregard of
the *re-* in most cases. Not used by Chaucer, it appears in the contemporaneous *Sir Gawain and the
Green Knight*, with the same idea of "rallying to pursue the game." There, the shortened *rechated* means
"rallied to pursue" the boar when he has broken from
covert (1446), when he has again been driven from
bay (1466), and in the form *rechatande* "rallying,
sounding the rally" for the hunters at the death of
the fox (1911). For this word *recheat (rechat, re-
chet)* the *NED.* gives the correct meaning as a noun
in "the act of calling together the hounds [properly
men and hounds] to begin or continue the chase of
the stag [or other game], or at the close of the hunt."

Turbervile figures this *rechate* in his "measures for blowing." For the signal itself in the body of his *Booke*, he uses "blow for the hounds" (p. 108), or "blowe a Rechate to their houndes to comforte them" (p. 111).

There remain to be explained two parts of the action in Chaucer's hunting scene. On *rused* (381) Skeat has no note, but his glossary misleads by his "roused herself, rushed away," for this place. The *NED*. gives the correct meaning and etymology "to make a detour or other movement in order to escape from the hounds," OF. *ruser*, with this Chaucer quotation first. The word is frequent in the *Master of Game*, as in chapters iii, v. xxxi, among others. The hart has turned suddenly from his course to throw the hounds from the track. Doubtless something like that described in the *Master of Game* (ch. iii, p. 31) has taken place: "He maketh a ruse on some side, and there he stalleth or squatteth until the hounds be forth." Or it may be he had let the hounds and hunters pass, and then doubled upon his track and run back the way he came. In any case, the hart "stal away . . . a prevy way," as Chaucer puts it.[20]

---

[20] The *Master of Game* deals with ruses of the hart in the same chapter "Of the Hart and his Nature," especially on p. 30, where he begins "An old hart is wonder wise and felle ('cunning') for to save his life." Turbervile, in chap. xl, "Certaine observations and suttleties to be used by Huntesmen in hunting an Harte at force," mentions many "suttleties" of the hart to escape his pursuers, and the procedure in such cases.

The hart's ruse results in a second action of the hunt at this point. The running hounds do not at first perceive the deer's change, "overshoot" the scent, and so lose it for a time. Besides, in *overshote* (383) of this realistic scene, Chaucer again uses for the first time another hunting term in its technical sense. This he follows by still another technical word of the hunt when he adds of the hounds, they "were on a defaute y-falle," the first example of *default* in its hunting sense in our literature. Skeat defines the phrase *on a defaute y-falle* as "had a check," and the *Master of Game* regularly uses the native expression *on a stynt* "at a stop" (pp. 169, 170), and *fall upon the stynt* (p. 165). The hunting game is temporarily at a standstill. The hounds, it is true, would soon perceive that the scent was lost, and would go about, often aimlessly, to find it. If they fail, as they must have done in this case, the lymer, or tracking hound, must be brought up to find the scent again and put the running hounds "to rights." That the hunt was temporarily stayed at this time is clear from the lines which follow at once:

Therewith the hunte, wonder faste,
Blew a forloyn at the laste.

The word *forloyn* has been almost as badly treated as Chaucer's *embosed* of this passage. The *NED.* says "a note of recall," with this use in Chaucer as the first quotation. Skeat says, with less certitude, "a

recall (as I suppose; for it was blown when the
hounds were all a long way off their object of pursuit.)" He follows this with a none too clear quotation from the *Book of St. Albans*. In fact, the *Book
of St. Albans* illustrates only one of several meanings of the word. Etymologically *forloyn*, OF.
fort+logne, is an adverb, meaning, as Cotgrave gives
it, "verie farre off (a hunting term)." Often, perhaps
usually, the derived noun meant that the hounds
were far off the scent, away from the hunted animal,
as also the measure blown on the horn to indicate
that fact—the use in this place. But forloyn might
mean that one hound, with the deer, had outstripped
all the others, as indicated by the verb in this passage from Turbervile (p. 245):

> When a hound meeteth a chase [that is a
> hunted animal] and goeth away with it farre
> before the rest, then we say he forloyneth.

Again, if a hunter had lost track of the chase, or as
the *Master of Game* says (p. 173), if he have

> been at any time out of hearing of hound and
> horn, he should have blown the forloyn; . . and
> whoso first heard him so blow should have
> blown to him the "perfect," if it be so that he
> were in his rights;

that is, on the right track of the hunted animal. All
these meanings, it will be seen, easily go back to the

adverbial "verie farre off" of Cotgrave and Old French, here become a noun *forloyn*.

Light is thrown on the development of meaning by that of the ME. verb *forloinen*. This meant transitively "to leave very far off, to forsake," and intransitively—doubtless the earlier—"be very far off, stray, err." Both transitive and intransitive uses occur in the *Clannesse* of Chaucer's contemporary. Further illustrations of the forloyn may be cited from the English *Twici* (A. Dryden, p. 23), which also gives the signal on the horn:

> And afterwards, when they are gone ahead of you, you ought to call in the manner as I tell you; you ought to blow trout, trout, trourourout, trout, trout, trourourourout, trourourourout, trourourourout. "Hunter, why do you blow in that manner?" Because I was on my right [line, of course], and the Hart is unharboured, and I do not know what has become of the hounds, nor of the company; and for this I blow in that manner. "And what chase do we call this?" We call that chase the chase of Forloyng.

> And when he [the hart] is fer fro me y schall blow in other manner, & that is this, trout, trout, trororout, trout, trout, trororout, trorororororout, v tymes this late mote. "Syre huntere, whi blowest thou thus?" For as muche as y have no knowyng, but am al uncerten where the hert is

bycome, & y wote never where myn houndez bun bycom, ne the men, & therfore y woll blow in this manner . . . "Syre, what maner chace clepe that?" We clepen it chace forloyne.[21]

In the passage before us it is the deer that has stolen away, the dogs that are very far off, and forloyn the signal means that a check, stynt, or default has resulted. Chaucer himself interpreted the situation in lines 539–41:

> "Sir," quod I, "this game is doon;
> I holde that this hert be goon,—
> Thise huntes conne him nowher see."

The forloyn, therefore, is not strictly a recall, as Skeat surmised and the *NED.* says with confidence. How entirely the forloyn indicated a check or delay in the hunt, is clear from Turbervile (p. 108):

> If it shoulde happen that the Harte, turning counter uppon the houndes in the thicket, had come amongest chaunge, then let all the huntesmen menace and rate their houndes, and couple them up againe untill they have gone backe eyther to the layre, or to [the] last blemish made upon any Slotte or viewe [that is, of the hart], and so hunt on againe untill they may finde the Harte.

If the difficulty were great the lymer was called up,

---

[21] So the *Craft of Venery* (A. Dryden, p. 108).

as I have said, the lymerer having followed the chase in the more open ground, according to Turbervile in the same chapter, "to helpe them at default if neede require." The *Master of Game* is equally explicit regarding the check to the hunt (p. 170) :

> And if it be great danger (that is, a serious default as the context shows), they ought to blow a mote for the lymer and let him sue till he hath retrieved him, or else till he hath brought him [the hunted hart] out of danger [that is, out from among the other deer].

It may be assumed that when a check resulted from the loss of the scent in any other way, the procedure was essentially the same.

The discussion so far shows that Chaucer was describing the hunting scene in the *Book of the Duchess* with much more of realism than has usually been supposed. How then must we understand his further account, the dropping of the hunt for a considerable time, and the return to it at the close of the poem? Now, there is no evidence that Chaucer was actively engaged in the hunt. Skeat, it is true, explains *my tree* of line 387 by saying, Chaucer "dreamed that he was one of the men posted to watch which way the hart went, and to keep the bounds." This seems to me wholly impossible, since it would imply an almost menial service for a king's valet. Indeed, the *Master of Game* (p. 188) tells us explicitly that the "stable," or men set to keep the boundaries, were "set by the foresters or parkers," and must themselves have been under-foresters or woodmen. Nor is there any indication that Chaucer was an attendant of the king in this king's hunt,[22] since in that case he could not have been free to act as he did. We must assume he dreamed of being an unattached observer, and meant by "my tree" merely the one at which he had stationed himself to view the hunt as an onlooker. Since the *forloyn,* or check, in the hunt has occurred—a check that might even mean the end of the hunt for that day—Chaucer feels free to wander off through the wood. The *forloyn* is thus used in the poem for an artistic purpose.

May I pause to note in this relation Professor Kittredge's explanation of "the quality of artlessness or naïvete" in the *Book of the Duchess (Chaucer and his Poetry,* ch. ii) as a sort of "dream psychology," an explanation that has continued to seem very attractive. Here Professor Kittredge applies it par-

---

[22] Such a position would have been entirely proper for Chaucer in 1369, but would have made impossible such freedom of action as he had planned for his poem. Besides, the Master of Game (p.190) shows that special care was taken for the disposition of the king and queen with their attendants: "For it is to be known that the attendants of his [the king's] chamber and of the queen's should be best placed, and the two fewterers ought to make fair lodges of green boughs at the tryste to keep the king and the queen and the ladies and gentlewomen, and also the greyhounds, from the sun and bad weather." Under such circumstances, Chaucer, a king's attendant, could not have withdrawn, even for the sorrows of a prince.

ticularly to the lack of further reference to the horse
on which Chaucer rode to the *forest-syde,* and to the
whelp which, the poet says, "cam by me," "fauned
me as I stod," and ran away when he tried to catch
it. The minute accuracy of Chaucer's description of
the hunt perhaps suggests some modification of a
·most interesting exposition. Reference to Turbervile
would seem to show that horsemen were regularly
supplied with pages for their horses, and that they
often took up their positions on foot.   Thus (p. 101–2)
horsemen of the relay

> shall place their houndes in some faire place
> at the foote of some tree, forbiding [that is bid-
> ding] the varlet that he uncouple them not with-
> out their knowledge and commaundement . . .
> Then shall they go three or foure hundreth paces
> from thence on that side that the hunting is or-
> deined, and shall hearken if they heare any thing
> or can discover the Harte. . . As also the horse-
> man shall withdraw himselfe aside for another
> reason. And that is because the pages and they
> which holde the horses do commonly make such
> a noyse that he can not heare the crye.

Perhaps Chaucer felt he could not make poetic material of such a page as he must have had in this age
of many servants.

The incident regarding the young hound, "That
hadde y-folowed and coude no good," is somewhat

different.   A young hunting hound was too valuable
to be lost, as shown by the discussion of the various
kinds of dogs and their elaborate care in the *Master
of Game* and Turbervile.   Young hounds, too, naturally trained with the old dogs, as Turbervile tells us
on p. 36, were also sometimes employed in the regular hunt, as implied on p. 103.   Now the blowing
of the forloyn, as already indicated, meant the coupling of the hounds.   It was the most natural thing,
therefore, that the poet, seeing such a hound running loose, "wolde han caught hit," not perhaps as
Professor Kittredge assumes, "to take him up in his
arms,[23] but to turn over to some keeper for coupling
up until the hounds were again let loose on the track
of the hart.   On the other hand, Chaucer's whelp
was to run away for a particular purpose, leading
the poet into a deep forest away from the hunt, and
finally to a prince of the blood.   When he came upon
the latter, clearly in distress, even a valuable hound
might be disregarded.

Before this latter event leads Chaucer, somewhat
tardily as in his early manner, to the real subject of
the poem, he was to give some further evidence of
acquaintance with hunting terms.   Along with the
native names of the deer he sees in the wood—the
hert, hind, buck, doe, roe—Chaucer uses for the first

---

[23] Quite possible for a running hound (ratch) if a kenet,
but not likely with a greyhound or other variety of hunting
dog.

time in our literature, so far as the *NED.* quotations indicate, the Anglo-French *foun* (OF. *faon*) "fawn, young deer of the first year," and *sour "sore,* a buck of the fourth year."[24]   Moreover, whether Chaucer was the first to use these words or not, we can hardly believe he did not employ them in their exact hunting significance.

When Chaucer came upon the "man in blak," whom we know as John of Gaunt, the bereaved husband of Blanche of Lancaster, the hunt was entirely put aside for a time.   It would have been distracting to us, as to them, if either poet or prince, in the interview which follows, should have been interrupted by hunting horns or hunting cries, by renewal of the chase, or by the clamor of huntsmen or hounds at the death.   Yet, from the later reference we are now to discuss, it must be clear that the hunt went on.   The ruse of the hart may be conceived to have led the hunters some distance away, or the poet's walk through the wood may have taken him far enough to be undisturbed.   This is in entire accord with hunting possibilities, quite apart from the poet's right to subordinate the minor to the major action.

In the abrupt close of the poem, when the poet—

---

[24] Chaucer again used *foun (fown)* in *Troilus and Criseyde* I, 465–7, where it has the figurative meaning of "a new thought, or emotion conceived."   The passage reads:
>Ne in him desyr noon othere fownes bredde
>But arguments to this conclusioun,
>That she on him wolde han compassioun.
This use of the word is not recorded in the *NED.*

for poetic purposes less quick than he must have been
in life — finally understands the great loss of his
patron and friend, the hunt is again introduced in
the following lines:

> And with that worde, right anoon,
> They gan to strake forth; al was doon
> For that tyme, the hert-hunting.

On these lines Skeat has no comment, but *strake* is
defined in his glossary as "move, proceed," with reference to this place, the only occurrence in Chaucer
apparently.[25] Doubtless *strake forth* has here the

---

[25] The etymology of *strake* is difficult, as indicated by the
NED. The special difficulty lies in the fact that we have not
only a ME. strong verb *striken* with past tenses *strǫke* and
strāke, but two ME. weak verbs *strāken—strāked* and *strǫken*
—strǫked, all with essentially the same meanings: 1) "to go,
move, proceed"; 2) "to sound a horn (sometimes at least indicating movement)." The first, or strong verb is clearly OE.
strīcan "strike," with an irregular past *strāke* beside the regular *strōke*, as we have today another irregular past *struck*
in the same verb. For the *strāke* form cf. *drave* beside *drove*,
even in Elizabethan English. These are not Nth. forms, since
they clearly belong to the South, as shown by many references. They may be shortened forms of the OE. pasts *drāf*,
strāc.

Of *strāke* wk., with the meaning "sound upon a horn," the
NED. says "of obscure origin." It regards the word as a
hunting term only, failing to include *strāke* "go, proceed" of
Piers Plowman's Crede, 82, or even this Chaucer example. For
its etymology I suggest an unrecorded OE. wk. vb. *stræcan*
"cause to go," with derived intransitive meaning, making it
parallel in purport with OE. *strican*. Such a *stræcan* by
shortening of the root vowel would give ME. *strāke*, as OE.
wræc f. "vengeance" with similar phonology gave ME. *wrāche*.

The wk. *strǫke*, with meanings similar to those of the other verbs, as in *Master of Game*, pp. 194–5, is probably a de-
scendant of OE. *strācian* "stroke," with special derived senses,

23

broader sense of "proceed homeward," as shown by
the context. The hunt has ended for the day. Yet
the abrupt transition from prince and poet to the
hunters of lines 345–386 (*they* of line 1312 must
refer to the latter) requires some further explanation. How are the hunters and the king himself
(1314) brought into more immediate contact with
the somewhat distant poet? Or how had the hunt
gone on, as we must believe it did, without disturb-
ing the colloquy between the poet and the "man in
blak," and yet now become evident to both?

The explanation is in the second meaning of
strake, well authenticated by examples in our literature, although not given by Skeat. Just as *rechase,
recheat (rechate),* and *forloyn* mean both the act itself and the corresponding signal upon the hunter's
horn, so *strake* means not only "proceed, go home-

---

perhaps influenced by the other verbs. Such, at least, is a con-
sistent and possible scheme for these difficult words.

Incidentally, the *NED.* puts Malory's use of *strāke (Morte
d'Arth.* X, lii) under the noun, such a noun as does occur in
Turbervile under "Measures of Blowing" and elsewhere. Malory's example, however, is the infinitive of the verb. To Sir
Tristrem is attributed the origin of all "measures of blowing," and these are enumerated as follows: "First to the uncoupling, to the seeing, to the rechate, to the flight, to the
death, and to strake." Here *to strake,* not *to the strake,* it
will be noticed, is the measure blown as the hunters set out
homeward after the hunt, the meaning derived from the literal one of going homeward itself. *To strāke* also meant "to
proceed to the field," or "from covert to covert," as shown by
Turbervile's "measures" which gives the accompanying sig-
nals upon the horn. In Malory, too, the *rechate* can not be a
"recall" as ordinarily defined, but the rallying to the chase, as
I have defined it.

ward," but "sound the signal for proceeding," in this case, going home after the killing of the hart. The situation is explained by this passage from the *Master of Game* (ch. xxxiv, pp. 178–9):

> And when there is nought left [that is after the rewarding of the hounds] then shall the lord, if he wishes, or else the master of the game or in his absence whoso is greatest next him stroke in this wise, that is to say blow four motes and stynt not half an Ave Maria, and then blow other four motes a little longer than the first four motes. And thus should no wight stroke but when the hart is slain with strength. And when one of the aforesaid hath thus blown, then should the grooms couple up the hounds and draw homeward fair and soft. And all the rest of the hunters should stroke in this wise: "Trut, trut, tro-ro-row, tro-ro-row," and four motes all of one length, not too long and not too short. And otherwise should no hart hunter stroke from thenceforth till they go to bed.[26]

That such signaling was kept up on the journey home is not only implied by the *Master of Game*, but clearly stated in *Sir Gawain and the Green Knight* 1363–4 and 1922–3. I quote the latter:

---

[26] This passage is in one of the chapters original with the Duke of York, and thus clearly gives the English as distinct from the French practice.

And þenne þay helden to home, for hit watz
nieȝ nyȝt,
Strakande ful stoutly in hor store hornez.

Thus the noise of the hunt, which has been going on at a distance, again comes within hearing of the poet, and the character of the measure heard shows that the hunt is over for the day.[27]

Again, another measure on the horn indicated that the king would hunt no more, as the *Master of Game* explains (ch. xxxvi, pp. 194–5):

And if the King will hunt no more then should the master of his game, if the King will not blow, blow a mote and stroke with a mote in the middle. And the sergeant, or whoso bloweth next him and no man else, should blow the first mote but only the middle, and so every man as often as he likes to stroke, if they have obtained that which they have hunted for. And the middle mote should not be blown save by him that bloweth next the master. And thereby may men know, as they hear men stroke homeward, whether they have well sped or not.

Thus Chaucer, still in the wood with the sorrowing prince, but hearing the appropriate signal for the return after the hunt, could add the lines beginning,

With that methoughte that this king
Gan [quikly] homeward for to ryde.

---

[27] Turbervile figures "A strake of nyne, to drawe home the companie. With twoo windes."

Thus, too, unity is given to the poem, not only through the character of the interview between the poet and prince, but through an entirely proper and explainable return to the hunt with which the dream began.

The castle to which the king rode was, as we know, a dream castle, the description playing upon the names of John of Gaunt, Lancaster, Blanche, and the Richmond connected with both John and his Duchess in the period when the poem was written.[28] The castle suggested the bell, the stroke of twelve, and Chaucer awoke at midnight, to find the book he had been reading and resolve upon making his most important early poem.

One minor bit of possible realism remains to be mentioned. The hunt of which Chaucer dreamed is placed in May. Now the frequent use of May by the medieval poets is known to have been to some extent a convention. Here, for example, if the *Book of the Duchess* was written in 1369, as usually assumed, the opening of the scene in May must have been merely conventional. Yet it is not impossible that the poem was not composed before the spring of 1370. John of Gaunt was not home from command of the French expedition until November. If he requested Chaucer to write the poem, as Professor Kittredge suggests,

---

[28] In speaking of it as a dream castle, I do not mean that there may not have been reminiscences of an actual castle or castles which Chaucer may have known. See Tupper in *Mod. Lang. Notes* XXXI, 250, 442; XXXII, 54.

the composition could not have been undertaken until late in the year, and the completion of the poem may well have reached into 1370. Or possibly the request of the bereaved husband was not made in the ecstasy of his grief, but some months after the Duchess Blanche had passed away. Be that as it may, the hunting of the hart in the month assigned may have had a realistic basis. The *Master of Game* (ch. iii, p. 35) informs us:

> The harts have more power to run well from the entry of May into St. John's tide [June 24] than at any other time; for then they have put on new flesh and new hair and new heads for [that is, on account of] the new herbs and the new coming out of trees and of fruits, and be not too heavy. For as yet they have not recovered their grease, neither within nor without, nor their heads, wherefore they be much lighter and swifter.

There is, therefore, some reason to believe Chaucer was as realistic in this as in other respects, when describing the hunting scene of this poem.

Nor is it wholly impossible Chaucer has introduced still another realistic touch in his May hunt. The early failure of the hounds to keep the scent, the ease with which the hart had succeeded in his ruse, may have some relation to the time in which the hunt is placed. In the chapter "Of Running Hounds and their Nature," the *Master of Game* informs us that keeping the scent was more difficult in this very period. He says (ch. xiv., p. 112) :

> Also the hounds scent worse from May until St. John's time than in any other time of all the year, for as I shall say the burnt heath and the burning of fields taketh the scent from the hounds of the beasts that they hunt. Also in that time the herbs be best, and flowers in their smelling, each one in their kind, and when the hounds hope to scent the beast that they hunt, the sweet smelling of the herbs takes the scent of the beast from them.

I make no attempt to press these latter points, but, it must be admitted, the coincidence of these two characteristics of a May hunt might have had its basis in the same realism that has seemed so clear in the whole description of the hunting scene in the *Book of the Duchess*, and the realism that will appear in other passages in Chaucer's poetry still to be discussed.

The lines in the *Book of the Duchess* are the most explicit of those in which Chaucer deals with hunting. Yet here and there in other places are shorter passages relating to the subject, and in them some technical terms of the hunt, so that these also warrant some words of interpretation. The most considerable of these references are in the *Knight's Tale* which, although based on Boccaccio's *Teseide,* shows great freedom in the use of its source. Indeed, in the parts of the Tale with which I shall deal there are scarcely more than hints of the original. Chaucer has represented hunting as he knew it in his native land.

For example, in lines 780–88 *(CT,* A 1638–46), the allusion to Arcite's likeness to a lion, as he comes to fight with Palamon, is made more specific in relation to northern latitudes by addition of the bear.[29] The scene is then worked out more realistically as an actual hunting incident by the introduction of the spear, the standing at the gap in the wood *(gappe,* twice mentioned) through which the bear—*him* of 793 must refer to that animal rather than to the lion —comes rushing,

And breketh bothe bowes and the leves.

From him there is now no escape, and hunter or hunted must succumb as Arcite makes clear by his remark. So, to the likeness of Palamon to a lion and Arcite to a tiger in the fight, Chaucer has added, in lines 800–1 *(CT,* A 1658–9) the realistic figure that would appeal to Englishmen more readily:

As wylde bores gonne they to smyte,
That frothen whyte as foom for ire wood.

A still more important passage for which there is little basis in the *Teseide (KT.* 815–37, *CT,* A 1673–

_____
[29] Compare *Teseide* Bk. vii, st. 106,119.

95)[30] describes the coming of Theseus, the mighty hunter,

For after Mars he serveth now Diane.

One can but wonder, from the applicability of the whole scene, whether this is not also a reminiscence of Edward III and his characteristic fondness for war and hunting. In this passage we first meet the hunting term *grete hert* "great hart, hart worthy to be hunted," a compound not recognized by Skeat and the *NED.*, but frequent in the *Master of Game* and not uncommon in other places. For instance, chapters xxiii–v of the *Master of Game* all deal with "How a Man should know a Great Hart," and the following quotation (p. 131) indicates the specific use:

And also if a man find such a hart [a "great hart and an old one" as already described], and men ask him what hart it is, he may answer that it is a hart chaceable of ten that should not be refused.

The compound is again used by Chaucer in line 823, when he mentions the "joye and appetyt" of Theseus,

To been himself the grete hertes bane.[31]

---

[30] See *Teseide*, ll. 77–8. The scene in its distinctive references is practically all Chaucer's.

[31] The *NED.* gives to *great*, under 7, the meaning "grown up, full grown," but cites first a quotation from Caxton's *Charles the Great*. The use in the above compound falls under that meaning, and the example in Chaucer is one of the earliest I have found. Compare also *Destr. of Troy* 13,557:

A grete herte in a grove, goond hym one;

Attention has already been called to the May time
as one peculiarly appropriate for hunting the hart,
so that it is not strange Theseus was especially "desirous" of hunting "the grete hert in May."   Thus,
there is no lack of realism in his pursuing his own
purpose, and still coming upon Arcite and Palamon,
the former of whom had gone out for another reason,

> For to doon his observaunce to May,
> Remembering on the poynt of his desyr.

Again, it is perhaps a knowledge of English hunting
that made Chaucer represent Theseus as riding "to
the launde," or plain,

> For thider was the hert wont have his flight.

This, at least, would fit in with what the *Master of
Game* tells us in chapter iii, p. 36:

> And all the time from rutting time [middle
> of September to middle of October] into Whit-
> sunday great deer and old will be found in the
> plains.

The "clothed al in grene" of line 828, applying to
Theseus, the Queen, and Emily, and for which there
is nothing in the original *Teseide,* is doubtless another
realistic touch of Chaucer's time.   By the time of
Turbervile hunting dress seems to have changed or

---

and Gower, *Conf. Amant.* I, 2299,
> The grete hert anon was founde.

Turbervile (ch. xxxvii, p. 100) has *great deer* in the same
sense: "But if he find Slot that seem of a great Deare, he
may say a Hart of ten without any addition of words."

been less regarded, but his reference to the matter is proof of the earlier custom; he says in chap. xxxviii, p. 101:

> Phoebus[32] sayth that they ought to be clad in greene when they hunt the Hart or Bucke, and in russet when they hunt the Bore, but that is of no great importance, for I remitte the coloures to the fantasies of men.

In the same passage of the *Knight's Tale* also occurs the specific hunting phrase "han a cours . . . with houndes," that is, "have a run (at a hart) with hounds," for which this Chaucer quotation is the first cited by the *NED*.

In lines 1290–94 *(CT*, A 2148–52) Chaucer is responsible for introducing the English hunting dogs, the "whyte alaunts" "as grete as any steer,"[33] to the

---

[32] Gaston de Foix, called from his manly beauty Gaston Phoebus, wrote the *Livre de Chasse* on which the Duke of York's *Master of Game* was based.

The Knight's "yeman" in the *Prologue* to the *Canterbury Tales* (100 ff.), whom Chaucer guesses to be "a forster" and is shown to be a hunter by his bow and arrows, his horn and "bawdrik," has also his "cote and hood of grene." So the apparently similar "gay yeman" of the *Friar's Tale (CT*, D 1380 ff.), besides his similar bow and arrows, has his "courtepy of grene," while his hat was probably also of that color, though "with frenges blake."

[33] On this passage A. S. Cook has an elaborate and interesting note in, 'The Last Months of Chaucer's Earliest Patron' *(Trans. of Conn. Acad. of Arts and Sciences* xxi, 128 ff.). He there suggests that Chaucer first saw alaunts at the wedding feast of Lionel, Duke of Clarence, in Milan June 5, 1368. Apart from the uncertainty about Chaucer's being at that feast, the suggestion rests on the idea that there could have been no alaunts in England before 1381 when the *Knight's Tale* was written. The latter fact seems to me as unlikely

description of which the *Master of Game* gave chapter xvi. He confirms Chaucer regarding their color by saying (p. 116) ;

> And though there be alauntes of all hues, the true hue of a good alaunte, and that which is most common, should be white, with black spots about the ears.

That the *mozel* "muzzle" of 1293 was also important for such an animal, the chapter fully implies, especially the sentence,

> In all manner of ways alauntes are treacherous and evil understanding, and more foolish and more harebrained than any other kind of hound.

Such traits the author confirms by saying, "For men have seen alauntes slay their masters." The "colors of gold" on the alaunts are quite in accord with what we have been told of those sometimes placed on valuable lymers. The "torets," a word first used by Chaucer, were swivels to allow free play of the leash as already explained, not "small rings on the collar of a dog," as in Skeat's glossary.[34] One further touch

---

as that there were no lymers in England before Chaucer wrote the *Book of the Duchess*, because Chaucer in that poem is the first to have used the name in English. At any rate, our main purpose here is to point out that the allusion of the alaunts is original with Chaucer, and that it apparently falls in with his considerable knowledge of medieval hunting.

[34] Skeat does refer to the other form of the word, *turet*, found in the description of the *Astrolabe*, and a note by Wharton "which seems to make the word equivalent to a swivel." The *NED.* defines it clearly as "a swivel ring on a

of English hunting interests occurs in describing the feast given by Theseus, before the tournament, to Palamon, Arcite, and their supporters from many countries. This feast the poet refrains from describing at length, but among other details alludes to

What haukes sitten on the perche above,
What houndes liggen on the floor adoun,

as they perhaps often did in Edward Third's castle halls. The *Teseide* (vi, st. 8) mentions hounds, falcons, goshawks, but the scene in this and other particulars is essentially English.

A brief hunting scene occurs in the *Franklin's Tale* (*CT*, F 1190–94), where Aurelius is shown by the magician:

Forestes, parkes ful of wilde deer;
Ther saugh he hertes with hir hornes hye, . . .
He saugh of hem an hondred slayn with houndes,
And somme with arwes blede of bittre woundes.

Then follow three lines devoted to hawking, with which we are not dealing in this paper. The hunting part is true to English practice, deer being run down by the hounds, or killed by bowmen stationed at various plases along the course of the hunt. Of the use of the bow *La Chace dou Serf* tells us (Dryden's translation, p. 130):

---

dog's collar." The word *toret (turet)* "little tower" had acquired this secondary meaning because the ring was set and moved in a little tower-like structure fixed in the collar itself. For these examples in Chaucer the meaning should be, "a swivel ring set in a tower-like form."

Make your varlets carry bows, for no one
ought to kill the hart with a sword after he is
frayed [that is, after the hart's antlers are well
grown, implying full growth of the animal]. I
advise you that you shoot from afar.

The Franklin himself, it will be remembered *(Prol.*
347–8),

After the sondry sesons of the yeer
So chaunged he his mete and his soper,

a change doubtless partly dependent upon hunting.

Among significant references to hunting in the
Canterbury Tales, one must not forget the description of the Monk, since with total disregard of the
canons of the church,

He yaf nat of that text a pulled hen,
That seith that hunters been nat holy men.[35]

He was, we remember *(Prol.* 166–92),

An out-rydere that lovede venerye;

. . . .

Therefore he was a pricasour aright;
Grehoundes he hadde as swifte as fowel in
    flight;
Of priking and of hunting for the hare
Was al his lust, for no cost wolde he spare.

Here *pricasour* (for which Chaucer is alone responsible) whatever its exact etymology, must mean
"huntsman," as the *NED.* suggests with a "perhaps,"

---

[35] Compare my article 'Some of Chaucer's Lines on the
Monk,' *Mod. Phil.* I, 105, and above, pp. 39ff.

rather than merely a "hard rider," as Skeat defines it. So *priking* is not simply "riding," but "riding in the hunt," and here more specifically "tracking (the hare)."[36] Probably the use of the word in this latter meaning depends on the swiftness of the hare in her flight, for the *Master of Game* (ch. xxxv, p. 181) calls the hare "the king of all venery." Turbervile, in some verses before chap. lviii, p. 160, makes her say,

> For running swift, and holding out at length,
> I beare the bell above all other beasts.

Very properly, therefore, Chaucer provided the Monk with greyhounds "as swifte as fowel in flight."

The Monk's fondness for hunting the hare, rather than some other animal, depended not on her swiftness alone. The Duke of York not only introduced the hare first among animals to be hunted, but says (ch. ii, p. 14):

> Much good sport and liking is the hunting of her, more than that of any other beast that any man knoweth. . . . And that for five reasons. The one is, for her hunting lasteth all the year as with running hounds without any sparing, and this is not with all the other beasts. And also men hunt at her both in the morning and

---

[36] See *Master of Game* ch. xvi, p. 116: "If a man prick a horse," that is, "hunt a horse." The noun *pricking* meant "the footprints of a hare," as in *M. of G.* ch. xxxv, p. 185. For *pricasour* we may also compare Turbervile's "a good priker or huntsman on horsebacke" (ch. xxxviii, p. 101).

in the evening. . . . That other reason is . . .
for hounds must need find her by mastery, and
quest point by point. . . . And when she is
started it is a fair thing. And then it is a fair
thing to slay her with strength of hounds, for
she runneth long and ginnously [that is, cun-
ningly].

Turbervile is equally strong in praise of hare hunting (ch. lix, p. 162) :

I might well maintaine that of all chases the
Hare maketh greatest pastime and pleasure,
and sheweth most cunning in hunting, and is
meetest for gentlemen of all other huntings, for
that they may find them at all times and hunt
them at most seasons of the yeare, and that with
small charges.

Twici's *Art of Venerie* begins with the hare, and explains it as follows (Dryden's modernization of the
Middle English text, p. 19) :

Now will we begin with the Hare. "And why,
Sir, will you begin with the Hare, rather than
with any other beast?" I will tell you; because
she is the most marvellous beast which is on
this earth; . . . and since all the fine terms [of
hunting] are based upon it (that is, upon the
chase of the hare).

Again, Chaucer follows English custom of the
period when he has the Monk possess "grehoundes"

for coursing the hare. The *Master of Game* says explicitly (ch. ii, p. 22) :

> Men slay hares with greyhounds and with running hounds by strength as here in England, but elsewhere they slay them also with small pockets, and with purse-nets, and with small nets with hare-pipes, and with long nets, and with small cords. . . . But, truly, I trow, no good hunter would slay them so for any good.[37]

The modern editors of the *Master of Game* remind us, too (see Hare, *App.* p. 122), that hunting customs have changed since Chaucer's time, greyhounds being no longer used in hare hunting.

Some minor allusions in the *Canterbury Tales* indicate Chaucer's acquaintance with specific terms of hunting, or with the lore of game animals. In the *Shipman's Tale*, line 104 *(CT*, B 1294) reads,

> As in a forme sit a wery hare,

where *forme* is the hunter's name for the lair of a hare. Skeat has no note, but Turbervile explains in his chapter lix "Of the Subtilities of an Hare when she is Runne and Hunted" (p. 165) :

> I have also seene an Hare runne and stande up two houres before a kennell of houndes, and then she hath started and raysed an other

---

[37] The expressions "As here in England" and "Truly I trow etc.," are the Duke of York's additions to the original of Gaston de Foix.

freshe Hare out of her forme and set her selfe
downe therin.

So in the *Nun's Priest's Tale* 517 *(CT,* B 4527) it is
said of the fox,

For yet ne was ther no man that him sewed,

where *sewed* "sued" is used in its specific sense of
"pursued as game."

Passages in the *Friar's Tale* 71ff. *(CT,* D 1369ff)
and the *Merchant's Tale* 769–70 *(CT,* E 2013–14)
show Chaucer using another hunting term for the
first time, a *dog for the bow.* They are, in the order
above:

For in this world nis dogge for the bowe,
That can an hurt deer from an hool y-knowe
Bet than this Somnour knew a sly lechour,
Or an avouter, or a paramour;

and of Damien the young lover:

And eek to Januarie he gooth as lowe
As ever dide a dogge for the bowe.

Skeat's notes on "dogge for the bowe" in these passages are valuable, but leave something to be desired. Such a dog was especially trained to accompany the bowman on a deer hunt, in order to follow
and bring down a stricken deer only. Unlike a running hound, he must be absolutely subservient to
his master, as silent as a lymer, making his attack
only when so ordered, and only upon a deer already
wounded by the bowman's arrow. The latter careful

discrimination is indicated in the first passage, with figurative application to the Summoner. The quality of subservience is shown in the second quotation, to illustrate which the *CtDict.* refers to T. L. O. Davies, *Supplementary English Glossary* (1881), and says: "Such dogs, being well trained and obedient, were taken to typify humble and subservient people."

In the *Maunciple's Tale* 79–82 *(CT,* H 183–6) is a noteworthy bit of folklore regarding one of the game animals:

A she-wolf hath also a vileins kinde;
The lewedeste wolf that she may finde,
Or leest of reputacion wol she take
In tyme whan hir lust to han a make.

This allusion, Skeat asserts with great definiteness, is taken from *Romance of the Rose* 7799–7804. Such may be the source but, as Skeat admits, it occurs in an entirely different part of that work from the lines used in the *Maunciple's Tale* just before. It is interesting, therefore, that a fuller account of this supposed characteristic of the she-wolf occurs in the *Master of Game,* chap. vii, pp. 54–5, so that this bit of animal lore may have been known to Chaucer, as to hunter and forester in England, quite apart from any literary source.[38]

---

[38] The allusion to the Summoner as "wood were as an hare" *(Friar's Tale* 29, *CT,* D 1327), slight as is its relation to hunting, seems to be the earliest use of the expression "mad as a hare," "mad as a March hare." The latter form is first recorded as used by More in 1529. Doubtless the idea is con-

Apart from the *Book of the Duchess* and the *Canterbury Tales,* some significant references to hunting are to be found in *Troilus and Criseyde.* In Book ii, lines 962–4, the cynical Pandarus replies to the question of Troilus "shal I now wepe or singe" (l. 952) by saying:

> Hir love of freendship have I to thee wonne,
> And also hath she leyd hir feyth to borwe;
> Algate a foot is hameled of thy sorwe.

Skeat's note explains *hameled* as "cut off, docked," but adds in his glossary, "it refers to the mutilation of dogs that were found to be pursuing game secretly. They were mutilated by cutting off a foot." This is apparently not quite accurate, since the process of hameling (hambling) was rather to cut off the balls of the feet,[39] and is therefore less applicable to the single foot of the *Troilus* reference. Skeat's explanation would make the line mean that "sorwe" as a

---

nected with that of melancholy attributed to the hare. For example, Turbervile says: "The Hare first taught us the use of the hearbe called wilde Succorye, which is verie excellent for those whiche are disposed to be melancholike; she hir selfe is one of the moste melancholike beastes that is."

The proverb in *Troilus* iv, 1373–4,

> . . . men seyn that hard it is
> The wolf ful and the wether hool to have,

also has its basis in the animal lore of a game animal. More remote is that of *Troilus* iv, 1453–4,

> . . . men seyn "that one thenketh the bere,
> But al another thenketh his ledere."

Both these proverbs are original with Chaucer. They are not in his source.

[39] See *NED., CtDict.* etc., under *hamble.*

hound could no longer pursue Troilus so effectively, and in that case the line seems to have little direct connection with the preceding. Indeed, Skeat indicates its separation by a period after *borwe*. I suggest the possibility of another explanation. The deer was sometimes *hameled,* as in training of young hounds,[40] so that it is possible the line means a foot of thy sorrow (cause of thy sorrow) has been hameled. That is, Criseyde has already given her friendship and "leyd hir feyth to borwe," thus becoming *hameled* and more easily pursued. See the figure of pursuit in line 959. In any case, *hameled* is still another hunting term used by our poet.

The interpretation I have just given of line 964 seems more likely, because Pandarus again uses a hunting figure in lines 1535–36 of the same book. He there still further encourages Troilus by saying:

> Lo, holde thee at thy triste cloos, and I
> Shal wel the deer unto the bowe dryve.

From this, *tryst (trist)* as a hunting term must mean, not simply an appointed place as usually given, but a place at which the bowman stood to shoot the deer. The *Master of Game* (chap. xxxv, p. 190) uses both "standing" and "tryste," as in "And when the king is at his standing or tryste, whichever he prefers." The former seems to be defined in the reference on p. 189 to "the king's standing, if the king

---

[40] See Turbervile ch. xiv, p. 36.

would stand with his bow," while on the next page
we are told,

> that the fewterers ought to make fair lodges
> of green boughs at the tryste to keep the king
> and queen and ladies and gentle-women, and also
> the greyhounds, from the sun and bad weather.

Tryst would seem to mean, then, not only the place
of a bowman as in Chaucer, the "standing" in native
English, but also a more elaborate place appointed
for king and queen when he took a less active part
in the hunt.[41]   Both these examples are original with
Chaucer.

In the *Legend of Good Women* 1188–1217, describing the hunt by Dido and Aeneas and based on the
Aeneid iv, 129–59, Chaucer has unified the scene, and
in some particulars made it conform to English hunting practice.   While nets and spears are mentioned
(1190) as by Virgil,[42] the goats and the boar of the
Latin poet are omitted, and the hunt is mainly con-
fined to the hart—the appropriate game for a royal
hunt—as in the *Book of the Duchess* and the *Knight's*

---

[41] Minor allusions to hunting in *Troilus* occur in iii, 1779–81:
> In tyme of trewe on haukinge wolde he ryde,
> Or elles hunten boor, bere, or lyoun,—
> The smale beestes leet he gon bisyde;

but this is from Boccaccio's *Filostrato*.   In l. 1238, where
Troilus dreams of "a boor with tuskes grete," the dream notion is Chaucer's, as well as the kissing of the lady in his
arms.   The boar, however, belongs to Boccaccio.

[42] Nets were sometimes used in England, in order to confine
the hunt within certain boundaries, as indicated in a footnote
to *Master of Game* p. 30.

Tale. Here, too, Chaucer again uses the specific hunting term *find* for the discovery of the game animal, and adds at once his only example of true hunting cries:[43]

> The herd of hertes founden is anoon,
> With "Hey, go bet, prik thou, lat goon, lat
>> goon."[44]

Nor must we forget, among the allusions to hunting in the *Legend of Good Women,* some of the gifts which Dido gave to Aeneas. None were too good for him, we are told in lines 1114 ff., and among them

---

[43] Very different these from the cries and shouting when the fox is pursued by the widow, her daughters, and "many another man," by the dogs of the farm and the maid Malkin, in the *Nun's Priest's Tale (CT,* B 4565 ff.).

[44] The punctuation should show, as does that of the Globe edition, that the hunting cries proper conclude with this line. I suggest, also, that the next two lines are specifically what the "yonge folk," as distinct from their elders, boastingly say, and that this fact should be more adequately indicated by new marks of quotation inclosing lines 1214–5, as perhaps a dash after the latter. Chaucer then concludes the account of the royal hunt with "and up ('upon that') they (the elders, not the boastful youth) kille
These wilde hertes and han hem at hir wille."
The *bestys wilde* or *wild(e) bestes* of some MSS. may be explained as a misunderstanding of this conclusion, as if it belonged to what is said by both old and young. Chaucer, I take it, meant to emphasize the hart hunting, and as I have pointed out above, no other animals are included in the description by him. Besides, this foolish boast was surely not spoken by Dido or "this Troyan by her syde" while actually engaged in hunting the royal game.
The hunting cry "Hey" occurs in *Sir Gawain and the Green Knight* (1158), where with "war" it is used to hold in the hinds. "Go bet, prik thou" are terms of encouragement, as Skeat says, but they seem here to apply specifically to the setting on of the "finders," while "lat goon" must be the cry at the uncoupling of the running hounds after the finding of the hart.

Ne gentil hautein faucon heronere,
Ne hound for hert or wilde boor or dere,
the latter especially an appropriate gift for a royal
hunt.

There are, besides, a number of minor allusions
to hunting in Chaucer. In the Prologue to the
Legend of Good Women (131B), the "smale foules"

That from the panter and the net ben scaped

rejoice in their escape, and sing "the fouler we de-
fye." The Host in the *Canterbury Tales* addresses
the poet in a hunting figure *(CT*, B 1886) :

Thou lokest as thou woldest finde an hare,
For ever upon the ground I see thee stare.

Sir Thopas and the Marquis Walter in the *Clerk's
Tale* were hunters, as indicated in lines B 1296–9,
E 81, 234.[45] The Christmas time in the *Franklin's
Tale* (F 1255) brings "braun of the tusked swyn,"
a product of the hunt. The Maunciple uses a figure
from hunting in his *Prologue* (H 77), and the Phebus of his *Tale*, Apollo the archer (H 108, 129), is
made to kill his wife with bow and arrow, which he
later breaks in grief when he realizes he has used
them so disastrously (H 264, 269).

The illustrations and interpretations of this paper
indicate that Chaucer knew much more of medieval
hunting practice than has usually been supposed. It

---

[45] The humorous pursuit of the fox which carried off Chan-
ticleer in the *Nun's Priest's Tale* contains no technical hunting language.

shows, too, that he used hunting terms in their strict hunting senses, in other words, with a realism quite in keeping with that shown in so many other particulars throughout his work. Once again did the poet return to the subject in what might have been an extremely interesting presentation. When the Monk has wearied his audience with his doleful tales of misfortune, and the Knight has stopped him with "good sir, namore of this," the Host suggested something more in keeping with the Monk's character (B 3995):

Sir, sey somewhat of hunting I yow preye.

But for some reason Chaucer was not ready with a hunting tale, and the Monk is allowed to put us off:

"Nay," quod this Monk, "I have no lust to pleye."

SOME NOTES ON CHAUCER AND SOME CONJECTURES*

I. 1. *Book of the Duchess 309–11*

So mery a soun, so swete entunes,
That certes, for the toune of Tewnes,
I nolde but I had herd hem singe.

The word *entunes* is considered a noun by Skeat, the Globe edition of Chaucer, and the dictionaries generally. Yet it is the only example of the noun in all our literature, so far as records show. It is said to be derived from the verb *entunen*, OF. *entoner*, no OF. equivalent for a noun of this form being known. Such derivation of noun from verb in so early a period is unusual, to say the least, no other similar noun from a verb being recorded among the *en-* or *em-* compounds in the Bradley-Stratmann *Dictionary*. Two centuries after, such a derivative would not have been strange. Besides, the noun *tune (tun)* existed in Middle English, since it is used by Gower *(Conf. Amant.* viii, 830) and other writers.

I suggest that *entunes* is the verb in the occasional Northern third singular present indicative in *-es*, and that the present tense is here used in rime for the past which we should expect, as *look* is used for

* *Phil. Quar.* Vol. II, pp. 81–96 (1923).

looked in the rime of line 840. Such use of one inflectional form for another in rime is not unknown in Middle English poets, as in *juele* for *jueles* (Pearl 929), *outfleme* for *outflemed* (1,177), possibly *adyte* for *adytes* (349). Not unlikely Chaucer was here influenced by the rime word *Tewnes*, already in his mind for the couplet. This explanation of *entunes* would make it accord with the two Northern -*es* forms of the verb in the rimes of this poem, those in lines 73–4 *(elles-telles)*, and 257–8 *(falles-halles)*.

Two also occur in the *House of Fame*, probably composed not many years after the *Book of the Duchess*, those of lines 425–6 *(elles-telles)*, and 1907–8 *(tydinges-bringes)*. The similar rime in the *Reeve's Tale, thinges-bringes (CT*, A 4129–30), the only example of this sort in the *Canterbury Tales*, is naturally in keeping with the Reeve's more Northern dialect.

The suggestion, it seems to me, makes the line smoother—"so merry a sound so sweetly chimes (or is entuned)." It avoids a plural *entunes* as appositive of the singular *sown*, while it makes *so merry a soun* more exactly parallel to *so swete a steven* of line 207, *hir song* of 297, and *the moste solempne servyse* of 302. The birds unite in a single tuneful effort, as especially stated in lines 304–5. *Swete* as an adverb as well as an adjective is not exceptional, and is paralleled by Chaucer's *swote* in both uses.

2. *Lines 866–69*

Hir eyen semed anoon she wolde
Have mercy; fooles wenden so;
But hit was never the rather do.
Hit nas no countrefeted thing.

The punctuation above is Skeat's, except that he connects the last line with what follows. The Globe edition agrees, but places *fooles wenden so* between dashes. The four lines seem to me to belong together, the last one completing the idea. I would paraphrase: Her eyes seemed as though she would at once show pity (or favor), and fools thought so; but favor was not more quickly shown on that account— her glance (of pity or favor) was no counterfeited (or feigned) thing. The poet goes on to say it was her own "pure," that is natural, manner of looking, and seems to confirm the interpretation above by line 874,

Hir loking was not foly sprad,

"Her glance was not foolishly spread or dispensed." I would keep the semicolon after *mercy*, put a comma after *so*, and a comma or dash after *do*. Separation of the first line of the couplet from the second is common in Chaucer, as in lines 15, 43, 51, 61, 75, 89, to take some especially good examples in this poem.

II. *Complaint of Mars 113–4*

Now fleeth Venus unto Cylenius tour,
With voide cours for fere of Phebus light.

In the second line *voide* was explained by Skeat as "solitary; Mars is left behind in Taurus. Besides (according to l.116) there was no other planet in Gemini at that time." Manly ('On the Date and Interpretation of Chaucer's Complaint of Mars,' *Harvard Studies and Notes in Phil. and Lit.* Vol. V, p. 120) says:

> "With voide cours" is a technical phrase meaning that, after separating from the conjunction, Venus passed through the rest of the sign without coming into familiarity with any planet.

A footnote refers to Wilson *(Dict. Astrol.)* under *voide of course,* and so also the *NED.* explains the word.

Neither of these interpretations takes account of the closely connected latter half of the line, *for fere of Phebus light,* and of the secrecy the situation naturally requires. Such secrecy is implied in the command of Mars in line 195:

> But bad hir fleen lest Phebus hir espye;

by the words of the tear-bedewed Venus in 90–91,

> Alas, I dye!

> The torch is come that al this world wol wrye;

and by lines 25–9, which tell us beforehand what was to happen because of Phebus *with his fyry torches rede.*

I suggest, therefore, that perhaps the commentators have gone too far in finding a special astrological sense for *voide*. The OF. *voide* "sachant, fin, rusé" (Godefroy), that is, "cunning, artful," would better suit the whole line, and be quite in keeping with what we should expect of a woman who has sought her lover's abode at night, and finds the day dawning upon her—a situation implied by the allegory. *Voide* in this sense is not otherwise found in Chaucer, but in its origin is not an unnatural development of *voide* "empty, vacant, vacated for the purpose of eluding." Compare *avoid* "make empty, shun, elude"; and *voidance* "act of emptying," then "evasion, subterfuge," the latter older meanings.

III. *Parlement of Foules 204–18*

Skeat's note on line 183, adding to Tyrwhitt's statement about Chaucer's use of Boccaccio's *Teseide*, here says:

> In fact, eleven stanzas (183–259) correspond to Boccaccio's *Teseide*, Canto vii, st. 51–60; the next three stanzas (260–280) to the same, st. 63–66; and the next two (281–294) to the same, st. 61, 62.

The statement is altogether too sweeping. Bilderbeck notes *(Chaucer's Minor Poems,* p. 87) that lines 201–3 are original with Chaucer. Lines 188–9 are quite as truly Chaucer's, as well as 191, describing the singing of the birds.

With voys of aungel in hir armonye.

Bilderbeck, too, might have begun his note on Chaucer's additions to Boccaccio with lines 199–200:

That God, that maker is of al and Lord,
Ne herde never better, as I gesse.

Finally, and most important of all, the whole stanza 204–10 is Chaucer's own, a point Skeat and Bilderbeck failed to mention.[1]

This last stanza is most interesting, because in it Chaucer extended the beauty of Boccaccio's garden to that of an earthly paradise. There was neither heat nor cold, neither sickness nor age, neither darkness nor night, while there grew also "every holsom spyce and gras," and there was "joye more a thousand fold Then man can telle." It is not necessary to attempt a definite source for the passage, since the earthly paradise had been so frequently described, but only to call more special attention to the unlikeness to Boccaccio in this place.[2] In the latter the only hint of this immediate stanza is in the lines (*Tes.* vii, st. 53),

Ripieno il vide quasi in ogni canto
Di spirite, che qua e la volando
Gieno a lor posta.

---

[1] Cary, in his translation of Dante's *Divine Comedy* (1805), had noted lines 201 ff. as parallel to *Purg.* xxviii, 9 ff. See my brief note in *Poems of Chaucer*, p. 59.

[2] On earlier descriptions of the earthly paradise see Cook's *Old English Elene, Phoenix, and Physiologus*, p. lvi, where the editor also makes general reference to this passage among others.

Here *spirite* may possibly have suggested Chaucer's *wind* of line 201, which in its turn may have reminded the poet of Dante's *Purg.* xxviii, 9, and especially of line 18 in that place. The latter reads in Longfellow's translation, "That ever bore a burden to their (the birds') rhymes," a close parallel to Chaucer's

> Acordant to the foules songe on-lofte.

Chaucer, it is to be added, had been approaching this description of the earthly paradise—or shall we rather say preparing for it—in two anticipatory passages. These are the comparison of the song of the birds with "voys of aungel" (191), and the emphasis upon the "ravisshing swetnesse" of the "instruments of strenges" by the lines 199–200, "That God, that maker is" etc. Neither of these allusions, as I have noted above, is in the Boccaccio stanzas Chaucer was following.

IV. *Troilus and Criseyde* II, 1228–9; *Knight's Tale* A 979–80

The lines of the first passage read,

> And doun she sette hir by him on a stoon
> Of jaspre, upon a quisshin gold y-bete.

In his notes on these lines Skeat translates the last phrase, "a cushion beaten with gold; cf. KT, A 979." The reference in the latter place is to Theseus's pennon,

Of gold ful riche, in which ther was y-bete
The Minotaur, which that he slough in Crete.

On *y-bete* in this place Skeat has this longer note:

> y-bete, beaten; the gold being hammered out into a thin foil in the shape of the Minotaur; see Marco Polo, ed. Yule, I, 344. But, in the Thebais, the Minotaur is upon Theseus' shield.

In his glossary Skeat also defines *y-bete* of the *Knight's Tale* as "formed in beaten gold."[3]

Skeat's note on Theseus's pennon has been generally followed and sometimes extended. Thus, Liddell translates *of gold ful riche* "rich with gold, having the Minotaur embossed upon it," as if the whole pennon was of gold. Child definitely says as much: "The pennon was of gold hammered thin in the shape of the Minotaur." Pollard's note is less clear, but the last part seems to imply thinly beaten gold. The whole reads:

> y-bete, stamped. Lydgate *(Chron. Troy* I, ix) speaks of arms "branded or bete" upon coatarmour. Cf. also *Anelida* l. 24, where we are told that the car of Theseus was "gold-bete."

The car (char) of Theseus we must assume was covered with thin plates of gold.

The dictionaries have followed the same or similar leads. The *NED.* places the *Knight's Tale* line under

---

[3] The reference to Yule's *Marco Polo* is curiously inadequate for Skeat's definition. A banner with a cross upon it is mentioned, but with no intimation of beaten gold.

"beat *v.* **21** To work metal or other malleable material by frequent striking; to hammer." Under the separate article *beaten* **5. c.**, however, it does add "embroidered" to such more literal meanings as "overlaid, inlaid, embossed, damascened with gold or other precious metal." All these meanings it illustrates by one of the *Sir Gawain* passages among others, but no clear distinction of the exact use of the word is made, and no origin suggested. The *CtDict.*, under **17**, has the definition, "in medieval embroidery, to ornament with thin plates of gold or silver," with quotation from Rock's *Textile Fabrics.* Unfortunately Rock had relied mainly upon such late works as Dugdale's *Baronage* and *Onomasticon* of the late seventeenth century. Besides, Rock is no longer regarded as an authority on textiles, though still often quoted.[4]

All this is the more remarkable because Morris, in his edition of the *Prologue and Knight's Tale* (1872), had given "ornamented" as one meaning of *bete* "beat," and in his edition of *Sir Gawain and the Green Knight* (1864, 1869) had used the meanings "worked, embroidered" for the pp. *beten* in that poem. Moreover, he there added a hint of the origin of the word, though without making clear the relationship. Maëtzner, too, in the *Wörterbuch* to his *Altenglische Sprachproben* (Vol. I, 1878) had given the secondary

---

[4] My authority is Mr. W. M. Milliken of the Cleveland Museum of Art.

meanings of "besetzt, verziert" to ME. *bẹ̄ten,* though here, also, without explaining its origin or clearly distinguishing its uses.

The examples in *Sir Gawain,* which had led Morris to define *beten* as "worked, embroidered," should have made clear a use of the word in which no metal plates were employed. Thus, in lines 77–8 the Gawain poet speaks

> Of Tars tapites innoghe
> Þat were enbrawded and beten wyth þe best
>   gemmes;

and lines 2027–8 describes Gawain's *cote,* with its cognizance on velvet, as with

> vertuuus stonez
> Aboute beten and bounden.[5]

Here, clearly, no metal plates are employed, while the union of *beten* with *embrawded* and *bounden* indicates some kind of embroidery or sewing upon cloth. The third example in *Sir Gawain* (1832–33) describes the girdle given the hero by the lady of the castle:

> Gered hit watz with grene sylke and with golde
>   schaped,
> Noȝt bot arounde brayden, beten with fyngrez.

In this passage *beten with fyngres* not only can not

---

[5] Compare the description of Emetrius in the *Knight's Tale,* A 2160–1:

> His cote-armure was of cloth of Tars,
> Couched with perles whyte and rounde and grete.

mean "flattened into a thin plate," but as certainly shows the manner of "embroidering or adorning," as by sewing or weaving.[6] The lady is emphasizing the simplicity of the girdle as a reason why Sir Gawain might accept it. A large number of other examples might be brought together in which *bẹ̄ten* is used with textile fabrics, and with no indication of metal plates.

It might be surmised that OE. *bēaten* "beat" had assumed a secondary meaning like "work, embroider, adorn" when used with cloths, as some other verbs of rapid motion had acquired similar meanings in relation to textiles. Compare *braid* from OE. *bregdan* "move to and fro"; *weave* in its relation to *wave* "fluctuate, move back and forth"; or the modern verbs *whip, whip-stitch* for a certain kind of sewing. Yet OE. *bēatan* had no such meanings, so far as accessible examples show. Only ME. *bẹ̄ten* had acquired the new uses, though in conditions under which we should naturally expect textile fabrics, as in tapestries, banners, clothing, coat-armor, that is the cloth-covering of armor, girdles, cushions, and the like.

Yet in this case, development within the language does not account for the new Middle English meanings of *bẹ̄ten*. As said above, Morris gave a hint of

---

[6] *Noȝt bot arounde brayden* has been missed in idea by the translators and commentators. It means "not embroidered (or adorned) except around [the edges]"; that is, not elaborately adorned with embroidery or other figure work.

their oi .n, although it is not clear that he fully understoc 1 the history of the word. At least, when he added to his definition of *bęten* in *Sir Gawain* the words "Fr. battu," he seems not to have had before him any examples of the Old French original. Now, however, Godefroy's *Supplement* (1895) supplies the lacking information. There we find that OF. *batre* "beat, batter" had already acquired the same meaning of "adorn [textile fabrics]," at least when combined with *or* "gold." Godefroy gives:

> or batu, or martelé et réduit en fil; par alté-
> rat., la loc. *à or batu,* qui signifiait: (orné) avec
> de l'or battu, est devenue une expression adjec-
> tivale qui a pris l'accord du substantif auquel
> elle se rapportait et s'est même transformée en
> *batu à* (ou *en*) *or.*

This meaning he illustrates with such examples as *ensegnes batues à or arrabiant (Naissance du Cheva-lier au Cygne* 3162) ; *vestemens batus en or (Perce-for.* iv, fol. 59b) ; *robbe de pourpre, qui toute estoit a or battue (Lancelot* t. ii, fol. 112c).[7] Littré explains

---

[7] To the forms by Godefroy may be added Anglo-Norman *batu d'or,* as in the following quotations from a list of the possessions of Henry VI *(Rot. Parl.* IV, 229, year 1423):

vi Trappur' d'or Bokerain noier, chescun Trappur' ovec iiii scochons du arm' du Roy, batuz d'or, & i escochon de Seint George.

i autre cloth de tarterin blanc, linez de lienge toil, batuz d'estoillez d'or.

Doubtless earlier uses of the expression might be found in English records.

In one of the oldest church inventories of vestments, the

under *battu:* "Brocart battu d' or, brocart dans le quel il entre beaucoup d'or."

Direct connection of ME. *gold y-bẹ̄te (bẹ̄te, bẹ̄ten)* with OF. *à (en) or batu (batu d'or)* would seem to be conclusively proved from Chaucer's translation of some lines in the *Romaunt of the Rose.* Lines 824–26 of the original, describing Sir Mirthe's garments, read:

> D'un samit portret a oysiaus,
> Qui ere tout a or batus,
> Fu ses cors richement vestus;

and are translated by Chaucer, lines 836–8:

> And in samyt, with briddes wrought
> And with gold beten fetisly,
> His body was clad ful richely.

Here both the OF. *portret,* beside the English *wrought,* and the *à or batus,* beside the English *gold beten,* are conclusive proof that there were no gold plates on the robe of Mirthe. The ME. *gold beten* is an evident translation of OF. *à or batus.*

ME. *gold bẹ̄teñ (gold y-bẹ̄te),* then, and similar

Inventories of Christchurch Canterbury by J. W. Legg and W. H. St. J. Hope (1315–16), the description of the copes, albs, and other vestments is in Latin, but the figure work is almost invariably described as *brudatus (breudatus, broudatus)* "embroidered." There is no reference to anything that could be regarded as beaten in the ordinary sense. I cite two examples from pp. 53 and 68:

Item Capa R. de Kylwardy Archiepiscopi brudata ubique auro cum ymaginibus stantibus.

Item Alba ejusdem cum paruris et amictu de viridi velvetto brudato cum rosis aureis.

expressions are a transfer from Old French idioms which applied, first of all, to gold (or metallic) thread used in textile fabrics. This metallic thread was employed in both weaving and embroidery, in the latter of which there was considerable English development in the thirteenth and fourteenth centuries.[8] Whether OF. *batre* was used for embroidery or ornamentation with precious stones, as in *Sir Gawain*, is not clear from examples accessible to me, but at least ME. *bēten* had this meaning. The latter, therefore, and its Modern English equivalent *beaten*, should have the special meanings when used with textiles of "woven, embroidered, adorned, trimmed," the use with cloth being distinctly separated from that with metal or other substance which might be beaten or hammered in the ordinary sense. The meaning "stamped," which Pollard used for the *Knight's Tale* line, is not justified. The Lydgate reading, *branded and bete,* should be *brauded and bete* (see the *NED.* under *branded),* so that the Lydgate passage belongs with those in *Sir Gawain.*[9]

To return to the passages in Chaucer, the cushion

[8] England was especially famous in this period for an embroidered work known both at home and abroad as *opus Anglicum* or *Anglicanum.* This may have been in Chaucer's mind in his use of the expressions noted above.

[9] It is not to be denied that thin bits of gold or silver were sometimes sewed on cloth, but such use was extremely rare, so far as I can learn, compared with that of gold or metallic thread in weaving and embroidery.

A good example of the modern use of beaten "embroidered,

"gold y-bete," on which Criseyde sat to soften the
"stoon of jaspre" on which it was placed must have
been of down or other soft material, and covered
with some valuable textile, embroidered or ornamented with gold thread. So, also, the pennon of
Theseus was of some rich cloth, woven or embroidered with the figure of the Minotaur in gold thread.
We may safely dismiss in these cases all idea of thin
plates of gold attached to textile fabrics, or of cushions or pennons made entirely of such plates. Examination of many similar examples in Middle English,
in which *bęten (bęte, y-bęte)* is used with textile fabrics, indicates a similar explanation.

V. *Prologue to Canterbury Tales* 164,
"and preestes thre"

Various commentators have tried to explain the
apparent inconsistency between this reference to
three priests and the number of pilgrims Chaucer
seems to have had in mind for his Canterbury pilgrimage. Modifications of the text have been proposed by Bradshaw *(Coll. Papers,* p. 110), Herzberg
(Canterbury Geschichten, p. 581), Ten Brink *(Mar-
burger Universitätschrift),* and Kastner *(Athenæum,* 1906, I, 231. Tyrwhitt *(Introd.* vi) explained
the apparent discrepancy as due to an interpolation

---

adorned," occurs in Baker's *Chronicle of the Kings of England,*
p. 236: "A red fiery Dragon, beaten upon white and green
sarcenet." This also forms an admirable illustrative passage
for the *gold y-bęte* of the *Knight's Tale.*

by some scribe or copyist, and Skeat *(Notes to Cant. Tales)* agrees. The idea of an inadvertent slip on Chaucer's part was suggested by Liddell *(Chaucer, Notes)*, and such is perhaps the more commonly accepted explanation.

Let it be said at once that probably no interpretation can entirely eliminate the inconsistency in Chaucer's references to the number of the pilgrims. To preserve the text, however, and present an interpretation least conflicting with what the poet is believed to have intended, and least untrue to a natural psychology, is perhaps all that can be done. Yet even this is decidedly worth while. We begin with the generally accepted idea that Chaucer intended thirty pilgrims as narrators of tales in his great poem. If each had told four tales before the return to London, as the Host of the Tabard proposed, the number of tales would have been one hundred and twenty, an English great hundred, a not unnatural plan for the poet. It is not to our purpose that Chaucer found such an elaborate plan impossible, and greatly modified it in the end. The necessary element in any proposal is to find in the received text a company of narrators numbering exactly thirty.

The crux of the matter centers around the expression "and preestes thre" of the *Prologue* 164. A possible explanation of the difficulty has recently occurred to me. Chaucer, it is clear, makes some attempt to group his pilgrims, as he describes them in the *Prologue*. He begins with a group of the upper classes represented by the Knight, Squire, and attendant Yeoman. Then comes a group of the more prominent church people, the attractive Prioress, her Chaplain, the three priests, as usually explained, the Monk, and the Friar. Something like a professional class is represented by the Merchant, Clerk, Sergeant of the Law, and Franklin, and this is followed by a guild or fraternity group, the Haberdasher, Carpenter, Weaver, Dyer, and Upholsterer, with their Cook. A sort of provincial group includes the Shipman of Dartmouth, the Doctor, the Wife of Bath, the Parson, and the Plowman his brother. Only the Doctor might seem to be out of place in this group, but he may also have been from some city other than London. It is perhaps unlikely that Chaucer would have so satirized a physician of the capital city. Finally, the poet enumerates a miscellaneous group of six in the Reeve, Miller, Summoner, Pardoner, Maunciple, and himself.

In general Chaucer describes his pilgrims, as we know. Yet he neither describes himself, nor gives any specific reason for his making the pilgrimage.[10] The Nun's Chaplain is not described, nor the priest later called the Nun's Priest in the *Prologue* to his

---

[10] From the words of the Host in what is called the *Prologue to Sir Thopas* and his criticism of Chaucer's first offering in the *Prologue to Melibeus*, especially after the definite refer-

Tale. No member of the Guild group is individually
described, except the attendant Cook. Description of
each narrator was therefore not intended, except as
some general idea of the character was to be given in
the narrator's *Prologue,* or Head-link. Yet while each
member of the Church group is not described, it is
surprising that two of that group, as it is usually understood, are never again mentioned in any way.

The Church group, as Chaucer has been thought to
intend it, consisted of seven persons, the Prioress,
Chaplain, *preestes thre,* the Monk, and the Friar.
Yet the *Tales* themselves reveal as narrators only
five members of such a group, the Prioress, Second
Nun (her Chaplain), the Nun's Priest, the Monk, the
Friar, with no mention or suggestion of any other.
Besides, by later mentioning the single *Nonnes
Preest* specifically *(CT,* B 3999), Chaucer has him-
self excluded the possibility of two other priests who

---

ence to the poet made by the Man of Law in his *Prologue,*
it is clear that Chaucer was unknown to the Host and the
Pilgrims. He has joined the pilgrims without revealing his
identity, doubtless in order to observe them in their freest
and most natural manner. Had they known a reporter was
among them, they would have been more constrained, to say
the least.

Would Chaucer himself have made a pilgrimage, and might
this have been in 1387? The religious spirit of *Truth,* probably composed in the last part of 1386 or the beginning of
1387, would seem to answer the first question in the affirma-
tive, while the fall of his fortunes with those of Philip La
Vache and others would have furnished the occasion for such
a Canterbury pilgrimage in the spring of 1387. Possibly the
illness which, later in 1387, caused the death of Chaucer's
wife may also have begun early enough to furnish the occasion for a religious pilgrimage.

could have borne that title. This reference, too, is fairly early in the poem, before the poet could have made any considerable change in his original plan. I suggest, therefore, that the Monk and Friar were intended from the beginning to be the other two members of the Church group. In that case, the *with hir* of line 163 applies in particular to the Nun's Chaplain, and in a less definite way to the Nun's Priest, the Monk, and the Friar, the last two of whom are "with her" only in a general sense. Compare, for example, how the Franklin is said to be in the company of the Man of Law (line 331), although they seem to have no special connection with each other. Note also the general *with us* in the case of the Doctor and the Summoner, as if Chaucer separated them somewhat from those mentioned immediately before.

No one would contend that the Monk and the Friar were not priests in the fullest sense. Nor would any others of the Pilgrims so naturally fit into a typical Church group. The Parson, a parish priest it is true, is anything but a typical representative of churchmen of the time, while he would have been the last to associate himself with the Prioress or the other more prominent representatives of the church. In fact, by the extraordinary praise accorded him, he is distinctly separated from most priests of his time, as his little town is far removed from the chief places in the state religion.   The Pardoner, too, does not belong to a typical Church group.   Though perhaps attached to an English house, he was just back from Rome to play upon the fears, credulities, and super-stitions of the English folk in a manner thoroughly disapproved of by Chaucer, as doubtless also by many churchmen. The same may be said of the Sum-moner.   Finally, there is no need to account for a nat-ural desire on the part of the Monk and the Friar to associate with the Prioress and the Second Nun, or with the Nun's Priest, as he is later described in the Head-link to his *Tale*.

What will at first seem a great objection to this in-terpretation of *preestes thre* must of course be met. In meeting it, however, let us remember the very considerable objection to the usual interpretation. Three priests in addition to the Monk and the Friar, or seven in the Church group, make with Chaucer thirty-one pilgrims, when he tells us himself in *Prol.* 24 that there were only twenty-nine. Much less great is the difficulty in regarding the Church group as made up of five persons, making with himself the twenty-nine pilgrims he first mentions.   In describ-ing the groups of pilgrims, he places himself in the last division—"a maunciple and myself, ther were namo"—as if he had now completed the company of twenty-nine he had already enumerated.   Looking back to lines 19–27 of the *Prologue* we can well believe this. He has reached the Tabard before the others who need not be supposed to have arrived together, in spite of "in a companye" (25-6), for that expression he has virtually corrected in "by aventure y-falle in felawshipe." All, including Chaucer, are bent on the same journey for the same purpose, a pilgrimage to Canterbury's shrine. It is as if the poet had written:

> At night was come into that hostelrye
> Wel nyne and twenty in a companye
> Of sondry folk, by aventure y-falle
> In felawshipe, and pilgrims were *we* alle.

I do not suggest the change of *they* to *we* in the last line, but merely point out how slight a turn would have united Chaucer with the other pilgrims in essential relations. Indeed, he has joined himself and the company in the following lines by a similar confusion of pronouns. In lines 30-34 he begins with *I* and closes with a *we* clearly implied in *our* of the last line:

> And shortly, whan the sonne was to reste,
> So hadde I spoken with hem everichon,
> That I was of hir felawshipe anon,
> And made forward erly for to ryse,
> To take our wey, ther as I yow devyse.

Here "And made forward" means "and we made forward," not only because it takes two to make a bargain, but because of the "our wey" in the following line. The *I* has become *we* within the sentence, as *they* of line 26 as naturally became *we* in line 29, uniting Chaucer with the other pilgrims

That toward Caunterbury wolden ryde.

It is at least in favor of this new interpretation of *preestes thre* that Blake and Stotherd, in their pictures of the Canterbury pilgrims leaving the Tabard Inn, have intentionally or unintentionally followed the same idea. They portray thirty persons in the procession, including of course the Host of the Tabard, that is twenty-nine pilgrims inclusive of Chaucer. They also place together five persons only in the Church group, the Prioress, Second Nun, Nun's Priest, Monk, and Friar, taking no account of any other two priests such as Chaucer has been thought to imply. There is no reference, so far as I know, to either artist's reason for so numbering and arranging the pilgrims, but the result is what I now propose in explaining the difficult *preestes thre* of the Prologue. The pilgrims who set out from Southwark, as the pilgrims who had gathered the evening before for the pilgrimage, were twenty-nine in number.

This new interpretation makes possible a new and surprisingly excellent assumption regarding Chaucer's plan for the *Tales* as a whole, one not alone creditable to his art, but indicative of his ingenuity, and fully accordant with his later realism. No

satisfactory explanation has ever been proposed for
his introduction of another narrator during the journey to Canterbury, as when the Canon and the Canon's
Yeoman suddenly join the company on the road, and
one of them remains to tell his *Tale*. Tyrwhitt comments (*Introd.* xxxviii) :

> The introduction of the Chanouns Yeman to
> tell a tale, at a time when so many of the orig-
> inal characters remain to be called upon, ap-
> pears a little extraordinary. It should seem that
> some sudden resentment had determined Chaucer
> to interrupt the regular course of his work, in
> order to insert a satire against the alchemists.

Skeat quotes Tyrwhitt with apparent approval, but
makes the suggestion that "the poet has boldly im-
proved upon his plan of the pilgrims' stories as laid
down in the prologue." Yet it is by no means pleasant to believe Chaucer the diplomat, the comptroller
of customs, the knight of the shire, had been buying
a medieval gold brick, and was now salving his
wounded vanity by exposing the fraud. Nor is it
more creditable to think the poet was now altering a
well-laid plan, in order to round out the number of
his narrators to thirty.[11]

Only Professor Kittredge, so far as I have found,
has suggested a different view of the introduction of

---

[11] We need not here consider whether the poet had now
altered the original plan as to the number of tales each pilgrim should tell. Without regard to that point the twenty-

the Canon's Yeoman's tale from that of Tyrwhitt
and Skeat. In a short paper upon the "Canon's Yeoman's Prologue and Tale" in *Transactions of the
Royal Society of Literature,* Vol. XXX, Professor
Kittredge protested against considering this episode
as an after-thought. He says:

> What is there to indicate that the Canon and
> his Yeoman are after-thoughts? Nothing at all
> except the silence of the Prologue, and in this
> instance the *argumentum ex silentio*—seldom a
> very trustworthy support — is perfectly falla-
> cious. Assume for a moment that Chaucer in-
> tended, from the outset, to subserve variety and
> liveliness by making a couple of unlooked-for
> travellers join the calvacade on the road. Would
> he have registered his intention in advance?
> The question answers itself. To speak of the
> Canon and his Yeoman in the Prologue would
> have been to defeat his own object. . . . To be
> sure this silence is consistent with the theory
> that the Canon and his Yeoman were after-
> thoughts; but it is equally consistent with the
> theory that they were not.

Yet Professor Kittredge made no attempt to show
how the *Canon's Yeoman's Tale* might be fitted into

---

nine narrators at the beginning need to be increased to thirty,
in order to reach the number generally assumed to have been
in Chaucer's mind, and most natural under the circumstances.
26

the preconceived plan which the poet is believed to have had in mind.

To assume that *preestes thre* included the Monk and the Friar, and that the twenty-nine pilgrims included himself, returns to Chaucer the credit of having originally planned one of the most dramatic incidents of the whole poem. Nor is it less realistic than dramatic. No travelers who saw such pilgrims on their way could have failed to join them, not only for protection on the road, but for the same "felawshipe" that had first prompted the poet to become one of their number. Making *preestes thre* include the Monk and the Friar reveals Chaucer's more perfect and much richer plan. The twenty-nine pilgrims who begin the journey were to be rounded out to thirty by one narrator who should join them on the journey. The time and place are admirably chosen. An earlier addition to the pilgrim groups would have been less appropriate, and less effective as a surprise. The disappearance of the Yeoman's master is fully and ingeniously accounted for by his fear of exposure. The new character and the new tale fit perfectly into an original scheme, without any implication of change of that scheme or new circumstance in Chaucer's life. Surely the poet was capable of such a plan.

As has long been noted, the *Canon's Yeoman's Prologue,* or Head-link, fits exactly into the previous scheme. It mentions the "lyf of Seint Cecyle" as having been told on the morning of leaving Ospring, as we feel confident from other circumstances it must have been. It tells in an entirely natural manner the arrival of the two horsemen, eager to join such a "mery companye." Under the guise of wonder regarding these new accessions, the poet describes the Canon in some such lines as he had used in his *Prologue* for other characters. After his plan in presenting the Pardoner and the Wife of Bath more vividly, he allows the Yeoman to become the chief exponent of his own character and circumstances. Every detail fits into an otherwise well-arranged design, which it enhances by new elements of surprise and pleasure.

The purpose of this note is to relieve Chaucer of what has been regarded as an error on his part, and that without proposing any textual emendation. Not one of the emendations so far suggested has satisfied many more than the original proposer. Standing as it does in rime, *preestes thre* is most likely to be what Chaucer wrote and intended to write. It is not flattering to believe either that he could not count correctly as far as thirty, or that having altered his original plan he did not change line 164 in so slight a particular. I would relieve him of all but the slight inadvertence—if so it may be called—of not making clearer the inclusion of the Monk and the Friar in the Church group, without specifically attaching them to the entourage of the Prioress. If the interpretation reveals, as it seems to do, a more ingenious design of the great poet than has usually been assumed, so much the better.

SAINT AMBROSE AND CHAUCER'S LIFE OF ST. CECILIA[*]

The reference to Saint Ambrose in Chaucer's *Life of St. Cecilia (CT*, G 271 ff.) has never been explained. Although Chaucer in this reference was clearly following his Latin source, Tyrwhitt regarded these lines as an awkward interruption of the narrative and wished that he could find reason for omitting them. Skeat gave up the problem with the words: "I cannot find anything of the kind in the works of St. Ambrose."[1] Professor Lowes, in his admirable article upon the interpretation of the two crowns,[2] does not mention this Ambrose passage, nor attempt to explain the expression the "palm of martirdom." His only reference to Ambrose is incidental to his relation of the story of the bee lighting on the infant's lips, from the sermon on St. Ambrose by Jacobus de Voragine.[3]

---

[*] *PMLA*. Vol. XLI, pp. 252–61 (1926).

[1] Skeat's *Works of Chaucer* V, 409. Skeat does refer to the story of the basket of roses, typifying martyrdom, in a sermon of Jacques de Vitry on St. Dorothea, a story which begins with "Beatus Ambrosius narrat," and in this respect is similar to the lines in the Life of St. Cecilia.

[2] "The 'Corones Two' of the Second Nun's Tale," *PMLA.*, XXVI, 115 ff., XXIX, 129 ff.

[3] The only other reference to Saint Ambrose by Chaucer, that in the *Parson's Tale of Vices and Virtues*, was easily discovered by Skeat, as he shows in his note to *CT*, I 84.

I propose to show, not only that the expression the "palm of martirdom" was used by Saint Ambrose, but that he was the source of the symbolism in the "corones two," and is thus peculiarly connected with the St. Cecilia story.

To begin with the latter, the allusion to the symbolic character of the flowers of the two crowns is found in the *Commentarius in Cantica Canticorum* of Ambrose, *Cap. Sec.* (Vers. 1 and 2).[4] These two verses, which Ambrose combined for his Commentary, read in the Vulgate:

> Ego flos campi, et lilium convallium; sicut lilium inter spinas, sic amica mea inter filias;

or in the King James version: "I am the rose of Sharon and the lily of the valleys," etc.

On this passage Ambrose comments in six paragraphs, the first two general from our point of view, with reference to Christ and the Church and the general nature of flowers. In the third paragraph he points out that lilies do not live "in asperitatibus montium incultisque silvarum, sed in hortorum amoenitate," which leads him to say:

> Sunt enim horti quidam diversarum pomiferi virtutum, juxta quod scriptum est. Hortus con-

---

[4] Migne, *Patr. Lat.* XV., *Opera Sancti Ambrosii* I, col. 1559. I use the column number of the Benedictine edition inset in the Migne edition, here col. 1967 of the latter. The full title of the work is *Commentarius in Cantica Canticorum e Scriptis Sancti Ambrosii a Guillelmo, quondam Abbate Sancti Theoderici, postea Monacho Signiacensi, Collectus.*

clusus etc. *(Cant.* 4, 12)[5] eo quod ubi integritas, ubi castitas, ubi religio, ubi fida silentia secretorum, ibi claritas angelorum est, ibi confessorum violae, lilia virginum, rosae martyrum sunt. Bene lilium Christus, qui est flos sublimis, immaculatus, innoxius, in quo non spinarum offendat asperitas, sed gratia circumfusa clarebit.[6]

The phrases *confessorum violae, lilia virginum, rosae martyrum,* which it was hardly necessary to italicize in the text, not only give the symbolism of the flowers in the "corones two," but in slightly different order, the words which Jacobus de Voragine used in speaking of the infant Saint and the bee that lighted on his lips. Clearly, in the time of the Bishop of Genoa, the symbolism of the flowers was well known as belonging to Saint Ambrose. To him, too, such symbolism peculiarly belongs. In no other commentary on the *Canticum Canticorum* among the Greek or earlier Latin Fathers is there any such symbolic interpretation of this passage. Indeed, Ambrose is the first of the Latin Fathers to comment at length on this highly poetical book.

In other respects, the *Commentarius* of Ambrose is

---

[5] "Hortus conclusus, soror mea sponsa, hortus conclusus, fons signatus."

[6] Ambrose goes on, referring to the *sicut lilium inter spinas* of the *Vulgate* (Verse 2), with something more of symbolism for the rose: "Sicut enim spina rosarum, quae sunt tormenta martyrum: non habet spinas inoffensa divinitas, quae tormenta non sensit."

a mine of symbolism. I illustrate from some further references to flowers, or to plants and the garden in which they grow. Continuing his comment on the first two verses of the second chapter, Ambrose applies the first verse more directly to Christ in his fifth paragraph, in part as follows:

> Flos enim humilitatis est Christus, non luxuriae, non voluptatum atque lasciviae, sed flos simplicitatis, flos humilitatis;

and on the second verse in his sixth paragraph:

> Nonne inter asperitates laborum contritionesque animorum boni flos odoris assurgit; quia contrito corde Deus placatus.

On verse eleven of this chapter, *Flores visi sunt in terra, tempus secandi advenit,* he has the comment:

> Ante adventum Christi hiems erat: venit Christus, fecit aestatem. Tunc omnia erant florum indiga, nuda virtutum; passus est Christus, et omnia coeperunt novae gratiae fecundari germinibus. . . . Imber impedit flores; at nunc flores videntur in terra. Boni flores apostoli, qui diversorum scriptorum suorum atque operum fuderunt odorem.[7]

Commenting on *Cant.* 6, 2, which he here introduces, *Qui pascitur inter lilia,* he again reiterates the symbolism of the lily and the rose:

[7] Migne, *Patr. Lat.* XV, 1568.

Lilium castitatem significat. . . . Bona pascua sacramenta divina sunt. Carpis lilium, in quo sit splendor aeternitatis; carpis rosam, hoc est, Dominici corporis sanguinem. Bona etiam pascua, libri sunt Scripturarum coelestium.[8]

Some examples of other symbolisms may be briefly given. On *Cant.* 4, 12 Ambrose comments as follows:

Ut in vite religio, in olea pax, in rosa pudor sanctae virginitatis inolescat. . . . Bona ergo anima fragrat odores justitiae.

The word *hortum* in *Cant.* 5, 1 leads Ambrose back to his comment on *Cant.* 4, 12, and he adds,

Quanto hoc pulchrius, quod anima ornata virtutum floribus, hortus sit. . . . Myrrha enim est sepultura mortuorum.

A comment on the mandrake accompanies that on *Cant.* 7,12 :

Ibi mandragorae dederunt odorem. Plerique discernunt quemdam inter mandragoras sexum; ut et mares et feminas putent esse, sed feminas gravis odoris. Significat ergo gentes, quae ante fetebant, cum essent infirmiores evirata quadam imbecillitate perfidiae, boni odoris fructus ferre coepisse, postquam in adventum crediderunt.

On *Cant.* 8, 13, *Qui sedes in hortis* etc., Ambrose suggests,

---

[8] Migne, *ibid.*, 1572.

Delectabitur enim quod in hortis Christus sedebat, et in hortis positi amici intendebant voci ejus.[9]

Such symbolism Ambrose made peculiarly his own by using it in other places in his works. Thus, in his *Expositio in Psalmum,* commenting on *Psalm* cxviii (cxix), 25, he quotes *flores visi in terra* from *Cant.* 2, 11, and uses part of his interpretation in that place:

Boni flores apostoli, qui diversorum scriptorum atque operum suorum fuderunt odorem.[10]

Again, Ambrose repeats his comment, quoted above, on *Cant.* 2, 1–2, practically in the same words, in his *Expositio in Lucam* (chap. vii, ll, 27, 28).[11]   In his *Liber de Institutione Virginis,* cap. xv, occurs another comment upon the lily:

Christi lilia sunt; specialiter sacrae virgines, quarum est splendida et immaculata virginitas.

Here again, too, Ambrose goes on to quote *Cant.* 1, 1–2, and 6, 1–2, and his interpretation of those passages.[12]

Evidence that the symbolism which Ambrose had so strikingly presented was to persist is found with-

_____

[9] Migne, *ibid.,* 1585, 1589–90, 1612, 1617, for the last four quotations respectively.

[10] Migne, *ibid.,* 1040.   I quote only that part of the commentary which refers to the symbolism of the flowers.

[11] Migne, *ibid.,* 1440–41.   The only difference is in the use of *illic* for *ibi* in the second sentence.

[12] Migne, *Patr. Lat.* XVI., 269.

in a half century of his death.   In the first half of the
fifth century Bishop Eucherius of Lyons wrote his
*Liber Formularum Spiritalis Intelligentiae ad Ura-
nium,* and in this he repeats and explains, somewhat
naïvely perhaps, the symbolism of Ambrose:

> In Salom.: Ego flos campi et lilium convallium
> *(Cant.* II, i).   Rosae martyres, a rubore san-
> guinis. . . . Violae confessores, ob similitudi-
> nem lividorum corporum.   In Cantico cant.:
> Flores in terra visi sunt *(Cant.* II, 12).[13]

Again, a little below, Eucherius adds: "Rosa, quod
rutilanti colore rubeat, martyres significat."

Essentially, too, Rabanus Maurus, whose active
life belonged mainly to the ninth century, followed
the example of Eucherius and the symbolism of Ambrose.   In his *De Universo Libri* XXII (XIX, chap.
viii) he has: "Rosa a specie floris nuncupata quod
rutilanti colore rubeat.   Significat autem rosa martyres"; and he adds a little below:

> Potest et in lilio virginitas exprimi: quia ex-
> cellentior est castitas virginalis, quam caeterae
> virtutes, sicut in Apocalypsi ostenditur.[14]

So, also, in his *Allegoriae in Universam Sacram
Scripturam,* under "R" Rabanus gives: "Rosa est

---

[13] Migne, *Patr. Lat.* L, 727 ff. for the whole work of Eucherius, col. 744, not 742 as in the Index, for the specific reference.

[14] Migne, *Patr. Lat.* CXI., 528.   The subject of chap. viii,
from which these quotations are taken, is *De Herbis aroma-
ticis sive communibus.*   Still further evidence that Rabanus

coetus martyrum ut in libro Ecclesiastici," referring to *Ecclesiasticus* xxiv, 18.[15]

To these we may add more significant references from St. Bernard of Clairvaux, who lived mainly in the twelfth century. It will be remembered that St. Bernard was introduced by Chaucer in the *Invocation* preceding the *Life of St. Cecilia*—a passage closely following Dante, who clearly knew Bernard's *Missus est, seu de Laudibus V. Mariae,* and its high praise of the Virgin. But Bernard also commented on the *Song of Solomon* in his *Sermones in Cantica,* and there and in other places used the Ambrosian symbolism. His *Sermo XLVII, De triplice flore* etc., quotes *Cant.* 2, 1 *(Ego flos campi)* and adds:

> Itaque juxta praefatam de floris statu partitionem, flos est virginitas, flos martyrium, flos actio bona. In horto virginitas, in campo martyrium, bonum opus in thalamo. . . . Idem flos campi, martyr, martyrum corona, martyrii forma.[16]

---

had the Ambrosian symbolism in mind is found in his reference to Confessors:
Viola propter vim odoris nomen accepit. . . . Violae quoque significant confessores ob similitudinem lividorum corporum.
He goes on to quote *Cant.* 2, 11, and comment further upon it, as Ambrose had done. The last clause of the comment on Confessors will be seen to be from that of Bishop Eucherius.

[15] Migne, *Patr. Lat.* CXII., 1040.

[16] Migne, *Patr. Lat.* CLXXXIII., 1429–30. Chaucer's reference to Bernard in the *Invocation,* as noted above, is pretty certain evidence that he had in mind other parts of Dante's *Paradiso,* as canto xxxi, in which Bernard is twice mentioned

In his *Cantica Canticorum Commentatio*, St. Bernard again comments on *Cant.*, 2, 1, part of which comment is as follows:

> Et sum lilium castitatis videlicet et puritatis exemplum: non superborum sed *convallium*. Castitas enim superba non castitas est, sed ornatum diaboli prostibulum.[17]

So in his *Vitis Mystica seu Tractatus de Passione Domini* St. Bernard has a chapter (xviii) called *De flore castitatis, quae est lilium*, in which he says:

> Non potuit deesse in Vite nostra florente flos lilium candentis, excellens castitatis insigne. Inter omnes virtutes castitas quadam speciali praerogativa flos meruit appellari, quae per lilium figuratur.[18]

Finally, St. Bernard probably had the Ambrosian comment in mind when, in his *Sermo XLI* of the *Sermones in Cantica*, he says of *Cant.* 5, 1, *Messui myrrham* etc.: "Ubi nunc martyres in myrrha . . . figurat?"[19]

In his second paper Professor Lowes showed how the symbolism of the lily and the rose, which we now know as Ambrosian, had become a part of the Church

by name, and whom Dante made the author of the prayer to Mary at the beginning of canto xxxiii; see Professor Carleton Brown's admirable article on the subject in *Mod. Phil.* IX, 1 ff.

[17] Migne, *Patr. Lat.* CLXXXIV., 279.

[18] Migne, *ibid.*, 452.

[19] Migne, *ibid.*, 138.

hymnology. Nor should it be forgotten that, in the
year of the appearance of the first article by Lowes,
Professor Tupper[20] had noted the same symbolism in
Ælfric's Homily, *In Natale Sanctorum Martyrum*
(ed. Thorpe, Ælfric Soc., II, 546). Professor Tupper
later observed the more important reference to the
symbolic interpretation of the flowers in Ælfric's
Homily *De Assumptione Beatae Mariae,* which deserves somewhat fuller treatment.[21] Ælfric speaks
of the Holy Spirit's telling of having seen Mary as-
cending to heaven like à dove. The following quotation contains the last words of the speech and
Ælfric's comment:

> "And, swa swa on lengctenlicere tide, rosena
> blostman and lilian hi ymtrymedon." Ðæra
> rosena blostman getacniað mid heora readnysse
> martyrdom, and ða lilian mid heora hwitnysse
> getacniað ða scinendan clænnysse ansundnes
> mægðhades.[22]

---

[20] *Riddles of the Exeter Book,* ed. F. Tupper, 1910 (Preface
1909), p. 166. Still earlier, Skeat had called attention to the
"earliest English life of St. Cecilia" in Cockayne's *Shrine*—
now more accessible in EETS. 116—and that of Ælfric in his
Lives of the Saints, not then in print, but now in EETS. 94,
357 ff. Both these mention the crowns of roses and lilies.

[21] *Homilies,* I, 444. Lowes in his second paper (footnote 6)
makes acknowledgment to Tupper for this second reference.

[22] Ælfric later explains that Mary did not actually suffer
"bodily martyrdom," but her mental anguish was equivalent
to it, and she thus deserved the roses of the martyr's crown.
Along with the adoption of these two symbolic interpretations
of Ambrose, it is worth noting that Ælfric, in his Homily
In Natale unius Confessoris (II, 548), makes no mention of
the Ambrosian symbolism of the violet.

The Ambrosian symbolism had come to England, though with no recognition of Ambrose as the originator. In fact, another Ambrosian symbolism, not hitherto pointed out, appears in a still different work of the Old English period. It is to be found in the prose version of the Old English *Salomon and Saturn,* where Saturn asks,

> Saga me, hwylc wyrt is betst and selust?

and Salomon answers:

> Ic ðe secge, Lilige hatte seo wyrt, forðam ðe heo getacnað Crist.[23]

With this should be compared the symbolic identification of the lily with Christ in one of the passages quoted from the *Commentarius* of Ambrose (cf. above, pp. 408–9).

It would be gratifying to be able to identify the *Preface* quoted in Chaucer's source, and to which reference is made by Chaucer himself *(Second Nun's Tale,* 271). Ambrose, however, so far as I can discover, wrote no such *Praefatio,* either in works recognized as his, or in those attributed to him. He apparently never mentioned Saint Cecilia or Tiburce or Valerian. On the other hand, Chaucer's use of the *Preface* is of importance for its slight evidence of originality and, as we shall see, for the additional symbolism of the "palm of martirdom."

---

[23] Kemble's edition in the *Ælfric Society Publications,* p. 186.

416 CHAUCER

In the first place, Chaucer's addition to his original, in which he calls Ambrose "this noble doctour dere," is the poet's own recognition of the high place Ambrose had come to hold in the Church. Thus, he is sometimes ranked with Augustine, Jerome, and Gregory the Great "as one of the Latin 'doctors,' "[24] or made "one of the most illustrious Fathers and Doctors" with Augustine, St. John Chrysostom, and St. Athanasius "as upholding the chair of the Apostles in the Tribune of St. Peter's at Rome.[25] Again, in the last line of the speech of Ambrose, summing up the virtue of St. Cecilia,

> Deuocioun of chastitee to love,

Chaucer has slightly modified his source and made clearer the real sacrifice. Paraphrasing the Latin,

> Viros virgo duxit ad gloriam, mundus agno-
> vit, quantum valeat devotio castitatis,

he has made more explicit the renunciation by adding "to love," with the rare use of *to* "against." The line means "devotion to chastity as against love."

The older use of *to* "against" in this place, on which I have seen no comment of like effect, is the only one that can explain the line. Although Skeat's great *Glossary* to Chaucer does not recognize it, and the *NED.* has no Chaucerian example, it is known not

---

[24] Rev. A. J. Grieve, *Encyc. Brit.* article.

[25] *Cath. Encyc., Ambrose.*

only in Old English (see *Toller-Bosworth* under "to
I, 1 f."), but appeared in various works of Chaucer's
own age as well.   It occurs in *Clannesse* 1230, *Piers
Plow.* A. III, 274, Wyclif's *Psalms* l, 6 and lxxxiv, 6.
The *Piers Plowman* instance was recognized by Skeat
in his *Glossary,* the other citations are from the
NED.[26]

Finally, the figure of the "palm of martirdom" is
one used by Ambrose, who so delighted in the allegorical interpretation of Scripture.   It is true that
he did not always interpret the palm in the same way.
When commenting on *Cant.* 7, 8, *Ascendam in pal-
mam* etc., he quotes the preceding verses 6 and 7,

---

[26] The proposed Middle English Dictionary should be on the
lookout for more illustrations of the word.   See the *NED.*
under "to, VII b."   I do not see that *to* "is used after words
denoting opposition or hostility," as the *NED.* says, and the
Toller-Bosworth.   The "opposition" is wholly in the *to* itself,
as shown by the examples.   It seems to be merely a retention
of an older meaning; compare its cognate Greek δέ "but," "usually having an opposing or adversative force" (Liddell and
Scott).   The *Cent. Dict.* does this better in recognizing under
"to, 8" the meanings "against, over against" and giving, besides three Elizabethan examples, one from Addison, and one
from Irving.   Under the same heading it places the present-
day examples like *hand to hand, two to one.*   The latter is
explained in the *NED.* definition of "to, III, 19" as "connecting the names of two things (usu. numbers or quantities)
compared or opposed to each other."   Unfortunately, it seems
to me, the *Cent. Dict.* does not connect its Middle English
examples of *to* with those of later times, but places
them under "to, 17.   In various obsolete, provincial or collo-
quial uses."   Under this heading it gives the *Piers Plow.* example of Skeat, and one from *Polit. Poems* (Furnivall):
        To thee only trespassed have I.
At any rate, enough has been said to justify giving Chaucer's
to in the *Second Nun's Tale* 283, the special sense of "against."

27

Quam pulchra etc., and interprets the palm as follows:

> Sed etiam ipsa charitas palma est, ipsa est plenitudo victoriae . . . Qui vincit, ascendit in palmam, et manducat fructus ejus.[27]

But in the *Sermones* ascribed to Ambrose is found the figure which Chaucer and his source attributed to him. In *Sermo XX* we read:

> Palmae, inquam, offeruntur vincentibus. . . . Per palmam dextera martyris honoratur. . . . Praemium enim quoddam est palma martyrii. . . . Est plane palma martyribus suavis ad cibum, umbrosa ad requiem, honorabilis ad triumphum, semper virens, semper vestita foliis, semper parata victoriae, atque adeo marcescit palma, quia martyrum victoria non marcescit.[28]

This does not mean that Ambrose was the first to use the "palm of martirdom," as he was the first to use the symbolism of the lily and the rose, for the former expression had been used two centuries before by Tertullian in the last paragraph of his *De Spectaculis*.[29] But it does mean that Ambrose, who was responsible for the symbolism of the "corones two," had also used this new expression with peculiar

---

[27] Migne, *Patr. Lat.* XV, 1610.

[28] Migne, *Patr. Lat.* XVII, 416–7.

[29] See also *Rev.* vii, 9, though without clear reference to martyrs.

force, and with direct application to such a martyrdom as that of St. Cecilia.

In the absence of any *Praefatio* directly attributable to St. Ambrose, it is not too much to conceive the manner in which his name became attached to the Life of St. Cecilia. The Ambrosian symbolism so permeates the story that some clerical writer may well have illustrated the *palma martyrii* in the last quotation from Ambrose by reference to St. Cecilia and Valerian. After that, the further incorporation of Ambrose as directly testifying to the worth of the principal characters in the Tale was a simple matter. While, too, Jacobus de Voragine and Chaucer following him, halted the story to cite authority for "the miracle of thise corones tweye," this is not so different from Chaucer's own digressive method in other places. Compare ll. 505–10 of the *Nun's Priest's Tale*, or the much longer digression on the bringing up of children in the *Physician's Tale* (ll. 72–104), to take two examples from his later works. May we not also say that Tyrwhitt's objection to the St. Ambrose reference is largely, if not entirely, removed by the proof here given of the much more important place of Ambrose in the whole story than has hitherto been suspected.[30]

---

[30] As I read the last proof of this article, *Mod. Lang. Notes* for May has come, with Mr. Parker's extremely interesting reference to the *duas coronas* given to Abel in the *Pseudo-Matthaei Evangelium*. These now seem to me a development of certain passages of Scripture, as 1 *Cor.* ix, 25; *Jas.* i, 12;

and *Rev.* ii, 10; iii, 11; iv, 4. At least, the material of which Abel's crowns were composed is not mentioned, nor any flower symbolism such as is made so important in Chaucer's *Life of St. Cecilia.* It is this flower symbolism of the *corones two* which I have traced to St. Ambrose, and for which he seems to have been responsible. The two crowns given to Abel are also different from the single crowns of individual types given to Cecilia and Valerian.

APPENDIX

STUDIES IN CHAUCER*

There has been no more important contribution to Chaucer literature in this country for many years than the three volumes of Chaucer studies by Professor Lounsbury of Yale. Indeed, outside the texts by the Chaucer Society, no such extensive contributions have appeared on either side of the water, great as has been the interest in Chaucer study of late. The volumes include eight monographs on points of importance in the life and work of Chaucer, the larger number being historical in treatment, departing somewhat from the original intention to embody the latest researches on all Chaucer questions. Professor Lounsbury also warns us in the Introduction, that he differs considerably from the opinions of most scholars; but apart from his opinion on *The Romaunt of the Rose,* these differences are not so much in new views as in the correction of misstatements. The essays deserve special mention, also, because they are not the dilettante work of popular periodicals now re-issued, but, fresh from the workshop of the scholar, they give evidence on every page of scholarly investigation.

---

* Studies in Chaucer. By Thomas R. Lounsbury. In 3 Vols. N. Y. Harper. See *The Dial,* Vol. XII, pp. 351–53 (February, 1892).

The first two chapters deal with the life of Chaucer, the real and the legendary. The life is treated in a way somewhat unique among biographers, and especially among biographers of our older poets. It neither attempts to establish conjectures that are attractive rather than probable, nor does it try needlessly to overthrow well established data. Professor Lounsbury is fair and impartial, while restraining with commendable temperance the natural desire to make too much of one's hero. As an evidence of his fairness may be cited the lengthy discussion of the poet's birth. In this, every argument for the date 1340, so commonly accepted, is given its full force, although with equal care are stated the many indications that a somewhat earlier date may be the true one. One noticeable feature of this chapter is the way in which incorrect statements are traced to their sources, thus allowing each reader to judge for himself of the value to be put upon them. It may be disappointing that no new facts are added to Chaucer's life; but, as the author points out, new facts can be obtained only by the most painstaking examination of past records, with the possibility that years of search may not reveal anything of value. On the whole, therefore, this treatment merits great praise for its attempt to give the exact facts known, unadulterated and unembellished by culpable conjecture.

The Chaucer Legend, as it is called, follows the same laborious method as in the previous chapter, every misstatement in regard to Chaucer being followed to its fountain-head in conjecture, in unfounded assertion or in the misinterpretation of some previous biographer's luckless paragraph. This is destructive criticism, yet the reader must admire the persistency of the effort, even if he sometimes wearies of the continual sarcasm hurled at the unwary biographer of the father of English poetry. But the work has been well done, and one feels secure in the beliefs established as in the overthrowal of that which is false. One early source of Chaucer fable is here given for the first time in English dress,— Leland's Latin biography of the poet being now first translated by Professor Lounsbury. Leland's is a naïve piece of work, full of inaccuracies and puerile in its artlessness. Both naïveté and inaccuracy may be best shown by quoting a few lines at the beginning of this remarkable biography:

> Geoffrey Chaucer, a youth of noble birth and highest promise, studied at Oxford University with all the earnestness of those who have applied themselves most diligently to learning. The nearness of that institution was in a measure the motive that induced him to resort thither; for I am led by certain reasons to believe that Oxfordshire or Berkshire was his native county.

He left the university an acute logician, a delightful orator, an elegant poet, a profound philosopher, and an able mathematician.

It is hardly necessary to point out that scarcely a single fact here set down has the remotest foundation in truth.

The title of the third study, 'The Text of Chaucer,' might lead us to expect some new interpretations, some elucidation of cruces, or some critical comments on the numerous allusions in Chaucer. But the author's plan has been different. We have instead, an historical account of the text and the various editions, with critical estimates of their value. For the general reader this is admirable, and perhaps more valuable than the other. We are here furnished with what may be called a history of the interest in the poet, as shown by the attempts to edit him. And editions of Chaucer are hardly less numerous or less various in value than those of Shakespeare himself. It is interesting to remember that the first printed edition of Chaucer was made by that patron-saint of English printers, the careful and conscientious Caxton; and that the second does credit to the painstaking patron of the new art, both in respect to his admiration of Chaucer and his desire to rectify his own first print, which, though he had made it, as he says, "according to my copy, and by me was nothing added ne minished," was found to be inaccurate in not a few particulars when compared with a better text. Then Chaucer is followed down through the editions of Thynne (1532), Stow (1561), Speght (1598, 1602), Urry (1721), Morell (1737), the famous Tyrwhïtt (1775), Wright (1847–51), Bell (1854–6), and so down to the Chaucer Society's critical "Six Text" in recent years. Some more recent editions are not mentioned, and a complete bibliography would have been an advantage to this chapter. Still, the care with which the various editions are discussed, and the exactness in pointing out their merits and demerits, make this chapter invaluable, without the dryness of the customary bibliography.

No question in connection with Chaucer will appeal more quickly to scholar or general reader than the question of what Chaucer wrote—what are his veritable productions. One turns with peculiar interest, therefore, to the lengthy treatment—almost a volume in itself—of this question. The chapter divides itself into three parts: a summary of the tests of genuineness, an enumeration of the poems attributed to Chaucer at various times, and a discussion of those considered doubtful. In the first part, the value of each test is estimated, with the purpose of showing that no single one is infallible, and that therefore it is impossible to assert on the strength of one or two such tests the spuriousness or genuine-

ness of a given work. The reason for devoting so
much space to this becomes apparent in the third
part, especially in considering the authorship of
The Romaunt of the Rose. In the second part the
historical treatment predominates, as in the chapters
already mentioned. Not only is a list given of everything at any time attributed to Chaucer, but the manner in which each was first published, together with
its subsequent history, is stated in full.

The third part of this chapter is peculiarly one
for the student of Chaucer. To the general reader,
this careful application of various tests, this painstaking comparison of word with word, rhyme with
rhyme, passage with passage, and all the close reasoning from linguistic facts, will hardly be appre-
ciable, and therefore hardly fascinating. To the
Chaucer student, on the other hand, this is perhaps
the most valuable contribution in the three volumes.
In the chief controversy as to *The Romaunt of the
Rose*, Professor Lounsbury takes the side of Chaucer's authorship, combatting the view independently
arrived at by Ten Brink and Skeat. It is not an easy
question to settle, however, and perhaps it never can
be settled, except as scholars range themselves on
one side or the other. Professor Lounsbury certainly makes the most of the arguments in favor of his
view. Clearly, Skeat has considerably overstated
certain arguments; while Lounsbury relies for the

force of some of his on the fact that the translation, if by Chaucer, shows the imperfections of early work,—a fact on which it is easy to lay too much stress. But the real decision must rest more on authority than on clear balance in favor of either side.

The volumes before us seem somewhat iconoclastic, as one finds some oft-repeated statement about the poet overthrown in nearly every chapter. In reality, this is only an attempt to set right much false statement and many inconsistencies. We see this especially in the chapter on the learning of Chaucer —a thorough investigation into the sources of Chaucer's material, as showing the authors with whom he was acquainted. In this it is not so much that new material has been added, as that all has been brought together in convenient form. The inaccuracies of former statements are pointed out, with the second-hand sources from which the poet took his stories in many cases, and in general the real meaning and extent of the assertion that Chaucer was a learned man. It is evident that the term "learned" applied to the poet may be much misunderstood, and has at best a relative signification. While knowing Latin, Chaucer could occasionally mistranslate it. He was guilty of considerable mistakes, in fact, quite apart from a goodly number of anachronisms so common in all our early poets. He has enriched our literature with a few names no one understands. Yet his fame rests securely on something far different from learning, and cannot be shaken by occasional evidences of ignorance or inaccuracy.

Under the discussion of Chaucer's relation to language and religion are treated two widely different subjects, the first somewhat scantily, the second with greater fulness. In the latter, are considered Chaucer's relation to the reforms of Wyclif, and to the church in general. Contrary to the frequently expressed opinion, Professor Lounsbury regards Chaucer neither as a follower of the reformer nor as a good churchman, but rather as one in whom the skeptical tendency was increasingly strong toward old age. He admits that there are few passages on which to base such an opinion, and that it must rest rather upon the general impression one gets from constant perusal of the author's works. In one sense, this conclusion may be accepted. Chaucer was an acute satirist of the church, and this shows him a keen observer of the abuses into which the church had fallen. While this is so, he also appreciates the best in the church, as shown by his sympathetic portrait of the poor parson; although this can hardly be said to ally him with the Wyclifites. To us there seems, also, little ground for asserting in Chaucer a decidedly skeptical tendency, in any modern sense of that term. He was broad and liberal-minded, with deep insight into men and affairs; he was a poet, and this implies an intuitive perception of men's motives; he was a satirist, and therefore a sharp critic of men's follies and foibles; but he was not characteristically a doubter, much less a demolisher of men's faith.

The third volume of these scholarly studies deals with Chaucer in literature, first in connection with literary history, and next as an artist. The historical treatment so common in these essays is taken in the first study. The opinion of Chaucer held by his contemporaries, and the numerous tributes since his time, find a place. Here are discussed at length the modernizations of the poet in the last three centuries, their misinterpretations and their failures. It is perhaps questionable whether the writer gives due force to these modernizations, in a certain way. No doubt they might have been rendered unnecessary by a knowledge of Chaucer's language, as it is equally true they are now poor substitutes for the poet himself. But looked at as an evidence of the appreciation of Chaucer, even in his "rude verse," as they understood it, they are overwhelming testimonies to the perennial power of the morning star of English poetry. In this sense, there is decided interest in the attempts to make Chaucer familiar, from the early emancipation out of the thraldom of the "black letter," to the attempted Latin version by Kinaston, and the paraphrases of Dryden, Pope, Wordsworth, with a host of lesser names.

The treatment of Chaucer as a literary artist starts out with an attempt to show that Chaucer met considerable criticism in his own time. It is scarcely proved; and the interpretation by which the conclusion is reached seems very much like that the author deprecates so much in other places. One or two points will hardly endure criticism. These are, the defense of those inaccuracies we call anachronisms, and of the originality of Chaucer. Doubtless a defense for anachronisms is often set up in the inaccuracy of the age; but this is extenuation, not defense, of the thing itself, and it should be so understood. In the same way, though we may deprecate any criticism of Chaucer's originality, it is unnecessary to go to the other extreme, and underrate the work of those who have sought to point out Chaucer's indebtedness to others for his material.

Apart from these points, however, the estimate of Chaucer is fair and appreciative; so that this last chapter, as well as those that have preceded it, will prove a valuable source of information and opinion to every student of "Dan Chaucer, well of English undefyled."

BIBLIOGRAPHY OF THE WRITINGS OF OLIVER FARRAR EMERSON

BY PROFESSOR CLARK S. NORTHUP, CORNELL UNIVERSITY

1888

1. Latin Verse Translation of Onward, Christian Soldiers from the English of Rev. S. Baring-Gould. *Education*, November, 1888, IX. 187.

1889

2. Browning [a Sonnet]. *The Cornell Mag.*, May, 1889, I. 363.

Also in *The Chautauquan*, February, 1890, X. 554.

3. Browning's Diction: a Study of The Ring and the Book. *MLN*, April, 1889, IV. 108–11.

Also in *Amer. Notes and Queries*, April 27, May 25, June 8, 1889, II. No. 26, III. Nos. 4 and 6.

4. The Development of Blank Verse.—A Study of Surrey. *MLN*, December, 1889, IV. 233–6.

5. Emerson's Private Life. Rev. of E. W. Emerson, Emerson in Concord. *The Dial*, July, 1889, X. 49.

6. English in Secondary Schools. *The Academy* [Syracuse], June, 1889, IX. [233]–244.

"This paper received a prize offered by *The Academy* for the best paper on English in the secondary schools."

7. Recent Books on the Study of English Literature. *The Dial*, November, 1889, X. 168.

8. Rev. of Browning's Asolando. *The Cornell Mag.*, April, 1889, II. 288–90.

9. The Ring and the Book. *Ibid.*, January, 1889, I. [205]–216.

10. Tenure of Office of Teachers. *The Independent*, August 29, 1889, XLI. 1106.

11. To H. C. [Hiram Corson: a Sonnet]. *The Cornell Era*, May 31, 1889, XXI. 315.

12. The Word Molinist in The Ring and the Book. *Amer. Notes and Queries*, July 13, 1889, III. 121.

13. To Wordsworth [a Sonnet]. *The Chautauquan*, March, 1889, IX. 339.

1890

14. Antony and Cleopatra [Barnes Shakespeare Prize Essay, Cornell University, 1889]. *Poet-Lore*, February–April, 1890, II, 71–7, 125–9, 188–92. [Supplement:] Antony and Octavius: a Comparative Estimate. *Ibid.*, October, 1890, II. 516–23.

15. English in Preparatory Schools. *The Academy* [Syracuse], March, 1890, V. [104]–108.

16. Nature: a Sonnet. *The Chautauquan*, September, 1890, XI. 722.

17. Rev. of Elene, Edited by Charles W. Kent. *MLN*, January, 1890, V. 20–2.

18. Sweet's Phonetics and American English. *MLN*, November, 1890, V. 202–4.

19. William Cullen Bryant. *The Dial*, June, 1890, XI. [31]–33.

A review of John Bigelow's Life in the American Men of Letters Series.

1891

20. The Etymology of English Tote. *MLN*, December, 1891, VI. 252.

21. Ezra Cornell (January 11, 1807–1891) [a Sonnet]. *The Cornell Mag.*, January, 1891, III. 150.

22. The Ithaca Dialect, | a Study of Present English. | By Oliver Farrar Emerson, A.M., | Instructor in English, Cornell University. | Presented to the University as a Thesis for the Degree of | Doctor of Philosophy. | Reprinted from *Dialect Notes*, Part III. | Boston: | 1891. |

23.5 cm., pp. (85–173). Cover-title. Rev. in *Nation* LIV. 54; in *N. Y. Daily Tribune*, January 10, 1892, p. 14.

23. James Russell Lowell, 1819–1891. *The Dial,* September, 1891, XII. 133–5.

24. Poesie [a Sonnet]. *The Chautauquan,* March, 1891, XIII. 176.

25. Rev. of Franz H. Stratmann, A ME Dictionary, Revised by Henry Bradley. *The Nation,* May 28, 1891, LII. 445–6.

26. September [a Sonnet]. *The Chautauquan,* September, 1891, XIII. 740.

27. Studies in English Literature. *The Dial,* February, 1891, XI. 309–11.

A review of Daniel G. Thompson, The Philosophy of Fiction in Literature, and 8 other volumes.

1892

28. The American Dialects. *Providence Sunday Journal,* October 16, 1892, p. 4.

29. Books on English Literature and Language. *The Dial,* August, 1892, XIII. 106–8.

A review of Hiram Corson, A Primer of English Verse, and 5 other volumes.

30. English Pronunciation. The "Guide to Pronunciation" Again. *MLN,* November, 1892, VII. 194–6.

31. On a Passage in the Peterborough Chronicle. *MLN,* December, 1892, VII. 254–5.

32. The Stone Cutter [a Sonnet]. *The Cornell Mag.,* June, 1892, IV. 324.

Emerson's sonnets (see Nos. 2, 11, 13, 21, 24, 26, 32) are reprinted in the Western Reserve Univ. *Bulletin,* July, 1929, N.S. XXXII. 13. 5–11.

33. Studies in Chaucer. *The Dial,* February, 1892, XII. 351–3.

A review of Lounsbury's Studies in Chaucer. Reprinted in the present volume as Appendix A.

34. The Teaching of English Literature. *The Nation,* April 14, 1892, LIV. 283.

35. The Teaching of English Literature and Language. *Ibid.*, April 28, 1892, LIV. 321.

36. Webster's International Dictionary. The New Webster and the "Guide to Pronunciation." *MLN*, January, 1892, VII. 17–20.
Rev. by S. Porter in same, pp. 118–21. E. replies, pp. 194–6. Porter rejoins, VIII. 202–6.

1893

37. English Prose Literature. *The Dial*, September 1, 1893, XV. 116–18.
A review of English Prose, Vol. I, edited by Henry Craik.

38. The Future of American Speech. *Ibid.*, May 1, 1893, XIV. 270–1.

39. Notice of English Classics for Schools, New York, American Book Company. *The School Rev.*, February, 1893, I. 120.

40. Prof. Earle's Doctrine of Bilingualism. *MLN*, November, 1893, VIII. 202–6.
Reply by Earle, *ibid.* IX. 61–2.

41. Relations of Literature and Philology. *The Educational Rev.*, February, 1893, V. 130–41.

42. Rev. of Bernhard ten Brink, History of English Literature, Vol. II, Part 1 (Wyclif, Chaucer, Earliest Drama, Renaissance), translated by William C. Robinson. *The School Rev.*, March, 1893, I. 311–13.

43. Rev. of Adams S. Hill, The Foundations of Rhetoric. *Ibid.*, January, 1893, I. 48–9.

44. Rev. of Charles F. Johnson, English Words. *Ibid.*, February, 1893, I. 119–20.

45. Rev. of Mrs. Sara E. H. Lockwood, An English Grammar, Adapted from Essentials of English Grammar by William D. Whitney. *Ibid.*, January, 1893, I. 53–4.

46. Rev. of Henry Sweet, A Short Historical English Grammar, and Leon Kellner, Historical Outlines of English Syntax. *Ibid.*, June, 1893, I. 375–6.

178

1894

47. Articles in Johnson's Universal Cyclopaedia, New Edition, New York, A. J. Johnson Co.: Lexicography, V. 209–12, 1894. Pronunciation, VI. 806–7, 1895. Punctuation, VI. 860. The Scottish Language, VII. 394.

In the edition of 1908, these articles are found in VII. 173–6, IX. 494–5, 548, X. 394, respectively.

48. The Doctrine of Bilingualism Again. *MLN*, November, 1894, IX. 212–14.

49. The History | of the | English Language. | By Oliver Farrar Emerson, A.M., Ph.D. | Assistant Professor of Rhetoric and English Philology | in Cornell University | New York | Macmillan and Co. | and London | 1894 | All rights reserved |

19.5 cm., pp. xii, [2], 415. Rev. by L. Morsbach in *Anglia Beibl.* VII. 321–38; by J. Ellinger in *ESt* XXII. 72–3; by F. Holthausen in *Litbl* XVII. 264–6; in *LCBl* XLVI. 954–5; by C. F. McClumpha in *MLN* X. 53–5; by Francis H. Stoddard in *Educ. Rev.*, May, 1895, IX. 509–12.

Second edition, 1895.

50. Rev. of Katherine L. Bates, The English Drama. *The School Rev.*, April, 1894, II. 242–3.

51. Rev. of The Gospel of St. Luke in AS, Edited by J. W. Bright. *MLN*, April, 1894, IX. 120–1.

1895

52. "Colleges" at Harvard and Elsewhere. *The Nation*, November 7, 1895, LVI. 327.

Comment by H., Wm. G. Brown, and A. Matthews, p. 346. E. replies ("College" Again), November 28, pp. 387–8.

53. Cornell University Summer School. University of the State of New York, *Regents' Bulletin* 29, pp. 456–9, 1894; *Extension Bulletin* 9, pp. 45–8, July, 1895.

54. Editor (with others). Word-Lists. *Dialect Notes* I. 8. 368–400. 1895.

55. History of Rasselas | Prince of Abyssinia | by Samuel Johnson | Edited with Introduction and Notes by | Oliver Farrar Emerson, A.M., Ph.D. | Assistant Professor of Rhetoric

and English Philology | in Cornell University | [Emblem.] | New York | Henry Holt and Company | 1895 |
17.3 cm., pp. lv, [1], 179. English Readings. Rev. by E. Koeppel in *Archiv* XCVII. 416–17; by K. D. Bülbring in *Anglia Beibl.* VII. 306; by P. Aronstein in *ESt* XXVII. 285–6.

56. History of the English Language, Second Ed. New York, The Macmillan Company, 1895. See No. 49.

57. A Parallel between the ME Poem Patience and an Early Latin Poem Attributed to Tertullian. *PMLA*, 1895, X. 242–8.

58. Rev. of Charles S. Baldwin, The Inflections and Syntax of the Morte d'Arthur of Sir Thomas Malory. *The School Rev.*, January, 1895, III. 43–4.

59. Rev. of William E. Mead, Elementary Composition and Rhetoric. *Ibid.*, April, 1895, III. 235–6.

60. Rev. of Selden L. Whitcomb, Chronological Outlines of American Literature. *Ibid.*, February, 1895, III. 117.

61. Rev. of Laura J. Wylie, Studies in the Evolution of English Criticism. *Ibid.*, May, 1895, III. 299.

1896

62. A Brief History | of the | English Language | By | Oliver Farrar Emerson, A.M., Ph.D. | Professor of Rhetoric and English Philology in Western Reserve | University; Late Assistant Professor in Cornell University; | Author of "The History of the English Language" | New York | The Macmillan Company | London: Macmillan & Co., Ltd. | All rights reserved |
18.8 cm., pp. x, [2], 267. Reprinted, with corrections, 1897, 1900. Rev. by F. Klaeber in *Anglia Beibl.* VIII. 233–5, 346; by E. E. Hale, Jr., in *School Rev.* V. 406–8.

63. Joint editor with E. H. Babbitt, Clark S. Northup, and others. Word-List. *Dialect Notes* I. 411–27. 1896.

64. Rev. of Otto Jespersen, Progress in Language with Special Reference to English. *The School Rev.*, October, 1896, IV. 633–5.

65. Rev. of Henry Sweet, A Primer of English Historical Grammar. *Ibid.*, April, 1896, IV. 236.

1897

66. American Dialects. *MLN*, April, 1897, XII. 127–8.
Same in substance in *Dial*, March 16, 1897, XXII. 177;
JEGP I. 110; *Nation*, March 18, 1897, LXIV. 202.

67. Readers for the American Dialect Society: Circular of
Directions. March 1, 1897. 8vo, pp. 4.
Reprinted in *Dialect Notes* II. 127–30.

68. Rev. of *Anglia* XVIII (N. F. VI). *JEGP* I. [83]–[88].
1897.

69. The Teaching of English Grammar. *School Rev.*,
March, 1897, V. 129–38.

1898

70. Athenæum Press Series | Memoirs | of the | Life and
Writings | of | Edward Gibbon | Edited, with Introduction and
Notes | by | Oliver Farrar Emerson, A.M., Ph.D. | Professor
of Rhetoric and English Philology in | Western Reserve Uni-
versity | Boston, U. S. A., and London | Ginn & Company |
Publishers | The Athenæum Press | 1898 |
19 cm., pp. lxxv, [1], 279.

71. Editor, *Dialect Notes*. 1898–1905.

72. The Letters of Edward Gibbon. *JEGP* II. 363–9. 1898.

1899

73. The Gibbon Arms. *The Athenæum*, February 25, 1899,
p. 243.

74. The Legend of Joseph's Bones in Old and Middle English. *MLN*, June, 1899, XIV. 166–7.

75. The Place of the Novel in Literature. Introduction to
Papers Read Before the Novel Club of Cleveland. Published
by the Club. 1899. 8vo, pp. xx, 108.

76. Report as Chairman of the Committee on Readers.
Dialect Notes II. 76–8. 1899.

77. The Text of Johnson's Rasselas. *Anglia* XXII. 499–509.
1899.
Reprinted with slight changes in Western Reserve Univ.
Bulletin, April, 1899, N.S. II. 2. 40–48.

1900

78. Transverse Alliteration in Teutonic Poetry. *JEGP* III.
127–37. 1900.
Rev. by C. M. Lewis in *MLN* XVI. 43–4. E. replies, pp.
91–2. L. rejoins, p. 128. E. responds, p. 160.

1901

79. Address at the Unveiling of the Memorial Tablet to
President Charlès Backus Storrs. Western Reserve Univ.
Bulletin, November, 1901, N.S. IV. 131–40.

80. A Correction. *The Nation,* February 21, 1901, LXXII.
Refers to comment by Brander Matthews on Emerson's His-
tory of the English Language in *Harper's,* February, 1901,
CII. 431–6.

1902

81. The Work of the American Dialect Society. *Dialect
Notes* II. 269–77. 1902.
Reprinted in *Proceedings* Mod. Lang. Assn. of Ohio 1900–2,
1903, pp. 55–66. An abstract appeared also in *PMLA* XVII.
xxvii–xxviii.

1903

82. Some of Chaucer's Lines on the Monk. *MPh* I. 105–15.
1903.

1904

83. (With Calvin Thomas and others.) Report | of a | Joint
Committee | Representing the National Educational Associa-
tion, | The American Philological Association, and the | Mod-
ern Language Association of America | on the Subject of | a
Phonetic English | Alphabet | Printed by | The Publishers'
Printing Company | 32–34 Lafayette Place, New York | 1904 |
23 cm., pp. 53. 3 plates. The other members of the Committee were Calvin Thomas, George Hempl, Charles P. G.
Scott, and E. O. Vaile.

84. A Middle English | Reader | Edited, with Grammatical
Introduction | Notes, and Glossary | by | Oliver Farrar Emer-
son, A.M., Ph.D. | Professor of Rhetoric and English Phi-

lology | in Western Reserve University | New York | The Macmillan Company | London: Macmillan & Co., Ltd. | 1905 | All rights reserved |

19 cm., pp. cxix, [1], 475. Rev. in *The Athenæum*, July 29, 1905, p. 144; by H. Littledale in *MLR* I. 133–6; by B. S. Monroe in *JEGP* VI. 319–23; by H. Spies in *ESt* XL. 94–103; by J. von der Warth in *Anglia Beibl.* XX. 203–5; by W. A. Read in *Litbl* XXVIII. 152–3; by W. H. in *LCBl*, February 3, 1906, LVII. 213; by H. Jantzen in *Neue Phil. Rundschau*, 1906, pp. 327–8.

Reprinted 1908, 1909, 1912. 2d edition, 1915.

1906

85. Cain and the Moon. *Athenæum*, August 18, 1906, pp. 186–7.

86. Legends of Cain, Especially in Old and Middle English. *PMLA*, 1906, XXI. 831–929.

87. An Outline History | of the | English Language | By | Oliver Farrar Emerson, Ph.D. | Professor of Rhetoric and English Philology in Western Reserve | University; Author of "The History of the English | Language," "A Brief History of the English | Language," " A Middle English Reader" | New York | The Macmillan Company | London: Macmillan & Co., Ltd. | 1906 | All rights reserved |

19.5 cm., pp. 208. Rev. in *Neue Phil. Rundschau*, 1907, pp. 166–7.

1909

88. The American Scholar and the Modern Languages. *PMLA*, 1909, XXIV. lxxiii–cii.

Address as chairman of the Central Division of the MLAA at Chicago, December 28, 1908.

1910

89. Milton's Star that Bids the Shepherd Fold. Western Reserve Univ. *Bulletin* XIII. 32–48. 1910.

90. A New Note on the Date of Chaucer's Knight's Tale. Studies in Language and Literature in Celebration of the

70th Birthday of James Morgan Hart, New York, Holt, 1910, pp. [203]–254.

91. The Suitors in Chaucer's Parlement of Foules. *MPh,* July, 1910, VIII. [45]–62.
Rev. by J. Koch in *Anglia Beibl.* XXII. 274–5.

1911

92. A New Chaucer Item. *MLN,* January, 1911, XXVI. 19–21.
Correction by E., p. 95; by S. Moore, XXVII. 79–81. Rev. by J. Koch in *Anglia Beibl.* XXII. 265–6.

93. Poems of Chaucer | Selections from His Earlier and Later Works | Edited with Introduction | Biographical and Grammatical | Notes and Glossary | by | Oliver Farrar Emerson, Ph.D. | Professor of English in Western Reserve University | Author of "The History of the English Language" | "A Brief History of the English Language" | Editor of "A Middle English Reader," etc. | New York | The Macmillan Company | 1911 |
18 cm., pp. vii, xi–lviii, [2], 257.

94. The Suitors in The Parlement of Foules Again. *MLN,* April, 1911, XXVI. 109–11.

1912

95. Chaucer's First Military Service—a Study of Edward Third's Invasion of France in 1359–60. *The Romanic Rev.,* October–December, 1912, III. 321–61.

1913

96. Chaucer's Testimony as to His Age. *MPh,* July, 1913, XI. 117–25.

97. A Note on the Poem Patience. *ESt* XLVII. 125–31. 1913.

98. Rev. of Patience, Edited by Hartley Bateson. *MLN,* June, 1913, XXVIII. 171–80, 232.

1914

99. Two Notes on Patience. *MLN,* March, 1914, XXIX. 85–6.
100. What is The Parlement of Foules? *JEGP,* October, 1914, XIII. 566–82.

1915

101. The Earliest English Translations of Bürger's Lenore: a Study in English and German Romanticism. Western Reserve Univ. *Bulletin*, May, 1915, N.S. XVIII. 3. 1–120. Western Reserve Studies I. 1.

102. A Middle English Reader. New and Revised Edition. 1915. See No. 84.
19.2 cm., pp. cxxvii, [1], 478, [1]. Rev. in *Nation* CI. 331; by G. P. Krapp in *Educ. Rev.* LI. 99–100; by J. W. Bright in *MLN* XXXI. 61–2.
Reprinted 1916, 1919, 1921, 1923, 1924, 1927, 1928.

103. A Note on the ME Cleanness. *MLR*, July, 1915, X. 373–5.

104. Scott's Early Translations from Bürger. *JEGP*, July, 1915, XIV. 351–6.

1916

105. English or French in the Time of Edward III. *Romanic Rev.*, April–June, 1916, VII. 127–43.

106. Miscellaneous Notes. i. Iraland (Alfred's Orosius, I. 1). ii. Trẹson (Treason). iii. Afterdiner, Aftermete, Aftersoper. *MLR*, October, 1916, XI. 458–462.

107. More Notes on Patience. *MLN*, January, 1916, XXXI. 1–10.

108. A Note on the Dialectal Use of College. *Dialect Notes* IV. 299–300. 1916.

109. Seith Trophee. *MLN*, March, 1916, XXXI. 142–6.

110. The Shepherd's Star in English Poetry. *Anglia*, January 15, 1916, XXXIX. [495]–516.

1917

111. At-After and Iraland. *MLR*, October, 1917, XII. 493–4.

112. A New Word in an Old Poet. *MLN*, April, 1917, XXXII. 250–1.
On underlay in Spenser.

113. The OF Diphthong ei (ey) and ME Metrics. *Romanic Rev.*, January–March, 1917, VIII. 68–76.

114. Spenser, Lady Carey, and the Complaints Volume. *PMLA*, June, 1917, XXXII. 306–22.

115. Trẹson in the Chronicle Again. *MLR*, October, 1917, XII. [490]–492.
Reply by H. Bradley, pp. 492–3.

1918

116. Spenser's Virgil's Gnat. *JEGP*, January, 1918, XVII. 94–118.

117. The West Midland Prose Psalter 90:10. *MPh*, May, 1918, XVI. 53–5.

1919

118. Chaucer's Opie of Thebes Fyn. *MPh*, September, 1919, XVII. 287–91.

119. ME Clannesse. *PMLA*, September, 1919, XXXIV. 494–522.

120. Notes on OE. *MLR*, April, 1919, XIV. 205–9.

121. Rev. of Patience, Edited by H. Bateson, 2d Ed. *JEGP*, October, 1919, XVIII. 638–41.

122. Two Notes on Jane Austen. *JEGP*, April, 1919, XVIII. 217–20.

1920

123. Mead-Meadow, Shade-Shadow, a Study in Analogy. *MLN*, March, 1920, XXXV. 147–54.

1921

124. Beguiling Words. *Dialect Notes* V. 93–7. 1921.

125. Grendel's Motive in Attacking Heorot. *MLR*, April, 1921, XVI. [113]–119.

126. Imperfect Lines in Pearl and the Rimed Parts of Sir Gawain and the Green Knight. *MPh*, November, 1921, XIX. 131–41.

127. Rev. of Purity, Ed. by Robert J. Menner. *JEGP*, April, 1921, XX. 229–41.

128. (Jointly with R. G. Whigam.) Sonnet Structure in Sidney's Astrophel and Stella. *StPh*, July, 1921, XVIII. 347–52.

129. Two Notes on Sir Gawain and the Green Knight. *MLN*, April, 1921, XXXVI. 212–15.

1922

130. Chaucer and Medieval Hunting. *Romanic Rev.*, April–June, 1922, XIII. 115–50.

131. Milton's Comus, 93–94. *MLN*, February, 1922, XXXVII. 118–20.

132. Notes on Sir Gawain and the Green Knight. *JEGP*, July, 1922, XXI. 363–410.

133. Some Notes on the Pearl. *PMLA*, March, 1922, XXXVII. 52–93.

1923

134. Monk Lewis and His Tales of Terror. *MLN*, March, 1923, XXXVII. 154–9.

135. Notes on OE. *MLN*, May, 1923, XXXVIII. 266–72.

136. Shakespeare's Sonneteering. *StPh*, April, 1923, XX. 111–36.

137. Some Notes on Chaucer and Some Conjectures. *PhQu*, April, 1923, II. 81–96.

138. Some Old Words. *MLN*, June, 1923, XXXVIII 378–80.

1924

139. The Battle of the Books. *PMLA*, March, 1924, XXXIX. lvi–lxxv.
Presidential address, MLAA, Ann Arbor, December 27, 1923.

140. The Early Literary Life of Sir Walter Scott. *JEGP*, January–July, 1924, XXIII. 28–62, 241–69, 389–417.

141. John Dryden and a British Academy. *Proc.* Brit. Acad. 1921–3, X. 45–58. [1924.]
Rev. by F. Liebermann in *Archiv* CXLIV. 281–2; by W. van Doorn in *Engl. Studies* IV. 214.

142. Notes on Gilbert Imlay, Early American Writer. *PMLA*, June, 1924, XXXIX. 406–39.

1925

143. Dryden and the English Academy. *MLR*, April, 1925, XX. 189–90.

144. Pudding-Time. *AmSp*, October, 1925, I. 45.

145. Shakespearean and Other Feasts. *StPh*, April, 1925, XXII. 161–83.

1926

146. The Crux in the Peterborough Chronicle. *MLN*, March, 1926, XLI. 170–2.

147. The Date of Adam Davy's Dreams. *MLR*, April, 1926, XXI. 187–9.

148. Originality in English Poetry. *RESt*, January, 1926, II. 18–31.

149. The Punctuation of Beowulf and Literary Interpretation. *MPh*, May, 1926, XXIII. 393–405.

150. Saint Ambrose and Chaucer's "Life of St. Cecilia." *PMLA*, June, 1926, XLI. 252–61.

151. Spoon-Bread. *AmSp*, March, 1926, I. 310.

152. Two Notes. *AmSp*, August, 1926, I. 616.
On pudding-time and compounds of blind.

1927

153. More Notes on Pearl. *PMLA*, December, 1927, XLII. 807–31.
Thence reprinted in a pamphlet of 32 pages, with an obituary notice by Clark S. Northup and the first edition of the present bibliography. 1928.

154. Rev. of St. Erkenwald, edited by Henry L. Savage. *Speculum*, April, 1927, II. 224–5.

155. Rev. of Sir Gawain, Ed. by J. R. R. Tolkien and E. V. Gordon. *JEGP*, April, 1927, XXVI. 248–58.

156. Two Lexical Notes. *MLN*, April, 1927, XLII. 244–6.
On lake, "pits" and verm, "strip between road and ditch."

BIOGRAPHY AND EULOGY

157. WHO'S WHO IN AMERICA since 1901.

158. NATIONAL CYCLOPAEDIA OF AMERICAN BIOGRAPHY, New York, 1906, XIII. 188–9.

159. THE CLEVELAND PLAIN DEALER. [An editorial.] March 12, 1927.

160. THE CORNELL ALUMNI NEWS. March 24, 1927, XXIX. 302.

161. WALTER GRAHAM. *Cleveland Town Topics*, March 26, 1927. Port.

162. CLARK S. NORTHUP. In the appendix to a reprint of More Notes on Pearl, pp. 25–6. See No. 153.
Reprinted in *Grinnell and You*, December, 1927, VII. 4. 8.

163. THE PHI BETA KAPPA KEY. January, 1928, VI. 658.

164. THE RESERVE ALUMNUS. Oliver Farrar Emerson Memorial. May, 1928, p. 9.

165. DAVID SILVERMAN. *The Reserve Weekly*, March 22, 1927.

166. A W.R.U. STUDENT. A Tribute. *The Cleveland News*, March 18, 1927.
Verse, ten 4-line stanzas.

167. ARTHUR F. WHITE. *The Reserve Alumnus*, April, 1927, III. 6. 7. Port.

LIST OF THE MORE IMPORTANT AUTHORS, BOOKS, AND ARTICLES REFERRED TO IN THE TEXT AND FOOTNOTES*

Compiled by Professor Sarah F. Barrow

Adam of Usk, *Chronicon*, ed. E. M. Thompson, pp. 75, 79, 141, 159.

Ælfric (Abt.), *Homilies*, ed. Thorpe (Ælfric Society), pp. 51, 414; *Lives of the Saints*, ed. Skeat, p. 414.

Alfred (King), *Boethius*, p. 51; *Bede*, p. 51; *Pastoral Care*, p. 52.

Allbutt, Sir T. Clifford, *Greek Medicine in Rome* (1921), p.315.

Ancient Laws and Institutes of England, ed. Thorpe (1840), p. 43.

Armitage-Smith, Sydney, *John of Gaunt* (1904), pp. 148, 163, 190, &c.

Baillie-Grohman, Wm. A., and F., Editors (1904), *The Master of Game* (1406–13), p. 322.

Baker, Sir Richard, *Chronicles of the Kings of England* (1643), p. 392.

Baluzius, E., *Vitae Paparum Avenionensium* (1693), pp. 71, 74, 140.

Baring-Gould, S., *Legends of the Patriarchs and Prophets*, p. 39.

Barnes, Joshua, *History of Edward III* (1688), pp, 190, 214.

Benedictine Rule, pp. 56, 57.

Berners, Juliana, *The Book of St. Albans* (1486), ed. W. Blades (1881).

---

* This is not intended to be either a complete index of proper names or an exhaustive list of the references to the numerous books and articles of various kinds mentioned in the text and footnotes of this volume. The purpose of the list is twofold: (1) to help readers get a clear conception of the comprehensiveness of Professor Emerson's reading and learning and of the thoroughness of his scholarship, (2) to offer perhaps some valuable hints and suggestions to students and investigators of Chaucer's life and works.

The items are arranged alphabetically without reference to the subject of each item, and they are mostly recorded as they appear in the book.

Bestiary (Middle English), p. 47.

Bethune, G. W., editor of Walton's *Angler*, pp. 40 ff.

Bilderbeck, J. B., *Selections from Chaucer's Minor Poems* (1895), pp. 58, 382 f.

Blake, William, "Canterbury Pilgrims," p. 399.

Boccaccio, G., *Teseide*, pp. 97, 124, 319, &c.; *Filostrato*, p. 374.

Bradley-Stratmann, *ME Dictionary*, p. 378.

Bradshaw, H., *Collected Papers*, p. 378.

Brown, Carleton, 'The Prologue of Chaucer's "Life of St. Cecile" (*Mod. Phil.*, IX), p. 412.

Burton, R., *Anatomy of Melancholy*, pp. 314, 318.

Butler, Samuel, *The Elephant in the Moon*, p. 327.

Canons of Edgar (No. 64), pp. 39, 43.

Catholic Encyclopaedia, p. 416.

Caxton, William, *Jason*, p. 342; *Charles the Great*, p. 361.

Century Dictionary, pp. 328, 417, &c.

Chamberlayne, C. G., *Die Heirat Richards II mit Anna von Luxemburg* (Halle, 1906), pp. 135, 160.

Chaucer, Geoffrey, *Life and Times*, pp. 58–90, 123–173, 174–262, 271–297, 320–377; *Prol. to Cant. Tales* (ll. 177 ff), pp. 39–57; *Parlement of Foules*, pp. 58–90, 123–173, &c.; *Knight's Tale*, pp. 123–173, 312, 319, &c.; *Monk's Tale*, pp. 39–57, 263–270, &c.; *Second Nun's Tale*, pp. 405–430, &c.; *The Clerk's Tale*, p. 97; *Parson's Tale*, p. 53; *House of Fame*, pp. 623, &c.; *Book of the Duchess*, pp. 105 ff., 320–359, &c.; *Troilus*, pp. 289, 301, &c.; *Legend of Good Women*, pp. 94, 123, 304, &c.; *Romance of the Rose*, p. 279; *To Adam Scriveyn*, p. 260; *Complaint of Mars*, pp. 100, 102, 121, 380, &c.; *Lack of Steadfastness*, pp. 97, 122; *Truth, To Bukton, To Scogan, Complaint of Venus*, p. 122; language notes, including many references, pp. 298 ff. and 378 ff.

Child, C. G., *Selections from Chaucer* (1912), p. 385.

Chronicon Anglicae (Rolls Series), pp. 132, 136, &c.

Clannesse, (ME poem, ed. R. Morris), pp. 417, 346.

Cockayne, T. O., *The Shrine* (EETS), p. 414.

Comptes de l'Argenterie, pub. by L. Donet-d'Arcq *(Société de l'histoire de France)*, p. 177.

Cook, A. S., 'The Last Months of Chaucer's Earliest Patron' *(Trans. of Conn. Acad. of Arts and Sciences, XXI)*, p. 363; *The Old English Elene, Phoenix, and Physiologus* (1919), p. 383.

Cotgrave, Randle , *Dictionarie of the French and English Tongues* (1611), pp. 329, 345.

Coulton, G.G., *Chaucer and his England*, p. 103.

Cursor Mundi (ME poem), pp. 54, 55, 340.

Crumpe, S., *An Inquiry into the Nature and Properties of Opium* (1793), p. 316.

Dante (Cary's and Longfellow's translations), pp. 383, 384, 412.

Davies, T. L. O., *Supplementary English Glossary* (1881), p. 371.

Davis, H. W. C., *England under the Normans and Angevins* (1905), p. 296 (In C.W.C. Oman's *History of England*, Vol. II).

'Decretals', pp. 41 ff.

Delachenal, R., *Histoire de Charles V* (1909), pp. 174, 177, 209, 258, &c.

Denifle, H. S., *La désolation des églises, monastères, et hôpitaux en France pendant la guerre de cent ans*, pp. 204, 222.

Deschamps, Eustache, *Miroir de Mariage*, p. 236; *Vie de Deschamps* in Deschamps, *Oeuvres complètes*, p. 236.

Dictionary of National Biography, pp. 69, 135, 150, &c.

Dioscorides of Anazarbo (ca. 77), p. 314.

Dryden, Alice (editor), *The Art of Hunting, or, Three Hunting MSS.* A revised edition of *The Art of Hunting*, by Wm. Twici, Huntsman to King Edward the Second. By H. Dryden (1844).

—— *The Age of Venery*, A translation of *La Chasse du Cerf*, an Old French Poem (written about 1250), translated into English by H. E. L. Dryden (1843), edited and corrected by Alice Dryden, Northampton (1908).

Du Cange, Charles, *Glossarium* (1840–50), (1st ed. 1678), p.51.

Dugdale, Sir William, *Baronage* (2nd ed. 1682), p. 386.

Duke of York, *Maystre of the Game* (ca. 1400; ed. Baillie-Grohman, 1909), pp. 320 ff.